:
:
:
:

SPACES,

WORLDS,

AND GRAMMAR

•
•
•
•

COGNITIVE THEORY OF

LANGUAGE AND CULTURE

A SERIES EDITED BY

GILLES FAUCONNIER,

GEORGE LAKOFF, AND

EVE SWEETSER

PREVIOUSLY PUBLISHED:

CONSTRUCTONS: A CONSTRUCTION GRAMMAR

APPROACH TO ARGUMENT STRUCTURE

ADELE E. GOLDBERG

SPACES, WORLDS, AND GRAMMAR

Edited by   **GILLES FAUCONNIER AND EVE SWEETSER**

THE UNIVERSITY OF CHICAGO PRESS

CHICAGO AND LONDON

GILLES FAUCONNIER is professor in the Department of Cognitive Science at the University of California, San Diego.

EVE SWEETSER is associate professor in the Department of Linguistics at the Universtiy of California, Berkeley.

THE University of Chicago Press, Chicago 60637
The University of Chicago Press, Ltd., London
© 1996 by The University of Chicago
All rights reserved. Published 1996
Printed in the United States of America
05 04 03 02 01 00 99 98 97 96   1 2 3 4 5

ISBN: 0-226-23923-3 (cloth)
ISBN: 0-226-23924-1 (paper)

Library of Congress Cataloging-in-Publication Data

Spaces, worlds, and grammar / edited by Gilles Fauconnier and Eve
  Sweetser.
      p.   cm. — (Cognitive theory of language and culture)
    Includes index.
    ISBN 0-226-23923-3 (cloth : alk. paper). — ISBN 0-226-23924-1
(pbk. : alk. paper).
    1. Psycholinguistics.   2. Space and time in Language.
3. Cognition.   4. Grammar, Comparative and general.   5. Semantics—
Psychological aspects.   I. Fauconnier, Gilles.   II. Sweetser, Eve.
III. Series.
P37.S63   1996
401'.9—dc20   96-12878
                                                  CIP

CONTENTS

ACKNOWLEDGMENTS

At cognitive linguistics workshops held in the early 1990s at the University of California, Berkeley, and the University of California, San Diego, a number of us found we were converging on a common theme. We kept turning up cases where a central function of linguistic form was to mark aspects of mental space structure and of the mappings and relations between spaces. We agreed that it would be useful to gather this research in a single volume. And so this collection was born.

We would like to thank all of the contributors for their insightful comments on each other's papers, as well as for their patience and care in revising their own. Thanks are also due to Gene Casad, Aaron Cicourel, John Dinsmore, Ron Langacker, Jeff Lansing, and David Zubin for their ideas, comments, and general support of the workshops. An anonymous reviewer for the University of Chicago Press also gave us extensive, careful, and useful input. Finally, to the cognitive linguistic communities of Berkeley and UCSD, thank you—this book would not have happened without your work to inspire it and your energy to support it.

Gilles Fauconnier and Eve Sweetser

Eve Sweetser and Gilles Fauconnier

1 Cognitive Links and Domains: Basic Aspects of Mental Space Theory

-
-
-
-

Cognitive Structure and Linguistic Structure

This volume focuses on the interaction between grammar and cognitive structure: in particular, on the principled relationship between mental space structures and syntax and semantics. The various contributors provide much evidence for the systematic, pervasive, and often subtle role played by natural language in expressing and guiding the setup of cognitive constructs. From a linguistic perspective, this provides substantive explanations for the forms and meanings of many grammatical constructions. From a cognitive science perspective, it shows how rich language data, if properly understood, can serve to reveal aspects of higher-level mental representation.

Our goals in this introduction are twofold: to give a general overview of the cognitive and linguistic framework underlying most of the scholarship in the volume, and to give some expression to potential dialogues both among contributors to the volume and between contributors and the rest of the cognitive science and linguistic communities. We begin our overview by examining some systematic aspects of human cognitive structure and move from those to the question of parallels in linguistic structure. This will lead us specifically to the theory of mental spaces and to how such a theory can help us motivate the observed structure of human languages. We then discuss the particular contributions to cognitive and linguistic theory made by individual contributors to the volume and relate them to each other and to the field at large. We see this volume as evidence of the broad utility of the mental spaces framework in analyzing divergent aspects of linguistic and cognitive structure. The result is recognition of real complexity, but also of genuine parallels between these divergent phenomena. The parallels help us to understand how humans find certain kinds of complexity effortless to process and other kinds impossible.

Cognitive Connections

It has long been recognized that humans access and process similar or identical information differently in different contexts; the very existence of psychological "priming effects" is overwhelming evidence of this. While objectivist semantics has focused narrowly on aspects of meaning which seemed to be analyzable as independent of contextual differences (relegating the rest of meaning to pragmatics), more and more evidence has come to light that it is a basic function of linguistic structure to both exploit and depict the differential information accessibility that attends on cognitive viewpoint.

If human cognition is so contextually configured, it is crucial to examine what sorts of connections our minds tend to make, and what sorts of effects are produced by different contexts. The examination of linguistic usage is a powerful tool for such cognitive study. What sorts of connections between domains allow us to use a word or expression from one cognitive domain as a *trigger* to refer to another *target* entity in another cognitive domain, for example? A few of the sorts of connections that are relevant just to referential uses of language are pragmatic functions, metonymy, metaphor, analogy, connections between roles and values, and understanding of identity and counterpart relations.

Pragmatic functions (cf. Nunberg 1978), link domains to one another. For example, authors and books are linked by the function associating each book with its author. With this function in place, a name or description of the author (trigger) can serve to identify books (target), as in *Plato takes up half of the top shelf of that bookcase.* In the example *The ham sandwich wants a second glass of coke,* the pragmatic function linking customers to their orders allows *the ham sandwich* to identify a customer. *Ham sandwich* is a good trigger for reference to the target entity, the customer, because food in restaurants is made precisely so that customers can eat it, and the employee's central task is to get the right food to the right customer. Books and articles exist only because some author writes them, and a reader has multiple important reasons to keep a mental record of the connection (interest in reading more of the same author's work, need to cite correctly in publishing her own work, and so forth). Perhaps even more basic and older is the connection between representation and thing represented (as in Jackendoff's (1975) celebrated example, *In the picture, the girl with the green eyes has blue eyes*). Any concept of representation inherently involves two mental spaces, one primary and the other dependent on it. Entities in the two spaces may be *counterparts* of each other, as is the case with the green-eyed girl and her blue-eyed image in the picture. In such well-established contexts of close relations between spaces, description of a trigger can exploit existing structure to set up a specific *connector* between the trigger (e.g., ham sandwich) and the target (the relevant customer).

In no case is it necessary for us to posit the real existence of entities connected by pragmatic functions. We could look at a painting of a boat, and have no idea whether there was a physical boat such as that represented. A restaurant employee could make up a fictitious customer, ask the kitchen for a ham sandwich to take to this customer, and subsequently request a coke for the same purpose. The point is that the cognitive structures of our domains of customers and orders, or of paintings and objects in the world, are inherently connected by our understanding of the world we live in. We reflect these basic cognitive links by using a linguistic expression for an item in one domain (like *ham sandwich* or *the girl with green eyes*) to refer to a connected item in another domain (like the customer who ordered it, or the blue-eyed painting of the girl).

Another basic cognitive connection which humans cannot usually escape making is the understanding that the same person is very different at different times of his or her life, but is nonetheless "the same," so that five-year-old Mary and fifty-five-year-old Mary are a necessary example of identity (and shared name) between divergent entities in differing worlds. In other words, the understanding of object permanence which we develop in early childhood will naturally incline us to make cognitive connections between entities in quite remote temporal and spatial contexts. Humans also share an understanding of role playing and the ability of people to represent the actions of others, as in theater. We are inevitably aware, too, of the ability of humans to entertain multiple world views and functional world views, and of the difference between any two persons' views of the same aspects of the world. The world as we think it "is" is not the same as the world as we wish it were, or as we fear it might be, or as we think another person sees it. Yet there are crucial links between these different structures: when we say *I wish Joe had come to the meeting,* we mean that we view as preferable a world that is much like ours except that Joe came to the meeting. Crucially, the speaker does not mean that he or she would prefer a world in which Joe came to the meeting only to die of a heart attack on the spot, or in which Joe came to the meeting and World War III was announced over the radio at the same moment. The wish space inherits partial but significant structure from our beliefs about reality.[1]

It should be noted that it is not obvious that links like customer-order or author-book should be cognitively similar to links between represented world and representation or to the relations between beliefs and "reality." Yet all these cognitive connections have similar linguistic consequences in that they allow transfer of descriptions (and of other grammatically indicated structures such as presupposition and inference) from one domain to another.

Many pragmatic functions overlap with the phenomena discussed in the context of the traditional, or the more recently extended, domain of **metonymy.** Saying *hands* to mean "workers" is based on two essential experiential connections: all, and only, humans have hands as parts of their bodies—and human work is prototypically done with hands, making *hands* a good trigger for ultimate successful reference to a worker. An extended "frame metonymy" analysis might claim that the restaurant customers and foods are both parts of a larger whole (a "restaurant frame"), and that one part of the frame here stands for another; or that authors are part of a frame which includes their works.

Metaphor and analogy reflect the universal human ability to link domains on the basis of experiential connections of many different sorts, certainly not all as evident as the metonymic ones mentioned above. Take, for example, everyday idiomatic metaphoric usages like *Finding that reference was just the icing on the cake* and *Sandy shot down Lou's proposal*. There is no inherent metonymic connection between a reference and icing on a cake; in fact, we are not aware of any pragmatic link at all. But the mapping allows us to see aspects of the paper-writing world (or of a broader world of achievements and activities) in terms of the world of food. A cake is a delicacy, presumably a valued item in the food world. Supposing that icing adds further deliciousness and value to the cake, icing on the cake can be seen as something which is unnecessary but nice—the cake would have been good without it, but is even better with it. A reference which adds an interesting but not essential example to an already well supported scholarly argument could also be seen as unnecessary to the basic achievement, but nice to have. However, there is no need to mention necessity or pleasantness overtly. By metaphoric identification of the reference with the icing, we have evoked an understanding of one domain in terms of the other, which includes and transcends the literal analysis of the metaphor given above.

Similarly, Sandy's criticism of Lou's proposal has little to do with shooting. But as Lakoff and Johnson (1980) have pointed out, the salient metaphorical structuring of argument as combat allows us to see the criticism as an act of violence, albeit perhaps involving no more violent action than scribbling on the margin of a piece of paper. Even when metaphor is based on experiential correlation (this one probably is based on a genuine, if partial, correlation between arguments and possible violent behavior), it need not be based on the kind of close contiguity of domains that generally underlies metonymy.

Analogy, like metaphor, need not be based on a close connection between the two domains connected. Metaphor, unlike analogy, crucially allows access between the two domains in a way that permits direct transfer of naming conventions. Gentner (1983) has discussed examples such as the atom as analogous to a solar system, and Gentner and Gentner (1983) have shown in some detail that metaphor and analogy have real cognitive consequences for human reasoning. Gibbs (1980) and Gibbs and O'Brien (1990) have also shown that idiomatic metaphorical expressions are genuine parts of cognitive processing. Metaphor and analogy thus allow us to make mental connections, to shape cognitive mappings, in complex and powerful ways which must be taken into account as factors in setting up mental models.

Cognitive connections between roles and the values filling those roles are very basic, as Hofstadter (1986), Fauconnier (1985, 1991), and others have pointed out. As with the idea of representation, the idea of roles carries along with it the idea of multiple possible mappings between a role and its filler. Roles include, but are not limited to, human roles such as *Sara's mother* or the *president of the United States,* each of which could be filled by some individual (perhaps the same individual, Janet Smith). Our general human cognitive capacities appear to include the ability (and the need) to set up **frames,** or structured understandings of the way aspects of the world function (Goffman 1974, Fillmore 1985). These frames allow us to make maximal use of the data we are given in crucial respects; for example, if someone talking about a house mentions *the front door, the bathroom,* or *the driveway,* we don't ask *What front door?* We know that there is probably a front door, simply from a complex understanding of the kind of object in question. Or if a wedding is under discussion, speakers can refer not only to *the groom* and *the bride,* but also to *the ushers, the guests, the cake, the dress,* and *the rabbi,* all in the certain knowledge that such references will successfully be understood with respect to the hearer's understanding of a wedding scenario. Frames thus typically include **roles** for participants, such as *bride* and *groom* and *cake,* or the now-classic cases of *customer* and *waiter* and *menu* in a restaurant (Schank and Abelson 1977), or *buyer* and *seller* and *goods* in a commercial event. Roles are created by general social or physical framings of experience; for example, *parent* or *president* or *student* exists against our understanding of family structure, political or corporate hierarchy, or educational institutions. Roles, like individuals, can have properties or attributes. For example, *The president has been commander in chief since 1776* depicts command of the armed forces as a legally defined attribute of the role of president, not of some individual who has filled that role.

It is part of our understanding of roles that certain roles have only one value at a time: there can be only one president of a given country at a time, a person can only have one husband or wife at a time, and so forth. However, the same individual is almost certain to fill multiple roles—e.g., president, parent, and wife. There are thus at least some roles which are in a one-to-one connector mapping with their values, while most values are in a one-to-many mapping structure with respect to roles. These constraints make it easy to cognitively access information in certain ways. Knowing a role may allow rapid and easy identification of its unique filler, while reference to the filler may saliently fail to identify the role. The structure of frames and roles thus gives us a salient example of differential cognitive accessibility. And this is reflected linguistically: we can readily say things like *The president has blue eyes* (the eyes belong to the individual, not to the role), while it is usually much more difficult to use names of individuals to refer to their roles.[2] Finally, the notion of the role is relative. The same element, with the description *president*, may be a role for the value *Clinton* and a value for the higher role *head of state*, as in *In the United States, the head of state is the president*.

Identity and counterpart relations are another area where unnoticed complexity results from mental space structure. Identity and coreference are crucial aspects of semantics; the use of personal and reflexive pronouns in natural language has proven to be one of the most complex problems faced by linguistic analysis, largely because there appear to be no formal aspects of linguistic structure which will reliably predict the choice of one pronominal form over another. No structural metric will predict the possibility of using a reflexive in examples like *This article was written by Sandy and myself* (Ross 1970) or *He opened the drawer and there was a letter to himself* (Zribi-Hertz 1989). The speaker in Ross's example and the (implicit) observer or subject of perception in Zribi-Hertz's example are available for coreference via reflexive pronouns, despite the complete lack (or the syntactically inaccessible placement) of linguistic antecedents. An understanding of the mental space structure potentially available to linguistic processing shows why the postulation of purely formal constraints on the use of reflexive forms falls short of an explanatorily (or even descriptively) adequate account. As mentioned above, there are hundreds of reasons to identify one entity with another: we may believe that the two entities are the same individual at two different times (as with the five-year-old and her later fifty-five-year-old self), or that one is a theatrical representation of another (Chuck Yaeger and the role *Chuck Yaeger* in *The Right Stuff*), or that one is a photographic representation of the other, and so on through a long list of possible mental space connections.

In other cases, reflexive pronoun use seems to refer to "identity" involving complex and partial mappings between cognitive constructs. Take the case of the "bad daughter" who behaves outrageously toward her uncomplaining father, while if *she* were the mistreated parent, she would be furious. It might be said about such a daughter that *If she had been her father, she would have hated herself* (i.e., she (the father) would have hated herself (the daughter)). This does not involve a typical case of "hating oneself," where the same entity is both the hater and the object of hatred. Instead, we are invited to construct a situation wherein the daughter's subjective viewpoint is somehow attached to her father's body, emotions, parental role, and so forth, while the "rest" of her remains the daughter, and is just as annoying as ever.[3] The "real-world" daughter has no single counterpart in this imaginary situation; and the imaginary father and daughter are "identical" only in that each of them corresponds to a different part of the same "real-world" entity. As Lakoff's paper in this volume reveals in more detail, "identity" is a complex concept, depending on our complex understanding of human personality, psychology, and so forth. Yet it is regularly reflected in contrasts between linguistic forms.

Linguistic Reflections of Cognitive Connections

In principle, there is no reason why human cognitive structures like frames, metaphors, representational worlds, and so forth should be reflected in semantics or in grammatical structure. A very reasonable and convenient theory of meaning might posit that language directly represents the properties and relations of entities in the world. In that case, we would not expect meaning to be structured by human cognition. And even if we imagine that certain aspects of semantics must inevitably describe human categories, the more autonomous from semantics we assume syntax to be, the less reason we have to suppose that syntactic constructions should reflect any of the structure of human experience and understanding. And a syntax, or a grammatical domain, connected to an objectivist meaning system would of course have no reason at all to be affected by such nonobjective phenomena.

However, as is already evident from the examples cited so far, linguistic structure does reflect precisely the aspects of human cognition described above. Far from naming entities purely on the basis of their independent properties or actions in the world, we often name them on the basis of cognitive and experiential connections which we think will enable our interlocutor to access the desired referent. Most interesting of all, there appear to be very general principles which regulate the relationship between an entity and the linguistic expression used to refer to it. Central among these is the **Principle of Access** (also known as the ID Principle),[4] which states that an expression which names or describes one entity (the trigger) can be used to access (and hence refer to) an entity (the target) in another domain only if the second domain is cognitively accessible from the first, and if there is a connection between trigger and target. Thus the domain of restaurant food orders allows ready cognitive access to a domain of customers placing orders, and there is a specific cognitive connection between a given customer and that customer's chosen dish. A representational painting of a seascape allows ready cognitive access to a hypothesized ocean and shore which is thus represented; and there may be a specific cognitive connection between a depiction of a given boat and a real or imagined model for the depiction.

The theory of mental spaces provides a model of the connection between semantics and cognition which allows us to address these important issues and offers theoretical concepts intended to account for the regularities observed in the cognition-language relationship. As we shall see elsewhere in this volume, mental space theory can thus elucidate a wide range of linguistic and philosophical problems, from the difficulties of indirect reference discussed above (which include classic issues such as referential opacity)[5] to choices of grammatical construction, of tense or aspect, and of pronoun form. Far from being independent of experiential structure, syntax and grammar, as well as lexical choice, are centrally involved in expressing and constructing human understanding of the world.

Mental Spaces

The discovery (or sometimes rediscovery) that cognitive connections of the sort outlined above play a central role in semantics, and more generally in the organization of thought, had important consequences for the research on meaning undertaken after the mid-seventies. Emphasis was shifted from the study of logic-like sentence meaning to that of the cognitive constructions which sentences help to set up—metaphoric projection, frame organization, roles, figure-ground configurations, metonymic pragmatic functions, mental space links, cognitive schemas, and cultural models.

Fauconnier's work on mental spaces provided a general model for studying the rich interplay between cognitive connections and natural language, and it prompted other research in a multitude of areas where this interplay has a major role. The realization that many superficially different kinds of problems were being dealt with by different people within a unified perspective was one of our strong motivations for preparing this book. We hope that the diversity and richness of the phenomena that lend themselves to the approach will bring out the generality, perhaps the universality, of domain connection in human thought and language.

Before moving on to other aspects of the volume, we will go over some basic notions and examples that initially motivated the mental space approach. As already pointed out, language is remarkable in allowing us to talk not just about what is, but also about what might have been, what will be, what is believed, hoped for, hypothesized, what is visually represented, make-believe, fiction, what happened, what should have happened, and much more. Objectively, none of these are the same. We are referring to very different kinds of things: time periods, possible and impossible worlds, intentional states and propositional attitudes, epistemic and deontic modalities, pictures (i.e., blobs of paint on paper or cloth), and so on. And yet it turns out that there is a level at which similar cognitive constructions are set up for all of them. This is revealed by the fact that they pattern identically in a wide array of cases from a grammatical and logical point of view.

So, for example, as insightfully noted by Jackendoff (1975), one finds the opaque/transparent ambiguities of propositional-attitude sentences like (1) in picture sentences like (2) as well.

(1) Max believes that the man with the gray hair is behind the fence.
   (*de re:* the man has gray hair, but Max may believe otherwise)
   (*de dicto:* Max believes the person is a man and has gray hair, but may be mistaken)

(2) In Max's painting, the man with gray hair is behind the fence.
   (the man has gray hair, but in the painting you can only see his nose and arms sticking out from behind the fence, or again perhaps he is represented with a different color of hair)
   or
   (what you see in the painting is a man with gray hair, perhaps an incorrect representation of a man with brown hair, or again not a representation of anybody in particular)

In Fauconnier 1979, 1981, 1985, and 1988, these observations are generalized to all cases for which domain connections apply. Examples of other domains which are associated with similar linguistic manifestations include the following.

Time

(3) In 1952, the man with gray hair headed the CIA.
   (Did he have gray hair then? Does he have gray hair now?)

Theater

(4) In the movie, the man with gray hair is a spy.
   (Who has gray hair? The actor? The character? Both?)

Counterfactuals

(5) If Jack were older, his gray hair would inspire confidence.
(Does Jack already have gray hair, or would he have it only in the counterfactual situation?)

Ambiguities like these are a simple consequence of the Access Principle, as we are about to show in more detail. The more general question they raise, along with analogous generalized patterns for presupposition and for constructions such as comparatives, is this: what are the mental representations that lend themselves to a broad application of operations like the Access Principle? And what is their status with respect to language use and language structure?

Mental space research seeks to provide answers to that double question in the form of a detailed model of the meaning construction that takes place under pressure from language forms, context, structured background knowledge, and other pragmatic factors.

The informal idea is straightforward in the case of simple examples like (1) through (5). When such sentences appear at some point in a discourse, they open a new domain (set up to contain structured information and inferences "about" beliefs or time periods or pictures, etc.). Phrases such as *in 1952* or *in the picture* or *Max believes* are all thus *space builders*—overt mechanisms which speakers can use to induce the hearer to set up a new mental space. They provide in themselves very little explicit information about that new domain, or what it purports to refer to. And for that reason, any additional structure that may be needed in the domain for reasoning purposes will typically be inherited according to default mechanisms from other domains, and ultimately often from background knowledge. In the same fashion, counterparts for elements in existing domains will be created in the new domains. Connectors link domains, and domains may be linked in more than one way. They allow a continuity of reference to hold throughout the discourse, but crucially they also allow a partitioning of information, such that an element and each one of its counterparts can be associated with different frames and properties.

In example (3), for instance, *man with gray hair* may identify an initial element in the base space. A new mental space is set up for the time period 1952 in which the initial element has a counterpart, possibly associated with different properties ("young man with brown hair"). The Access Principle will allow the counterpart to be accessed through a description of the initial element. In other words, we can be talking about the man who now has gray

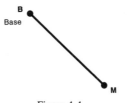

Figure 1.1

hair, and what he was doing back in 1952 (when his hair may have been of a different (and perhaps irrelevant) color).

Example (5) sets up a counterfactual space. The expression *his gray hair* may describe the hair Jack has now (base space) or the hair he would have if he were older (counterfactual space).

Of course, the elements in spaces are not themselves referents in the standard sense, and the descriptions are not descriptions of the mental elements. If a mental space partially fits the world, then an element and its construed descriptions will match reality in certain (complex) ways. In the simplest case, an element will be matched with a real referent, and a description will be matched with that real referent's real properties.

The dynamics of mental space construction and space linking are technically abstract, but conceptually straightforward. The basic idea is that, as we think and talk, mental spaces are set up, structured, and linked under pressure from grammar, context, and culture. The effect is to create a network of spaces through which we move as discourse unfolds. Because each space stems from another space (its "parent"), and because a parent can have many offspring, the space network will be a two-dimensional lattice. Motion through the lattice typically takes the following forms.

Starting from an initial (base) space (B), we generate a new ("child") space (M), and structure it in various ways, as shown in figure 1.1.

More generally, if a space is current,[6] we can generate a new space (M_j) relative to the current space (M_i), as shown in figure 1.2.

We can also move from higher spaces to lower spaces, or move back from lower to higher spaces.

Structure in any given space is simple in the sense that it is partial and involves no logical operators. But it incorporates frames and schematic conceptualizations. The space elements thus fit into cognitive models that are imported from background knowledge and typically elaborated locally during any particular discourse. Space elements may or may not have external referents. Whether they do or not, spaces are linked to the world by the presumption that "real" situations can be matched with space configurations by humans in systematic ways. The logical properties of thinking, first- and

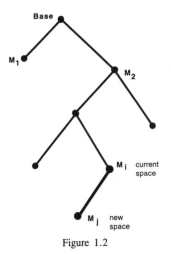

Figure 1.2

higher-order, follow from the ways in which spaces are linked, rather than belonging to an abstract mathematical system independent of thinkers. Elements (including frame-based roles) have counterparts in connected spaces, and structure in one space is related to structure in another.

Because the explicit structure set up in spaces is minimal, and because the default structure is always revisable as discourse unfolds, spaces are very different sorts of things from worlds (such as logicians' possible worlds, or the fictional worlds of narratives). Also, logical operations such as entailment or disjunction do not operate within spaces. Rather, they correspond to links and matching conditions between spaces.[7]

The dynamic and subjective view of meaning construction that emerges includes key concepts which are absent in the more narrow logical tradition. First, at any given point in discourse, one or (usually) several mental spaces have been set up and linked to each other; one of those spaces is singled out as the *viewpoint* (the space from which, at that point in discourse, others can be accessed or created). Second, some particular space (possibly the same one as the viewpoint space, but not necessarily) is in *focus;* it is the space to which structure is being added, and it is accessed from the current viewpoint space. Third, motion through the network of spaces consists in starting from a *base,* which provides the initial viewpoint, and then shifting viewpoint and focus, using the appropriate Space Connectors.

If this is the kind of conceptual organization that underlies the construction of meaning via discourse, then discourse participants must be able to keep track of the discourse dynamics, for purposes of reasoning and of communication. Since language is the direct overt manifestation of the process, we expect it to highlight some of the mental space structure. In particular, we expect that grammars of natural languages will include the means of giving participants (partial) answers to questions such as the following. What is the starting point (the base space)? What space is currently the viewpoint? How is the viewpoint located with respect to the base? What space is the focus of attention—the space being accessed and receiving additional structure? What are the connections between the spaces? What are the internal configurations within spaces?

Such questions define an important realm of application for grammatical and reasoning processes. An overarching notion that runs through it all is that of *access*. Because of the partitioning and subjectivity inherent in mental space building, some spaces will be used to access others, viewpoints and sometimes even bases will change, and some mental spaces will become inaccessible to others.

Ample evidence is offered in this book that grammar does indeed serve exactly such purposes, and that access is the key to understanding some logically mysterious properties of language.

Here are some simple, classic examples of access. Bear in mind that such examples would normally occur in larger discourses with preexisting mental space configurations. We treat them here essentially as minidiscourses.

(6) Max believes the woman with green eyes has blue eyes. (cf. Jackendoff 1975)

In the Base space, we have "a woman with green eyes," i.e., an element **a** associated with the properties "woman" and "green eyes." What sentence (6) does is open a new space M, in which structure representing something about Max's beliefs is going to be set up. In that new space, there is a counterpart **a'** for the element a initially set up in the base. And that counterpart is associated with the property "blue eyes" via the English expression *has blue eyes,* as shown in figure 1.3.

However, the linguistic expression which identifies **a'** is *the woman with green eyes.* And this description is appropriate for the base element **a,** linked to the property "green eyes."

It is easy to see how the Access Principle works here: spaces B (the base) and M are connected; element **a'** in space M is accessed through its counterpart in the base. The description *the woman with green eyes* picks out **a** and identifies its counterpart by virtue of the general Access Principle.

Notice that now **a'** is linked to a property (blue eyes) different from that of its counterpart (green eyes). There are now two ways of accessing **a'**: either through its counterpart, or directly in terms of the properties linked to

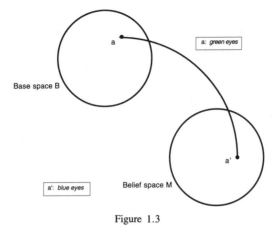

Figure 1.3

it in space M. So if Mary is the woman in question and if Max believes he will marry Mary, there are two ways to say it in the present context.

(7) Max believes he will marry the woman with green eyes. (access from the base)

(8) Max believes he will marry the woman with blue eyes. (access from M directly)

In the first case, although M is in focus, viewpoint is still from the base. In the second case, viewpoint has been shifted to the new space M.

A sentence like (6) might of course occur in a different context where *the woman with green eyes* is an appropriate description in M, rather than B. In that interpretation, **a'** is accessed directly in M, and is linked to the two properties "green eyes" and "blue eyes," yielding a reading closer to a contradiction: Max believes that Mary has blue eyes, and that she has green eyes.

In a case like (6) in which only two spaces are set up, mental space access explains why we find two readings (the traditional *de re* and *de dicto,* incorrectly viewed as logical properties of propositional-attitude sentences in many philosophical treatments). It is certainly gratifying to see referential opacity fall out as just a special case of Access. Even more important, perhaps, when seen in this light, opacity phenomena are just one case of ambiguity stemming from the availability of complex accessing strategies, combined with access principles. Typically, there will be more than two mental spaces in a discourse configuration, and correspondingly a linguistic description (such as *the woman with green eyes*) may well have one, two, or more possible identification paths within the structure.

Accessing principles depend on space configurations and the degree of accessibility of such spaces, sometimes marked grammatically or pragmatically. The type of space involved is much less relevant, and so we find ambiguities similar to those of (6) in (9), (10), (11), and many other similar forms where mental spaces are set up to talk about pictures, time, wishes, and so on.

(9) In the picture, the woman with green eyes has blue eyes. (Jackendoff 1975)

(10) When she was born, the woman with green eyes had blue eyes.

(11) I wish the woman with green eyes had blue eyes.

The sentence in (12) is another example that illustrates the same basic principles.

(12) In *Uneasy Rider,* Jane Fonda's brother takes a cross-country motorcycle trip with his sister.

A new space M is set up relative to the base B by the expression *In Uneasy Rider*. This new space serves to structure information, inferences, etc. about the movie (what happens to the characters in the story). Several configurations are compatible with sentence (12). In one, *Jane Fonda* accesses the actress in the base, *Jane Fonda's brother* picks out her brother, Peter Fonda. This in turn gives access to the character he plays, by connection to M. That character, Jack, has a sister, Jill; the corresponding element in M is accessed by *his sister*. Sentence (12) is saying, in effect, that Jack travels with Jill. Notice how the Base provides Viewpoint, with the movie space M in Focus, as shown in figure 1.4.

Another possibility, after Peter Fonda is picked out in the Base, is for the description *his sister* to pick out Peter's sister Jane. That in turn will provide Access from the Base to the movie character played by Jane, say Joy, who is not Jack's sister (we assume now that Jane Fonda is also starring in the movie). Sentence (12) is now accessing both characters from the Base, and its content is that Jack travels with Joy, as shown in figure 1.5.

Suppose now that the movie is actually about the Fonda family. Then the descriptions can be interpreted as applying directly to space M. Sentence (12) tells us that Peter travels with Jane (in the movie, of course!). The actors

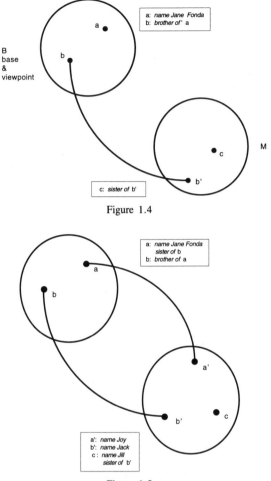

Figure 1.4

Figure 1.5

playing the parts of Peter and Jane might be Tom Cruise and Meryl Streep, but we do not access the characters via the corresponding actors in the Base. Viewpoint has been shifted to M, as shown in figure 1.6.

But this type of context also allows Access from the Base, because we now have a second link between the spaces: they are connected by the Actor-Character function (Meryl → Jane), and also by the Identity connector (''real'' Jane → ''movie'' Janc). The difference would come out if the movie were a ''film a clef'': it is still about the Fonda family, but names have been slightly altered—Meryl Streep now plays a character called Fane Jonda.

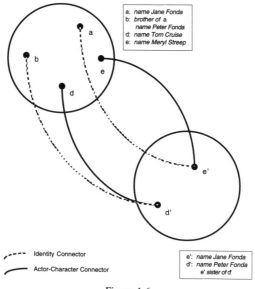

a: *name Jane Fonda*
b: *brother of* a
   name Peter Fonda
d: *name Tom Cruise*
e: *name Meryl Streep*

- - - -   Identity Connector

⌐‾‾   Actor-Character Connector

e': *name Jane Fonda*
d': *name Peter Fonda*
  e' *sister of* d

Figure 1.6

Sentence (12) remains applicable, telling us now that Feter travels with Fane. The Access Principle has been applied again, but this time via a different connector, as shown in figure 1.7.

Further intepretations could be devised. They are not a matter of vague or fuzzy pragmatics. To compute an understanding of (12), one must choose among several connecting paths, based on current configurations, background knowledge, and target inferences. Examples involving explicit representations like movies and pictures probably make the ambiguities more apparent, but it is easy to show (Fauconnier 1985) that the access possibilities are the same with other mental spaces (beliefs, time, hypotheticals, counterfactuals, fiction, quantification, etc.). Sentences (13), (14), and (15), have the potential to build up space configurations and connecting paths like those of (12).

(13) Henry believes that Jane Fonda's brother took a cross-country motorcycle trip with his sister.

(14) In 1983, Jane Fonda's brother took a cross-country motorcycle trip with his sister.

(15) I wish Jane Fonda's brother had taken a cross-country motorcycle trip with his sister.

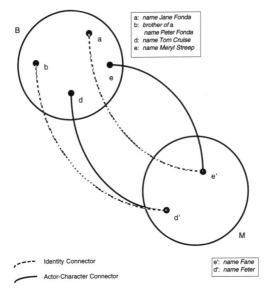

Figure 1.7

As in examples (1) through (5) above, multiple access strategies are available. Henry may or may not believe that Jane has a brother, or that the brother is the traveler, and so forth.

The above examples are meant to give a flavor of the initial motivation for the mental space framework. Later research has explored many other aspects and areas of application. This volume presents some of the most recent work bringing mental space theory together with analysis of the structure of language. Like other research in cognitive semantics, the work is based on, and motivated by, the following powerful idea: complex, high-level cognitive constructions lie behind our everyday reasoning, our social behavior, and our use of language, and such constructions can be uncovered and scientifically investigated by using the evidence provided by grammar, i.e., grammatical markings and grammatical organization. Typically, the cognitive construction process is driven by much more than language alone, so that the link to grammatical structure is anything but direct. The contributions to this book reveal the subtle yet systematic role played by natural language grammar in setting up the kinds of connections evoked informally above (e.g., for time, belief, images, etc.).

Access and Viewpoint

Assuming, then, that we construct mental spaces by some of the mechanisms outlined above, how does that help us understand the relationship between linguistic structure and viewpoint? As mentioned above, it is an inherent property of human cognition to contextualize, to access information differentially in different contexts. Much recent linguistic work has analyzed the ways in which semantic and pragmatic structure reflects and makes use of differential accessibility. Langacker (1987, 1991, 1993) and Talmy (1978, 1988) have both argued at some length that everyday syntax and semantics are constantly and centrally creating viewpoint in ways that are inextricably intertwined with their other functions. Fauconnier (1985) has argued that the French subjunctive in a relative clause marks that clause's content as being part of the irrealis world depicted by a higher subjunctive clause, and prevents the information contained in the relative clause from being taken as a description of a real-world situation. This choice of mood could thus be said to both mark the speaker's viewpoint and prevent direct access to the information in the relative clause from a base "reality" mental space. The technical notion of focus space has been developed by Dinsmore (1991), who develops a general theory of discourse management, subsuming Reichenbach's (1947) temporal reference system as a subcase of a general mental space partitioning framework. He shows that not only differing temporal spaces, but differing access to and focus on those temporal spaces, are essential components of the semantics of tense and aspect categories in English. Banfield (1982), Fleischman (1990), Silva-Corvalan (1983), and others have laid out ways in which tense, aspect, deixis, choice of referential description, and other formal linguistic markings structure the presentation of viewpoint in literary texts. Chun, Li, and Zubin (n.d.) have further demonstrated the relationship of other grammatical markings (such as reflexive morphemes) to the subjectivity structure of oral and written narrative. Much of this work seems highly compatible with a mental space framework. Subjectivity structure, for example, involves the multiple clues indicating what mental space we are in at a given point in the text. Even more recent work by Michelle Cutrer (1994) has developed these ideas extensively using the mental space framework to show the fundamental unity and elegance of the disourse-construction principles in narrative and in everyday talk.

Many of the papers in this volume are thus centrally focused on the issue of how grammar structures cognitive access and viewpoint. Deixis and tense being inherently viewpoint phenomena, it is not surprising that these show pervasive interaction with mental space structure. Rubba's paper demonstrates the use of spatial deictics (*this, that, here,* and *there*) to refer not only directly and literally to the physical space of the speech environment, but indirectly (via metaphor and metonymy) to the social space and social relations associated with that environment. Our evidently differential access to space, depending on location, is thus used to mark differential access to and connection with social and cultural domains. Van Hoek uses data from American Sign Language (ASL), a language which uses physical space as the medium of its "phonology," to show that in this different modality, and despite superficially dissimilar systems of reference in ASL and spoken languages, very general accessing principles nonetheless apply in ASL as they do in spoken languages. For example, ASL reference systems demand the initial establishment of a location as connected with a referent; subsequent reference to that entity will be accessible only via this established location, unless another reference location is established by appropriate mechanisms.

Matsumoto provides an example of the way viewpoint of a static situation can be changed by mapping it onto a space involving dynamic change processes. Whether or not this mapping is viewed as metaphorical, it clearly changes subjective viewpoint by setting up contact between mental spaces. When a border is described as "running from point X to point Y," although the viewer does not see the border as physically in motion (shifting its location), the mapping of a line onto a directional vector path creates the effect of viewpoint: the speaker is accessing the border from the vantage of X.

Familiar examples of "transparent" and "opaque" reference of definite descriptions show the opposite effect. The same linguistic material can serve as an access point to evoke more than one cognitive entity. Uses of subjunctive forms to show mental space subordination to an irrealis space is one way of limiting this potential for accessing extra, irrelevant readings. Mejías-Bikandi's paper shows that the Spanish subjunctive is used as a way of limiting access to referents and presuppositions which would be accessible using indicative clauses. Sweetser similarly demonstrates that English "backshifted" counterfactual verb forms can be used to mark the application of a definite description inside a conditional space, rather than in a base mental space.

Another way in which one linguistic expression can access multiple referents is via basic structural connections such as that present between roles and their values. Sakahara shows that the distribution of the Japanese particles *wa* and *ga* and other aspects of copula-sentence structure in Japanese follow from an understanding of semantic predication and identification as involving roles and values. The difference between predicating a role of a value (*Homer is the author of the Iliad*) and identifying the value of a known role (*The author of the Iliad is Homer*) is crucially marked in the grammar, thus showing the important role of information access in the syntax and morphology of the copula construction.

Sanders and Redeker continue the tradition of examining viewpoint in narrative structure. They explore the ways in which access between mental spaces, as marked by linguistic structure, provides narrative viewpoint and they show how the interpretation of narratives is influenced by the choice of implicit and explicit markers of viewpoint. The relevant markers include the choice of description from one subject's belief space rather than from the narrator's space, and implicit rather than explicit attribution of information to some particular subject's mental state.

The impression left by this body of work is that the dependence of interpretation on viewpoint is a ubiquitous phenomenon, which is exactly what we would expect, given the psychological evidence that human information processing is strongly context-influenced. Deixis, for example, is a norm, not an oddity, in language. But forms once thought to have much more "straightforward" meanings—past tense is a salient example—can be seen to fit into a network of linguistic functions having to do with creating, maintaining, and interpreting information from particular points of access.

Semantic Freeloading

Natural language has a striking potential for making rich and extensive meaning available on the basis of very little overt linguistic structure. Consider, for instance, the comment made about one 1992 U.S. presidential candidate (George Bush) by another (Tom Harkin).

He was born on third base and he thinks he hit a triple.

What would it take for someone who knows about baseball, politics, and American society to automatically set up an appropriate domain mapping, find the right counterparts, and derive the rich set of inferences intended by the speaker? It might seem like improbable mental acrobatics, and yet it is the stuff of our everyday thinking and talking. One salient feature of such processes is that they make extensive use of preexisting structure derived from our culture, experience, and local background knowledge. This preexisting structure comes with its built-in inferences, which do not require reprocessing each time they are used anew; and, perhaps even more remarkably, the mappings allow them to be projected wholesale on domains of different content.[8] In Rubba's paper, for example, the inherited knowledge of the cultural map of San Diego is shown to be present for exploitation in the nonliteral use of distal deictics such as *that part of the city,* referring to a part that is culturally alien to the speaker rather than physically distant.

This is just one of the ways in which significant and rich meaning is obtained at very little cost. Grammar combines with mental space construction to provide several others, and many of the contributions to this book provide striking examples of this natural-language capacity.

Claudia Brugman examines the interaction between mental space phenomena and the basic constructions linked to English HAVE: Causative, Resultant State, Affecting Event, and Attributive. Analyzing examples like (16) and (17), Brugman shows that superficially different senses linked to such constructions actually fall out from the interplay of grammatical properties with the higher level of conceptual semantic organization reflected in mental space construction.

(16) Chandler had Marlowe give up Brigid without a shred of remorse.

(17) *The Chronicle* has the Giants winning the pennant next season.

Cross-domain mappings of this type are a very general source of creative context-bound polysemy. Laura Michaelis finds that they generate multiple (and productive) senses of *still* and *already,* as in examples (18), (19), and (20).

(18) I was still there when he arrived.

(19) He may have apologized, but he still shouldn't have done that.

(20) Macy's is still within Joe's price range, though Saks is too expensive.

The mapping theory accounts for the multitude of senses that can emerge when operators corresponding to words like *still* are applied to new domains. Semantics is generative not by virtue of grammar, but by virtue of the building principles for cognitive constructions.

Sweetser, in her paper, employs the same general strategy to reduce the systematic but idiosyncratic properties of English conditionals described by Fillmore (1990a, 1990b). It turns out once more that the relevant grammatical markers are faithful indicators of conditional mental space constructions, from which the observed semantic properties are easily derivable. Thus, for example, conditional structures mark the setting up of several different kinds of mental spaces, and the choice of verb form within a conditional structure reflects both relative tense and embedded status within mental space constructions.[9]

Another very general discourse mechanism which provides the partitioned spaces with the required structure for proper inferencing and local elaboration is the phenomenon of *Spreading*. Pragmatic and grammatical conditions allow structure from one space to be automatically (but sometimes conditionally) transferred to one or many other spaces simultaneously.

The case of Spreading that has perhaps received the most attention in the literature is Presupposition Float. In mental space terminology, the dynamics of Float can be expressed straightforwardly: if a substructure is introduced into a space by means of a grammatically presuppositional construction, it will float up into higher spaces until it meets itself or a contradiction of itself. For example, *Laura's husband* is a grammatically definite description presupposing that Laura is married. This presupposition spreads differently in the following examples:

(21) Bill says that Joe wants to meet Laura's husband.

(22) Bill says that Laura is single but that Joe wants to meet Laura's husband.

(23) Bill says that Laura is married and that Joe wants to meet Laura's husband.

All three examples involve a minimum of three spaces (the base space, and those evoked by *say* and *want*). In example (21), the presupposition that Laura is married is satisfied by default in all three spaces (in the absence of further discourse structure). In (22), the presupposition is satisfied only at the level of *want;* it gets blocked at the higher level of *say* by an explicitly incompatible structure (*Laura is single*). In (23), the presupposition does make it up to the *say* space, where it meets an explicit copy of itself (*Laura is married*), which blocks it from floating all the way up to the base. The speaker of (23) does not indicate whether Laura is actually married.

Presupposition Float is another phenomenon for which grammatical information will often provide decisive clues. Mejías-Bikandi's paper provides a very clear case of subtle meaning differences produced by the interaction of Spreading with grammar. Mood in this study of Spanish linguistic contexts is analyzed as a grammatical marker that indicates whether a particular space is *accessible* to another. An important consequence of this type of analysis is that grammatical devices are available not only to mark certain space structures as presuppositional and hence floatable, but also to control spreading within configurations.

Other instances of Spreading (structure propagation) show up in the analogical counterfactual phenomena displayed in Fauconnier's contribution. Default structuring occurs in a "nonrealistic" way to yield intended inferences, but the structures remain cancelable in later discourse, and if cancellation does occur, the entire configuration is liable to shift radically (through a sort of instantaneous reverse spreading) and yield a sharply different interpretation. This effect is apparent, for example, in the punch lines of jokes, when the listener is forced into a sudden reinterpretation of immediately preceding discourse (cf. the comic-strip example in Fauconnier's paper).

Meaning is also obtained "for free" when covert spaces are set up without explicit grammatical information. Covert spaces are needed to provide a complete understanding of the analogical counterfactual examples. This constitutes another case in which the cognitive constructions go well beyond the surface grammar.

The Cultural and Experiential Nature of the Models

The single biggest source of "meaning for free" is our rich understanding of experience and culture. In this collection, we have Rubba's analysis of the language of spatial deixis giving expression to cultural understandings of similarity and difference, thus vastly extending its central physical range of meaning. (Fleischman (1990) has argued that temporal reference is similarly extended from basic time structure to social and epistemic distancing.) Crucially, such an extension is not only tapping into a general cultural model of social distance as physical distance (people are "close" socially if they have an important social relationship, "distant" if they have none or only a peripheral one), but also into the experiential basis for this cultural model. There is a real experiential correlation, from early contact with nurturing parents onwards, between social relationship and physical proximity, and indeed spatial structure in the physical world. All of this structured understanding of the world, more and less cultural, provides a basis for linguistic usages like extending the *this/that* contrast to mark "my kind of social group" and "not my kind of social group." We don't have to create such structure to interpret such expressions, we merely have to access extant structure. What Rubba shows is that this structure is exploited linguistically to allow expression of a complex mental space construct involving cognitive linkups between maps of geographic areas, social identities, and deixis in both domains.

Lakoff's paper, in displaying the ways in which grammatical markings of coreference mark different aspects of our understanding of identity, displays our mental models of selfhood and personhood. The grammar need not create a concept of a human as having differentiable, if not separable, mental and physical attributes: the culture has such a concept, available for evocation and marking by grammatical phenomena. Thus *I dreamed I was Brigitte Bardot and I kissed me* evokes an image of my consciousness in Brigitte Bardot's body, engaged in kissing my body, while *I dreamed I was Brigitte Bardot and I kissed myself* evokes a scenario in which my consciousness is again in Brigitte Bardot's body, but Brigitte Bardot's body gets kissed rather than mine. Grammatical structures for coreference, such as the control (or EQUI) construction also have different properties from pronouns, and again pick out certain aspects of our understanding of identity. If grammar creates mechanisms for marking recurrent reference to the same entity (e.g., pronouns and reflexives), then it is cost-free to extend such mechanisms to more complex understandings of identity and sameness between entities, often at very abstract levels.

Pragmatic scales are perhaps the ideal example of culturally based semantic freeloading. Basic precultural experience allows all humans to extract scales from the physical environment: degrees of variable physical attributes such as weight, length, and so on, are among obviously scalar phenomena. Scalar correlations (such as lighter-hotter or darker-colder in the physical world) are extremely useful, since they allow us to reason from the degree of one aspect of a situation to the degree of some other aspect of the situation. However, grammatical constructions which expoit scalar models are by no means restricted to general experientially based scales. Instead, we construct and constantly make use of cultural understandings that department stores exist on a scale of expensiveness, jobs on a scale of authority within an organization (or on a pay *scale*), foods on a scale of exoticness, and so forth. Michaelis' paper on *still* shows that the use of this expression reflects assumed structures of this kind, as in *Aunt Amanda would probably enjoy the Italian restaurant, but not the sashimi place: in fact, even Indian food is* <u>*still*</u> *a bit far out for her*. The speaker of such an utterance crucially does not need to do all the cultural building up of a model which includes an understanding of Anglo and ethnic cuisines, a cline between the two ends of the spectrum, and so forth.

Frames, and the roles they bring with them, are likewise part of our general human and culture-specific experience. They make pervasive cognitive connections, and permit motivated but rampant use of one linguistic form to refer to multiple referents. Sakahara's paper on role and individual readings of Japanese noun phrases explores some of the ways that grammar reflects our cultural and contextual understanding of roles, values, and frames. Rubba invokes cultural frames and roles to account for the use of generic *you* in speakers' scripts for assimilation of immigrants to the United States.

Other built-in mappings like metaphors and pragmatic functions are often deeply rooted in culture and in experience, and can bring along huge amounts of information and structure at no extra cognitive cost. Although this volume does not focus on metaphor, or on the identification and categorization of new pragmatic connectors, Matsumoto's paper is an example of metaphorically structured mappings (in this case, probably based in physical experience). These meanings are there to be evoked—they need not be arbitrarily specified or created for the specific usage in question.

The initially overwhelming complexity of linguistic usages is, then, not an independent and autonomous complexity. It is a reflection of the complex—and economically interrelated—structure of cognition.

Notes

1. With respect to inheritance, we should also mention the Parsimony Principle of Kay (1983). Kay basically claims that hearers construct interpretations of texts in such a way as to rely maximally on inherited information or already set up information, rather than constantly setting up new entities for no reason.

2. For example, *George Bush is commander in chief for only a few more days* is most readily understood as meaning that the individual will no longer fill that role, rather than that the office of president will be dissociated from the office of commander in chief.

3. The example is adapted from the following line in a play by Samuel Beckett, reported by Michel Charolles (p.c.): *S'il avait été son père, il se serait détesté.*

4. Fauconnier 1979, 1985.

5. Sentences such as *Oedipus wants to marry his mother* have two classes of readings. In one class, Oedipus is supposed to want to marry someone (perhaps Jocasta), whom he does not believe to be his mother but whom the speaker characterizes as his mother. In the other, Oedipus's wish is to marry someone whom he (as well as the speaker, perhaps, though not necessarily) would describe as his mother. The latter class of readings, where the description is that given by the subject and not that given by the speaker, is traditionally characterized as *opaque* or *de dicto*, the former as *transparent* or *de re*.

6. As discourse unfolds, focus and viewpoint may shift from one space to another; this shift corresponds to an abstract motion of the discourse participants through the lattice of spaces. A space is current when it serves as viewpoint, or when it is in focus.

7. Discourse Representation Theory, as developed by Kamp and his colleagues (cf. Kamp 1984), involves partial and augmentable structure, and in this respect resembles the theory of mental spaces.

8. Fauconnier and Turner (1994) show that the sentence in (16) is an example of conceptual blending, in which two initial mental spaces give rise to a third, which uses structure from the input spaces and from background knowledge to create novel structure, and allows central cognitive work to be performed.

9. See also Cutrer 1994.

References

Banfield, Ann. 1982. *Unspeakable Sentences: Narration and Representation in the Language of Fiction*. Boston: Routledge and Kegan Paul.

Chun, S., Naicong Li, and David Zubin. n.d. Subjective Mental Spaces in Story Worlds. In preparation.

Cutrer, Michelle. 1994. Time and Tense in Narrative and in Everyday Language. Ph.D. diss., University of California, San Diego.

Dinsmore, John. 1991. *Partitioned Representations*. Dordrecht: Kluwer Academic Publishers.

Fauconnier, Gilles. 1979. Mental Spaces: A Discourse Processing Approach to Natural Language Logic. Manuscript, University of California, San Diego.

———. 1981. *Sull'anafora: atti del Seminario, Accademia dell Crusca, 14–16 dicembre 1978*, 129–46. Firenze: Presso l'Accademia della Crusca.

———. 1985. *Mental Spaces: Aspects of Meaning Construction in Natural Language*. Cambridge, Mass.: MIT Press. Reprinted 1994, Cambridge: Cambridge University Press.

———. 1988. Quantifiers, Roles, and Domains. In Umberto Eco, Marco Santambrogio, and Patrizia Violi, eds., *Meaning and Mental Representation*, 61–80. Bloomington, Ind.: Indiana University Press.

———. 1991. Roles and Values: The Case of French Copula Constructions. In Carol Georgopoulos and Roberta Ishihara, eds., *Interdisciplinary Approaches to Language: Essays in Honor of S.-Y. Kuroda*, 181–206. Dordrecht: Kluwer Academic Publishers.

Fauconnier, Gilles, and Mark Turner. 1994. Conceptual Projection and Middle Spaces. Technical Report no. 9401, Department of Cognitive Science, University of California, San Diego.

Fillmore, Charles J. 1985. Frames and the Semantics of Understanding. *Quaderni di Semantica* 6(2):222–54.

———. 1990a. Epistemic Stance and Grammatical Form in English Conditional Sentences. *Papers from of the Twenty-Sixth Annual Regional Meeting of the Chicago Linguistic Society*, 137–62. University of Chicago.

———. 1990b. The Contribution of Linguistics to Language Understanding. In Aura Bocaz, ed., *Proceedings of the First Symposium on Cognition, Language and Culture*. 109–28. Santiago: Universidad de Chile.

Fleischman, Suzanne. 1990. *Tense and Narrativity: From Medieval Performance to Modern Fiction*. Austin, Tex.: University of Texas Press.

Gentner, Dedre. 1983. Structure-Mapping: A Theoretical Framework for Analogy. *Cognitive Science* 7:155–70.

Gentner, Dedre, and Donald R. Gentner. 1983. Flowing Waters or Teeming Crowds: Mental Models of Electricity. In Dedre Gentner and Albert L. Stevens, eds., *Mental Models*, 99–129. Hillsdale, N.J.: Lawrence Erlbaum Associates.

Gibbs, Raymond. 1980. Spilling the Beans on Understanding and Memory for Idioms in Conversation. *Memory and Cognition* 8:449–56.

Gibbs, Raymond, and J. O'Brien. 1990. Idioms and Mental Imagery: The Metaphorical Motivation for Idiomatic Meaning. *Cognition* 36:35–68.

Goffman, Erving. 1974. *Frame Analysis*. New York: Harper and Row.

Hofstadter, Douglas. 1986. Analogies and Roles in Human and Machine Thinking. In *Metamagical Themas*, 547–603. New York: Bantam Books.

Jackendoff, Ray. 1975. On Belief Contexts. *Linguistic Inquiry* 6:53–93.

Kamp, Hans. 1984. A Theory of Truth and Semantic Representation. In Jeroen Groenendijk, Theo M.V. Janssen, and Martin Stokhof, eds., *Truth, Interpretation, and Information: Selected Papers from the Third Amsterdam Colloquium,* 1–41. Dordrecht: Foris Publications.

Kay, Paul. 1983. Three Properties of the Ideal Reader. Cognitive Science Technical Report no. 7, Institute for Cognitive Studies, University of California, Berkeley.

Lakoff, George, and Mark Johnson. 1980. *Metaphors We Live By.* Chicago: University of Chicago Press.

Langacker, Ronald W. 1987. *Foundations of Cognitive Grammar.* Vol. 1: *Theoretical Prerequisites.* Stanford, Calif.: Stanford University Press.

———. 1991. *Foundations of Cognitive Grammar.* Vol. 2: *Descriptive Application.* Stanford, Calif.: Stanford University Press.

———. 1993. Reference Point Constructions. *Cognitive Linguistics* 4:1–38.

Nunberg, Geoffrey. 1978. *The Pragmatics of Reference.* Bloomington, Ind.: Indiana University Linguistics Club.

Reichenbach, Hans. 1947. *Elements of Symbolic Logic.* New York: MacMillan.

Ross, John Robert. 1970. On Declarative Sentences. In R. Jacobs and P. S. Rosenbaum, eds., *Readings in English Transformational Grammar,* 222–72. Waltham, Mass.: Ginn & Co.

Schank, Roger C., and R.P. Abelson. 1977. *Scripts, Plans, Goals and Understanding: An Inquiry into Human Knowledge Structures.* Hillsdale, N.J.: Lawrence Erlbaum Associates.

Silva-Corvalan, Carmen. 1983. Tense and Aspect in Oral Spanish Narrative: Context and Meaning. *Language* 59:760–80.

Talmy, Leonard. 1978. Figure and Ground in Complex Sentences. In Joseph H. Greenberg, ed., *Universals of Human Language.* Vol. 4: *Syntax,* 625–49. Stanford, Calif.: Stanford University Press.

———. 1988. The Relation of Grammar to Cognition. In Brygida Rudzka-Ostyn, ed., *Topics in Cognitive Linguistics,* 165–205. Amsterdam: John Benjamins.

Zribi-Hertz, A. 1989. Anaphor Binding and Narrative Point of View: English Reflexive Pronouns in Sentence and Discourse. *Language* 65:695–727.

2 Mental Spaces, Constructional Meaning, and Pragmatic Ambiguity

.
.
.
.

In the sentences in (1), the main verb, HAVE, appears to be expressing the depiction of an irrealis situation or the prediction of a future situation.[1]

(1) a. The movie had him dying in the end.
    b. The play has him lonely and old when he dies.
    c. "Lefebvre had Canseco running all the way."[2]
    d. "Dearborn has [Henry Miller] die on June 7, Fergusen on June 4."
    e. Imelda's count has Ferdinand as the victor.
    f. Jeane Dixon has Dan Quayle winning the nomination in 1996.
    g. Wayne Walker has the A's finishing outside of first in the division.

In this paper I demonstrate that the "predictive" or "depictive" semantics of these sentences do not result from a distinct sense of the verb HAVE, but rather follow from more general principles for the cross-space interpretation of individuals and relations—and do so, for the most part, via pragmatics, or "invisibly," in the sense of Fauconnier 1990.

In addition to the basic concepts and constructs of the mental spaces framework, I employ a lexically based approach to the constructions in question (along the lines of Fillmore, Kay, and O'Connor 1988 and Norvig and Lakoff 1987). I will describe some of the general semantic properties which are associated with the construction as lexical properties of its head. Those constructional semantic properties, plus the invisible aspects of meaning which are recovered via pragmatic and real-world knowledge, account for the interpretation of these examples in a generally straightforward and elegant way.

I will also discuss an extraposition-type construction (*The Bible has it that woman was made from man*), which shares the lexical head and many of the semantic properties but which differs in both its syntactic and its space-building properties. By contrast with the constructions exemplified in (1), the semantics of the extraposition-type construction necessarily involves the creation of a daughter space. The existence of this construction shows that a specific complementation pattern may be a criterion for space building; this is a possibility not explicitly mentioned in other discussions of space builders (Fauconnier 1985, 1990, 1991; Rubba, chapter 8 in this volume).

I will first outline the essential properties of four basic constructions headed by the verb HAVE, properties which must be assigned to these constructions independent of the creation of another space. This overview is intended merely to introduce the notion that HAVE heads four constructions which show distinct semantic properties and which impose morpholexical constraints on the form of their complements which reflect their semantic differences. I then show that the use of HAVE with the depictive or predictive semantics exemplified in (1) is simply the product of a composition of one of the four basic constructions with an irrealis mental space. I also discuss some conditions on the constructed space, and the concomitant constraints on the semantico-pragmatic construal of the complements of HAVE. In a final data section, I then discuss the extraposition-type construction and its semantico-pragmatic interpretation, which invokes an irrealis daughter space. I conclude with a summary and some speculations as to the larger significance of these findings.

The Semantics of HAVE Constructions

The constructions which are at issue comprise a proper subset of those headed by English HAVE. They form a natural subset, since they have superficially identical structural properties and differ from each other in easily defined aspects.

I use the expression *construction* in accordance with the usage of Fillmore and Kay n.d. and Fillmore, Kay, and O'Connor 1988, inter alia. (I also use *reading* roughly synonymously with *construction* when I wish to emphasize the frame semantics associated with the construction.) In this usage, a construction is any conventional pairing of formal properties with semantic properties.[3] For the examples discussed here, the grammatical construction may be thought of as equivalent to the lexical entry of its head, HAVE. One can describe the formal conditions of co-occurrence between HAVE and its complements, and one can also describe a frame-based semantics (or "ontological semantics," after Nirenburg and Levin 1991) which the use of each such construction invokes. The latter is what I mean by its *constructional* semantics. The description of the construction also contains semantic properties which must hold of its complements individually (such as their semantic roles and aspectual properties of the predicational complement—what Niren-burg and Levin call the "syntax-driven" semantics). Both kinds of semantic information will be relevant to the description of these data, and both are included in a lexically headed grammatical construction as conceived by Fillmore, Kay, and O'Connor (1988).

The range of semantic interpretations of sentences whose matrix verb is HAVE has been the subject of a great deal of discussion, both within and outside the generative paradigm (see, for example, Anderson 1971, Bach 1967, Bendix 1966, Cattell 1984, Fillmore 1968, and Kearns 1988). Many of these studies have been concerned with the "problem" of isolating the lexical semantics of HAVE itself, or with supporting one or another version of the claim that HAVE has no lexical semantics.[4] The examples in (2) show why it has appeared to some that the relations coded by HAVE are too diverse, and too dependent for their specific interpretation on the semantics of their complements, to be given a lexical definition (I exclude from this part of the discussion any sentence which is readily given a depictive or predictive construal, as in (1)).

(2) a. I had my baby kissed by the president.
     b. I had him climbing the walls.
     c. Albany has an express bus running to it.
     d. She has children coming to her house this Sunday.
     e. I had him bring chips to the party.
     f. She has children come to her house every Sunday.
     g. I have a tooth missing.
     h. I had him in the palm of my hand.
     i. I have five dollars in my pocket.
     j. "No one will have this person as chairman."
     k. "A neighbor had at least two wives pass away before anyone thought anything of it."
     l. I had him angry the minute I walked in the door.
     m. I have my husband to keep honest.
     n. I have my husband to keep me honest.
     o. We have to grade exams this weekend.
     p. We have eaten already.
     q. I have two sons.
     r. I have no more patience.

However, in Brugman 1988 I argue that most constructions headed by HAVE fall into one of four classes.[5] I will not recapitulate those arguments here; rather I describe the four classes which together I call the "basic" constructions, and I argue that the depictive and predictive semantics of the sentences in (1) can be derived from these basic constructions.

These basic constructions are those exemplified in (2a) through (2l). They share certain syntactic properties which may be schematized as in (3).[6]

(3) $[_s [NP_1] [_{VP} HAVE [NP_2] [XP]]]$

Throughout the following discussion, I refer to the subject noun phrase as NP_1 and to its denotatum as NP_1'; similarly the postverbal nominal is NP_2, and its denotatum NP_2'. The expression *XP* is as usual a variable over all major phrase types, any of which can appear in the third (or "predicational") complement position in all four readings; for simplicity, I confine my discussion to sentences with a VP in this position. The situation or state of affairs which the syntactic sequence $NP_2 + XP$ denotes will be notated as *S*. All the data to be considered here share the semantic property that NP_2 is construed as the notional subject of XP (in contrast with (2m)).

The sentences in (2a) through (2l), which exemplify the structures primarily discussed here, all express relationships between an individual (NP_1') and some situation *S*—an event, an action, or a state.[7] These sentences contrast in various ways with the other examples in (2): those in (2q) and (2r) express relations between individuals; (2m) and (2o) express relations between an individual and an event where NP_1 denotes a participant in *S*, where there is a control relation into the embedded predicate; and I treat the HAVE of the perfect construction in (2p) as an operator on an event.

The "Basic" Constructions

In Brugman 1988 I argue that the sentences in (2a) through (2l) fall into four classes, distinguishable ultimately on semantic grounds. The semantic differences are constructional—that is, they involve differences of interpretation at the sentence level—and there are concomitant differences in the co-occurrence constraints placed on the complements of HAVE.

I call the four construction types Causative, Resultant Event, Attributive, and Affecting Event. These are just names for lexical entries, intended to be mnemonic for the constructional semantics of each type. Their collective status as "basic" constructions is not justified here; I use the term as a reminder that these are the four constructions whose frame-based and syntax-driven semantics are most readily describable as a projection of their sub-categorization properties and to which other constructions can be easily related. In the next four subsections, I outline the semantic constraints on the complements in each construction and talk briefly about the constructional semantics of each.

CAUSATIVE

The use of HAVE which is most easily isolated is the one I have labeled the Causative, exemplified in (4).

(4) a. I had the children make dinner last night.
   b. I had the president kiss my baby. (cf. (2a))
   c. I had him bring chips to the party. (= (2e))
   d. She has children come to her house every Sunday. (= (2f))

An often-noted semantic property of the Causative HAVE construction is that it is never used to describe a situation of typical (direct or billiard-ball) causation. It generally is used to describe a situation of indirect, and often verbal, causation. Even when the causation is verbal, it usually must refer to an indirect verbal (persuasive) causation rather than an order (cf. Rader 1981).[8] The semantics of the Causative construction is restricted further, in ways not relevant to the current discussion.

It follows from the fact that this construction denotes an act of persuasive causation that NP_1' must be human—must, in fact, be a possible agent of the activity of S. The other important semantic constraint, on the aspectual structure of the XP complement, is best discussed in the context of the next construction.

RESULTANT EVENT

Often confounded with the Causative is the Resultant-Event reading of HAVE. Examples like (5) show this semantic type, in which the existence, presence, action, appearance, or demeanor of NP_1' results in the situation denoted by the sequence NP_2 + XP. The resulting situation need not be intended, nor indeed desired, by NP_1'.

(5) [Despite my best efforts,] I had him angry the minute I walked in the door.

Notice that the sort of nondeliberate instigation emphasized here by the sentence adverbial is not compatible with the semantics of the Causative construction.[9]

(6) #[Without knowing it,] I had the children wash the dishes.

Since NP_1' is not an agent, naturally NP_1 need not be animate.

(7) The boss's foul mood had the steno pool quaking in their pumps.

Another difference in the semantic conditions placed on the complements of the two constructions concerns the aspectual type of the predicational complement. If we take as demonstrated that a human can be the referent of the subject of either construction, but a nonhuman can be NP_1' only of the Resultant Event, the following contrast is highly suggestive:

(8) a.   I had the children wash the dishes last night.
    b.   I had the children washing the dishes in no time.

(9) a.   *My glowering countenance had the children wash the dishes last
        night.
    b.   My glowering countenance had the children washing the dishes in
        no time.

This contrast in acceptability indicates that the Causative construction requires a perfective XP complement, while the Resultant-Event reading requires an imperfective XP. When XP is a perfective VP, this condition may be manifested in bare-stem infinitive morphology, and when it is imperfective, the VP will have the morphology of the present participle (for other forms, see Brugman 1988). The distribution of temporal adverbials is correlated with the aspectual type of the XP constituent, as shown by (8a) and (8b).

Another formal difference between the Causative and Resultant-Event constructions follows from the difference in their constructional semantics: under many circumstances, having NP_2 coreferential with NP_1 in the Causative construction renders a pragmatically marked sentence, whereas a corresponding Resultant-Event sentence is unremarkable ((10b) is an example of Resultant Event, while (11) is a Causative).

(10) a.   I had the children get out of bed promptly.
     b.   I had myself out of bed promptly.

(11)   #I had myself get out of bed promptly.

This is presumably because there are circumstances in which it is odd to imagine exerting indirect agency on oneself. However, one can initiate upon onself an act which results in the state of one's being out of bed, the resulting state being the situation focused on by the Resultant-Event construction.

Essentially the same fact accounts for the difference in the potential identity of the understood proximal cause of XP' in two of the readings which Chomsky (1965:21–22) isolates for the sentence *I had the book stolen* (i.e., the control properties of the embedded clause). *I had the book stolen (for the insurance money)* requires that the book thieves be distinct in reference from NP'_1; in contrast, the sentence *I had the book stolen (in no time)* strongly favors a reading in which NP'_1 is also the book thief (i.e., NP_1 controls the understood embedded subject).

We can readily see, then, that identity of formal properties at the first order gives way to some semantically based differences in the conditions on the complements and modifiers of the two constructions, and that these differences follow directly from their constructional semantics: the difference between causing and initiating or instigating a situation. This description also accounts for the similarities in their constructional meanings, since in both cases the XP denotes a situation resulting from some other situation, a fact which can be notated by giving it the semantic role *resultative* in both constructions (following Rothstein 1984 I use *circumstantial* and *resultative* as names for the semantic roles of predicational complements).

Two other HAVE constructions, the Affecting Event and Attributive/Existential, show similarities and differences corresponding to those which characterize the Causative and Resultant Event constructions, though of course their frame-based semantics are substantially different.

THE AFFECTING EVENT

The Affecting Event construction, exemplified in (12), is used to express a situation in which some event is seen as affecting NP'_1 (the optional expression *on me* forces a "malefactive" construal, which is a subcase of this reading and precludes the Causative reading).

(12) I had my dog die (on me).

There appears to be a strong preference for animate subjects in this construction. Note the oddness of (13).

(13) #?Main Street had four dogs die at its busiest intersection last month.

This is odd even if one can imagine, for example, Main Street being affected by traffic jams at that intersection as a result of the accidents. Inanimate subjects are much more likely to occur in the Attributive construction, as I show below.[10]

As is the case for the Causative construction, having an animate subject correlates with the requirement that the XP denote a perfective situation.[11] This accounts for the fact that sentences which most clearly provide this reading are those in which XP is a bare infinitive VP, since those are always perfective. However, the Affecting-Event construction differs from the Causative in that there is a substantial difference in their frame-based semantics, since the XP denotes a circumstantial rather than a resulting state of affairs.

THE ATTRIBUTIVE

Sentences like those in (14) exemplify the construction I call Attributive.

(14) a. I have keloid tissue on my back.
     b. He has a fly resting on his nose.

Here, the state of affairs S, expressed by the sequence $NP_2 + XP$, is presented as (if it were) a property of NP_1'. This state of affairs is often a state, as it is in (14), but in fact may be any imperfective situation, as in (15), where XP denotes an event type repeated regularly.

(15) Albany has an express bus running to it.

This construction may just as readily be used to impose an attribution upon NP_1' (as in (14b)) as it does to express an objective property of NP_1', as in (14a). The Attributive construction may thus be deployed in order to impose a particular point of view on a situation (cf. Fillmore 1976).

As the examples suggest, the differences between this construction and the Affecting-Event reading are twofold and interconnected. There is an animacy requirement on NP_1' in the Affecting-Event construction which does not hold for the subject of the Attributive construction, and the XP complement must be perfective in the Affecting-Event construction and imperfective in the Attributive construction.

A Word About the Semantics of the Constructions

In the preceding sections, I have implicitly taken the position that what we have here is a case of polysemy, rather than a single highly abstract meaning, on the part of the lexical head HAVE. While I have not proven that proposition here, I have shown that the four uses impose substantially different conditions on their complements, evoke discernibly different semantic frames, with different entailments, and hence are most elegantly considered different "meanings" of HAVE. The fact remains that, as many linguists have observed, a great deal about the specifics of interpretation of each of these constructions is filled in by the complements.

Assuming the distinctions presented in the previous section to be generally correct, I will now discuss sentences which, with the addition of space creation, can easily be assimilated to these four basic constructions.

The Depictive Cases: HAVE Constructions Involving Cross-Space Connectors

In this section, I consider examples of HAVE sentences in which S holds in some space other than the origin space, and NP_1' brings about that situation (as it holds in that space) or the situation is treated as a property of NP_1'. The examples I consider first are given in (16) through (25), some of which are the same examples as given in (1).

(16) Wayne Walker has the A's finishing outside of first in their division.

(17) Jeane Dixon has Quayle winning in 1996.

(18) "Dearborn has [Henry Miller] die on June 7, Fergusen on June 4."

(19) Imelda's count of the votes had Ferdinand being the winner.

(20) "Another scenario had *thirtysomething* returning as a TV movie."

(21) "Lefebvre had Canseco scoring all the way."

(22) LaRue had me bringing chips to the party.

(23) John Sayles has Happy Felsch throw the 1927 World Series.

(24) The movie has him dying in the end.

(25) In *The Maltese Falcon*, Raymond Chandler had Philip Marlowe give up Brigid O'Shaughnessy without an iota of remorse.

These sentences appear to manifest a constructional semantics in which HAVE is used to convey either the prediction of a situation in a future world (as in (16) and (17)), or where the (real-world) facts are subject to dispute or confirmation (as in (18) through (20)), where the world is a declarative one (as in (22)) or a fictional one (as in (23) through (25)). One strikingly different property of these examples as contrasted with the basic ones discussed previously is that, in all uses described in the first section, the situation S must hold in the origin space. In sentences (16) through (25), the corresponding situation need not, or is not known to, hold in the origin space. But despite the superficial semantic similarities among this set of sentences and its obvious semantic distinction from the four constructions discussed in the first section, these do not constitute a fifth construction type. Rather, they are all instances of one or another of the four constructions plus the creation of a daughter space.

There are both descriptive and explanatory advantages to this solution, as compared to one which simply identifies a fifth HAVE construction. We have seen one of them just above: despite the shared semantic property that S is irrealis, the kind of nonrealis situation denoted varies, although there is no formal signal of that variation. (This aspect of the interpretation results directly from the kind of space invoked, which is a product of pragmatic principles arising from knowledge about the referents of the complements; see the next section.) In the ensuing discussion I also show that these "depictive" uses (as I call this set of examples) impose the same correlated conditions on complements that the four basic constructions have. Furthermore, since on this solution these sentences may instantiate different constructions, it accounts for semantic differences among depictive sentences apart from the character of the daughter space. Simply put, the depictive uses have the syntactic and semantic properties of the four basic HAVE constructions, with the additional condition—imposed pragmatically rather than semantically—that they involve the building of a daughter space.

The obvious explanatory advantage of this analysis is that we will not have to posit another construction based on the exceptional semantic properties of these sentences, since we will instead identify those exceptional aspects of their semantics as general possibilities of interpretation underdetermined by the syntactic form of the construction. As I show in the discussion of the extraposition construction below, this independence of space creation from constructional semantics differentiates these uses of HAVE from the use which heads the extraposition-type construction.

The fact that HAVE constructions are so easily accessible to cross-space interpretations—that is, interpretations in which a daughter space is created—follows naturally from the semantics of those constructions. If indeed the space-crossing aspect of the meaning is independent of the construction, it follows that all four HAVE constructions should be able to have space-crossing instantiations (although general pragmatic principles should make space-crossing versions of some of these constructions less accessible); as I show below, this prediction is borne out.

The Constructed Spaces of Depictive Sentences

In each of the sentences in examples (16) through (25), NP_1 refers either to a created space or to a person or institution which can construct a world corresponding to a mental space. This space (no matter whether it is named directly or evoked via its "author"[12]) can be an interpretive space (e.g., a theory or a declarative space), a belief space, a fictional text, or a future or hypothetical counterpart to the origin space. Following Fauconnier 1985, I use M to talk about any non-origin space evoked by these sentences, and R when talking about the origin space. I call the interpretation in which both NP_1' and S hold in R the R-space interpretation, and the one in which S holds in M the M-space interpretation. In a sentence with an M-space interpretation, NP_2' and XP' may or may not have counterparts in R, but for our purposes NP_2' and XP' and the relations between them all exist by definition in the M space, whatever its nature may be. In other words, NP_1 evokes another space either directly or indirectly, and the situation S holds in that space. In the cases at issue, NP_1' exists in R.

As noted above, nothing about the sentences in (16) through (25) besides encyclopedic knowledge about the referent of NP_1 signals that the S holds in a space other than R. Most of these sentences have a strongly preferred interpretation involving a space M. However, sentences like (21) show an ambiguity over an interpretation in which the embedded predicate holds in R or in some M. This sentence was uttered by a radio announcer to describe the then third-base coach of the Oakland A's waving then right-fielder Jose Canseco into home, but actually Canseco only reached third base on the play. Only by extralinguistic knowledge can we identify (21) as instantiating the depictive interpretation rather than an R-space resultant-event interpretation. In the space of Lefebvre's intentions, Canseco's counterpart reached home as a result of Lefebvre's instigating act. Another utterance of this same sentence could describe a situation in which Canseco reached home in R.

Sentence (21) therefore involves an intention space. Other kinds of spaces may be evoked as well: sentence (17) is readily interpreted as involving a future hypothetical (or predictive) space because of our encyclopedic knowledge that Jeane Dixon is a psychic. Sentence (16) has the same predictive interpretation, since Wayne Walker is a sportscaster. Sentence (22) can describe a situation in which the departmental secretary has constructed a future intended world in which everyone is to bring an assigned food. That S does not necessarily hold in R is again shown by a possible continuation of (22).

(22′) LaRue had me bringing chips to the party, but since everyone's on a diet I've brought rice cakes instead.

The examples discussed so far involve a NP_1 which denotes an animate participant, an "author" of a space in the sense that he or she is the creator of a non-origin space in which S holds. The other examples, (19), (20), (24), and (26), show that NP_1 can denote a "text" which corresponds directly to the space.

(26) The 1967 theory had COMP hanging from S.

One discourse-pragmatic property of these depictive sentences is their frequent occurrence in a context of explicit or implicit contrast with a situation holding in R, or in another non-origin space, holding of the counterparts to NP_2' and XP' in the M space. Sentences (22) and (22') provide such an environment, where the contrast is between M (LaRue's intention space) and R. Similarly, (26) could be continued as in (26').

(26') The 1967 theory had COMP hanging from S, but by 1973, it hung from S'.

The Properties of Depictive Sentences

All the examples in (16) through (25) describe situations in which, in some space M, a situation holds as a result of an action, property, or disposition of some individual NP_1' in R. As noted, some of those examples have animate ("author") and some have inanimate ("text") subjects. What is interesting for our purposes is that the properties of the four basic constructions hold for the examples we have here; that is, the examples with animate subjects have either perfective or imperfective predicational complements while those with inanimate subjects may properly have only imperfective predicational complements. This follows from the general constraint that the Resultant-Event constructions may have an animate or inanimate subject while the Causative may only have an animate subject, and that these are correlated with imperfective and perfective predicational complements respectively. Therefore, the examples we have seen so far are all most readily interpreted as examples of the Causative or the Resultant-Event constructions with the understanding that the situation described holds in the space M, and that that space itself is invoked by NP_1.

Let us look at this in more detail. In the two examples with bare-stem infinitive embedded VPs, i.e., (23) and (25), NP_1 denotes an "author" who (our encyclopedic knowledge tells us) creates a text in which S holds. Sentence (23), on the intended interpretation, describes a situation in which the mention of John Sayles evokes the film *Eight Men Out* in virtue of his being its director and having had some control over the content of the story. *John Sayles* therefore denotes the "author", in my sense, of the text which builds the film space. In the film, Happy Felsch engineers his team's loss of the 1927 World series.[13] Sayles has caused this event to take place in the space of his film—he could have changed the script so that the team pulls a victory out of the jaws of defeat. Only hearers who know that John Sayles is a film director, and not a crooked manager or the wealthy owner of the rival team, will interpret this sentence as intended, i.e., as involving a film space.

On the other hand, the text may be named explicitly, as it is in (25); the *in* phrase is a space builder, in the terminology of Fauconnier 1985. However, we can get an equivalent interpretation of the sentence without the space-building *in* phrase, assuming some knowledge of Raymond Chandler (or perhaps merely knowledge that the other two NPs denote fictional characters) and knowledge of the semantics of the construction. On either interpretation, NP_1' is the agent of a caused situation. Needless to say, the kind of causing that exists in the real-world situation described in (25) or (23) is different from the causing act described using a sentence like (8a), *I had the children wash the dishes* (on its R-space interpretation). This results from the differences in the properties of NP_2 in such cases: neither Philip Marlowe nor (these days) Happy Felsch is subject to being acted on in R. However, given the fact that the R-space HAVE Causative is not appropriately used to describe either direct manipulative causation or causation from a direct order, it is natural to use this construction to describe causation that takes place in virtue of the creation of a fictional world. In the absence of supporting context, the M-space Causative interpretation is most readily available when there is no counterpart to NP_2 in an R-space. This is because, given the marked nature of the causation described by the M-space causative, the R-space interpretation will always be more accessible if there is an individual in R corresponding to NP_1. There is a certain set of HAVE sentences which may not receive an R-space interpretation: if the subject NP denotes a "text," it may be that the participants are understood to exist only in M. In (26′), for instance, we do not understand that speakers' R-space linguistic behavior changed between 1967 and 1973; this is rather necessarily a statement about linguistic theory, about the M-space counterparts to the R-space entities COMP, S, and S′.

Let us now look at the other examples, those with an imperfective embedded VP. In these sentences, NP_1' may be animate or inanimate, but either way, it is a property, a disposition, or an event which triggers the resulting event S. As we noted for the R-space examples of the resultant-event construction, the subject referent may bring about the event deliberately or inadvertently. Both possibilities hold as well in the M-space sentences (17), (19), and (22).

(17) Jeane Dixon has Quayle winning in 1996.

(19) Imelda's count of the votes had Ferdinand being the winner.

(22) LaRue had me bringing chips to the party.

In (17), Jeane Dixon brings about the prediction-space situation by her psychic powers and irrespective of her political leanings, so (17) describes a (nonrealis) situation which results from a disposition of Dixon. Similarly, in (19) Imelda just counts the votes and from that action Ferdinand becomes the winner (in a nonrealis space). Notice with this example and with (22) that the text which evokes the space may be purely declarative, constructed solely for the purposes of establishing that XP' holds of NP$_2'$. Another example of this kind is (27).

(27) The first-base umpire had him$_i$ holding up, while the home-plate umpire had him$_i$ swinging through.

The intended interpretation here is that according to the first-base umpire the batter stopped swinging before he broke his wrists (which means it doesn't count as a strike), while in the judgment of the home-plate umpire he executed a complete swing. Since the call *ball* or *strike* depends on the determination of the swing, the umpires here have a dual role: they observe the event in R, then in their individual belief spaces make a judgment about the batter's action. Note that a single action of the batter in R corresponds to one event in each of the two declarative spaces and that those two events are incompatible in any single space. In other words, the observation and judgment of the umpire bring about the determination in his declarative space. This, I suggest, is an example of the Resultant-Event reading across spaces.

Just as we saw in the first section, the Causative and Resultant-Event readings have semantic properties in common, and there are situations which could be accurately and appropriately described using either of them, such as (22) (the resultant-event form with an inflected VP complement) and (22'') (the causative form with a bare infinitive VP complement). (The parenthetical forces the M-space interpretation since the situation *S* cannot hold in R.)

(22)   La Rue had me bringing chips to the party.

(22'') La Rue had me bring chips to the party (but I won't be able to come at all).

Interestingly, however, the M-space uses of the Causative and Resultant-Event constructions do not so strictly adhere to the animacy conditions as do those constructions describing situations holding in R. There are two classes of examples where this constraint seems to have been relaxed. First, there are examples in which animate subjects are inappropriate in M-space causatives. Observe the difference in acceptability between (27) and (27').

(27') #The first-base umpire had him hold up, while the home-plate umpire had him swing through.[14]

This example is odd simply because the semantic conditions of the Causative construction cannot be fulfilled: the umpires are not agentively, deliberately bringing about these events in their judgment spaces. In fact, example (6) is odd for the same reason (on this reading, and where S holds in R).

Sentences like (28) and (29) are genuine counterexamples to the animacy constraint on NP_1 of causatives.

(28) The movie version has him die at the end.

(29) ?Bill's theory has INFL attach to S'.

These are less than perfect for many speakers, but they are not as bad for anyone I know as (10a), repeated here as (30).

(30) *My glowering countenance had the children wash the dishes.

There are two possible explanations for this difference between M-space and R-space instances of the causative. One is that a metonymy of work-for-author is operating here: since NP_1 in these cases will always denote a work of an author, they will always provide an author-causer of the event. The disadvantage of this account is that the work-for-author metonymy appears rarely if at all outside this construction, so this solution lacks generality, and seems ad hoc.[15]

A more plausible explanation is that—whether overall or just in the M-space case—the correct level of generalization is not with animacy but with the directness of causation. Perhaps, properly stated, the conditions on the directness of causation may entail animacy in R, rather than animacy itself being a condition. Perhaps if the "author" or "text" requires that S hold in M, either can serve as subject referent of a causative construction, whereas if the properties of the "author" or "text" merely bring S about, that situation is properly expressed using the Resultant-Event construction.

This apparently vanishingly subtle distinction in the frame-based semantics may simply reflect the real-world situation, since for some of these, like (29) and (29′), the real-world difference between the two situations described is barely discernible.

(29′) Bill's theory has INFL attaching to S′.

The Resultant-Event reading appropriately expresses a range of situations which includes those situations also expressed using the Causative (see Brugman 1988, sections 3.3 and 3.4). This semantic property of the two constructions is independent of space crossing.

The Other HAVE Constructions and Their M-Space Instances

If, as my discussion suggests, the depictive sentences we have seen so far can simply be assimilated under the Causative or Resultant-Event construction, then the Attributive and Affecting-Event HAVE constructions should also have M-space instances. This in fact is so: the Attributive reading is quite common with "text" subjects and somewhat less so with "author" subjects. The Affecting-Event construction, which appears to be limited in use to animate subjects, also finds some instances in M-space sentences. That interpretation is obviously pragmatically marked, probably because it is used to describe situations which are simply rarer in the world.

THE AFFECTING-EVENT READING

If my claims so far are right, it should be possible to get instances of the Affecting-Event reading in which S holds in M. Recall that in this construction NP_1' is (portrayed as) being affected as a result of the situation described in the matrix VP complements. Novelists occasionally report the situation of being taken aback by some act of the characters which the writer has created, which would qualify the sentence in (31a), where NP_1 denotes the author, as being of the Affecting-Event type.

(31) a. In *The Maltese Falcon*, Raymond Chandler had Philip Marlowe give up Brigid O'Shaughnessy without an iota of remorse.
    b. In my dream last night I had a pack of angry wolves chase my little dog Fluffy.

Here the fictitious event S is presented in its potential to affect NP_1', the author of the text in which S holds.[16]

THE ATTRIBUTIVE CASE

The sentences in (32) are examples of the attributive construction with a cross-space interpretation.

(32) a. "The standard-theory way of representing a PP would just have PP immediately dominating P and NP."

    b. "He doesn't have himself participating in the [rape and murder], he has himself observing the situation."

    c. "A folk tale in deaf culture has a man and a woman sitting at different tables in a restaurant."

In the examples in (32), the situation holding in M and expressed by $NP_2 + XP$ is presented as an attribute of NP'_1, who exists in R. Sentence (32b), for instance, was uttered by an attorney in defense of his client, who was claiming diminished capacity. The speaker claims that in the client's belief space, he is observing but not participating in the crime. Sentence (32a) says that the standard theory has the property that the mentioned situation holds in that theory. Sentence (29′) also, and perhaps preferably, has this reading.

Two Dimensions of Ambiguity: Pragmatic and Semantic

I mentioned in the first section that while the formal differences between HAVE constructions could be traced directly back to differences in their semantic requirements, there are semantic differences which are not formally notated in the description I have given here, and which in fact find no morphosyntactic expression. Many individual sentences are perceived as ambiguous between two R-space interpretations, an example being *I had the book stolen*. This is because the morphosyntactic properties which distinguish constructions are not sufficient to identify their constructional semantics (semantic-role assignment is one formal, though invisible, means of distinguishing them). Sentences like (31a) are ambiguous in just the same way, because they meet the formal and the semantic requirements for both the Causative and the Affecting-Event readings. Similarly, example (29′) may express an Attributive situation, where INFL being attached to S′ is a property of the theory. It may also express a resultant-event situation, where the attachment of INFL to S′ is a consequence of some other property of Bill's theory, e.g., some version of X-bar theory. The ambiguity in such sentences is independent of the fact that a daughter space is invoked by the subject. The constructional ambiguity of the verb HAVE is the source of this sentence ambiguity.

The question arises whether there is actual ambiguity or mere vagueness in these examples. It is hard to decide, in some cases, whether a sentence is an example of the Attributive or the Resultant-Event reading, especially when NP_1 denotes a text. Is there really a difference in the situation holding within the world created as opposed to the situation in which the state of affairs named is a property of that text?

The attested (32b) provides a specific case in which one reading and precisely not the other is intended. This sentence, given in evidence of diminished capacity, must be read as asserting that the perceived state of affairs was a property of NP'_1 and not under his control, rather than a result of his intentional cognitive construction. The apparent vagueness or indistinguishability of the two readings in many specific sentences follows from the underdetermined nature of the daughter spaces themselves: since the texts are constructed by some author, the understanders can either see them as constructed with S as a property (with an Attributive reading) or as constructed such that S follows from other properties (giving it a Resultant-State construal). Similarly, when NP'_1 is an author, we can either see the situation holding in his belief or intent space as his properties, or as something that holds (in that space) as a consequence of other beliefs or other properties. (It is possible that the degree to which the two readings can be distinguished by the hearer is a function of the kind of M-space created.) This kind of ambiguity, in which both readings are compatible with the situation described, has been discussed in Norvig 1988, and can be found in sentences which do not involve multiple spaces.

A second dimension of ambiguity is along the axis of space building. Many examples we have seen are readily given either an R-space interpretation or an M-space interpretation.

(21)   ''Lefebvre had Canseco scoring all the way.''

(18′)   Dearborn had Miller get married on August 23.

(24′)   The movie had us dying at the end.

In the R-space interpretation of (24′), we in the audience (in R) are dying of laughter by the end of the movie. In the M-space interpretation, *us* refers to characters in the movie who die at the end. In the R-space interpretation of (18′), Dearborn brings about Miller's actual marriage, while in the M-space reading, Dearborn reports the date of Miller's marriage in his biography.

It is also possible that an ambiguity can result from the underspecification of the daughter space being invoked (that is, that there is ambiguity between two M-space interpretations). We can imagine, for instance, that a third-base coach will give the "hold up" sign, in the hope of influencing the third-base umpire, and that the coach will actually believe that the batter checked his swing. We also know that those two spaces can hold incommensurable propositions, as when the coach believes that the batter actually swung through. Similarly we can imagine that a jury will declare a defendant not guilty because he is not guilty in their belief spaces; or the declaration can be because of a technicality, although in the jury's belief spaces the defendant did commit the crime. Any HAVE sentence which can invoke one of these scenarios can in theory invoke the other, and hence can be ambiguous between a declarative-space interpretation and a belief-space interpretation.

It is the dimension of ambiguity involving the construction of spaces that I identify as pragmatic with the intention of further extending the utility of this construct, originated by Donnellan (1966) and expanded upon by Horn (1985, 1989) and Sweetser (1990). Donnellan appealed to the notion of pragmatic ambiguity to account for referential and attributive understandings of definite descriptions, while Horn used this construct to illuminate the distinction between propositional, or descriptive, negation and metalinguistic negation. (Sweetser took it up in the same direction as Horn to discuss corresponding differences in uses of modals and connectives.) As with all of the phenomena discussed in these works, I believe that the ambiguities exhibited in the sentences examined in this paper cannot be reduced to a kind of vagueness, since S must hold in *some* space or other, and that the ambiguity cannot be ascribed to anything semantic, lexical, structural, or scopal. (Horn 1989 (pp. 375–77) provides more candidates for pragmatic ambiguity and additional references.)

Since these two dimensions of ambiguity are independent, it follows that we should be able to find sentences which are ambiguous along both dimensions. Sentence (24'), for example, is constructionally (semantically) ambiguous over the Attributive and Resultant-Event readings, and is also pragmatically ambiguous over M-space and R-space interpretations. In practice, some subset of possible readings will be ruled out, either by extralinguistic knowledge or in consequence of composing the conditions imposed by the constructional semantics with the conditions which can possibly hold in some space.

The Extraposition Construction

The "extraposition" HAVE construction can be distinguished from the ones discussed in the first two sections on both syntactic and semantic grounds. The important part of the semantic difference is that it can only be used when NP_2 allows the construction of a space builder and the embedded predication holds in the invoked space. In other words, the cross-space reading which is available to the four basic constructions but attributable to independent principles appears here as a necessary semantic condition on the use of this structure.

The syntactic properties of this construction can be schematized as in (33), and exemplified in (34).

(33) $[_S [NP_1] [_{VP} HAVE \; it \; [_{S'} that \; [_S NP_2 \; XP]]]]$[17]

(34) Rumor has it that Reagan's aides wanted to invoke the twenty-fifth amendment.

Of course, *Rumor has it* is the most common and most idiomatic instance of the schema in (33). However, (33) does not simply describe the constituency of the idiom *Rumor has it that* S: the sentences in (35) (which seem odd for some speakers but unremarkably good for others) instantiate the same syntactic schema.[18]

(35) a. The grapevine has it that Nolan Ryan is pitching next week.
b. The scuttlebutt around town has it that they had to get married.
c. "A new joke has it that after 450 years, the next member of the royal family to be executed in the Tower of London will be Princess Michael of Kent."
d. "A new theory has it that the U.S. wanted to keep the Contadora contract from being signed."
e. "The description [of verb gapping] had it that a verb in a nonfinal conjunct gets omitted."

For at least some speakers, then, (33) gives the syntactic specifications of a productive construction form; it is apparent that there are concomitant semantic requirements on the lexeme heading the NP_1 slot, as I discuss briefly below.

This construction has only an M-space interpretation. So while (36) has available both an R-space interpretation (in which, in R, the children clean their rooms as a result of hearing the story) and an M-space interpretation (in which, in the story about the rampaging mother, the children clean their rooms), (36') has only the M-space interpretation.

(36) The story about the rampaging mother had the children cleaning their rooms immediately.

(36') The story about the rampaging mother had it that the children {were cleaning/cleaned} their rooms immediately.

The examples so far have involved the two readings Resultant Event and Attributive. In fact neither of the other readings is available, since for most speakers, no agent or patient participant can be the referent of NP_1.

(37) ?Glenn Dickey had it that Nolan Ryan was pitching this week.

Some speakers may find this sentence acceptable on the construal that *Glenn Dickey* metonymically refers to his column (he is a columnist for the San Francisco *Examiner*). But, in general, an "author" NP_1 cannot appear in this construction if there is no actual text—that is, this construction with an "author" NP_1 cannot be used to convey a belief or intention, as can the basic HAVE constructions, as exemplified in (21), (22), (27), and so forth. This fact may or may not fall out from more general constraints on the semantics of the construction. In any case, a true Causative or Affecting-Event reading is not available to any sentence with the syntactic form shown in (33).

While this construction appears to be roughly synonymous to the basic Attributive or Resultant Event in its M-space construal, its circumstances of use are rather different. The extraposed version seems to be used when the veracity (in R) of the embedded predication is in doubt: its implication is that the situation described in the embedded clause, holding in M, does not hold in R. (It also occurs with NP_1 denoting a text which is assumed *not* to hold in R, as a joke.) This amounts to a restriction on the frame-based semantics of the nouns that can appear in NP_1 position: the NP must refer to a text whose veracity (or accuracy in describing a situation in R) is subject to disconfirmation or at least dispute. Note the oddness of (38), and the pragmatic effect of conveying the speaker's disbelief in the veracity of the Bible in (39).

(38) #The truth has it that the earth is round.

(39) The Bible has it that woman was made from man.

In any case, it is evident that this construction is only appropriate when the subject denotes the text and not the author. This is true for most speakers. However, the following utterance, unplanned speech that was broadcast over the radio, suggests that some speakers may be generalizing the construction to M-space causative readings as well.

(40) "Spike Lee had it such that Angie did it [had an affair with Flipper Purify] out of curiosity."

It is possible that in (40), as in (37), NP_1 metonymically refers to the movie *Jungle Fever;* however, the surrounding context does not support this construal, since the utterance appeared within a larger discursus criticizing Lee's attitudes rather than critiquing the movie itself. (Also worth noting is the inclusion of the word *such* between *it* and the complementizer.) This is the only example I have encountered which unambiguously provides an animate referent for NP_1 (and which, consequently, would be analyzed as a Causative construction). Otherwise it appears that only the Resultant-Event or Attributive readings are available to this extraposition structure.

Even if this construction were to generalize, however, it will, I predict, generalize only to M-space uses. That is, a sentence like (41) will never appropriately describe a situation which wholly holds in R (compare (41′)).

(41)   %Spike Lee had it that Wesley Snipes drove Annabella Sciorra to the studio every morning.

(41′)   Spike Lee had Wesley Snipes drive Annabella Sciorra to the studio every morning.

It is worth looking at other verbs which have this complementation pattern of extraposition from direct-object position. Included in this class are some space-building predicates like BELIEVE and most factive verbs such as LIKE, APPRECIATE, etc., suggesting that the structure is statistically, though not deterministically, associated with some space-building property. The HAVE construction differs from all of these in not allowing a simple *that*-clause complement pattern analogous to those in (42) (cf. (43)), which demonstrates that while this complementation pattern is structurally quite regular and common, HAVE is uncommon in that it does not exhibit the other lexical properties normally found in lexemes with this complementation pattern.

(42)   a. I believe (it) that he said it.
       b. I like (it) that he sent me flowers.

(43)   Rumor has *(it) that he said it.

Thus, this HAVE extraposition construction is similar to the basic uses discussed in the first section in that a specific complementation pattern is associated with a constructional semantics similar to those of the Resultant-Event and the Attributive constructions. However, it has an additional and unique condition on it that the named situation S holds only in some M-space and that space is invoked, generally by direct reference, by NP_1—hence the denotational possibilities of NP_1 will constrain the possibility of this interpretation. There are also conditions on what kind of space is invoked thereby; rather than finding another case in which the nature of the daughter space is entirely unconstrained, as we found in the M-space uses of the basic constructions, here the daughter space must be fictive, or understood to be fictive. Because it is only within this syntactic form for HAVE that an M-space interpretation is required, we can say that this (partially lexically filled) syntactic pattern is a space builder.

Summary and Conclusions

I have shown that an apparently distinct meaning of HAVE which is in the business of expressing a prediction or a depiction is instead an unremarkable conjunction of independent sets of interpretive principles. For the examples discussed in the second section, the principles exist at two levels: the first is the lexical level in which one of four senses of the polysemous lexeme HAVE is invoked, while the second is at a much higher level of conceptual-semantic organization, that of mental space construction. The apparent idiosyncrasy of using HAVE as a verb of prediction dissolves when one realizes that a daughter space may be set up, with or without an explicit signal to the hearer to do so (as noted by Fauconnier (1985, 1990)). In the service of this notion that the construal of depiction or prediction is not a constructional property of these sentences, I have invoked the idea of pragmatic, as distinct from semantic, ambiguity.

I have shown that there is also a construction which is dedicated precisely to the depiction of some situation in a nonrealis M, and whose syntactic properties are unique to this meaning of HAVE and are compatible only with that meaning.

The case of HAVE is interesting both for construction grammar and for the theory of mental spaces. For construction grammar it shows that a multi-functional lexical network can have a varied internal landscape. Here, one lexical entry in the complex of HAVE has frame-based semantics which closely resembles the semantics of other senses of HAVE and additionally requires the construction of a daughter space. In contrast, other HAVE constructions must be semantically described so that their normal usage is compatible with M-space interpretations, but is not confined to them. The interesting question remains as to how to notate the difference between the two sorts of construction, a question which we should generalize to a theory of the difference between conventional pragmatic and semantic constraints on lexical meaning.

One consequence of these data for the theory of mental spaces is that a description of a mostly skeletal construction such as HAVE extraposition may criterially include daughter-space construction. It would be interesting to investigate further the question of how common it is for a sentential skeleton to require that one of its complements be a space builder.

The moral for semantics is a familiar one, that to the interpretation of an utterance in a particular context the hearer must bring all kinds of knowledge, from the lexically specific to very high-level principles of organization, and that encyclopedic knowledge must often be brought to bear on specific interpretations.

Notes

1. This paper is a considerable expansion and explication of ideas suggested in Brugman 1988; an earlier, condensed version of it appeared as Brugman 1992.

Part of the writing of this paper was done with support from NEH fellowship number FA-30259-91, and with the technical support provided at the Center for Research in Language, University of California, San Diego. Thanks go to M. Catherine O'Connor, Michele Emanatian, Gilles Fauconnier, and Robert Kluender for useful comments.

2. Throughout this paper I place attested examples in double quotation marks.

3. See also Lakoff 1987 (p. 467) and Langacker 1987 (p. 58) on the "symbolic unit." Langacker takes the position that syntax is largely or completely epiphenomenal; one need not take such a radical position to deploy the notion of the construction, or any similar form-meaning pairing.

4. For simplicity's sake I assume here an equivalence between "lexical semantics" as conceptualized in the generative paradigm and "constructional semantics" as conceptualized within the current framework. This simplification does some damage to the latter construct. However, given the rough equation made above between constructions and lexical entries, it is readily apparent that each construction will correspond to a distinct lexeme, or a distinct "sense" of HAVE. The only conceptual problem then remaining is whether such abstract characterizations of the constructional meanings for HAVE as I give below can count as bona fide senses.

5. The exceptions in (2) are (2m) through (2r).

6. This paper is not concerned with syntactic structure except as it defines the subset of HAVE constructions I consider here. In Brugman 1988 I show that no purely syntactic test (if such there be) proves the existence of a "small clause" constituent sister to HAVE within the matrix VP which dominates NP_2 and XP, rendering the structure in (i):

(i) $[_S [NP_1] [_{VP} \text{HAVE} [_? [NP_2] [XP]]]]$

However, nothing in this paper would be affected if such an additional constituent were discovered, or even if it were demonstrated that the various readings were associated with different constituent structures. See Stowell 1981 and Rothstein 1984 for a conclusion different from mine, and Williams 1980 and Alsina 1992 for arguments in favor of the constituent structure adopted here.

7. Note that I do not use the term *situation* in the sense in which it is used in Situation Theory.

8. It is also compatible with a situation in which the causee is not unwilling to perform the caused act. This is in contrast to causative verbs like MAKE and FORCE, where the causee must be reluctant.

9. The symbol "#" here means "unacceptable on the intended reading." This sentence does have an available reading, described below, which I call the Affecting Event construction; it cannot, however, describe the children's act of dishwashing through my inadvertent instigation.

10. In natural discourse one often finds the Affecting Event construction used presentationally, that is, used to introduce as a new or transitional topic of conversation an event which may have only been of interest to NP'_1. In this respect, the Affecting Event construction resembles the presentational HAVE construction discussed in Lambrecht 1988.

11. I believe this is essentially the same observation that Gruber (1967) made, that perfective events take agentive subjects. From this kind of observation the predicate-decomposition style of deriving participant roles was developed (cf., e.g., Dowty 1979).

12. "Author" and "text" are purely convenient notations for the two participant types and should not be misconstrued as, e.g., semantic-role assignments. In fact the semantic-role assignments are somewhat complicated, but whatever they are, they will play out as more general roles than "author" and "text". By *author* I will mean the person with predictive powers, the author (director, etc.) of a fictional narrative work, the maker of a theory, or the person in authority to create states of affairs by declaration (as a baseball umpire or the person who gives out assignments for the departmental potluck). The term *text* will correspondingly (and respectively) refer to the future world, the narrative work, the theory, or the declared state of affairs.

13. To simplify matters, I exclude from consideration here any sentence in which the individual NP'_2 in M is referred to using an expression which denotes the counterpart of NP'_2 in R, such as (i).

(i) John Sayles has Charlie Sheen throw the 1927 World Series.

This sentence can describe the same situation as (23), where John Sayles is the "author" and Happy Felsch throws the World Series in M. In R, Charlie Sheen is the actor playing Happy Felsch. The Access Principle (Fauconnier 1985) allows us to use the counterpart in R to refer to any individual in M. The sentence in (i) is just (23) plus a cross-space ID connector between the individual in M and his counterpart in R. Hence all sentences of the type (i) will be accounted for by my analysis plus Fauconnier's analysis (1985, chapter 1) of metonymy.

14. This sentence has a Causative reading, but it is pragmatically highly marked

since it describes a situation which is impossible in baseball, unless we are identifying as first-base umpire and second-base umpire two people who are acting as batting coaches, describing their causing acts in their respective intention spaces.

15. The author-for-works metonymy (as mentioned in Fauconnier 1985 and Lakoff and Johnson 1980, inter alia) is much more common; one way to analyze examples like (23) is that they utilize this metonymic principle.

16. In Brugman 1988 (p. 152) I probably created the impression that NP_1' must be the "author" as well as the sufferer. While I have found no grammatical reason why this condition should hold, it is difficult to imagine using this construction to describe a range of possible situations in which S, occurring in M, affects some participant other than the "author". One logical candidate for the subject of the affecting-event construction would be the reader of the text through which M is constructed; another would be the counterpart in R to some role in M, denoted by NP_2. One would imagine that the affecting-event construction could be pressed into service for either scenario; however, neither of these sentence types is easily constructed, and neither type is attested.

(i) ??[When I read *The Maltese Falcon*,] I had Philip Marlowe heartlessly let Brigid O'Shaughnessy take the fall.

(ii) ?[Elizabeth's just beat!] She had Cleopatra get bitten by the snake at two o'clock and at eight o'clock today.

I have no explanation for why such sentences should seem unnatural. There may be some as yet undiscovered semantic constraints on the subject participant in this construction which preclude certain participants in cross-space instances.

17. Capital letters indicate lexemes, and italics indicate word forms. The lexeme HAVE can be inflectionally altered, but the other fillers of this skeleton cannot. This constituency is argued for in Brugman 1988 (p. 261).

18. Adele Goldberg has pointed out that the collocation *I have it on good authority that* S shares the critical syntactic elements of this construction, but differs both in lexical conditions (where NP_1 is animate, and typically first person, and also in that a phrase like *on good authority* is required) and in its constructional semantics.

References

Alsina, Alex. 1992. The Monoclausality of Causatives: Evidence from Romance. Paper presented at the annual meeting of the Linguistic Society of America.

Anderson, J.M. 1971. *The Grammar of Case: Towards a Localistic Theory*. Cambridge: Cambridge University Press.

Bach, Emmon. 1967. *Have* and *Be* in English Syntax. *Language* 43:462–85.

Bendix, Edward H. 1966. Componential Analysis of General Vocabulary: The Semantic Structure of a Set of Verbs in English, Hindi, and Japanese. *International Journal of American Linguistics* 32(2), part 2.

Brugman, Claudia. 1988. The Syntax and Semantics of HAVE and Its Complements. Ph.D. diss., University of California, Berkeley.

———. 1992. Mental Spaces and Constructional Meaning. *CRL Newsletter* 7(1): 3–10. Center for Research in Language, University of California, San Diego.

Cattell, Ray. 1984. *Composite Predicates in English.* Syntax and Semantics, vol. 17. New York: Academic Press.

Chomsky, Noam. 1965. *Aspects of the Theory of Syntax.* Cambridge, Mass.: MIT Press.

Donnellan, K. 1966. Reference and Definite Descriptions. *Philosophical Review* 75: 281–304.

Dowty, David. 1979. *Word Meaning and Montague Grammar.* Dordrecht: Reidel Publishing Company.

Fauconnier, Gilles. 1985. *Mental Spaces: Aspects of Meaning Construction in Natural Language.* Cambridge, Mass.: MIT Press. Reprinted 1994, Cambridge: Cambridge University Press.

———. 1990. Invisible Meaning. *Proceedings of the Sixteenth Annual Meeting of the Berkeley Linguistics Society,* 390–404. Berkeley, CA: Berkeley Linguistics Society.

———. 1991. Roles and Values: The Case of French Copula Constructions. In Carol Georgopoulos and Roberta Ishihara, eds., *Interdisciplinary Approaches to Language: Essays in Honor of S.-Y. Kuroda,* 181–206. Dordrecht: Kluwer Academic Publishers.

Fillmore, Charles J. 1968. The Case for Case. In Emmon Bach and R.T. Harms, eds., *Universals in Linguistic Theory,* 1–88. New York: Holt, Rinehart and Winston.

———. 1976. Frame Semantics and the Nature of Language. In S. Harnad, H. Steklis, and J. Lancaster, eds., *Origins and Evolutions of Language and Speech,* 20–32. New York: New York Academy of Sciences.

Fillmore, Charles J., and Paul Kay. n.d. On Grammatical Constructions. In preparation.

Fillmore, Charles J., Paul Kay, and M.C. O'Connor. 1988. Regularity and Idiomaticity in Grammatical Constructions: The Case of *let alone. Language* 64:501–38.

Gruber, Jeffrey. 1967. *Look* and *See. Language* 43:937–47.

Horn, Laurence R. 1985. Metalinguistic Negation and Pragmatic Ambiguity. *Language* 61:121–74.

———. 1989. *A Natural History of Negation.* Chicago: University of Chicago Press.

Kearns, K. 1988. Light Verbs in English. Manuscript, MIT.

Lakoff, George. 1987. *Women, Fire, and Dangerous Things: What Categories Reveal about the Mind.* Chicago, University of Chicago Press.

Lakoff, George, and Mark Johnson. 1980. *Metaphors We Live By.* Chicago: University of Chicago Press.

Lambrecht, Knud. 1988. Presentational Cleft Constructions in Spoken French. In John Haiman and S. Thompson, eds., *Clause Combining in Grammar and Discourse.* Amsterdam: John Benjamins.

Langacker, Ronald W. 1987. *Foundations of Cognitive Grammar.* Vol. 1: *Theoretical Prerequisites.* Stanford, Calif.: Stanford University Press.

Nirenburg, S., and L. Levin. 1991. Syntax-Driven and Ontology-Driven Lexical Semantics. In James Pustejovsky and S. Bergler, eds., *Lexical Semantics and Knowledge Representation: Proceedings of a Workshop Sponsored by the Special Interest Group on the Lexicon of the Association for Computational Linguistics,* 9–19. Association for Computational Linguistics.

Norvig, Peter. 1988. Interpretation under Ambiguity. *Proceedings of the Fourteenth Annual Meeting of the Berkeley Linguistics Society,* 188–201. Berkeley, CA: Berkeley Linguistics Society.

Norvig, Peter, and George Lakoff. 1987. Taking: A Study in Lexical Network Theory. *Proceedings of the Thirteenth Annual Meeting of the Berkeley Linguistics Society,* 195–207. Berkeley, CA: Berkeley Linguistics Society.

Rader, M. 1981. The Temporal Frame of *get* and *have* and Its Contribution to the Comprehension of *get*-Causatives. Master's thesis, University of California, Berkeley.

Rothstein, Susan. 1984. The Syntactic Forms of Predication. Ph.D. diss., MIT. Distributed by the Indiana University Linguistics Club.

Stowell, Timothy. 1981. Origins of Phrase Structure. Ph.D. diss., MIT.

Sweetser, Eve. 1990. *From Etymology to Pragmatics: Metaphorical and Cultural Aspects of Semantic Structure.* Cambridge: Cambridge University Press.

Williams, Edwin. 1980. Predication. *Linguistic Inquiry* 11:203–38.

Gilles Fauconnier

3 *Analogical Counterfactuals*

- •
- •
- •
- •

How does language tie in with reasoning? One reasonable and fairly widespread view is that sentences yield meanings and that such meanings can serve as input to higher-level forms of reasoning like deduction, induction, and analogy.[1] Under that view, the important function of language is to provide information that can be exploited by the reasoning processes, for example, premisses for a deductive argument, or the specification of a structure that will be used analogically.

The research reported on in this book leads to a different conception. Language is actively involved in setting up construals, mappings between domains, and discourse configurations, with the fundamental properties of Accessing, Spreading, and Viewpoint. The formal properties that we find at the most basic semantic-pragmatic level of meaning construction are the same as the ones found in general reasoning, narrative structure, and other high-level forms of thinking and communication. The mental operations which allow us to construct meanings for the simple-looking words and sentences of our everyday life are also the ones at work in what we recognize more consciously as creative thought and expression.

A clear example of the hidden unity of micro and macro meaning-construction processes can be found in counterfactual phenomena. The importance of such phenomena has long been recognized. To quote from Nelson Goodman's seminal (1947) article, "the analysis of counterfactual conditionals is no fussy little grammatical exercise. Indeed, if we lack the means for interpreting counterfactual conditionals, we can hardly claim to have any adequate philosophy of science."

What Goodman pointed to were hidden logical complexities in commonly used sentences like (1):

(1) If that piece of butter had been heated to 150°F, it would have melted.

Goodman's work started a long and interesting tradition of developing a logical semantics that might accommodate such expressions and overcome a host of noted difficulties.[2] Counterfactuals are typically associated with the kind of grammatical construction exemplified in (1), although, as we shall see, they show up in other guises as well. Here are some typical examples of forms that have received attention:

(2) If we were on the beach, we would be having fun.

(3) If I had been Reagan, I wouldn't have sold arms to Iran.

(4) If I was a writer (who votes for the Cy Young) and looking at the numbers and how the pitchers have performed throughout the year, I would say I would be the leader. (pitcher Saberhagen, a Kansas City right-hander, in an interview)

(5) If the tau lepton had existed in the 1 GEV range, I would have discovered it. (disappointed physicist Zichichi)

(6) If all circles were large, and this small triangle △ were a circle, would it be large? (example from Moser 1988)

Several different techniques have been applied to such examples, but in most cases, the spirit of the approach has been essentially this: a counterfactual sets up an imaginary situation which differs from the actual one in one fundamental respect, expressed in the antecedent part (A, the protasis) of the *if A then B* construction. Its meaning consists in linking the apodosis (B) to this imaginary situation as a consequence: change the world just enough to make A true, and B will also be true.[3] As it turns out, this is easier said than done. The change produced by making A true instead of false typically ripples through the entire situation and it is a formidable problem to characterize what is and what is not immune to change in trying to build the counterfactual situation. Take, for example, sentence (2) above, and assume (i) that people always have fun on the beach, except when it rains; (ii) that "we" are currently not having fun; and (iii) that it is not raining. The understanding of (2) is based on preserving (iii) and changing (ii) as a consequence of being on the beach plus (i) and (iii). One could just as well, however, preserve (ii) and abandon (iii), which would yield the counterfactual in (7).

(7) If we were on the beach, it would be raining.

But this statement, in contrast with (2), does not sound like a natural one to make in the chosen context. As Goodman observed, the logically possible changes from the actual to the imagined situation, when A is assumed, are not equal candidates for computing the counterfactual.

But suppose that this obstacle could be overcome, that we could systematically find the intended imaginary situation from which B is deemed to follow.[4] Would that tell us what the expression means? It would not, because the imaginary situation would still not be linked to reality, and the consequences to be drawn would not appear. For instance, having the minimum change from actuality that would replace Reagan by myself, and having ascertained that in such a situation arms would not be sold to Iran, what could we conclude as to the actual situation? How could this fanciful invention entail the sort of thing it typically does, e.g., that I disapprove of the arms sale, or of Reagan, or that I am proud of my high moral standards, or that I wish I could come up with smart ideas like Reagan's, etc. Well, that's pragmatics, some will say, and indeed it is—but the counterfactual story is pointless if we don't know how to link it to the intended meaning. We need to know what the point is of constructing an alternative situation: what does the alternative situation have to say about the one we're in?

As it turns out, Goodman's problem and the pragmatic issue are linked. In spite of appearances, the structure of counterfactuals is not truth functional (entailment from an alternative set of premises); it is analogical: projection of structure from one domain to another. The theoretical import of these characteristics is significant. Expressions of natural languages are best viewed as maximally economical means of triggering complex projection of structures across discourse domains (here, mental spaces). This fundamental feature of language and thought, neglected in traditional accounts,[5] ties in very nicely with contemporary research on the role of metaphorical mappings in core semantics,[6] the extraction of abstract schemas in semantic construction,[7] the analysis of analogical thought and its connection to seemingly more elementary linguistic processes,[8] frame semantics,[9] and recent advances in the study of conceptual development.[10]

This paper examines several examples of counterfactuals in different grammatical constructions, and analyzes the analogical mappings that come into play when such counterfactuals are understood via the construction of appropriate mental spaces. But first, a few words about analogy.

Analogy

The aspects of analogy that are relevant for present purposes have been studied insightfully in work such as Hofstadter 1986, Gentner 1983, Gick and Holyoak 1983, and Turner 1991. They include domain mapping from a *source* onto a *target;* extraction of an *induced schema* (or *frame*); and *exten-sion, fluidity,* and *reanalysis.*

Domain Mapping

Analogy maps partial structure of a source domain onto partial structure of a target domain. In a famous example studied by Gick and Holyoak, the medical problem of operating on a cancerous tumor using rays so as to avoid damaging healthy tissue is solved by analogy to the military problem of taking a fortress. The fortress maps onto the tumor, the general onto the surgeon, the columns of soldiers onto the rays. To take the fortress is to destroy the tumor, to send small convergent columns from different directions is to direct weak rays of different orientation that will converge on the same body area. The *source domain* of military strategy is mapped onto the *target domain* of medical surgery. Clearly the mapping is restricted to a few counter-parts, and a very restricted amount of structure.

As Hofstadter emphasizes, the domains need not be different. For example, in a *Momma* comic strip, Momma's son Francis and his friend Jack are talking to Momma and showing her a credit card. Francis intends that his mother, Momma, will reason by analogy and draw appropriate conclusions, transferring the way that Jack and his mother use Jack's mother's credit card to Francis and Momma. The comic strip maps a social domain onto itself.

Jack:　This Visa card, Mrs. Hobbs? I use it and my mother pays the bills . . . so I never have to bother her for money!
Francis:　Momma, can't I do that too?
Momma:　It's fine with me.

Then, last panel:

Momma:　Check with Jack's mother.

Induced Schemas

The structures mapped onto each other are mappable by virtue of being instances of a common, more abstract schema. The schema is a *frame* with *roles* that can be filled by elements of one or the other domain. The associated structures both fit the schema, and the schema specifies the mapping. In the Momma example, Francis intends the following schema to be extracted:[11]

son uses **credit card** of **mother,** who pays **bills**

There are (at least) four roles, **son, mother, credit card,** and **bills,** interconnected by various relations. The relations fit into a rich inferential structure available through background knowledge. In the source situation, they are filled respectively by Jack, Jack's mother, Jack's mother's credit card, and Jack's bills. In the target situation intended by Francis, they would be filled by Francis, Momma, Momma's credit card, and Francis's bills.

Extension

For an induced schema to project structure from one domain to another, there has to be a partial mapping between the two domains. In the above example, the frame structure **son, mother, credit card, bills** allows Jack to be mapped to Francis, Victoria (Jack's mother) to be mapped to Momma, Visa card number 112 to be mapped to Master Charge number 333, and so on.

The specific situation *Jack uses Visa 112 of Victoria to pay Jack's bills* is interpreted, via the corresponding roles, as an instance of the abstract schema:

son uses **credit card** of **mother,** who pays **bills**

and that schema in turn gives a specific situation in the other domain, *Francis uses MC 333 of Momma to pay Francis's bills.*

Once the analogy has been triggered by a partial mapping, it is natural for further structure to get mapped, if this is possible. If Victoria, Jack's mother, pays the rent of Jack's sister, Annabelle, then perhaps Momma could pay the rent of Francis's sister, Mary-Lou and so on. A more extensive induced schema is produced. Besides being common in everyday reasoning, analogical extension is a crucial component of scientific innovation.[12]

Extension may also lead to the creation of new structure in the target domain. Suppose Mary-Lou is still living at home. The extended mapping requires a counterpart for Annabelle's apartment, i.e., an apartment for Mary-Lou, not already present in the target domain. Finding such an apartment for Mary-Lou creates the required new structure (under analogical pressure) and allows the analogical reasoning to proceed (i.e., Momma must pay the rent on the new apartment).

Or *extension* may lead to reinterpretation of old structure in the target. Perhaps Mary-Lou owns a boat and pays for its upkeep. Annabelle's apartment can be mapped onto the boat, and the rent onto the cost of the upkeep, triggering the inference that Momma should pay for the boat. Under that extension, the boat is now *thought of* as the equivalent for Mary-Lou and Momma of the apartment for Annabelle and Victoria. New structure has been imposed on the target domain of Momma and her family. And this is possible through projection from the source domain of Victoria and her family.

Fluidity and Reanalysis

The case of the boat also illustrates the flexibility of analogy. Reanalysis of the structural correspondences and extraction of new induced schemas are always possible. Deep analogy (Hofstadter 1986) is achieved by discovering and exploiting more abstract and less obvious schematic mappings.

There is never a "right" answer to the mapping problem, although given contexts will favor some mappings over others, as a function of the goals pursued, and in keeping within general heuristics favoring structural relationships over simple attributes (Gentner 1983). Again, the Momma comic strip provides an illustration of this point. Guided by her own purpose in the conversation, Momma chooses to interpret her son's suggestion through a mapping which runs counter to our expectations and to Gentner's higher-structure principle. In effect, Momma disregards the frame structure outlined above, and selects the more superficial schema:

young man uses Victoria's credit card and Victoria pays **bills**

That schema involves only *two* roles, **young man** and **bills,** which are filled by Jack and Jack's bills in the source, and by Francis and Francis's bills in the target, yielding:

Francis uses Victoria's credit card and Victoria pays **Francis's bills.**

Victoria and her credit card are constants in this alternative schema, and do not change when the roles receive different fillers.

The characteristics outlined above are central to analogical reasoning. But they show up more generally in other kinds of *structure projection,* such as metaphor (whether entrenched or novel), metonymy, and pragmatic-reference functions. The focus of this paper is the presence of the very same characteristics in mental space constructions, and specifically in those associated with counterfactual phenomena. Such phenomena, as it turns out, are based, just like analogy and other structure projections, on domain mappings, induced schemas, extension, and reanalysis.

Basic Observations: Counterfactuals and Frames

The analogical counterfactual phenomenon was pointed out in passing in Fauconnier 1990a on the basis of examples like (8).

(8) In France, Watergate wouldn't have done Nixon any harm.

Interpreting (8) as a comment on French politics and society is not a matter of examining the imaginary world in which Nixon was born or lived in France. Rather, it involves the extraction of a common frame for the American and the French sociopolitical domains, and structure projection from the two domains to a third. The relevant triggering frame might include elements like the following, in which boldface elements stand for roles. Such a frame is typically part of an idealized cognitive model (ICM),[13] and it will bring in a huge amount of background-knowledge structure in addition to the components crudely outlined here using English words and sentences.

F (Western democracy frame):
country has a **president** elected by **citizens**
president is **head** of **political party** competing with others for leadership of **country**
president's actions are constrained by **laws, public reaction,** etc.
action brings harm to **president** if
—it triggers negative **public reaction**
—it is unlawful and **president** is punished

Sentence (8) builds up mental spaces in discourse in the following way. The initial space, B, is relative to the American political system at the time of Watergate. It contains frame F, with fillers (*values*) for the various roles:

president → Nixon
country → United States
citizens → Americans
law → no break-ins
punishment → impeachment

Space B furthermore contains information about Watergate itself, which can be understood as a specific instance of a generic break-in frame:

break-in:
president secretly orders **break-in; break-in** fails and it is discovered that **president** was the instigator

The role **president** is already filled by Nixon; the role **break-in** is filled by Watergate. As before, the frame is actually much more complex than outlined here; the simplification should not alter the main characteristics of the process.

Finally, the initial space B contains information regarding the outcome of the specific events, which, again simplified, might include:

public reaction → outrage
punishment → impeachment
Watergate does harm to Nixon understood as an instance of the subframe:
break-in does harm to **president**

Notice that all of this elaborate structure, which will be essential in order to make sense of sentence (8) when it comes along in some conversation or other form of discourse, is *not* in any way conveyed by sentence (8); it is purely background.

When sentence (8) is actually processed as part of a discourse, it starts with the space builder *in France*. This is going to bring in two new spaces. First, it brings in a space G (as in Gallic) corresponding to relevant partial background information about the French political system. This space will include a frame F′ sharing much of the structure of frame F in the base space: it will include roles like **president, laws, country, public reaction,** and so on. The identical structure allows a mapping from space B to space G: shared roles and relations get mapped. The common structure of F and F′ is the *induced schema* that allows an initial mapping to be established. It corresponds to the basic **mother, son, credit card** schema in the Momma example (**mother** of **son** has **credit card; son** has **bills** to pay).

After space G is set up, the sentence could proceed in the regular past tense, as in (9).

(9) In France, Watergate did not do Nixon any harm.

A sentence like (9) would be saying something about the consequences of Watergate for Nixon in France. It would not use the extracted frames, it would not be analogical, and it would not be counterfactual.

Sentence (8), in contrast, because of the grammatical form *would not have done, is* counterfactual. And in terms of discourse construction, that translates into the introduction of a *third* mental space C (as in counterfactual). Space C is counterfactually bound to G: it is setting up a (partially defined) situation in which, contrary to current knowledge, something ''similar'' to Watergate happens in France.

The process functions in the following way. The space-builder *in France* indicates that relevant background structure in C will be inherited from space G. This includes frame F'. The words *Watergate* and *Nixon,* however, *do not* point to elements of space G (France). They point to elements w and n of the base B (United States). Since C is the space being structured, the words *Watergate* and *Nixon* must ultimately identify elements of C.[14]

Now, it is a fundamental property of mental spaces that such access is possible from one space to another when counterparts are mapped by connector functions. The general principle (Fauconnier 1985; Encrevé 1988; van Hoek, chapter 12 in this volume; and Lakoff, chapter 4 in this volume) is a generalization of Jackendoff 1975 and Nunberg 1978.

Access Principle[15]
If connector Γ maps element a onto element b, element b can be identified by a linguistic expression pointing to a.

It follows that in the example at hand, *Watergate* and *Nixon* will identify counterparts of w and n (from space B) in the focus space C. How are such counterparts obtained? This is where analogical mapping plays a key role: mental space C has inherited the "political" frame F' from G (France). It is therefore (partially) mappable onto the base (United States) which included frame F. Values (role fillers) are mapped onto values of the corresponding roles. This allows a straightforward mapping of n (Nixon) onto the value n' of the role **president** in space C. If there is a value for that role in G (e.g., Mitterrand), n' will also be the counterpart of that value in C (intuitively, Mitterrand in the counterfactual situation). If G is less specific (referring to French politics in general, independently of its particular instantiations), element n' has no counterpart in G. Informally speaking, n' is then a hypothetical French president involved in a Watergate-like situation.

Schematically:

	Space B	Space C	Space G
	Frame F	Frame F'	Frame F'
role:	**president**	**president**	**president**
value:	n (Nixon)	n'	Mitterrand
			or
			unspecified

Now, Watergate is not a value in the initial triggering frame F. But it is a value in the relevant additional frame BI (break-in). In order for Watergate to have a counterpart in C, this frame must be projected onto C, providing new structure:

	Space B	Space C	Space G
	Frame F	Frame F'	Frame F'
role:	**president**	**president**	**president**
value:	n (Nixon)	n'	Mitterrand
			or
			unspecified

	Frame BI	Frame BI
role:	**break-in**	**break-in**
value	w (Watergate)	w'

The cognitive construction illustrated above is required before the content of sentence (8) can even start to be assessed. That content, relative to the counterfactual focus space C, is expressed by:

Watergate not do Nixon any harm

The phrase *in France* and the grammatical aspect and tense (*would, have +* past) indicate what spaces are set up, with respect to which this content is to be evaluated. And by virtue of the Access Principle, this content reduces in space C to "w' not harm n'." That content is in opposition to the consequence of BI in space B, namely "w harm n."

At this point, space C is a "blend" of spaces B and G, with additional relations found in neither. What is the use of C in the discourse? It does not give direct information about actual situations, and it does not represent existing frame configurations. However, besides being counterfactual, C is also *conditional*. The semantics linked to C include the general *matching* conditions on hypothetical spaces (Fauconnier 1990a). The matching condition (an extended form of modus ponens) specifies in general that a space matching the defining structure of a conditional space fits it in all other respects.

In the present case, the defining structure of C is frames **F'** and **BI,** and its additional structure, introduced explicitly, is "w' not harm n'."

It follows therefore from matching with C that a space with frames F' and BI will also have the additional structure "w' not harm n'." This amounts to saying that frame F' when combined with BI yields different consequences from frame F combined with BI. Not surprisingly, then, the whole process ends up highlighting an important difference between the *existing* French and

American political systems, based on their potential consequences, when confronted with similar contexts. It is of course notable that sentence (8) does not in itself tell us what these differences might be; it is up to the listener (and the speaker for that matter) to infer from background knowledge what existing differences might account for the different consequences. But conversation participants do not have to go through this extra inferencing in order to understand (8). Sentence (8) under this interpretation is falsifiable to the extent that a new situation might arise in which the French president *is* harmed by a secret break-in, yielding a factual basis for constructing a space that violates Matching with C. It is also considered falsifiable in argumentative discourse by constructing such nonmatching spaces (counterfactually) by deductive or analogical reasoning from existing background knowledge.

One could counter (8), for instance, with (10).

(10) You're wrong. Look at all the harm the Greenpeace incident did to Mitterrand.

The Greenpeace incident was not a break-in,[16] but it was widely believed to have been secretly and illegally approved by the French president.[17] A sentence like (10) widens frame BI, replacing the role **break-in** by a more general one. Real consequences become available to assess the "truth" of the counterfactual (8).

The theoretical implications of examples like (8) are far-reaching. The analysis above suggests that, as discourse unfolds and mental spaces are set up, the recovery of meaning fundamentally depends on the capacity to induce shared structures, map them from space to space, and extend the mappings so that additional structure is introduced and exported. This picture is quite different from the classical view that core literal truth-conditional meaning is first produced, and later altered by more peripheral "pragmatic" operations.

Are the mechanisms operating in the interpretation of (8) representative of natural-language semantics? The remainder of this paper will show that indeed they are pervasive and basic, and that they show up in various grammatical guises. I will discuss relevant examples, using mental space construction and linkage as exemplified throughout this volume and in, for example, Fauconnier 1985, Lakoff 1987, Sakahara 1990, Dinsmore 1991, and Marconi 1991.

Such construction makes use of the following assumptions and operating principles:

(i) background knowledge in the form of frames, idealized cognitive models, cultural models, folk theories, etc. is available;

(ii) local framing and (extensive) pragmatic information is available—for example, whether we are reading a story, watching a play, having an argument, or reporting information; where we are, who we're interacting with and why, etc.;[18]

(iii) discourse construction starts in a *base space* (also called *origin* space or *current discourse* space[19]) from which a lattice of spaces related to each other will evolve;

(iv) the spaces are used to build up cognitive structure and information relative to "objectively" very different kinds of things: time periods,[20] beliefs,[21] pictures, hypothetical or counterfactual situations,[22] points of view,[23] quantifications, geographical locations,[24] and cultural constructions;[25]

(v) at any point in the dynamic unfolding of space configurations, one space and one space only is "in focus"; various grammatical and pragmatic devices exist to switch focus;[26]

(vi) the spaces are connected in two major ways:

    a. by the ordering relation on the lattice: each space is introduced relative to another (its "parent"), and only when a space is in focus can it serve to launch a new child space;

    b. by *connectors* that link elements across spaces, in accordance with the Access Principle outlined above;

(vii) structure is transferred across spaces, in a variety of ways, which include:

    a. *optimization:* transfer by default from parent to child: relevant structure not explicitly contradicted is inherited within the child space; this is a *downward* transfer in the space lattice (for example, *I wish Rosa's brother were kind* transfers to the "wish"-space properties satisfied in the base—features of the individual independent of kindness, such as appearance, being Rosa's brother, etc., even though such features are not themselves necessarily wished for);

    b. *access:* creation of counterparts via the Access Priniciple, as in the Watergate example above (for example, Rosa and her brother have counterparts in the wish space);

    c. *projection* of entire frames following the creation of a counterpart in a counterfactual space, as in the Watergate example: the break-in frame was projected along with the counterpart of element w; more generally, *projection* by extended mapping on the basis of initial partial mapping, as in metaphor and analogy;

    d. *matching conditions* for certain spaces (like hypotheticals), which allow additional structure to be transferred on the basis of partial fit (for example, *If Maxine loves Max, then Max is happy* sets up a hypothetical space with the matching condition LOVE (Maxine, Max). The satisfaction of this condition in an appropriately related space will allow transfer of the remaining structure, HAPPY (Max));[27]

e. *upward* floating of presuppositions through the space lattice, until they meet themselves or their opposite (This is the "projection problem" for presuppositions. In (i) *Sue believes that George's son is bald,* the presupposition that George has a son floats up to the Base, but not in (ii) *If George was a father, his son would be bald,* or in (iii) *George has a son and Sue believes that George's son is bald.* Sentence (ii) neither entails nor presupposes that George has a son; (iii) entails but does not presuppose that George has a son).

Optimization (downward) and floating (upward) are both cases of more general *Spreading,* which is a very powerful mechanism of structure building in natural language that allows large amounts of structure to be transferred without explicit specification.

I now turn to cases which illustrate aspects of the relevant phenomena.

Spreading and Cancellation

The following dialogue is taken from a *Drabble* comic strip:

Dad (watching wrestling on TV): When I was in my prime, I could've pinned Hulk Hogan in a matter of seconds!
Son (to mother): Is that true, Mom?
Mom: Probably.
Mom (next and last frame in the strip): Of course, when your Dad was in his prime, Hulk Hogan was in kindergarten.

Understanding this strip requires among other things that we understand the father to be saying that he used to be a top wrestler, and that we understand the mother's answer, superficially in agreement, as actually casting doubt on the "top wrestler" conclusion. Although the piece of discourse does not contain the typical grammatical markers for counterfactuals (*if, would*), it is understood through counterfactual mapping.[28]

Let us take a look at the space-building processes behind the dialogue. The following notational conventions will be useful. If a linguistic expression brings in a frame F, the notation Fxy will stand for "x and y fit frame F." So, for example, *Romeo is in love with Juliet* brings in a frame LOVE. If the expression is structuring some mental space M, and if *Romeo* and *Juliet*

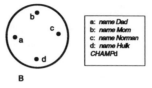

a:	*name Dad*
b:	*name Mom*
c:	*name Norman*
d:	*name Hulk*
	CHAMPd

Figure 3.1

identify a and b in space M, then we will write "LOVE a b" for the structure added to space M by the linguistic expression. A frame in this sense differs from a standard logical relation, in that it may bring with it large amounts of background knowledge and inferences, and it will typically contain many roles (e.g., *rival, parents, meeting place,* etc.).

The expression PRIME x will abbreviate the content of x fitting the frame brought in by *to be in one's prime.* Such a frame typically carries inferences regarding an age range, a corresponding peak in health, physical abilities, and so on.

The expression "PIN x y" will correspond to *pin someone in a matter of seconds,* with the corresponding implications (possibly by default) that x is stronger, a better wrestler, etc., than y. "CHAMP x" will stand for being a talented wrestler, a champion, or as good as a champion.

The mental space construction for the dialogue unfolds in the following way:

First space: the *base* B, in which we have prior or inferred information about Mom, Dad, Norman, their son, and Hulk Hogan, the wrestling champion, is shown in figure 3.1. Italics symbolize background or default structure. The comic strip does not say explicitly at the outset that the characters are a family or that Hulk Hogan is a champion.

Second space: when I was in my prime is a "past" space builder, which sets up a new space T relative to the base. There is a counterpart for Dad in this space, accessed through the pronoun *I.* This counterpart, a new element a_1 in T, is therefore linked to a by the Identity Connector I. Figure 3.2 reflects that a_1, but not its original counterpart, a, satisfies the conditions associated with the PRIME frame.

Third space: With *I could,* the possibility modal *can* opens a new space of possibility P, relative to the time space T, as shown in figure 3.3. Gramatically, the modal is in the past tense (*could*); this is because the corresponding new space P has opened "within" a past space.[29] By virtue of the Access Principle, the pronoun *I,* subject of *could,* sets up a counterpart, a_2, for a_1 and a in the newly opened possibility space P, which is now in focus.

Fourth space: Another grammatical past now comes along in the form *have pinned.* The function of this second past tense is not to mark time, but

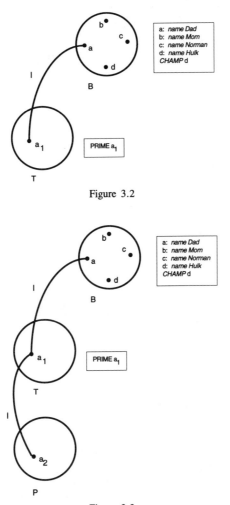

Figure 3.2

Figure 3.3

rather to mark distance along another dimension; it is a *distal* in the sense of Langacker 1978, used here to set up a counterfactual space relative to P. Compare (11) and (12).

(11) In my youth, I could pin Hulk Hogan in seconds.

(12) In my youth, I could have pinned Hulk Hogan in seconds.

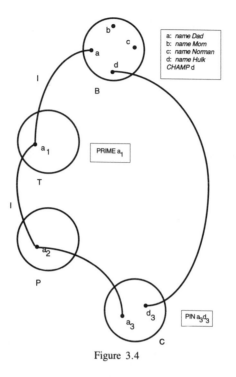

Figure 3.4

The present infinitive in (11) suggests that the pinning of Hulk Hogan actually did occur. The past in (12) implies strongly that it did not.

After the distal past has applied, a fourth space C is set up, with counterparts for Dad and Hulk Hogan, as shown in figure 3.4.

The counterfactual space C includes a counterpart, d_3, of d in the base (Hulk Hogan). At this point in the construction, new structure is brought into C by Optimization: this is the default procedure that transfers structure associated with an element in one space to its counterpart in another. Optimization applies only if it does not lead to internal incompatibilities. In this example, element d_3 inherits structure from its counterpart in the base, element d; this is the structure "CHAMP d_3."

Background knowledge of the form "he who pins down a champ is a champ" will add more implicit structure to space C, namely "CHAMP a_3." At that point, the space configuration will be as in figure 3.5.

In this way, structure has been built in the lowest space, the counterfactual C. This implicit structure can then be propagated upwards by *Spreading*. It will go up to the possibility space P, and then up again to the time space T, as shown in figure 3.6.

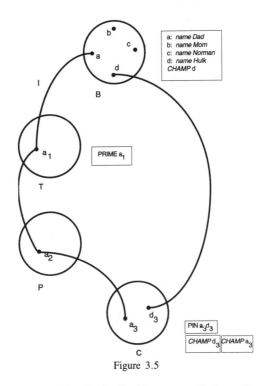

Figure 3.5

Spreading is halted either logically (if a contradiction arises) or pragmatically, as in this example: space T ("when I was in my prime") is explicitly set up as a focus of inference, and the inferred structure is understood to be time dependent—being a champion wrestler is a state that is liable to change from youth to old age (according to our default cultural model). Hence, the structure will not propagate beyond space T; we can infer that Dad was good in his prime, not that he still is. This aspect of Spreading is (unfortunately) not derivable from the space configurations alone; compare our example with sentence (13).

(13) Don't make me mad. Remember that yesterday, I could have knocked you out.

One interpretation here is that if it was possible yesterday, it still is today. The relevant inference (e.g., "I am stronger than you") will (or at least can) spread all the way up.

The two similar examples with different spreading properties show that inference propagation takes the conceived real world into account. This stands

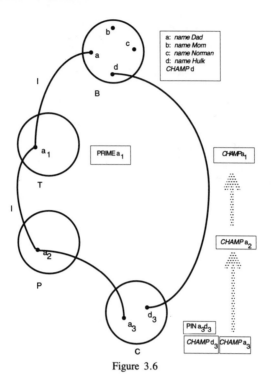

Figure 3.6

in contrast to the structure propagation downward into the counterfactual—the championhood of Hulk Hogan projected from the base to a space linked to a remote time period.

To recapitulate, the important feature of this construction is the inheritance by default of the CHAMP structure for the counterparts of d in space C. This follows from Optimization, the default principle that transfers structure from the base to the new spaces T, P, and C. The structure obtained for C through this process, (PIN a_3 d_3) [CHAMP d_3], warrants the crucial inference [CHAMP a_3], which in turn gets propagated back to space T. To put it less formally, counterparts for Hulk Hogan in the new spaces remain associated with the property of being a champion wrestler. To beat Hogan is therefore also to be a champion wrestler. Space C is *counterfactual*, because the father will not and did not fight Hogan. This is why [PIN a_3 d_3] cannot be transferred back to space T. The CHAMP structure, on the other hand, which holds for a_3 in C, does propagate to T (and it gets associated with a_1). As we might expect, then, the counterfactual construction yields the "real" past inference that the father used to be an outstanding wrestler.

The mother's contribution modifies the space construction. As pointed out

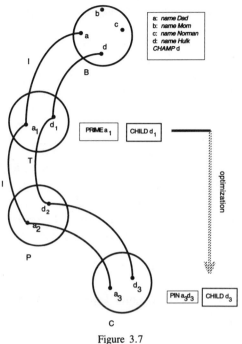

a: name Dad
b: name Mom
c: name Norman
d: name Hulk
CHAMP d

PRIME a₁   CHILD d₁

optimization

PIN a₃d₃   CHILD d₃

Figure 3.7

by Y. Takubo (p.c.), the mother's construction has counterparts d_1 and d_2 for d in the intermediate spaces T and P. The frame for d_1 linked to "_____ be in kindergarten," and abbreviated as CHILD, is explicitly added to space T. The time difference between B and T that was left vague in the first construction is now inferred to be large by virtue of cultural knowledge about kindergarten and professional fighting. More importantly, the new explicit frame is incompatible with the implicit structure [CHAMP].[30] The explicit frame relations in T propagate to spaces P and C, effectively cancelling the incompatible implicit structure [CHAMP d_3]. After the mother has spoken, the construction has shifted to that shown in figure 3.7.

What is striking about the example is the way in which the default strategies operate. Structure linked to element d in the base B (Hogan is strong, in his prime, a champion, etc.) propagates in spite of the fact that we "know" that going back in time to make Dad young should make Hogan much younger as well and remove his relevant properties (the realistic strategy implicitly adopted by the mother to justify her alternative construction). This highlights a general and distinctive property of counterfactuals: they are not intended to refer to realistic worlds; their power seems to lie instead in the inferences (produced through local space building) that they can project back to other spaces. As we will see in later examples, analogical mappings are at work here in different guises. In the Drabble example, for instance, the father's interpretation could be corroborated if space C matched a subspace of T, i.e., if the father had indeed fought and beaten fighters "comparable to" Hogan: space C works as a schema with minimal structure, and element d_3 is minimally specified—while the relevant CHAMP structure does get inherited by default, other properties of Hogan (the color of his hair, his phone number, the nationality of his mother, etc., if they happen to be specified in B) are weakly inheritable, but do not count in assessing the truth value requested by the son. Even though the construction rests on what looks like a vivid and concrete image, the father fighting Hulk Hogan, it allows a much more abstract schema to be extracted and used for reasoning and corroboration. This is also known to be an essential property of metaphorical mappings: a correspondence between vivid source and target domains allows abstract schemas to be extracted, transferred, or modified for the purpose of reasoning and organizing thought.

Fictitious Elements and Truth Conditions

The Naked Lie

The following dialogue is found in a movie called *The Naked Lie*. In the movie, a prostitute has been found murdered. Webster, an unpleasant, self-centered character, shows no sympathy, and Victoria disagrees with Webster.

Victoria: What if it were your sister?

Webster: I don't have a sister, but if I did, she wouldn't be a hooker.

Later in the movie, Victoria is talking to someone else:

Victoria: You know that sister Webster doesn't have? Well, she doesn't know how lucky she is.

The word *sister* brings in an important kinship frame that has interesting properties of its own, but I will simplify that aspect of the structure for present purposes, assuming only that a *role* s_i in some space containing a_i corresponds to the informal "sister of a_i." As with any other role, s_i may have a value or not in its space. If e is such a value, we shall use the notation $s_i \rightarrow e$ to indicate that e is a value of role s_i.

The first part of the example, the dialogue between Victoria and Webster,

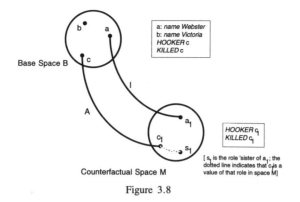

Base Space B

a: *name Webster*
b: *name Victoria*
HOOKER c
KILLED c

A

a_1

c_1

s_1

HOOKER c_1
KILLED c_1

Counterfactual Space M

[s_1 is the role 'sister of a_1'; the
dotted line indicates that c_1 is a
value of that role in space M]

Figure 3.8

amounts to negotiated space building. Victoria develops a model which carries the intended inference that Webster should show sympathy, and this
counterfactual model is analogical in interesting ways. Webster answers with
a counterfactual model of his own, designed to foil the inference. Webster's
model is also analogical.

Victoria's first contribution to the conversation sets up a space configuration in the obvious way, with the counterfactual space M, as in figure 3.8.
Notice that elements c and c_1 are linked by the *analogy* connector A, not by
identity. That is, we interpret Victoria's question as asking, "What if, *instead*
of happening to this girl, it had happened to your sister?" A very close
construction differing only in the type of connector would be produced by
the sentence *What if she were your sister?* This construal of this counterfactual would consist in keeping "the same" girl, but framing her as Webster's
sister. Victoria's counterfactual "replaces" the real girl analogically by Webster's sister.[31]

Once the counterfactual has been set up, new inferences can be drawn (in
space M) according to cultural models like "one should show sympathy if one's
sister is killed," and then, as in the Drabble example, the new inferences will
spread upward to counterparts in dominant spaces, as shown in figure 3.9. Although Victoria has not claimed that Webster has a sister, her use of the definite
description *your sister* could be interpreted as presupposing that Webster has a
sister. Element c_1 would then be linked by another connector (identity, I) to an
element c' in the base (Webster's sister), as in figure 3.10.

The diagram reflects that the base space B and the counterfactual space M
are linked by two connectors, analogy (A) and identity (I). The roles for
"Webster's sister" in the two spaces are s and s_1, linked by identity, I. The
values of these roles are c' and c_1, also linked by identity. The *analog* of c
(the "hooker" in the base) is c_1 in the counterfactual space M. This is a case

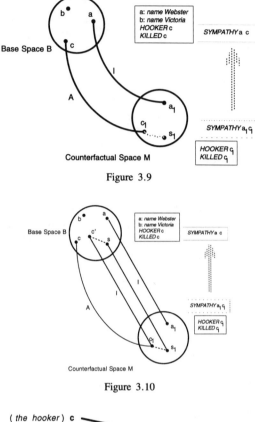

Figure 3.9

Figure 3.10

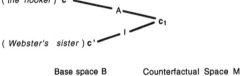

Base space B   Counterfactual Space M

Figure 3.11

of double linkage, with one element in the counterfactual space linked to two elements in the base, as shown in figure 3-11.

As in many counterfactual constructions, we get a frame-blending effect: element c_1 fits into the two frames for c (the murdered prostitute), and c′ (Webster's sister). And consequently, relevant properties of c_1 can be derived, e.g., deserving sympathy from Webster; such properties are in turn transferred back to the base via the analogical connector, **A**, and we get the

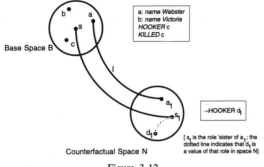

Figure 3.12

inference intended by Victoria that Webster should show sympathy for the murdered woman.

The dialogue at this point can be thought of as a competition between the participants to build appropriate spaces and connections, and thereby obtain intended inferences within the discourse. Webster proceeds by attacking and destroying the construction just set up by Victoria from two directions.

The first direction is a frontal attack. Webster says, "I don't have a sister." This amounts to removing c' from the base: the role s for *Webster's sister* no longer has a value. The transfer of the favorable "sister" frame to c_1 is blocked, and so it looks as if the corresponding inferences are blocked, in particular the need for Webster to show sympathy.

This is not entirely sufficient, however, since Victoria's counterfactual can be interpreted without the presupposition that Webster has a real sister. All that is needed is for c_1, the counterfactual element, to have the role s_1. In that alternative construction for Victoria's question, "What if it were your sister?," there is no value for the role *Webster's sister* (s) in the base, but in the counterfactual space the murdered woman is a value for the corresponding role (s_1). Webster's strategy to undermine inferences stemming from this alternate construction is to block the property "hooker" that would attach to his sister. This is done at the role level: no sister of Webster's could ever be a hooker. In the present formalism, this amounts to imposing the condition $\neg$ HOOKER (s_1) on the counterfactual space, which in turn prevents the counterpart c_1 from being linked to role s_1, because HOOKER (c_1) would contradict $\neg$ HOOKER (s_1).

In order to impose this condition, Webster has constructed a counterfactual space of his own, call it N, in which an imaginary sister makes an appearance, as shown in figure 3.12. This short exchange between Victoria and Webster (the first part of the dialogue) sets up three spaces: B, M, and N. It links B to M and N by means of counterfactual connectors, and links B to M by means of an analogical connector. B is thus linked to M in two ways). This is already fairly elaborate space construction for a perfectly ordinary piece of conversation.

The second part of the dialogue is less ordinary, and it is spectacular. *That sister Webster doesn't have* identifies an element in B, as confirmed by the use of the indicative in the next sentence. And this element d is presented as a counterpart in the base of d_1 in the counterfactual space N: indeed, since the difference between B and N is whether Webster has a sister or not, any counterpart of d_1 in B will necessarily *not* be the sister of Webster. Hence d is associated with the property of not being Webster's sister, and since this is the only available property, the implicature will naturally be that this is the reason for her being lucky. This will transfer back in turn to N in negative form: d_1 "is unlucky" by virtue of "being Webster's sister." This will feed in turn into surface pragmatics to yield the desired negative evaluation of Webster. Even though d is an element set up in B, it has no reference; it is entirely fictitious and used only for the purpose of producing the implicature. Endpoints of scales can also be fictitious in this way, with elements nevertheless set up in the base.[32] The twist in this case is Victoria's phrasing: *she doesn't know how lucky she is.* Although any referent chosen for d would normally know that she isn't Webster's sister and might also know that this is a good thing, she wouldn't know that she has escaped the fate of her counterpart in a world corresponding to space N.

Finally, there is a methodological point to be addressed in connection with examples like the ones discussed above. Clearly, they are facetious, and are meant to be. Should our theory account for them? Do they show anything interesting? I take the following strong position in this respect, following Moser and Hofstadter 1992 and Turner 1991: errors, jokes, literary effects, and atypical expressions use the same cognitive operations as everyday language, but in ways that actually highlight them and can make them more salient. As data, they have a status comparable to laboratory experiments in physics: things that may not be readily observable in ordinary circumstances, which for that very reason shed light on underlying principles. Notice that no specialized linguistic devices are invoked to explain the Webster/Victoria example. Rather it is claimed that the very same construction principles operate here as in other counterfactuals and analogies. But it's a powerful property of this model that it allows for the production and understanding of the strange, funny, or unusual cases, and that it displays the respects in which they are untypical.

The Missing Tree

A great example from insurance claims, reported by an advice columnist, is the sentence *Coming home, I drove into the wrong house and collided with*

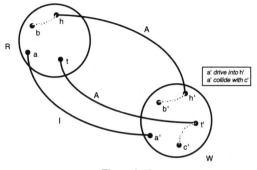

Figure 3.13

a tree I don't have. As in the previous case (*that sister Webster doesn't have*), we find a description here (of the tree) in terms of *non-existence* (of its counterpart). As usual, devious (but not deviant) descriptions like this are possible because of the Access Principle, which allows connecting paths across spaces. In the example, the counterfactuality and the analogy are triggered by the word *wrong.* Two domains are set up, one for the right house, one for the wrong one, as shown in figure 3.13.

Space R

h	role for a location ("house")
h → b	value for that role in space R
a	("speaker")
t	role for a tree in location h
t → ∅	(no value for the role—i.e., no actual tree in that location)

a drives safely into h

Space W

h'
h' → b'
a'
t'
t' → c'
a' collides with c'

A good description of t in R is *tree I don't have,* as in *Our houses are similar, except that I don't have that tree in the back* or *Your book has a chapter in it that mine doesn't have* (*not have* can express the absence of value for a role). The connecting path across spaces and from role to value will link t to its counterpart t' and then to the value c'. In this way c' will be identified (by the description for t).

The counterfactual here is space R (corresponding to what should have happened) as opposed to what did (space W). Relevant to this paper is the nature of the connector linking the two spaces: it is overtly analogical—the two houses and tree locations are in no way presented or conceived as identical, just analogous. A fascinating pragmatic feature that I do not go into here is the explanatory value of this construal for the insurance report.[33]

Mixing Frames and Blending Spaces

Another dimension of the phenomena studied in this paper is explored in Fauconnier and Turner 1994: the extent to which spaces that are connected analogically can give rise to new "blended" spaces in which cognitive work is effected. It is claimed that conceptual blending is a general instrument of cognition running over many linguistic and nonlinguistic cognitive phenomena, such as categorization, inference, grammatical constructions and functional assemblies, action frames, analogy, metaphor, and narrative. As noted above, space C in the Watergate-Nixon example is a blended space. So are space C in the Hulk Hogan case and space M in the *Naked Lie* case.

Blending is usually invisible to consciousness, but there are highly noticeable cases in cartoons and metaphors. Interesting discussion of such cases is found in particular in Talmy 1977, Hofstadter et al. 1989, and Moser and Hofstadter 1992. Goffman 1974 displays striking cases of frame mixing, viewed from a sociological standpoint.

The following attested example from everyday conversation in French shows the complexity of blended analogical counterfactual spaces:

Brigitte: Muriel pourrait facilement être la mère de son petit frère.
'Muriel could easily be the mother of her little brother.'
Catherine: Oh oui, moi à cet âge, je serais la mère de son petit frère.
'Oh yes, me at that age, I would be the mother of her little brother.'[34]

Brigitte in effect sets up a counterfactual space M, with two elements, "mother" and "son," mapped onto "sister" Muriel and her "brother" in space B. Age is the only relevant property, and is maintained across spaces. Notice that identification is in terms of roles *mère* and *frère*, each one from a different space.

Catherine sets up a time space for when she was Muriel's age. In that space, the element c' that refers to Catherine actually has the role *mother* with a corresponding child the same age as Muriel's brother. So it can get mapped onto a

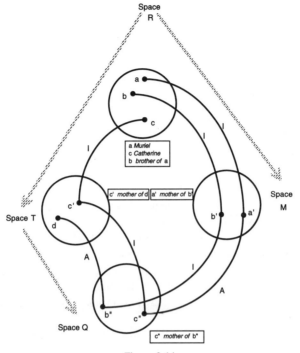

Figure 3.14

counterfactual in which the child becomes a counterpart of Muriel's brother, and the counterpart of c' inherits the ''mother'' property from c'.

In plain English, Catherine is saying (in French of course) that when she was Muriel's age, she had a child the same age as Muriel's brother. And this corroborates Brigitte's statement, by giving real evidence for the possibility of being Muriel's age and having a child the same age as her brother. Notice in particular how Catherine is *not* identifying with the mother of Muriel's brother, whose age is bound to be much greater, since she is also Muriel's mother.

Because the point of this dialogue happens to be relative ages of siblings on the one hand, and parent and child on the other, other properties are only weakly transferred: the mappings take place on the basis of age analogy and motherhood only, as shown in figure 3.14.

Space-building (simplified by leaving out all the roles)[35]

B (base)
    a name *Muriel,* age 24
    b brother of a, age 2
    c name *Catherine,* age 46

M (counterfactual possibility)
  a' mother of b', age 24
  b' son of a', age 2

T (past)
  c' name *Catherine,* age 24, mother of d
  d child of c', age 2

Q (counterfactual relative to T)
  c" age 24, mother of b"
  b" child of c", age 2

Connectors

Identity and analogy link b to b'; identity links c, c', and c" on the one hand, and b and b" on the other.

Crucially, analogy links d to b", and to b'. Analogy also links a' to c" (this happens because of the corresponding motherhood and age structures in spaces M, T, and Q). Linguistic evidence for the links is tied to the application of the Access Principle along the connecting paths: b" in Q is identified by the description *son petit frère* 'her little brother', which applies to b in the base space B.

It's interesting to note that while the purpose of the dialogue is to comment on the age difference between brother and sister, Catherine also makes the point that she was a young mother, compared perhaps to the next generation, exemplified by Brigitte and Muriel, who are 24 but have no children and are single. Believe it or not, in the real-life situation where this dialogue occurred, Brigitte was the daughter of Catherine (i.e., the analogical counterpart of Muriel's brother)!

Conclusion . . .

. . . insightfully provided by Anna Bosch, who noted the following country-music lyrics:

If you'd only put yourself in my shoes, you'd have some sympathy
And if I could put myself in your shoes, I'd walk right back to me.

Notes

1. Until recently, that view was standardly assumed in most of generative linguistics and model-theoretic semantics.

2. For an excellent critical review of this tradition, along with some original proposals, see Brée 1982. Detailed logical accounts are developed, for example, in Lewis

1973 and Goldstick 1978. Important linguistic treatments of the counterpart problem and world-creating predicates are found in McCawley 1981 and Morgan 1973.

3. B may already be true in the actual situation.

4. As pointed out in Goldstick 1978 and Fauconnier 1985, even Goodman's improbable counterfactual *If the match had been struck, it would not have been dry* (as opposed to *If the match had been struck, it would have lit*) is appropriate in the right context. Similarly, example (7) is fine in a context where the key assumption is that we never have fun, no matter what.

5. E.g., structuralist, transformational, generative, Gricean, Searlean, and Montagorean approaches.

6. See, e.g., Reddy 1979; Lakoff and Johnson 1980; Turner 1986 and 1991; Sweetser 1990 and 1996; Espenson 1991; and Goldberg 1995.

7. See, e.g., Langacker 1978, 1987, and 1991; Lindner 1982; Brugman 1982; Goldberg 1992; Talmy 1991; Maldonado Soto 1992; and van Hoek 1991.

8. See, e.g., Hofstadter 1986; Gentner 1983; Gick and Holyoak 1983; Orlich and Mandler 1991; Brown 1990; Turner 1991; and Sereno 1991.

9. See, e.g., Fillmore 1982 and 1985.

10. See, e.g., Bloom 1974 and 1991; and Mandler 1992.

11. I represent the schema in this ordinary language form for convenience. The psychological nature of frames is not crucial at this point.

12. This point is often noted by analogy theorists. Having developed a conceptual analogy between parts of two domains (e.g., hydraulics and electricity), scientists will attempt to test and extend it for other parts of the domains. See Gentner 1983, Hofstadter 1986, and Fauconnier and Turner 1994.

13. Cf. Lakoff 1987.

14. C is the focus space at this point in discourse.

15. Also called the Identification (or ID) Principle.

16. A bomb planted by French agents exploded on the ship Rainbow Warrior and killed a photographer.

17. Encrevé (1988) provides an insightful analysis of the mental space constructions and analogical connectors that were used by the daily newspaper *Libération* in reporting the Greenpeace incident.

18. All this sounds perfectly trivial and commonsensical, and it is indeed for participants in the process, which makes it all the more frustrating when we fathom its formal complexity and scientific intractability.

19. Cf. Langacker 1991.

20. Cf. Dinsmore 1991, Cutrer 1994, and Lansing 1992.

21. Cf. Mejías-Bikandi, chapter 6 in this volume, and Brugman, chapter 2 in this volume.

22. Cf. Sweetser, chapter 11 in this volume, and Lakoff, chapter 4 in this volume.

23. Cf. Sanders and Redeker, chapter 10 in this volume.

24. Cf. van Hoek, chapter 12 in this volume.

25. Cf. Rubba, chapter 8 in this volume.

26. Cf. Dinsmore 1991, Fauconnier 1991, and van Hoek, chapter 12 in this volume.

27. I call this extended modus ponens, because it is a generalisation of the simple case: if space H is connected to M, and H fits P and Q, and M fits P, then the additional structure Q is mapped onto M via the appropriate connector.

28. The expression *could've* is not counterfactual in examples like *Hurry, get some help, he could've hurt himself.*

29. When a grammatical tense marks a property of some space in the space lattice, it also applies to structures in all spaces dominated by the initial one.

30. Background cultural framing is necessary to obtain such incompatibilities.

31. Aspects of such counterfactuals are studied in Moser 1988, Fauconnier 1990b, and Lakoff, chapter 4 in this volume. The effect of the "it" construction used by Victoria is to build an analog of the situation where one element (the hooker) is replaced by another (the sister). Compare with the following sentences.

(i) My cheap earrings were stolen. Lucky *it* wasn't my pearls.

(ii)   *Lucky *they* weren't my pearls.

In the other construction, *What if* she *were your sister?,* a counterfactual is built with an identity connector. In the counterfactual, "she" is the same individual, but has different properties, as in the following sentence.

(iii) My earrings were stolen. Lucky *they* weren't genuine.

32. The following sentences do not entail that there actually is a "simplest problem," or that some stars are "the most distant."

(i) With this telescope, you can see *the most distant stars.*
(ii) Bart is incapable of solving *the simplest problem.*

The scalar endpoints are set up so as to trigger scalar quantification (you can see any stars; Bart is incapable of solving any problem). Cf. Fauconnier 1975.

33. A reviewer for this article points out the interesting use of the definite article in *the wrong house,* and notes the similarity to *I dialed the wrong number.* The definite signals the role, which is unique in the prototypical frame of "wrong versus right" number or house—you only dial *one* number, even though objectively the set of wrong numbers or wrong houses is very large. Here is a striking example of this use, from an article in the Los Angeles *Times,* under the headline *Error Reported in Breast Cancer Study:*

> The researchers had said heredity appears to account for about 2.5% of total breast cancer cases, but corrected that to 6%. . . . "We took the wrong number and multiplied it by the wrong number," said Dr. Graham A. Colditz, a co-author of the study.

34. The conditional *serais,* like its English counterpart *would be,* would be judged ungrammatical by native speakers. Nevertheless, it was produced in context, because the "grammatical" *aurais été* (would have been) carries extra (unwanted) referential implications.

35. With the roles:

B: σ sister of β
    β brother of σ
    σ → a
    β → b

M: μ mother of γ
    γ child of μ
    μ → a′
    γ → b′

T: μ → c′
   γ → d

Q: μ → c″
   γ → b″

This allows a more careful syntactic analysis: *la mère de son petit frère* is role $<\mu,b'>$, (mother of b′) with b′ identified via the role $<\beta,a>$ (brother of Muriel), and its value b in the base. The first sentence (Brigitte's statement) sets up M (*pourrait*), and identifies a′ as the value of role $<\mu,b'>$:

Muriel être *la mère de son petit frère*
a′   ← $<\mu,b'>$

And so on. We can link the grammar elegantly to the space building. Furthermore, the role structure brings out clearly the basis for the analogical mapping. In the structures for T and Q, we see d and b″ occupying the same structural positions.

References

Bloom, L. 1974. Talking, Understanding, and Thinking. In R.L. Schiefelbusch and L.L. Lloyd, eds., *Language Perspectives—Acquisition, Retardation, and Intervention,* 285–311. Baltimore: University Park Press.

———. 1991. Representation and Expression. In N. Krasnegor, D. Rumbaugh, R.L. Schiefelbusch, and M. Studdert-Kennedy, eds., *Biological and Behavioral Foundations for Language Development,* 117–40. Hillsdale, N.J.: Lawrence Erlbaum Associates.

Brée, D.S. 1982. Counterfactuals and Causality. *Journal of Semantics* 1:457–85.

Brown, A. 1990. Domain-Specific Principles Affect Learning and Transfer in Children. *Cognitive Science* 14:107–133.

Brugman, Claudia. 1988. *The Story of Over: Polysemy, Semantics, and the Structure of the Lexicon.* New York: Garland Publishing.

Cutrer, Michelle. 1994. Time and Tense in Narrative and in Everyday Language. Ph.D. diss., University of California, San Diego.

Dinsmore, John. 1991. *Partitioned Representations.* Dordrecht: Kluwer Academic Publishers.

Encrevé, P. 1988. "C'est Reagan qui a coulé le billet vert." *Actes de la Recherche en Sciences Sociales* 71/72.

Espenson, J. 1991. The Structure of the System of Causation Metaphors. Manuscript, University of California, Berkeley.

Fauconnier, Gilles. 1975. Pragmatic Scales and Logical Structure. *Linguistic Inquiry* 6:353–75.

———. 1985. *Mental Spaces: Aspects of Meaning Construction in Natural Language.* Cambridge, Mass.: MIT Press. Reprinted 1994, Cambridge: Cambridge University Press.

———. 1990a. Domains and Connections. *Cognitive Linguistics* 1:151–74.

———. 1990b. Invisible Meaning. *Proceedings of the Sixteenth Annual Meeting of the Berkeley Linguistics Society,* 390–404. University of California, Berkeley.

———. 1991. Subdivision Cognitive. *Communications* 53:229–48.

Fauconnier, Gilles, and Mark Turner. 1994. Conceptual Projection and Middle Spaces. Technical Report no. 9401, Department of Cognitive Science, University of California, San Diego.

Fillmore, Charles J. 1982. Frame Semantics. In Linguistic Society of Korea, ed., *Linguistics in the Morning Calm,* 111–38. Seoul: Hanshin.

———. 1985. Frames and the Semantics of Understanding. *Ouaderni di Semantica* 6(2):222–54.

Gentner, Dedre. 1983. Structure-Mapping: A Theoretical Framework for Analogy. *Cognitive Science* 7:155–70.

Gick, M.L., and K. Holyoak. 1983. Schema Induction and Analogical Transfer. *Cognitive Psychology* 15:1–38.

Goffman, Erving. 1974. *Frame Analysis.* New York: Harper and Row.

Goldberg, Adele E. 1992. The Inherent Semantics of Argument Structure: The Case of the English Ditransitive Construction. *Cognitive Linguistics* 3:37–74.

———. 1994. *Constructions: A Construction Grammar Approach to Argument Structure.* Chicago: University of Chicago Press.

Goldstick, D. 1978. The Truth Conditions of Counterfactual Conditional Sentences. *Mind* 87:1–21.

Goodman, Nelson. 1947. The Problem of Counterfactual Conditionals. *Journal of Philosophy* 44:113–28.

Hofstadter, Douglas. 1986. Analogies and Roles in Human and Machine Thinking. In *Metamagical Themas,* 547–603. New York: Bantam Books.

Hofstadter, Douglas, et al. 1989. Synopsis of the Workshop on Humor and Cognition. *International Journal of Humor Research.*

Jackendoff, Ray. 1975. On Belief Contexts. *Linguistic Inquiry* 6:53–93.

Lakoff, George. 1987. *Women, Fire, and Dangerous Things: What Categories Reveal about the Mind*. Chicago: University of Chicago Press.

Lakoff, George, and Mark Johnson. 1980. *Metaphors We Live By*. Chicago: University of Chicago Press.

Langacker, Ronald W. 1978. The Form and Meaning of the English Auxiliary. *Language* 54.

———. 1987. *Foundations of Cognitive Grammar*. Vol. 1: *Theoretical Prerequisites*. Stanford, Calif.: Stanford University Press.

———. 1991. *Foundations of Cognitive Grammar*. Vol. 2: *Descriptive Application*. Stanford, Calif.: Stanford University Press.

Lansing, Jeff. 1992. Mental Spaces and the English Progressive. Manuscript, University of California, San Diego.

Lewis, David. 1973. *Counterfactuals*. Cambridge, Mass.: Harvard University Press.

Lindner, Susan. 1982. What Goes Up Doesn't Necessarily Come Down: The Ins and Outs of Opposites. *Papers from the Eighteenth Annual Regional Meeting of the Chicago Linguistic Society*, 305–23. University of Chicago.

McCawley, James D. 1981. *Everything that Linguists Have Always Wanted to Know about Logic*. Chicago: University of Chicago Press.

Maldonado Soto, Ricardo. 1992. Middle Voice: The Case of Spanish *se*. Ph.D. diss., University of California, San Diego.

Mandler, J.M. 1992. How to Build a Baby: Conceptual Primitives. *Psychological Review* 99:587–604.

Marconi, D. 1991. Semantica Cognitiva. *Introduzione alla Filosofia Analitica del Linguaggio*, 431–82. Roma-Bari: Laterza.

Morgan, Jerry L. 1973. Presupposition and the Representation of Meaning: Prolegomena. Ph.D. diss., University of Chicago.

Moser, D. 1988. If This Paper Were in Chinese, Would Chinese People Understand the Title? Manuscript, Center for Research on Concepts and Cognition, Indiana University.

Moser, D., and Douglas Hofstadter. 1992. Errors: A Royal Road to the Mind. Manuscript, Center for Research on Concepts and Cognition, Indiana University.

Nunberg, Geoffrey. 1978. *The Pragmatics of Reference*. Bloomington, Ind.: Indiana University Linguistics Club.

Orlich, Felice, and Jean Mandler. 1991. Analogical Transfer: The Roles of Schema Abstraction and Awareness. Manuscript, University of California, San Diego.

Reddy, Michael. 1979. The Conduit Metaphor. In Andrew Ortony, ed., *Metaphor and Thought*, 284–324. Cambridge: Cambridge University Press.

Sakahara, Shigeru, ed. 1990. *Advances in Japanese Cognitive Science*. Vol. 3. Tokyo: Kodansha Scientific.

Sereno, M. 1991. Four Analogies between Biological and Cultural/Linguistic Evolution. *Journal of Theoretical Biology* 151:467–507.

Sweetser, Eve. 1990. *From Etymology to Pragmatics: Metaphorical and Cultural Aspects of Semantic Structure*. Cambridge: Cambridge University Press.

———. 1996. Reasoning, Mappings, and Meta-Metaphorical Conditionals. In Masayoshi Shibatani and S. Thompson, ed., *Topics in Semantics*. Oxford: Oxford University Press. Forthcoming.

Talmy, Leonard. 1977. Rubber-Sheet Cognition in Language. *Papers from the Thirteenth Annual Regional Meeting of the Chicago Linguistic Society*, 612–28. University of Chicago.

———. 1991. Path to Realization. A Typology of Event Conflation. Manuscript, State University of New York at Buffalo.

Turner, Mark. 1986. *Death is the Mother of Beauty*. Chicago: University of Chicago Press.

———. 1991. *Reading Minds: The Study of English in the Age of Cognitive Science*. Princeton, N.J: Princeton University Press.

van Hoek, Karen. 1991. Paths Through Conceptual Structure: Constraints on Pronominal Anaphora. Ph.D. diss., University of California, San Diego.

4 Sorry, I'm Not Myself Today: The Metaphor System for Conceptualizing the Self

•
•
•
•

What Would It Mean for Me to Be You?

In both logic and formal linguistics, it is commonly assumed that reflexives and other anaphoric pronouns indicate indentity of reference, which is represented in logical form by instances of the same logical variable. For example, *I washed myself* has the logical form "X washed X," where X designates the speaker of the sentence. Here *myself* is the reflexive pronoun and X is the logical variable.

Indeed, I am one of the culprits who helped bring that assumption into linguistics in the early 1960s, as part of what was called Generative Semantics. It is an assumption that works for some cases but, as we shall see, fails for many others.

But that is the least of it. The class of cases where it fails shows something far more important about our conceptual system and our language than the answer to the question of how reflexive pronouns work. Those cases contain the seeds of an understanding of how we conceptualize the Self—how we understand who we are and how we function.

We will begin with some sentences that do not fit this assumption. As we look into them further, we will be led away from narrowly linguistic issues, such as how to represent what pronouns mean, and into territory that is much more profound. But let us start where linguists usually start—with sentences.[1]

Consider the minimal pair in (1) and (2).

(1) If I were you, I'd hate me.

(2) If I were you, I'd hate myself.

These sentences mean very different things.

I first discussed these cases in a 1968 paper called "Counterparts, or The

Problem of Reference in Transformational Grammar." Back in those days it was common, at least among generative semanticists, to make the following assumptions: (i) *I, me,* and *myself* are all first person pronouns, and as such, they all refer to the same person, the speaker of that sentence; (ii) each sentence has a logical form that represents its meaning; and (iii) coreference is indicated in logical form by instances of the same variable. These days, of course, the same assumptions are made by a much wider community of linguists.

From these assumptions, it follows that sentences (1) and (2) should have the same logical form, very roughly "If X were Y, X would hate X." Clearly this cannot be the case, since (1) and (2) mean different things. Moreover, it was also assumed in those days, as it is widely assumed today, that a direct object is reflexive if and only if it is coreferential with its subject (except in certain well-known special constructions). This assumption suggests that when the direct object is *me,* it is not coreferential with its subject, whereas when it is *myself,* it is coreferential. But what does that say about logical form? Does it say that the logical forms are "If X were Y, Y would hate X" for *If I were you, I'd hate me* and "If X were Y, Y would hate Y" for *If I were you, I'd hate myself*?; or is it "If X were Y, X would hate X" for *If I were you, I'd hate myself*? None of these captures what these sentences mean. Take *If I were you, I'd hate myself.* Suppose I were you. That is, "Suppose X were Y." Then you would hate yourself. That would seem to opt for "Y would hate Y." But then you wouldn't be you; you'd be me, which would seem to opt for "X would hate X." Logical forms like these just don't seem to be up to the task of characterizing the meaning of these sentences.

These sentences all violate the condition that first-person pronouns refer to the speaker, but it seems that that assumption is just wrong for these cases, and some better way to handle the occurrence of first-person pronouns will be necessary. But what is that better way?

A clue to the solution lies in one of Jim McCawley's classic examples, cited in my 1968 "Counterparts" paper and shown in (3).

(3) I dreamt that I was Brigitte Bardot and that I kissed me.

In the dream, Bardot kisses McCawley. And, as McCawley reports, on his interpretation Bardot in the dream has Bardot's body, not McCawley's. In that case, what does it mean for McCawley to dream that he *was* Bardot? It means that in the dream, McCawley's consciousness is in Bardot's body. McCawley sees from Bardot's perspective, his will controls Bardot's body, his judgment determines how Bardot is to act in the world. McCawley's consciousness, with his accompanying judgment, capacity to feel, and will, replaces Bardot's consciousness, judgment, perception, capacity to feel, and will. Bardot, with McCawley's consciousness at the controls, kisses the physical McCawley when she encounters him. Any interpretation of the sentence short of this misses what the sentence means.

To understand sentence (3), to understand what it means for McCawley to *be* Bardot in the dream, one must be able to conceptualize a person as having two parts. Using the terminology of A. Lakoff and Becker 1991, I call these two parts the *Subject* and the *Self*. I will take the Subject to be the locus of subjective experience: consciousness, perception, judgment, will, and capacity to feel. The Self, for now, will be the body but, as we shall see below, the self is a lot more than just the body.

The interpretation of sentence (3) requires such a conceptualization of a person as split in two parts, with a Subject and a Self. One's Subject can then be understood as "projected" in a dream or in a hypothetical situation into someone else's Self. This is what is going on in the *If I were you* sentences. *I* is conceptualized as split into two parts; call them *Subject-of-I* and *Self-of-I*. Similarly *you* are conceptualized as split into *Subject-of-you* and *Self-of-you*.

Now in the "Counterparts" paper I suggested that natural language semantic representation, which linguists had taken as being made up of symbols alone up to that time, should include possible worlds, in Kripke's sense. I suggested using a variant of a Kripke possible-world semantics constructed by David Lewis (1968), which he called "counterpart theory." My suggestion was that counterfactual sentences should be understood in terms of two possible worlds, the real world and a hypothetical world. The clause *If I were you* sets up a counterpart relation between Subject-of-I in the real world and Subject-of-you in the hypothetical world. Thus, my locus of subjectivity—my consciousness, perception, judgment, will, and capacity to feel—in the real world replaces yours in the hypothetical world.

By the mid-1970s, Lewis's counterpart theory, which was framed within formal semantics, had pretty much disappeared from the field of formal logic for technical reasons. But the direct descendant of the counterpart semantics I had proposed has flourished in cognitive semantics—Fauconnier's theory of mental spaces (Fauconnier 1985). There mental spaces replace possible worlds, Fauconnier's "connectors" replace Lewis's counterpart relations, the reality space replaces the real world, and hypothetical spaces replace hypothetical worlds. With these adjustments, the theory of mental spaces adapts perfectly to the requirements of a cognitive semantics. The analysis suggested above for counterpart theory translates directly into the theory of mental spaces, as shown in figure 4.1.

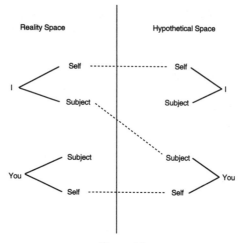

Figure 4.1

This form of representation of meaning differs in important ways from logical forms. There are no longer any variables. Binding is done by connectors, which can link entities across spaces. Cognitive structures, such as conceptual metaphors and other forms of conceptualization, can structure spaces.

We can now represent the meaning and characterize the grammar of the *If I were you* sentences. *If I were you* sets up a hypothetical space and a connector between my Subject in reality space and your Subject in the hypothetical space. This creates a counterpart of *you* in the hypothetical space that has my Subject paired with your Self. In the hypothetical space, my consciousness, perception, capacity for feeling, judgment, and will are in control of your Self—your body, your past, your social role, etc. Now consider again sentences (1) and (2).

(1) If I were you, I'd hate me.

Imagine a situation where a sentence such as (1) would be appropriate: suppose that I have done cruel things to you, but that you are a very forgiving, perhaps saintlike, person who doesn't feel badly toward me despite the cruelties. Suppose that I, on the other hand, am not particularly forgiving and harbor bad feelings for people who have hurt me. Now suppose you, instead of having your consciousness, perception, capacity for feeling, judgment, and will, had mine. The resulting hypothetical person, in the same situation that you are in, would hate me.

(2) If I were you, I'd hate myself.

Here is a situation where a sentence such as (2) would be appropriate: suppose that you are a really nasty person, and moreover that you have no moral sensibility at all. You feel no remorse at all. But I have a very considerable moral sensibility. Now suppose that you, instead of having your consciousness, capacity for feeling, judgment, and will, had mine. The resulting hypothetical person, given all the nasty things he's done, would hate himself—that is, his Subject with my values would hate his Self, with whom past actions are identified.

To my knowledge, such analyses cannot be done with anything like traditional logical forms, where persons are indivisible, where there are no hypothetical spaces, and where binding is done by using identical variable symbols, rather than connectors that can bind different entities across spaces. It was for this reason that I gave up on logical forms for representing meaning by 1968. The fact that mental spaces make such analyses possible provides support for including the theory of mental spaces within an adequate semantic theory. Similar conclusions about the inadequacy of standard logical forms have been reached by Ruwet (1991).

The Construction

Let us look a bit more closely at the proposed analysis of such sentences. These sentences are instances of a grammatical construction. The syntax of the construction is:

if NP_1 were NP_2, NP_3 would VP.
constraint: NP_3 is an anaphor and NP_1 is its antecedent.

The semantics of the construction is:

  (i) there are two mental spaces, the Reality Space, R, and a Hypothetical Space, H, dependent on R;
 (ii) the referents of NP_1 and NP_2 are in R, and the referent of NP_3 is in H;
(iii) each referent of an NP is conceptualized as having a Subject and a Self;
 (iv) NP_3's Subject is the counterpart of NP_1's Subject. NP_3's Self is the counterpart of NP_2's Self;
  (v) VP predicates the Subject properties of NP_3 that result from NP_2's Self being paired with NP_1's Subject;
 (vi) NP_2 VP is false in R; NP_3 VP is true in H; and

(vii) The antecedent-anaphor relationship indicates not full person identity, but rather Subject identity between NP_3 and NP_1.

A grammatical construction is an idiosyncratic pairing of a semantic content and the form in which it is expressed. *If I were you* sentences are not simple instances of the counterfactual conditional construction. The occurrence of *were* linking NP_1 and NP_2 is not a simple predication of identity. It is rather an instruction to form a hypothetical person by uniting NP_1's Subject with NP_2's Self. It requires a special construction to state this.

There are some details of the construction that we have not discussed yet. Consider the anaphoric relationship between NP_3 and NP_1. NP_3 cannot refer anaphorically to NP_2. Compare sentences (4) and (5), where sentence (4) meets the anaphoric condition and sentence (5) doesn't. Sentence (5) is decidedly strange.

(4) If I were you, I'd get upstairs this second!

(5) *If I were you, you'd get upstairs this second!

Another constraint on the construction is that VP must predicate Subject properties, not Self properties. Self properties include such things as physical characteristics, name, social role, religious affiliation, etc. Subject properties include consciousness, capacity to feel, judgment, and will. Thus sentences (6) and (7), which violate this condition, are strange, since they predicate the author's Self properties, rather than Subject properties of NP_3.

(6) *If I were you, I would be short and named George.

(7) *If I were Ross Perot, I would be Jewish.

If both the anaphoric and Subject-property conditions are violated, the resulting sentences are so odd that they become laughable.

(8) **If I were you, you would be short and named George.

(9) **If I were Ross Perot, he'd be Jewish.

Compare such sentences with sentences that obey the anaphoric constraint and predicate Subject properties, such as capacity to feel, judgment, and will, as in (10) and (11). In (10), judgment is projected, and *getting glasses* is the act based on judgment that is being suggested. In (11) *needing glasses* indicates a physical property, not an act resulting from a judgment. As a physical property, it is not a subject property and that violates the semantics of the construction.

(10) If I were you, I'd get glasses.

(11) *If I were you, I'd need glasses.

Note that in different sentences, different subject properties can be predicated. Depending on the kind of subject properties predicated, a different speech act will result. With a predication indicating a judgment as to what to do, the associated speech act is advice. Where the predication indicates a projection of will, the associated speech act is a directive. And if empathy is projected and the predication indicates a capacity to feel, an expressive speech act is indicated. Some examples are shown in sentences (12) through (14).

Projection of Judgment/Expression of Advice

(12) If I were you, I'd quit that job.

Projection of Will/Expression of a Directive

(13) If I were you, I would turn off the TV and come upstairs right this minute!

Projection of Empathy/Expression of Emotionality

(14) If I were you, I'd be angry too.

The distinction between these normal sentences and the odd sentences cited above supports the claim that what we are calling the Subject/Self distinction is a distinction between a locus of judgment, will, and empathy on the one hand and a locus of physical properties, social roles, real-world actions, etc. on the other.

It is important to understand that these distinctions have to do with construal—with how sentences are interpreted. Thus a single sentence may be construed as either predicating a Subject property or a Self property, depending on context. Compare sentences (15) and (16).

(15) If I were you, I'd hate that guy.

(16) *If I were you, I'd hate brussels sprouts.

Sentence (15) indicates a projection of empathy and an expression of emotionality. In normal contexts, sentence (16) is odd. Hating a person is a clear subject property, having to do with what one feels emotionally. But hating brussels sprouts is normally construed as physical, not a matter of judgment or emotionality. However, in certain contexts it can be construed as involving judgment and/or emotionality. For example, if one had been captured and tortured by having to eat five pounds of brussels sprouts a day for a month, one might well have an emotional reaction to brussels sprouts, and in such a context the sentence would be normal. In all of the examples given above, what is important is construal in context, and the construals I have given may, as one would expect on this analysis, be changed in far-fetched contexts.

Summary So Far

These examples suggest that there is something along the lines of what we have called a Subject/Self distinction, with the Subject being the locus of subjectivity and consciousness, including emotionality, judgment, and will, while the Self includes physical characteristics, social roles, etc. The use of anaphoric pronouns is based on this split. And the theory of mental spaces is required to express the meanings of sentences, given the Subject/Self split.

A Challenge To Formal Semantics

If this analysis is correct, the consequences are devastating for traditional, noncognitively oriented theories of semantics based on formal logic. Traditional accounts of semantics—whether characterized in terms of logical form, Montague-style formal semantics, situation semantics, or Kamp's discourse representation theory—simply do not have the conceptual resources to adequately characterize the sentences described in this section. Such theories, also lacking the tools of conceptual metaphor, are even less well equipped to characterize the phenomena in the following sections. This paper, therefore, presents a challenge to such theories—a challenge that I believe such theories cannot meet. The failure of such semantic theories is of considerable importance not just within linguistics, but within logic, philosophy, and cognitive science. I discuss just what that failure means below.

At this point I turn to other cases that require a Subject/Self split, or some such division of the person along those lines. As we shall see, what I call Subject and Self will vary somewhat from case to case, but in all cases what

I call the Subject will be the locus of subjectivity and consciousness (with variation as to whether judgment, emotionality, and will are included), while what I call the Self will always include physical characteristics and social roles—and in some cases past action, memory, etc. This variation of exactly what Subject and Self are is itself rather important for an understanding of how we conceptualize our own internal structure.

Metaphor

The analysis just presented is a metaphorical analysis, though I have not used that term yet. The analysis consists of two metaphors: *the Divided-Person metaphor,* according to which a person, a single entity, is understood as a group of two entities, which I refer to as Subject and Self; and *the Projected-Subject metaphor,* according to which a Subject can be projected onto someone else's Self in a hypothetical situation. As we shall see, the Divided-Person metaphor forms the basis of a whole system of metaphors for conceptualizing certain experiences that we commonly have, such as imagining ourselves as being someone else. The Projected-Subject metaphor makes use of the Divided-Person metaphor, but so do many other metaphors that I discuss below.

Before we proceed to the main body of the paper, let us consider a few more telling examples.

Some Coming Attractions

Here are additional cases where reflexives do not indicate coreference, that is, where a reflexive pronoun and its antecedent cannot be adequately represented as two instances of the same variable.

(17) You need to step outside yourself.

Sentence (17) cannot be adequately represented by ''*X needs to step outside of X.'' The relation ''outside of'' holds of two different entities, not the same entity. The same is true of *beside* in sentence (18).

(18) I'm beside myself.

Sentence (18) is not of the form ''*X is beside X.''
   Similarly, consider sentence (19).

(19) I'm not myself today.

This is not of the form "*X is not X today," which would, of course, be contradictory.

The same problem arises in the case of sentence (20).

(20) I lost myself in writing.

Sentence (20) is not of the form "X lost X in writing," again because *lose* is a relation between two different entities. But in this example, an even deeper problem arises. Given that *lose* and *find* are opposites, why isn't *I found myself in writing* the opposite of *I lost myself in writing*?

Sentences such as these raise a number of questions. Just what do they mean? Do they involve something akin to a Subject/Self distinction? Is there something systematic in these cases about the use of words such as *step, outside, look, beside, lose* and *find*?

The last question takes us into the realm of metaphor. If there is something systematic about the use of those words in the sentences above, the most likely possibility is that there are one or more conceptual metaphors that apply to the ordinary physical senses of those words and map them into some more abstract domain. If that is so, then those same mappings should not just account for what is systematic in the use of the words, but in addition, as conceptual mappings, they should tells us what is metaphorically entailed by those mappings, and hence also account for what the sentences mean. In addition, those mappings, if they are cognitively real, should be extendable to novel cases.

A. Lakoff and Becker (1991) began to answer these questions. They argued that there is an extensive system of conceptual metaphors that characterizes how we understand the internal structure of a person, and demonstrated that many of these metaphors have spatial source domains. As we shall see, this metaphor system accounts for both systematic word use and the meanings of such sentences.

In the following section, I take their work in some directions that they did not pursue, doubling the range of cases they considered. I will state the mappings, generalize over them as much as possible, and check for systematicities as well as inconsistencies across the mappings. Unfortunately, I do not have the space here to give these cases the full treatment they deserve; that would require a book-length discussion. For a discussion of the forms of evidence and argument used to arrive at analyses of the sort presented, see Lakoff 1993.

Some General Properties of the Self System

The Subject/Self distinction allows us to conceptualize and reason and talk about some of the most common of human experiences. Each conceptualization of such an experience raises a question that requires a metaphorical analysis as an answer.

Self-reflection, in which one reflects upon oneself, raises the question *Who is reflecting upon whom?* Absent-mindedness, in which you just aren't there for a while, raises the question *Who's not where?* For inner conflict, we ask, *Who's "in conflict with" whom?* And consideration of our "inner life" raises the question *What's "inside" what?* As we go through the system of metaphors, certain issues about one's "inner life" will keep recurring. Who's in control? Who's aware of what? Is there some internal incompatibility? Who sets the standards for action? The system is there to provide a way to conceptualize, reason about, and talk about such questions.

Questions about one's "inner life" are conceptualized and reasoned about in terms of physical relationships between two or more distinct individuals. Some of these physical relations are purely spatial; others have to do with the exertion of force. As we shall see, certain issues and general metaphorical themes keep recurring in the system: (i) normal functioning is nonself-conscious and controlled, with no internal incompatibilities; (ii) in normal functioning, the Subject and a single Self are in a canonical spatial configuration, with the Subject exerting force over the Self; (iii) the canonical spatial positions all have the Subject located in the same region of space as the Self; and (iv) the canonical configurations are either Subject inside Self, Subject directly above Self, or Subject in possession of Self.

From our tour of the metaphor system for the Self, we will find that, first, we do conceptualize a single person as divided. Second, the divisions are not consistent with each other. That is, we have a system of divisions that don't fit together into a simple general scheme. Third, we reason and talk about these internal divisions in terms of relations between external individuals.

What this means is that most accounts of our inner life are oversimplified. The Cartesian mind/body dualism is too simple-minded. There appears to be not one form of consciousness but many. The idea that there is just a single form of consciousness does not do justice to the complexity of our inner lives. The idea that there is no Subject/Self division at all does not fit our experiences, which show various kinds of Subject/Self divisions. In short, our inner lives are richer and more complex than most philosophers have realized. That is what makes the study interesting. Let us now look at the details.

The Metaphor System for Subject and Self in English

The Divided Person and the Objective Subject

A friend may tell you to take a good look at yourself, that you may look very different from the outside than from the inside. It is the external viewpoint, from which you see yourself as others see you, that is taken to be the objective viewpoint. Every time we try to see ourselves as others see us, we are conceptualizing ourselves as split in two, as if we were made up of an ensemble of at least two parts. There is a locus of consciousness and rationality, the center of all subjective experience—the Subject. The Subject normally resides inside the other half of us—the Self. The Self includes at the very least our bodies, our emotions, and that part of us that acts in the world.

When you step outside yourself and look at yourself, what might you see? You might see, for example, that you are selfish, that you are acting to satisfy your needs and desires rather than the needs and desires of others. But who is doing this seeing? You are, of course. You, the Subject, the locus of consciousness, rationality, and judgment, are looking at your Self, the locus of your needs, desires, and passions. Our culture tells us that the Subject, our locus of consciousness and reason, *should* be in control of our Self, so that our desires and passions do not get out of hand and lead us to harm others. Our culture also tells us that there is a way, a single way, we really are, and an objective viewpoint from which we could see who we really are, if only we can reach that place. This is a metaphorical folk theory that we all grew up with.

To state this view of the Self, we need two metaphors. First, we need the Divided-Person metaphor discussed above—the metaphor through which we conceive of ourselves as an ensemble of two or more entities. Second, we need a metaphor through which we conceptualize self-reflection as going outside of ourselves so that we can see ourselves.

THE DIVIDED-PERSON METAPHOR

Mapping:

(i) A person is an ensemble (containing one person, the Subject, and at least one other entity, a Self).
(ii) The experiencing consciousness is the Subject.
(iii) The bodily and functional aspects of a person constitute a Self.
(iv) The relationship between Subject and Self is spatial: the Subject is normally either inside, in possession of, or above the Self.

Details: The Subject is supposed to be in control of the Self. The Subject can reason, but cannot function directly in the world, as the Self can. The Subject is always the locus of consciousness, subjective experience, perception, reason, and judgment. The Self consists of other aspects of a whole person—the body, emotions, a past history, social roles, and much more.

Suppose we ask exactly what needs to be added to the general Divided-Person metaphor in order to account for the meaning of sentences like *You need to step outside yourself, You should take a good look at yourself,* and *I've been observing myself and I don't like what I see.* The mapping of the objective-subject metaphor needs to be added.

THE OBJECTIVE-SUBJECT METAPHOR

Mapping:

- (i) The Self is a container for the Subject.
- (ii) Being subjective is staying inside the Self.
- (iii) Being objective is going outside the Self.

Combined with:

- (iv) Knowing is seeing.

Knowledge Mapping:

Source Domain Knowledge: When one is inside a container one cannot see the outside of the container, the part that outsiders see. Only when one is outside the container can one see it. One is normally inside, and going outside takes more effort and more control than staying inside.

Target Domain Knowledge: When one is being subjective, one cannot know the self that others know. Only when one is being objective, can one know oneself as others do. One is normally subjective, and being objective takes more effort and more control than being subjective.

Loss of Self

What does it mean to lose yourself in some activity? It means to cease to be in conscious control and to cease to be aware of each thing one is doing. For example, suppose you are dancing. You might try to consciously control all your movements. But if it is a fast, complex dance, you may not be able to maintain conscious control of each movement. The dance may require you to let yourself go, to relinquish control, to allow yourself to just dance and experience the dancing without being consciously in charge of each movement. The effect can be exhilarating and joyful—a very positive experience, especially when losing oneself entails a freedom from stressful everyday concerns.

In the Loss-of-Self metaphor, conscious control is conceptualized as possession of the Self by the Subject, and ceasing to be in control is loss. But not all losses of control are positive, exhilarating experiences. A loss of control may be scary and negative. For example, you may lose control because of negative emotions, as when you are seized by anxiety or in the grip of fear. You may do more than you intended to do, with possible negative consequences, as when you get carried away. And perhaps the most scary experience of lack of control is when one feels that one's actions are being controlled by someone else, a hostile being, as when one feels possessed. The Loss-of-Self metaphor is thus a way of conceptualizing a wide range of very real experiences, both positive and negative.

THE LOSS-OF-SELF METAPHOR

Mapping:

(i) The Self is a possession of the Subject.
(ii) Control of Self by Subject is possession.
(iii) Loss of control is loss of possession.

Knowledge Mapping:

Source Domain Knowledge: If a possession of yours is taken, then you no longer have it.

Target Domain Knowledge: If something takes control of you, you no longer have control.

Subcase 1: Positive loss of Self: Freedom from normal concerns

Examples: *I lost myself in dancing. Only in meditation was she able to let go of herself. She let herself go on the dance floor.*

Subcase 2: Negative loss of self: emotional and demonic possession

Examples: *I don't know what possessed me to do that. I was seized by a longing for her. I got carried away. He's in the grip of an intense hatred. He was possessed by the devil. He's in the grip of his past.*

The Split Self

It is a common experience for people to have two or more inconsistent sets of values or needs that cannot be satisfied at once. For example, one may have religious values that are inconsistent with one's scientific values. Or one may have a need to make money and a need to create art. In general, inconsistent aspects of oneself are conceptualized as different Selves, for example, the businessman in you and the artist in you.

We have two common metaphors for conceptualizing such inconsistencies. In one, having the same values as someone is conceptualized as being in the same place. Thus, to go back and forth between the businessman and the artist in you is a form of indecision. When we have two needs that are incompatible, yet both strong, we conceptualize them as people in conflict. Thus, the saint in you may be in conflict with the scientist in you.

THE SPLIT-SELF METAPHOR

General Mapping:

(i) Incompatible aspects of a person are different people (that is, different Selves).

Special Case 1: Going back and forth

Mapping:

(i) Having the same values is being in the same place.
(ii) Indecision is going back and forth.

Knowledge mapping:

Source Domain Knowledge: You can't be in two places at the same time. Moving to a new place entails leaving the previous place.

Target Domain Knowledge: You can't have incompatible values. Adopting new values entails giving up old values.

Examples: *I keep going back and forth between my scientific self and my religious self. I keep returning to my spiritual self. I keep going back and forth between the scientist and the priest in me.*

Special Case 2: Being at war with oneself

Mapping:

(i) Incompatible strong needs or desires are people in conflict.

Examples: *He's at war with himself over who to marry. He's struggling with himself over whether to go into the church. He's conflicted.*

The True Self

It is common for people not to be satisfied with the kind of life they are leading. You may feel that your job is unrewarding or that your whole way of life is somehow not compatible with your judgment of what counts as living a rewarding life. In short, there is an aspect of you that is still unrealized and that is incompatible with those aspects that have been realized. As before, we conceptualize incompatible aspects of the Self as different people—different Selves. That Self which is compatible with your judgment as to what is important is called "the true Self." The Self which is realized is seen as being present to the Subject. That is not the true Self, which is not present to the Subject and must be "found." Realizing that aspect of yourself that is compatible with your judgment is conceptualized as "finding" your true Self. This may lead to a long-term quest, or search, for one's true Self.

THE TRUE-SELF METAPHOR

Mapping:

(i) Incompatible aspects of a person are different people (that is, different Selves).
(ii) Realized aspects of the whole person are a Self in the same place as the Subject.
(iii) Unrealized aspects of the whole person are a Self not in the same place as the Subject.

Lexicography: The "true self" names the Self that is compatible with the values of the Subject.

Entailment: Finding "one's true self" is realizing previously unrealized aspects of onseself that are compatible with judgments of one's experiencing consciousness.

Background Assumption: Most people have values that they have so far not been capable of realizing, but would like to realize in the future. It is considered a good thing to be able to function in a way that is compatible with one's values.

Examples: *He found himself in writing. I'm trying to get in touch with myself. He found his true self in writing. He went to India to look for his true self, but all he came back with was a pair of sandals.*

The Real Me

Suppose you are depressed or grumpy and you say something unkind to a friend. You may encounter the friend the next day and apologize by saying "I wasn't myself yesterday" or "I'm sorry, but you know that wasn't the real me." These cases are instances of a metaphorical model in which the Self that people normally see is compatible with the Subject's values—the real you.

It might appear that this metaphor is inconsistent with the True-Self metaphor. There the Subject has not yet found a Self that is consistent with its values. Here the Self that is consistent with the Subject's values is the one that one normally shows to the world. But the inconsistency is only apparent. The reason is that the two metaphors are about very different values. The Real-Me metaphor is about the everyday values involved in social interactions, while the True-Self metaphor is about the more cosmic values that determine the overall course of one's life—usually spiritual, artistic, moral, political, vocational, and intellectual values.

THE REAL-ME METAPHOR

Mapping:

(i) A person is a container with one Self outside and the Subject and other Selves inside.
(ii) The actions of the whole person are the actions of the exterior Self.

Assumptions: The values at issue are those concerned with everyday social interaction. One Self is normally on the outside, and it has values compatible with those of the Subject. This is the Self that other people normally see.

Lexicography: The "real me" is the Self whose values are compatible with the Subject's values.

Examples: *I'm not myself today. That wasn't the real me yesterday.*

The Two Inner Selves

It is common for people to be polite in public—to refrain from expressing their true feelings lest they hurt or offend someone. It is also common for people to act very differently in private than they do in public. Metaphorically, hidden is in and visible is out (as in *The truth came out* and *Keep your feelings in*). In addition, different aspects of oneself are conceptualized metaphorically as different selves. These metaphors come together in a conception of an inner, private self and an outer, public self. Add to this the common metaphor that essential is central (as in the central points of an argument), and you have a model of a person in which the inner, private self is the essential or "real" self, while the outer, public self is just a veneer. Thus, when we ask who a politician or an actress "really is," we are asking about their inner, private selves rather than their outer, public selves. Thus, revelations about someone's private life are commonly seen to be insights into a person's true character. This conception of a hidden, inner self is not consistent with the Real-Me metaphor, in which the "real" self is normally the visible, public self rather than the hidden, private self.

THE GENERAL INNER-SELF METAPHOR

Mapping:

  (i) Different aspects of a person are different selves.
  (ii) Hidden is in; visible is out.
  (iii) Essential is central; inessential is peripheral.

Entailment: The real Self (the one with the same values as the subject) is the inner, private self; the external, public Self is not real.

Examples: *Her sophistication is a facade. You've never seen what he's really like on the inside.*

The general Inner-Self metaphor has two special cases. In both cases, it is the inner self which is real and the outer self which is false. There is one case in which the inner self is not very nice, where it is indeed such a socially unacceptable self that it has to be kept from public sight. It may be mean, nasty, petty, jealous, angry, etc. The outer self is a socially acceptable veneer. It is the job of the subject to keep the inner self hidden, so that only the outer, socially acceptable self is made public and the nasty true self is not revealed.

Special Case 1: The Unacceptable Inner-Self metaphor

Constraint: The hidden inner Self has negative, socially unacceptable qualities. It is the job of the Subject to keep the inner Self from coming out.

Examples: *She's sweet on the outside and mean on the inside. The iron hand
in the velvet glove. Her petty self came out.*

There is a second version of the general Inner-Self metaphor in which the
real inner self is fragile and needs to be protected from the world by a false
outer self.

Special Case 2: The Fragile Inner-Self metaphor

Examples: *He won't reveal himself to strangers. He rarely shows his real
self. Whenever anyone challenges him, he retreats into himself. He retreats
into his shell to protect himself. He's outer-directed/inner-directed.*

These cases are, of course, not mutually exclusive: the inner self can be both
fragile and socially unacceptable.

Being True to Yourself

Suppose you are in a position of public responsibility and you are offered a
substantial bribe by someone who wants to act against the public interest.
Suppose you value honesty and integrity highly and have never taken bribes
in the past, but you need the money. If you take the bribe, you will betray
yourself. If you don't, you will be true to yourself.

The metaphorical model used in this case is one in which the Self is a
person who sets standards for the Subject. The Subject can fail to live up to
the Self's standards either by choice or not. If the failure is by choice, it
constitutes betraying the Self. If the failure is not by choice, it constitutes
letting the Self down.

What is particularly interesting about this metaphor is that here it is the
Self, not the Subject, who is setting the standards to be followed. Consider
the verb "disappoint." In *John disappointed his father,* John's father has set
standards that John has failed to meet. But in *John was disappointed in his
father,* John has set standards that his father has failed to meet. Now compare
the sentences *I disappointed myself* and *I'm disappointed in myself.* In *I
disappointed myself,* the Self is setting standards for the Subject and the
Subject fails to meet them. In *I'm disappointed in myself,* the reverse is true:

it is the Subject that has set a standard for the Self, which the Self has failed to meet. *I'm disappointed in myself* is an instance of a metaphor we will encounter below in which the Self is conceptualized as a servant for the Subject.

Why should it be the Self who is setting long-term standards of behavior? The reason is that it is the Self who acts in the world and who therefore has a past. The Subject—the experiencing consciousness—always exists in the present. The Self has the track record, and that track record constitutes a standard for present action.

THE TRUE-TO-YOURSELF METAPHOR

Mapping:

(i) The Self is a person who sets standards of conduct for the Subject.

Examples: *Don't betray yourself. Be true to yourself. I let myself down. I disappointed myself.*

Out to Lunch: The Absent Subject

It is normally expected that people will be able to consciously control their actions. One may fail to meet that expectation for a variety of reasons. One may be on drugs, or daydreaming, or mentally incompetent, or crazy, or euphoric, or overcome by passion.

There is a general metaphorical model that we use to conceptualize normal self-control by the Subject and the lack of it. It is a spatial metaphor: the Subject is exercising normal self-control when it is in a normal location or orientation. Among the normal locations are: on the earth, at home, at work, and on the ground. The normal orientation is upright.

There are three special cases of this metaphor. In the first, the normal location is in some bounded region. Being outside such a bounded region is seen as a lack of normal, conscious self-control. Among the bounded regions one can be outside of are the body (*beside myself*); the earth (*spaced out*); the workplace (*out to lunch*); home (*The lights are on, but no one's home*). The second special case involves vertical orientation, where the normal location for a person is on the ground. Lack of conscious self-control can thus be characterized as *floating off* or *the ground falling out from under you* or, in the case of euphoria, being *on cloud nine*.

One of the interesting aspects of this model is that the Self is never explicitly mentioned.

THE ABSENT-SUBJECT METAPHOR

Mapping:

(i) Normal Self-control is the Subject's being in a normal location.
(ii) Lack of normal Self-control is the Subject's not being in a normal location.
(iii) Degree of lack of Self-control is distance from normal location.

Subcase 1: Containers (bounded regions)

Mapping:

(i) Normal Self-control is the location of the Subject in a normal bounded region. Special cases of bounded regions where a Subject is normally located are the earth, home, a business, one's body, one's head.

Examples: *I was beside myself. He's spaced out. He's out to lunch. The lights are on but no one's home. Dude, you're tripping. Earth to Joshua, come in, Joshua. I'm out of it today. Are you out of your mind/head/skull?*

Subcase 2: Verticality

Mapping:

(i) Normal conscious Self-control by the Subject is the Subject's being located on the ground.
(ii) Lack of conscious normal Self-control by the Subject is the Subject's being above the earth.
(iii) Euphoria is being high.

Examples: *He's got his feet on the ground. He's down-to-earth. The ground fell out from under me. We'll kick the props out from under him. I kept floating off in lecture. He's got his head in the clouds. She reached new heights of ecstasy. I'm high as a kite. I'm on cloud nine. Her smile sent me soaring.*

The Scattered Self

It is hard to function normally when there are a lot of divergent demands on your attention—as when you have divergent needs, responsibilities, or interests—or when you cannot focus your attention on any one task, for example, when you are emotionally upset. In such a situation it is difficult to exert normal conscious self-control.

Metaphorically, the Self's attending to one concern is conceptualized as the Self being in one place. Aspects of the Self are conceptualized as parts of the Self. Thus, when different aspects of the Self are attending to different concerns, the Self is split into parts that are in different places. In short, the Self is scattered. When this happens, the Subject, if it wants to exercise control over the Self to achieve a single purpose, must get the Self together.

THE SCATTERED-SELF METAPHOR

Mapping:

(i) Aspects of the Self are parts of the Self.
(ii) Attending to one concern is being in one place.
(iii) When aspects of the Self attend to many different concerns, parts of the Self are in many different places.
(iv) Focusing attention on one concern is bringing parts of the Self together.

Knowledge Mapping:

Source Domain Knowledge: Only when the parts of an entity are together can the entity function properly.

Target Domain Knowledge: Only when the aspects of the Self are together can the Self function properly.

Examples: *He's pretty scattered. Pull yourself together. He's real together. He's all over the place. He hasn't got it together yet. He's not focused.*

Internal Causation

At this point, we can see how internal causation is conceptualized. Given the split of the person into Subject and Self, we can see that internal causation is just metaphorical external causation, with the Subject as cause and the Self as affected party. Since causes are understood metaphorically as forces, internal causation is conceptualized as the Subject exerting force on the Self. Thus, *I lifted my arm* is understood with *I* designating my Subject (my experiencing consciousness) exerting force on my Self (other aspects of me, in this case a part of my body) to make it move.

THE INTERNAL-CAUSATION METAPHOR

Mapping (A composition of the Causes-Are-Forces metaphor and the Divided-Person metaphor with the Subject as the Agent and the Self as the Patient):

(i) Internal causation is the successful application of force by the Subject on the Self.

Examples: *The yogi bent himself into a pretzel. I made myself get up early. I restrained myself from hitting him. I held myself back. I lifted my arm. I can wiggle my ears.*

The Self as Companion: Friend and Servant

Subject and Self are conceptualized as two people inhabiting the same body. That is, they are living in rather close quarters and in most ordinary cases, have the same interests. In short, the Self is naturally seen as the Subject's companion. But there are two very different kinds of companion possible. First, the Self can be a friend—an equal with whom you share your thoughts, discuss them, perhaps even argue. Secondly, the Self can be seen as a very different kind of companion—as a servant whose job it is to carry out the Subject's needs and desires. In this case, control of Self by Subject is exercised not by physical force but by speech-act force. The Self-as-servant is the only one who can immediately carry out the wishes of the subject. Moreover, the Self-as-servant may occasionally do something on his own when there is no time for the Subject to consciously reflect on a course of action. When the Self makes a mistake, the Subject may bawl him out. And when the Self cannot perform up to the standards of the Subject, the Subject may be disappointed in the Self.

THE SELF-AS-COMPANION METAPHOR

Special Case 1: The Self-as-Friend metaphor

Mapping:

(i) The Subject and Self are friends.

Examples: *I think I'll just hang out with myself tonight. I like myself and like being with myself. I debate things with myself all the time. I talk things over with myself before I do anything important. I was debating with myself whether to leave. I convinced myself to stay home. You need to be kind to yourself. I promised myself a vacation. I have a responsibility to myself to give myself time to exercise.*

Special Case 2: The Self-as-Servant metaphor

Mapping:

(i) The Subject is the master.
(ii) The Self is the servant.

Knowledge mapped: The Self is supposed to carry out the dictates of the Subject. The Subject is responsible for the care of the Self.

Examples: *I have to get myself to do the laundry. I told myself to prepare for the trip well ahead of time. I bawled myself out for being impolite. I'm disappointed in myself.*

Self-Sacrifice

The Self is the locus of needs, desires, purposes and ambitions. Since the Self, not the Subject, operates in the world, it is the Self who exerts effort to satisfy those needs and desires. The Self can also, at the direction of the Subject, exert effort to satisfy the needs and desires of others. Socially, people are expected to put a normal amount of effort into satisfying the needs of others.

Since one only has a limited amount of effort available, it is natural for effort to be metaphorically conceptualized as a limited resource—a kind of substance. Using your effort for someone else's benefit is conceptualized as giving that effort to that person. If you give it for no return, you are sacrificing it. If you give it to no effect, you are wasting it.

Since the Self is the locus of effort, it is possible to metonymically use the Self to stand for the Self's effort. Thus, giving of your effort is giving of your Self, sacrificing your effort is sacrificing your Self, and wasting your effort is wasting your Self. A person who is not willing to give of himself— one who uses his effort for his own benefit and not for the benefit of others is called "selfish."

THE SELF-SACRIFICE COMPLEX

Metaphor 1

(i) The Self's effort is a resource for the Subject.

Metaphor 2:

(i) Using effort for X's benefit is giving effort to X.
(ii) Using effort for someone else's benefit instead of your own benefit is sacrificing that effort.
(iii) Using effort without effect is wasting effort.

Metonymy 3:

(i) The Self stands for the Self's effort.

Composition of Metaphors 1 and 2 and Metonymy 3:

(i) Using one's effort for someone else's benefit is giving of one's Self.
(ii) Using effort for someone else's benefit instead of one's own is sacrificing one's Self.
(iii) Using one's effort without effect is wasting one's Self.

Examples: *She's giving of herself. She sacrificed herself for her family. You're wasting yourself on him. He's selfish.*

Self-Control is Up

The experiencing consciousness normally exerts control over what a person does. That is, the Subject normally controls the Self. Moreover, control is metaphorically up and lack of control is down, as in *They fell from power* and *She has power over me.* When these metaphors are combined, we get a composite metaphor in which the exertion of control by the Subject is conceptualized as the Subject's being above the Self, and losing control as the Subject's falling or being overcome.

There are two special cases of this metaphor. The first concerns consciousness, which is required for conscious control. When we become unconscious, we cease to exercise control. This is conceptualized as the Subject undergoing downward motion, as in *I fell asleep.* Thus, conscious is up and unconscious is down. The second special case concerns reason, whose locus is the Subject, versus passion, whose locus is the Self. When Subject is exerting control over the Self, reason is up and passion is down.

THE SELF-CONTROL-IS-UP METAPHOR

Mapping (A composition of the Control is Up metaphor and the Divided-Person metaphor):

(i) Control of Self by Subject is the Subject being above the Self.

Example: *He's got control over himself.*

Special Case 1:

(i) Consciousness is up.
(ii) Unconsciousness is down.

Examples: *He fell asleep. She slipped into a coma. He fell into a drunken stupor. Wake up!*

Special Case 2:

(i) Reason is up.
(ii) Passion is down.

Examples: *The argument fell to the emotional level. He kept control over his emotions. We had a high-level, rational discussion. A sudden impulse came over me to dye my hair green. He fell into a rage.*

The Structure of the System

This system of metaphors allows us to conceptualize the experience of consciousness. The system deals primarily with three issues: control, compatibility, and values. The metaphors used to conceptualize the internal structure of a person all involve functioning in space.

Certain submetaphors recur: compatibility is conceptualized as being in the same place; aspects of oneself are conceptualized as distinct selves; control is conceptualized in terms of spatial relations being above, being inside, being on the ground, and holding. Conceptual metaphors that exist independently of this system are also used within the system: Control is Up; Causes are Forces; Knowing is Seeing; Hidden is In; and Essential is Central.

The system also contains a dual—a possession-location dual. (For a general discussion of duals, see Lakoff 1993.) Self-control is conceptualized as either (i) possession, with the Subject's possessing the Self (the Loss-of-Self metaphor); or (ii) location, with the Subject's being located in the same place as the Self (the Absent-Subject metaphor).

In short, what we have here is not a random collection of mappings, but a highly structured system. However, the system is not self-consistent. That is, there are cases in which two mappings have contradictory entailments.

Inconsistencies

The Inner-Self metaphor: the real Self is internal and hidden.
The Real-Me metaphor: the real Self is external and visible.

The Absent-Self metaphor: control is being on the ground.
The Self-Control-is-Up metaphor: control is being up.

The Absent-Subject metaphor: moving outside the Self is decreased self-control.
The Objective-Subject metaphor: moving outside the Self is increased self-control.

The Self-as-Servant and Internal-Causation metaphors: the standard of behavior is located in the Subject.
The True-to-Yourself metaphor: the standard of behavior is located in the Self.

Philosophical Implications

How does all this inform philosophical theories of who we are? The first thing to bear in mind in all such discussions is that any account, philosophical or otherwise, of who we are must use language and must use concepts in our conceptual system. But our conceptual systems already include a built-in conceptualization of who we are—the one we have just discussed. It is what is presupposed by the very use of our language and our conceptual systems. It will play a role in all discussions, just as it has in the past.

Different philosophical discussions have focused on different parts of the system, with the Cartesian dualist tradition focusing on the Divided-Person metaphor and the postmodern tradition focusing on the lack of a single unified Self-concept. Recognizing that we have a built-in, unconscious, automatic way of conceptualizing the self that we use in everyday functioning raises the following questions. To what extent, if any, does functioning in terms of this conceptualization make the conceptualization real? If we function comfortably with this conceptualization daily, not even realizing that it is there most of the time, must it not reflect something real, or close to real?

Though we do not have a single, monolithic, unified conception of the Self, perhaps each member of the collection of conceptions that works for us does reflect some reality. In short, it may be the case that the collection of conceptions of the Self that have evolved to serve us well in our unconscious conceptual systems may give us the best account what the Self is that we can get using the kind of conceptual resources available to us in our unconscious conceptual systems.

The idea that we have multiple forms of consciousness makes good biological sense. PET-scan research indicates that, in different conscious tasks, different combinations of brain regions are activated. If we identify a combination of activated regions with a form of consciousness, that would suggest that we have not a single unified form of consciousness, but multiple forms with partial overlaps.

An important question to ask is whether this system of metaphors for the Subject/Self division is culturally specific, or whether it has a wider role across cultures. Not enough research has been done to know for sure, but as we shall see in the appendix below on the Japanese metaphor system, Japanese metaphors for the Self appear to overlap very considerably with the English system. What this shows is that the Self system is not just a product of Western culture. The mere fact that Japanese has a system of metaphors for the Self that is so similar to our own suggests that these metaphors are tapping into some sort of real human experience. This is an apparent counterexample to the postmodernist claim that conceptual systems are arbitrary and are mere historical contingencies.

However, the postmodernists are vindicated on an important issue. There is not just one single, monolithic, self-consistent, correct cultural narrative of what a person is. Instead, there are many partially overlapping and partially inconsistent conventional conceptions of the Self in our culture. This invalidates the traditional story in Cartesian philosophy of a monolithic subject/object distinction. However, the Cartesian tradition is partly vindicated by the existence of the Subject/Self distinction in the Divided-Person metaphor. But this is a far cry from the traditional subject/object distinction.

The conceptual system that we function with every day contains implicit philosophical theories. There are questions that we all need answers to in order to function, and our own unconscious conceptual systems have naturally evolved to provide them. The question to ask is just how much of the realities of our existence are captured by these systems that function so well for us that we barely notice them.

Implications for Formal Semantics and Philosophical Logic

The implications of this work for formal semantics and philosophic logic are quite dramatic. Logic has been understood as being independent of human cognition. It therefore cannot include such notions as metaphorical conceptualizations and mental spaces. Yet conceptual metaphors and mental spaces are required to handle the examples of identity of reference discussed in this chapter. This indicates, as has much other research in cognitive semantics, that formal semantics and philosophical logic, in anything like their present state, are grossly inadequate to the task of characterizing meaning in natural language. The fact that they are inherently incapable of handling coreference in the case of reflexive pronouns like those discussed in this chapter is especially telling.

Appendix 1: The Japanese System

The following examples were constructed by Yukio Hirose while he was visiting the University of California, Berkeley, as a postdoctoral fellow during the spring of 1993. They show the similarity between the English and Japanese systems of metaphor.

THE PROJECTIBLE-SUBJECT METAPHOR

(A1) Boku-ga   kimi dat-ta-ra,   boku-wa boku-ga iya-ni-naru.
I(male)-NOM you COP-PAST-if I-TOP   I-NOM hate-to-become
(Lit. 'If I were you, I (would) come to hate me.')
'If I were you, I'd hate me.' (In H, *you*'s Subject hate *I*'s Self.)

(A2) Boku-ga kimi dat-ta-ra, boku-wa **zibun**-ga iya-ni-naru.
                                  self-NOM
(Lit. 'If I were you, I (would) come to hate self.')
'If I were you, I'd hate myself.' (In H, *you*'s Subject hates *you*'s Self.)

THE OBJECTIVE-SUBJECT METAPHOR

(A3) Zibun-no kara-kara de-te,   **zibun**-o yoku mitume-ru koto-ga
Self-GEN shell-from get out-CONJ self-ACC well stare-PRES COMP-NOM
      taisetu   da.
      important COP
(Lit. 'To get out of self's shell and stare at self well is important.')
'It is important to get out of yourself and look at yourself well.'

THE SCATTERED-SELF METAPHOR

(A4) Kare-wa ki-ga   titte-i-ru.
he-TOP   spirit-NOM disperse-STAT-PRES
(Lit. 'He has his spirits dispersed.')
'He is distracted.'

(A5) Kare-wa kimoti-o   syuutyuu-sase-ta.
he-TOP   feeling-ACC concentrate-CAUS-PAST
(Lit. 'He made his feelings concentrate.')
'He concentrated himself.'

(A6) Kare-wa ki-o   hiki-sime-ta.
he-TOP   spirit-ACC pull-tighten-PAST
(Lit. 'He pulled-and-tightened his spirits.')
'He pulled himself together.'

THE LOSS-OF-SELF METAPHOR

(A7) Kare-wa akuma-ni   tori-tuk-are-ta.
he-TOP   the devil-by take-cling to-PASS-PAST
(Lit. 'He was taken-and-clung to by the devil.')
'He was possessed by the devil.'

(A8) Kare-wa dokusyo-ni **ware**-o   wasure-ta.
he-TOP   reading-LOC self-ACC lose[forget]-PAST
(Lit. 'He lost self in reading.')
'He lost himself in reading.'

(A9) Kare-wa ikari-no   amari   **ware**-o   wasure-ta.
he-TOP   anger-GEN too much self-ACC lose[forget]-PAST
(Lit. 'He forgot self because of too much anger.')
'He was beside himself with anger [had no control over himself].'

Note: The pronoun *ware* can be used in Japanese only in expressions that make use of either the Loss-of-Self metaphor or the Absent-Subject metaphor. These two metaphors are the duals in the system.

THE ABSENT-SUBJECT METAPHOR

(A10) Kare-wa yooyaku **ware**-ni kaet-ta.
he-TOP   finally   self-LOC return-PAST
(Lit. 'He finally returned to self.')
'He finally came to his senses.'

(A11) **Ware**-ni mo   naku kodomo-o sikatte-simat-ta.
self-LOC even not   child-ACC scold-PERF-PAST
(Lit. 'Not being even in self, (I) have scolded the child.')
'I have scolded the child in spite of myself (unconsciously).'

THE SPLIT-SELF METAPHOR

(A12) Kono mondai-ni   tuite-wa   watasi-wa kagakusya-tosite-no **zibun**-no hooni
this   problem-LOC about-TOP I-TOP   scientist-as-GEN   self-GEN   toward
katamuite-i-ru.
lean-STAT-PRES
(Lit. 'About this problem, I lean toward (my) self as a scientist.')
'I am inclined to think about this problem as a scientist.'

THE SELF-AS-SERVANT METAPHOR

(A13) Kare-wa hito-ni   sinsetuni-suru yooni **zibun**-ni iikikase-ta.
he-TOP   people-DAT kind-do   COMP self-DAT tell-PAST
'He told himself to be kind to people.'

THE INNER-SELF METAPHOR

(A14) Kare-wa mettani hontoono **zibun**-o das-na-i.
he-TOP   rarely   real   self-ACC get out-NEG-PRES.
(Lit. 'He rarely gets out (his) real self.')
'He rarely shows his real self.'

(A15) kare-wa hitomaede-wa itumo kamen-o   kabutte-i-ru.
he-TOP   in public-TOP always mask-ACC   put on-STAT-PRES
'He always wears a mask in public.'

THE TRUE-SELF METAPHOR

(A16) Kare-wa mono-o   kaku koto-ni   {**zibun**/hontoono zibun}-o miidasi-ta.
he-TOP   thing-ACC write COMP-LOC {self/true self}-ACC   find-PAST
'He found {himself/his true self} in writing.'

THE TRUE-TO-YOURSELF METAPHOR

(A17) **Zibun**-o azamuite-wa ikena-i.
self-ACC deceive-TOP bad-PRES
(Lit. 'To deceive self is bad.')
'You must not deceive yourself.'

THE REAL-ME METAPHOR

(A18) Boku-wa   kyoo-wa   **zibun**-ga **zibun** de-na-i   yoona kigasu-ru.
I(male)-TOP today-TOP self-NOM self   COP-NEG-PRES as if   feel-PRES
(Lit. 'I feel as if self is not self today.')
'I feel as if I am not my normal self today.'

Appendix 2: Metaphors for the Self and English Grammar

Here are two proposed principles of English grammar to account for the person marking in *If I were you, I'd hate me* and *If I were you, I'd hate myself* and in related sentences.

Principle 1: Subject and Self (the "aspects" of the person) take the same person marking as the entire person.

Principle 2: A reflexive pronoun and its antecedent must designate the same person, or aspects of the same person.

Refer back to figure 4.1. In figure 4.1, my real-world Subject corresponds to your hypothetical-world Subject. The sentences, of course, mean different things. *If I were you, I'd hate me* means that in H, YOU's Subject HATES I's Self, where YOU's Subject in H is the counterpart of I's Subject in R.

Since YOU's Subject in H is the counterpart of I's Subject in R, by Fauconnier's ID Principle it has the same person marking, namely, first person. By Principle 1, I's Self has the same person marking as I, namely, first person. By Principle 2, I's Self cannot be reflexive, since it is not an aspect of the same person as its antecedent, YOU's Subject. Hence, YOU's Subject surfaces as *I* and *I*'s Self surfaces as *me*.

Now consider the sentence *If I were you, I'd hate myself*. This means that in H, YOU's Subject hates YOU's Self, where YOU's Subject is the counterpart of I's Subject in R. By the ID Principle, YOU's Subject in H has the same person marking as its counterpart in R, I's Subject; namely, first person. By Principle 1, YOU in H has the same person marking as YOU's Subject in H, namely, first person. By Principle 1, YOU's Self in H has the same person marking as YOU in H, namely, first person. By Principle 2, YOU's Self is reflexive, since it is an aspect of the same person as its antecedent, YOU's Subject. Hence, in H, YOU's Subject surfaces as *I* and YOU's Self surfaces as *myself*.

To handle these sentences, Fauconnier's theory of mental spaces needs no revision. The Divided-Person and Projected-Subject metaphors plus the theory of mental spaces allows the meanings of such sentences to be represented in a straightforward manner, as shown in figure 4.1. Principles 1 and 2 account for the grammar of such sentences. But in order for such principles to be used, metaphors for the internal structure of the Self must be employed in the grammar of English.

Notes

1. This paper was inspired by an unpublished paper, "Me, Myself and I," by Andrew Lakoff and Miles Becker, written at the University of California, Berkeley, in December, 1991, for my course on metaphor. The Japanese examples are due to Yukio Hirose.

References

Fauconnier, Gilles. 1985. *Mental Spaces: Aspects of Meaning Construction in Natural Language*. Cambridge, Mass.: MIT Press. Reprinted 1994, Cambridge: Cambridge University Press.

Lakoff, Andrew, and Miles Becker. 1991. Me, Myself, and I. Manuscript, University of California, Berkeley.

Lakoff, George. 1968. Counterparts, or The Problem of Reference in Transformation Grammar. Manuscript, Harvard University. Distributed by the Indiana University Linguistics Club.

―――. 1993. The Contemporary Theory of Metaphor. In Andrew Ortony, ed., *Metaphor and Thought*, 2d ed., 202–51. Cambridge: Cambridge University Press.

Lewis, David. 1968. Counterpart Theory and Quantified Modal Logic. *Journal of Philosophy* 65:113–26.

Ruwet, Nicolas. 1991. *Syntax and Human Experience*. Chicago: University of Chicago Press.

Yo Matsumoto

5 Subjective-Change Expressions in Japanese and Their Cognitive and Linguistic Bases

- •
- •
- •
- •

There are some expressions in Japanese in which a state that did not actually come to exist as a result of a change is expressed as if it had.[1] This phenomenon is exemplified in sentences (1a), (2a), and (3a). These sentences contrast with (1b), (2b), and (3b), which are purely stative expressions that depict the same situation without appealing to such a possible change.

(1) a. Sono heya wa   maruku natte   iru.
       the   room TOP round   become RES
       (Lit. 'The room is in the state of having become round.')
       'The room is round.'

    b. Sono heya wa   marui.
       the   room TOP round
       'The room is round.'

(2) a. Kono empitsu wa nagaku natte   iru.
       this   pencil TOP long   become RES
       (Lit. 'This pencil is in the state of having become long.')
       'This pencil is long.'

    b. Kono empitsu wa nagai.
       this   pencil TOP long
       'This pencil is long.'

(3) a. Ie ga   ni-ken   kuttsuite   iru.
       house NOM two-CLASS stick.together RES
       (Lit. 'Two houses are in the state of having stuck together.')
       'There are two houses which (almost) touch each other.'

b. Ie ga   ni-ken   totemo chikaku ni aru.
house NOM TWO-CLASS very   close   be
'There are two houses very close to each other.'

Kunihiro (1985) discusses examples similar to these, and argues that sentences like (1a), (2a), and (3a) are based on what he calls the "resultative perception"—the human cognitive capacity to perceive the current state of an object as a result of possible past history (i.e., a change that is supposed to have produced the current state of the object). He claims that in sentences like these, this cognitive capacity is utilized even if the states being described did not actually come to exist as a result of a change.

In this paper, I examine the linguistic properties of such expressions to show that they do involve some sort of change that might be called "subjective change" (cf. the notion of "fictive change" in the work of Talmy (1990, 1996)) and explore the nature of this abstract process. In the first section, I provide evidence for the existence of subjective change, and propose my own characterization of it as the deviation from expectation or the norm, which is mapped onto a subjective change in a mentally constructed world or space (cf. Fauconnier 1985). I then compare the notion of subjective change with the notion of subjective (fictive) motion (Talmy 1983, 1989, 1990, 1996; Langacker 1987, 1988; Matsumoto 1996a, 1996b). I point out that there are some crucial differences between these two phenomena, despite Kunihiro's (1985) unified treatment of the two. I also point out that there are some expressions in which both processes are involved. In the third section, I compare subjective-change expressions to change-of-state expressions with the role interpretation of the subject (Sweetser 1990; cf. Fauconnier's (1985) notions of role and filler). Finally, I discuss some linguistic and cognitive bases for these expressions, and argue that expressions of subjective change are constrained by both linguistic and cognitive factors.

The Nature of Subjective Change

Subjective-Change Expressions versus Real-Change Expressions

In examples (1a), (2a), and (3a) above, the shape of a room, the length of a pencil, and the relative position of two houses are expressed with the use of the *-te iru* form of the verbs *naru* 'become' and *kuttsuku* 'stick together.' The *-te iru* form consists of the gerundive form of a verb marked by the suffix *-te* and an aspectual verb *iru*. It is used to mark a few different meanings, including the resultative, the progressive, and habitual recurrence, depending on the nature of the process denoted by the verb (see Kindaichi 1950, Fujii 1976, Takahashi

1969, Soga 1983, Teramura 1984, and Okuda 1985). As Takahashi (1969) and Okuda (1985) have argued, this form is interpreted as resultative when the verb represents a process that results in a change of state in the referent of the subject NP.[2] Since the verbs in the *-te iru* form in (1a), (2a), and (3a) are verbs that entail a change of state of the subject NP, the *-te iru* form is supposed to be interpreted as resultative. However, these *-te iru* predicates are different from typical resultative expressions involving a real change of state. As a resultative form of a verb, the *-te iru* form is used to express the current state of the referent of the subject NP in terms of the change that has produced that state. For example, sentence (4) expresses the state of leaves being on the ground under a tree as a result of the process that presumably produced that state.

(4) Happa ga takusan ochite iru.
　　leaf NOM　much　　fall　　RES
　　(Lit. 'Many leaves are in the state of having fallen.')
　　'There are many leaves (on the ground).'

A verb cannot be used in this resultative form if the state being described cannot be interpreted as being the result of the change denoted by the verb. Thus, sentence (5) cannot be used if stones are just on the ground unless there is a good reason to believe that they did fall from above.

(5) Ishi ga　　takusan ochite iru.
　　stone NOM much　　fall　　RES
　　(Lit. 'Stones are in the state of having fallen.')
　　'There are many fallen stones (on the ground).'

　　The peculiarity of examples (1a), (2a), and (3a) is that they are acceptable even though the changes denoted by the verbs are not the processes that have actually produced the states being described.
　　The impossibility of interpreting the possible change in these examples as a real change can be proved easily by the impossibility of the use of *moo* 'already' with (1a), (2a), and (3a), as shown in example (6).

(6) a. #Sono heya wa　moo　　maruku natte　　iru.
　　　　that　room TOP already round　　become RES
　　　　(Lit. 'The room is already in the state of having become round.')

　　 b. #Kono empitsu wa moo　　nagaku natte　　iru.
　　　　this　pencil TOP already long　　become RES
　　　　(Lit. 'This pencil is already in the state of having become long.')

   c. #Ie ga   ni-ken   moo   kuttsuite   iru.
       house NOM two-CLASS already stick together RES
       (Lit. 'The two houses are already in the state of having stuck
       together.')

The adverb *moo* 'already' presupposes the occurrence of a change in real time, and the incompatibility of this adverb with the *-te iru* expressions in (6) suggests that these *-te iru* expressions do not involve any change that takes place in real time. In contrast, the adverb *moo* can be used in a sentence like (4), which involves a real change. In this respect, sentences like (1a), (2a), and (3a) are crucially different from real-change sentences like (4).

Subjective-Change Expressions versus Simple Stative Expressions

Why, then, are such apparently resultative expressions like (1a), (2a), and (3a) possible? One view is that these *-te iru* expressions are not really resultative expressions, and do not involve any process at all. Rather, one might think, the *-te iru* form of a verb in these examples simply functions like an adjective, describing a state without reference to a prior process. In this view, *kuttsuite iru* 'be in the state of having stuck together' in (3a), for example, is a simple stative expression, and means something like 'be in the state typical of the result of something having stuck together'.

    This view might seem plausible in light of the existence of some *-te iru* expressions that are used to mark a state without reference to the process denoted by the verb (e.g., Kindaichi 1950, Teramura 1984). Examples include *bakagete iru* 'absurd', *sugurete iru* 'excellent', and *gotsugotsu shite iru* 'rugged'. These are apparently the *-te iru* forms of the verbs *bakageru* 'become absurd', *sugureru* 'become excellent', and *gotsugotsu suru* 'become rugged', though these simple nonpast forms are rarely used.

    These simple stative *-te iru* expressions are, however, different from the *-te iru* expressions under discussion in certain important ways. For many speakers, simple stative *-te iru* expressions cannot be used to modify nouns (i.e., attributively). Instead, the *-ta* form of a verb, which is the usual past-tense form, is used, as shown in (7a) and (7b) (Teramura 1984, Kinsui 1994). In this case, the *-ta* form does not entail a change in the past.

(7) a. ??bakagete iru hanashi
         absurd   story
         'absurd story' (intended)

b. bakageta hanashi
absurd story
'absurd story' (intended)

It is possible, however, to use the *-te iru* expressions *maruku natte iru,*
kuttsuite iru, and *nagaku natte iru* in (1a), (2a), and (3a) as modifiers of a
noun, as in (8a), (9a), and (10a). Morover, the *-ta* forms of these verbs are
interpreted only with a past-tense reading when used as modifiers of a noun,
as in (8b), (9b), and (10b).

(8) a. maruku natte iru heya
round become RES room
'a round room'

b. maruku nat-ta heya
round become-PAST room
'the room that became round'

(9) a. nagaku natte iru empitsu
long become RES pencil
'a long pencil'

b. nagaku nat-ta empitsu
long become-PAST pencil
'a pencil that became long'

(10) a. kuttsuite iru ni-ken no ie
stick.together RES two-CLASS GEN house
'the two houses that almost touch each other'

b. kuttsui-ta ni-ken no ie
stick.together-PAST two-CLASS GEN house
'the two houses that were attached'

In these respects, these resultative expressions are different from genuine
examples of simple stative *-te iru* expressions.[3]

Moreover, if these *-te iru* expressions do not involve any kind of process
and they are simple stative expressions, then *maruku natte iru* 'be in the state
of having become round' in (1a), for example, should be synonymous with
the adjective *marui* 'round'. However, these two expressions are different in
meaning. Consider the following examples.

(11) a. Sono heya wa   maruku natte   iru.
         that room TOP round   become RES
         (Lit. 'The room is in the state of having become round.')
         'The room is round.'

  b. #Sono heya wa   shikakuku natte   iru.
         that room TOP rectangular become RES
         (Lit. 'The room is in the state of having become rectangular.')[4]

(12) a. Sono heya wa   marui.
         the   room TOP round
         'The room is round.'

  b. Sono heya wa   shikakui.
         the   room TOP rectangular
         'The room is rectangular.'

As shown by these examples, the -te iru expressions can be used only for
the description of an unusual object (i.e., a round room rather than a rectangu-
lar one), while the simple stative adjectives are not constrained in this way.
   The same contrast can be found in the following examples.

(13) a. Kono biru wa   iriguchi ga   nikai ni   natte   iru.[5]
         this building TOP entrance NOM second.floor DAT become RES
         (Lit. 'As for this building, the entrance is in the state of having come to
         be on the second floor.')
         'This building has its entrance on the second floor.'

  b. #Kono biru wa   iriguchi ga   ikkai ni   natte   iru.
         this building TOP entrance NOM first.floor DAT become RES
         (Lit. 'As for this building, the entrance is in the state of having come to
         be on the first floor.')

(14) a. Kono biru wa   iriguchi ga   nikai ni   aru.
         the   building TOP entrance NOM second.floor LOC exist
         'This building has its entrance on the second floor.'

  b. Kono biru wa   iriguchi ga   ikkai ni   aru.
         the   building TOP entrance NOM first.floor LOC exist
         'This building has its entrance on the first floor.'

The difference between (13a) and (13b) again shows that the resultative form is possible only when it indicates some unusual situation. Examples (14a) and (14b) show that simple stative expressions are not restricted in such a way. If the *-te iru* expressions that I examine here are just simple stative expressions, there should be no reason why they are restricted to the description of unusual situations. Note also that simple stative *-te iru* expressions like *bakagete iru* do not have the implication of unusualness.

Thus, the *-te iru* expressions under discussion appear to be different from simple stative expressions.[6]

The Presence and Nature of Subjective Change

What, then, is the nature of *-te iru* sentences like (1a), (2a), and (3a)? I argue that it can be characterized as in (15).

(15) A *-te iru* expression can describe the unexpected (unusual) character of the referent of its subject NP as the result of a subjectively induced hypothetical process of change from its expected (normal) state to the state being described.

An object of an unexpected or unusual character is somehow felt to have undergone a change from its expected or usual state, and in this way an abstract process of change is induced in the mind of a conceptualizer. The resultative expressions under consideration are based on this kind of process. (I will examine what exactly is meant by ''the expected state'' in the next section.)

This view naturally explains why this kind of *-te iru* expression is limited to the description of unusual situations. It also explains another subtle aspect of these expressions: they describe an unusual situation as a special variation of an ideal or usual state. In this regard, consider (16a) and (16b) as possible descriptions of the geometric figure shown in figure 5.1.

(16) a. ??migi-ue no   kado ga   marui shikaku
      right-upper GEN corner NOM round square
      'a square the upper right corner of which is round'

Figure 5.1

b. migi-ue no   kado ga   maruku natte   iru shikaku
    right-upper GEN corner NOM round   become RES square
    (a square the right upper corner of which is in the state of having
    become round)
    'a square with a rounded upper right corner'

The expression in (16a) is contradictory for many speakers: the simple stative adjective *marui* 'round' may not be used to describe a square. The expression in (16b), on the other hand, is not contradictory; the resultative form in (16b) is used to describe the geometric figure shown in figure 5.1 as a (special) kind of square. The figure is expected to be a square, but it is an abnormal one that deviates from its expected (ideal) state. The *-te iru* form expresses the way in which a described entity deviates from its expected state (i.e., a corner is in the state of having become round). The contrast between (16a) and (16b) can only be explained by reference to the notion of subjective change (as a way of conceptualizing deviation from a norm).

The notion of deviation from a norm might not seem to be a good property to distinguish subjective-change resultative expressions from simple stative expressions, since the meanings of many adjectives also intrinsically involve comparison to a norm. For example, dimensional adjectives such as *big* and *small* are used relative to the normal size of object being described (Sapir 1944, Leisi 1953, Clark 1973). There are two differences, however, between adjectives of this type and subjective-change resultative expressions. First, relative adjectives are all gradable adjectives, while the *-te iru* expressions discussed here are not necessarily gradable. For example, *nikai ni natte iru* 'be in the state of having come to be on the second floor' in (13a) does not entail any gradability.

Second, subjective-change resultative expressions require the norm to be very specific, so specific that the state that deviates from the norm can be regarded as unusual (therefore inducing subjective change). Relative adjectives, on the other hand, allow the norm to be rather vague, and the state being described does not have to be unusual. The following sentences illustrate this point.

(17) a. ?Kono shinju wa chiisaku natte   iru.
        this   pearl TOP small   become RES
        (Lit. 'This pearl is in the state of having become small.')

    b. Kono shinju dake chiisaku natte   iru.
       this   pearl only small   become RES
       (Lit. 'Only this pearl is in the state of having become small.')
       'This pearl is exceptional in that it is small.'

The resultative form *chiisaku natte iru* 'be in the state of having become small' can be used when a very specific size of an object is assumed as the norm. Since it is not clear what is the normal size of pearls, one cannot easily use this form with respect to the size of pearls, unless the context specifies the norm. Thus, (17a) sounds strange out of context. (The adjective *chiisai* 'small' would create no problem in this regard.) One circumstance under which this subjective-change expression can be used is where only one pearl among many pearls strung together is exceptionally small and all the others are the same in size. Sentence (17b) is possible in such a context.

The subjective-change expressions are not as different from real- (objective-) change expressions as they might at first appear. Both kinds of expression involve the comparison of a described state with a reference state.[7] The major difference lies in the nature of the reference state. In the case of subjective-change sentences, the reference state is the expected or normal state.[8] In the case of real-change sentences, it is a temporally previous state.

Furthermore, the notion of the expected or normal state is utilized on many occasions with real-change resultative expressions. In many cases a speaker uses a resultative expression without really knowing what the previous state of the described object was (e.g., when a speaker describes an object that he or she has never seen before). On these occasions, the speaker often infers what the previous state must have been like on the basis of knowledge of the expected or normal prior state of the described object. For example, a speaker can utter (4), repeated here as (18), without really knowing the previous state of the tree, on the assumption that the leaves used to be on the tree (i.e., the normal position of leaves before falling), and that the process of falling must have produced this state.

(18) Happa ga takusan ochite iru.
　　　leaf NOM much　fall　RES
　　　(Lit. 'Many leaves are in the state of having fallen.')
　　　'There are many leaves (on the ground).'

Thus, a speaker sometimes appeals to the expected or normal state of objects for comparison in using real-change resultative expressions, just as in the case of subjective-change resultative expressions.[9]

Inference concerning a previous state and an assumed change of state on the basis of a current state is an important aspect of the use of resultative markers. This appears to be why a resultative marker, which can involve inference from a result, often develops into a marker of indirect evidence, which marks inference from reasoning (Bybee, Perkins, and Pagliuca 1994 (pp. 95–97).

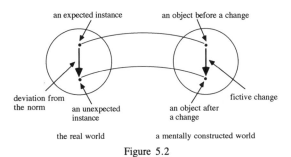

Figure 5.2

In the theory of mental spaces (Fauconnier 1985), the nature of subjective change can be understood in the following way. Subjective-change expressions are based on the process of change in a mental space. An unusual instance of the object being described and a normal instance in the real world are mapped onto an identical object at two different phases of a fictive change in a hypothetical world (i.e., after the change and before it) so that deviation from the norm is regarded as a change, as shown in figure 5.2. This mapping is characterized as the mapping of two different entities in the real world onto the same entity existing at different periods of time in a hypothetical world. This kind of mapping is discussed further in the section on cognitive bases.

Kinds of Reference States

I have argued that some resultative expressions in Japanese involve subjective change, or deviation from an expected state. What exactly is this expected state? There are several different sources for an expected state. In some cases the expectation comes from what people regard as ideal states. In other cases it comes from common assumptions about what objects are like in normal cases. In still other cases the expectation comes from speakers' (or hearers') personal assumptions about the particular object being referred to.

First, let us consider ideal categories as reference states for subjective change. It has been pointed out in the literature that some geometric figures such as a square and a straight line are cognitively simpler and more ''ideal'' than complex figures such as a gourd shape (Rosch 1975). These ideal categories of shape can serve as reference states in subjective-change resultative expressions. One example is (16b), in which a square as an ideal shape serves as a reference state. Other examples are (19a) and (19b) as descriptions of the shapes shown in figure 5.3.

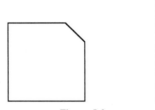

Figure 5.3

(19) a. Kado ga   {ochite iru / kakete iru / torete   iru}. (Kunihiro 1985)
corner NOM {drop RES / lack RES / come.off RES}
(Lit. 'A corner is in the state of having {dropped / lacked / come off}.[1])
'A corner is cut off.'

   b. Kono sen wa   kirete iru. (Kunihiro 1985)
this   line TOP be.cut RES
(Lit. 'This line is in the state of having been cut.')
'This line is broken.'

In these cases, the reference states are ideal shapes such as a square and a straight line, and shapes that deviate from those ideal shapes are described in terms of subjective changes from those ideal states. Similar examples are found in English as well.

(20) a. a square with a corner {rounded off / cut off}

   b. a broken line

In contrast, ideal shapes like a square and a straight line are not usually described in terms of subjective change from less ideal shapes. (21a) and (21b), for example, are not natural descriptions of a square and a straight line, although they are acceptable in some contexts, as I will point out later.

(21) a. ??Kado ga   tsuite   iru.
corner NOM be.attached RES
(Lit. 'A corner is in the state of having been attached.')
'A corner is attached.'

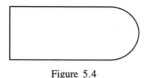

Figure 5.4

b. ??Kono ni-hon no sen wa   tsunagatte   iru.
    this   two-CLASS line TOP get.connected RES
    (Lit. 'These two lines are in the state of having got connected.')
    'These two lines are connected.'

Another illustration of the use of an ideal state as a reference state is the descriptions of the shape shown in figure 5.4 in examples (22a) and (22b).

(22) a.   migi-hashi ga   maruku natte iru   naga-shikaku
           right-edge NOM round   become RES long-rectangle
           (Lit. 'a rectangle the right side of which is in the state of having been rounded')

     b.   ??hidari-gawa ga shikakuku natte iru   kapuseru-gata
           left-side NOM   angular   become RES capsule-shape
           (Lit. 'a capsule shape the left side of which is in the state of having become square-like')

While both (22a) and (22b) are theoretically possible descriptions of the shape shown in figure 5.4, it is much more natural to describe that shape in reference to the more ideal shape of a rectangle, as in (22a), than to the less ideal capsule shape, as in (22b).

The second kind of expected state involved in Japanese resultative expressions is the commonly recognized object-specific normal state. Examples (1a), (2a), (3a), (8a), (9a), (10a), (11a), and (13a) have object-specific normal states as reference states. They are the normal shape of a room in (1a), (8a), and (11a), the normal (full) length of pencils in (2a) and (9a), the normal distance between two houses in (3a) and (10a), and the normal location of an entrance to a building in (13a). Other examples include the following.

(23) a.   Kare wa me ga   {dete iru   / tsuriagatte iru}
           He TOP eye NOM protrude RES / be.pulled.up RES
           (Lit. 'His eyes are in the state of having {protruded / been pulled up}.')
           'His eyes {protrude / turn up}.'

    b. Kono ie wa   hodoo ni   {tobidete iru / tsukidete iru}.
       this   house TOP sidewalk DAT project RES / stick.out RES
       (Lit. 'This house is in the state of having {projected / stuck out}.')
       'This house sticks out onto the sidewalk.'

    c. Kare no ji wa   migi ni   katamuite iru.
       his GEN character TOP right DAT incline   RES
       (Lit. 'His characters are in the state of having inclined to the right.')
       'His handwriting leans to the right.'

The examples in (23) are based on the normal position and shape of human eyes, the normal position of a house relative to a street, and the normal shape of handwritten characters.

    The third kind of source for the reference state for subjective change is a speaker's personal assumptions about the state of a particular object being referred to. Earlier I pointed out that sentence (11b), which is repeated here as (24), is unacceptable, since it does not refer to an unexpected (unusual) state.

(24) Sono heya wa   shikakuku natte   iru.
     that   room TOP rectangular become RES
     (Lit. 'The room is in the state of having become rectangular.')

However, this sentence is acceptable if the speaker has expected the room to be of some shape other than a rectangle. Examples (13b), (17a), (21a), and (21b) are also acceptable if they describe a state that is different from what the speaker has expected.

    In some cases the speaker's assumptions about the hearer's personal assumptions about the state of an object serve as the reference state. For example, a speaker who fully knows that the room being referred to is rectangular can say (24) on the assumption that the hearer expects it to be some other shape.

Subjective Change and Subjective Motion

Differences between Subjective Change and Subjective Motion

The nature of subjective change may perhaps be elucidated by comparison with subjective motion (abstract motion), which has been much discussed in recent cognitive linguistics literature (e.g., Talmy 1983, 1989, 1990, 1996; Langacker 1987, 1988; Honda 1994; Matsumoto 1996a, 1996b). This comparison is also important in light of Kunihiro's (1985) view, according to which subjective-change expressions and subjective-motion expressions are treated in the same way. In this section, I show that these two phenomena are crucially different in some important respects.

The examples in (25) are typical sentences involving subjective motion. Sentence (25a) is representative of what Talmy (1996) calls coverage path expressions, and (25b) is representative of access path expressions. In the following discussion, I restrict my comments to coverage path expressions, in which a verb of motion is used to represent subjective motion (see Matsumoto 1996b for a discussion of the nature of access path expressions).

(25) a. The highway runs from San Francisco to New York.

    b. There was a fire last night across the river, through the canyon, and over the mountain. (= example (5b) (p. 170) in Langacker (1987))

It has been claimed, first by Talmy (1983, 1989, 1990) and then by Langacker (1987, 1988), that sentences like these involve some subjectively induced process of motion.[10] That is, in uttering sentences like (25a) and (25b) the speaker (or the conceptualizer) mentally traces a path for the purpose of computing the configuration or the location of the entity expressed in the subject NP. These expressions allow several possibilities as to what the moving entity is. In some cases it is the movement of the focus of attention; in other cases the motion of some imaginary entity is involved; and in still other cases the mover is a specific person (e.g., a speaker or a hearer). Langacker argues that this difference is a matter of specificity: subjective motion is maximally unspecific, and an interpretation of a mover can differ in specificity according to context.

Subjective motion is also involved in some uses of Japanese verbs of motion. I give examples of these in (26) for comparison with Japanese subjective-change sentences.

(26) a. Sono sanmyaku wa   nanboku ni   hashitte iru.
       that   mountain range TOP south-north LOC run ASP
       'The mountain range runs from north to south.'

    b. Sono haiuee wa   sangaku-chitai ni   haitte iku.[11]
       that   highway TOP mountain area GOAL   enter go
       'The highway goes into a mountainous area.'

    c. Sono michi wa machi no mannaka o toot-ta.
       that   road TOP city GEN   center ACC go.through-PAST
       'The road went through the center of the city.'

Subjective change is different from the subjective motion involved in (26) in the following three respects. First, subjective change is a change that the referent of the subject NP is supposed to undergo, while subjective motion is the motion of something else (Langacker 1987:171). What is supposed to change in the subjective-change sentence (1a), for example, is the room itself. In the subjective-motion sentence (26b), on the other hand, what moves is not the highway, but the focus of attention or an imaginary or real person.

This point might not be so obvious, however, and requires careful examination. In fact, Kunihiro (1985), who treats subjective-motion sentences in the same way as subjective-change sentences, says that sentences like (26a) represent the extent of a mountain range in terms of the result (traces) of a possible process that the mountain range has supposedly undergone (i.e., running), on the assumption that it is the mountain range that has "run."

There is some evidence to support the view that the moving entity in these examples is not the referent of the subject NP but something else.[12] The use of motion verbs in subjective-motion expressions suggests that such expressions involve the image of the motion of something unexpressed in the sentence (Matsumoto 1996a, 1996b). In both English and Japanese, descriptions of linear entities in terms of subjective motion are restricted if such an image cannot be easily evoked and projected upon the described entity in the mind of a conceptualizer. This kind of restriction manifests itself in the description of untraversable linear entities. Consider the sentences in (27).

(27) a.   Sono {michi / haiuee} wa   heeya no mannaka o
          the   road / highway TOP plain GEN center ACC
          {iku / susumu / tooru}
          go / proceed / go.through
          'The {road / highway} {goes / proceed / passes} through the center
          (or middle) of the plain.'

     b.   Sono {kyookai-sen / densen / keeburu} wa heeya no   mannaka o
          the   borderline   / wire   / cable TOP   plain GEN center ACC
          {*iku / ?susumu / tooru}.
          go / proceed / go.through
          'The {border / wire / cable} {goes / proceeds / passes} through the
          center of the plain.'

     c.   Sono {kabe / jooheki   / saku} wa   kooen no mannaka o
          the   wall / castle wall / fence TOP park GEN center ACC
          {*iku / *susumu / *tooru}.
          go / proceed / go.through

'The {wall / castle wall / fence} {goes / proceeds / passes} through the center of the park.'

Sentence (27a) suggests that the three verbs considered here—*iku* 'go', *susumu* 'proceed', and *tooru* 'go through, pass'—can all be used to describe traversable linear entities such as roads and highways. Sentences (27b) and (27c) suggest that this is not true of untraversable linear entities. The verb *iku* cannot be used to describe a border, a cable, a wire, a wall, or a fence. The verb *susumu* is not acceptable for the description of a wall or a fence, though it is only somewhat unacceptable for a border, a cable, and a wire. While many verbs of motion in English can be used in all of the English equivalents of (27a) through (27c), there are some verbs, such as *proceed,* that cannot be used easily in the description of untraversable linear entities.

The fact that descriptions of untraversable linear entities in terms of subjective motion are restricted can be explained, once we recognize the motion of a moving entity distinct from the subject NP. Traversable paths can easily evoke an image of something moving along the path in the mind of a conceptualizer, while untraversable paths cannot. This suggests that when a concrete image of a moving entity cannot be evoked, some verbs cannot be used to describe paths in terms of subjective motion. (The verbs that can be used to describe untraversable paths, on the other hand, appear to require a less concrete image of a moving entity. That is, movement of the mere focus of attention is enough to license the use of such verbs.) Thus, subjective-motion expressions involve motion of an entity distinct from the subject NP and they are different from subjective-change expressions in this respect.

The second difference between subjective change and subjective motion concerns the basis of induction of the two processes. Subjective change is induced because of the unusual character of the objects being described; hence deviation from the reference state is recognized. Subjective motion, on the other hand, is induced by the configuration or extent of the described object. Subjective-motion sentences involving verbs of motion are used to describe objects which are extended in a certain way in space (in most cases one-dimensionally).[13] This extended configuration triggers the motion of some object or the focus of attention over the object in the mind of the conceptualizer.

The third difference between subjective motion and subjective change concerns the relevant stages of a process for the description of a state. Since subjective-motion expressions are used to describe spatially extended objects, all successive stages of motion along the entities are relevant to the description of the objects (Langacker 1987). In (26c), for example, the motion of an object is continuous as the object moves through the center of the city, and this continuous process as a whole represents the configuration and extent of the road. In the case of subjective change, on the other hand, the described state is the final stage of a change; all the intermediate stages of that change are irrelevant for the description of the object, and the initial state is relevant only in comparison to the final state. That is, the intermediate stages of the change of shape of the room in (1a) are irrelevant, and the final state of the change alone (in comparison to the initial state) is the object of description.

This difference in the relevant stage of a process is reflected in the possible verb forms that subjective-motion and subjective-change sentences can take. Since only the final state of subjective change is used for the description of an object, subjective-change expressions appear in the resultative -te iru form only. Verbs in the simple nonpast form like the one in (28), for example, cannot be interpreted as representing subjective change.

(28) Sono heya wa   maruku naru.
     that room TOP round   become
     'The room will become round.'

Subjective motion, on the other hand, is a continuous process, and the process as a whole is used to represent the configuration or extent of the described object. For this reason, its expressions are not limited to the -te iru form (cf. examples (26) and (27)).[14]

Expressions Involving Both Subjective Change and Subjective Motion

There are some interesting examples in which both subjective change and subjective motion are involved. Consider the following sentences.

(29) a. Michi wa soko kara hiroku natte   iru.
        road TOP there from wide   become RES
        (Lit. 'The road is in the state of having become wider from there.')
        'The road is wider from there on.'

     b. Michi wa soko de hiroku naru
        road TOP there   wide   become
        (Lit. 'The road becomes wider there.')
        'The road widens there.'

In these examples, a moving perspective (Talmy 1983, 1988) is taken, and the change is noted as the focus of attention moves (Talmy 1990). In (29a), for example, a road at (and after) the current point of attention is described as being wider than it was at previous points of attention. The change so noted is a subjective change that has the state of the object at the previous point of attention as its reference state. The motion of the focus of attention over the described object is subjective motion. That is, these expressions are based on the subjective change triggered by subjective motion.

The existence of both subjective motion and subjective change in this kind of example has also been noted by Langacker (1987), who states in relation to the English example in (30) that a conceptualizer "mentally traces downward along the artery and notes the 'changes' in its configuration that are encountered along the way. I analyze this motion as subjective motion by the conceptualizer" (p. 175).

(30) This artery branches just below the elbow.

Langacker, however, does not explore the notion of change involved in this example any further.

Other English examples in which both subjective motion and subjective change are involved include the sentences in (31), which are noted by Talmy (1983, 1988).

(31) a. The fence gets higher as you go down the road.

b. The telephone poles get taller as you go down the road.

Sentence (31a) is an example which is, like (30), based on the change of successive states of (different sections of) an object experienced as the focus of attention moves, while (31b) is an interesting case in which a change is noted when a set of spatially sequential objects are experienced as the focus of attention moves.

The examples in (32) also involve subjective change as well as subjective motion. They differ from the examples in (29) and (30) in that they are based on the change than an object as a whole (rather than successive sections of the object) appears to undergo as the focus of attention moves.

(32) a. The road extends from San Francisco to Los Angeles.

b. The vast field spreads to the north.

c. Highway 5 bisects the university campus.

In these examples, as the part of the object on which attention is focused shifts, the object as a whole (as the conceptualizer perceives it) appears to extend, stretch, or be bisected.

The Japanese expressions involving subjective change and motion in (29) are different from the canonical subjective-change expressions discussed in the first section in that their verb forms are not limited to the -*te iru* resultative form, as illustrated by (29b) (and therefore the statement about the possible verb forms of subjective-change expressions in the preceding section must be modified). There is a semantic difference between resultative sentences like (29a) and nonresultative sentences like (29b). Resultative forms are used to describe a certain section of an object as the final state of a subjective change on the basis of its comparison with another section which represents the initial state of a subjective change. Sentence (29a), for example, is a description of a section of a road (cf. "from there on") in comparison to another part of the road: the road is wider from there on. Nonresultative forms, on the other hand, are used to describe the configuration of a described entity in terms of the entire process of change that one can note during the movement of attention. For example, (29b) is a description of the configuration of a road as a whole: the road widens at an indicated point.

This difference explains the difference in the verb forms of these expressions. Since (29a) describes the final state of a change, it is in the resultative form; (29b) describes the configuration of a road in terms of an entire process of a change, so it is in the simple nonpast form.

The semantic difference that I noted above explains the fact that the nonresultative form cannot be used as a description of a part of an object, unlike the resultative form. Consider (33a) and (33b).

(33) a.   Michi no kono bubun wa   hiroku natte   iru.
          road GEN this   section TOP wide   become   RES
          (Lit. 'This section of the road is in a state of having become wider.')
          'This section of the road is wider.'

   b.   #Michi no kono bubun wa   hiroku naru.
          road GEN this   section TOP wide   become
          'This section of the road becomes wide.' (intended)

In (33a), the state of a section of a road is described in comparison to another part of the road. The nonresultative form cannot be used in this way, as can be seen from the unacceptability of (33b).

This difference between the resultative and nonresultative expressions of subjective change triggered by subjective motion is essentially the same as the third difference between subjective motion and subjective change noted above: the entire process of subjective motion is relevant for a description of an object, while only the final state of subjective change in comparison to its initial state is relevant for the description of the state of an object. In this respect, one might say that resultative expressions like (29a) inherit a property of subjective change in relation to the difference in the relevant stages of a process, while nonresultative expressions like (29b) inherit a property of subjective motion, although both involve subjective change as well as subjective motion.

Comparison to the Role Interpretation of Change Predicates

Sweetser (1990) mentions another use of change predicates to describe cases where no object is observed to change; in this section, I compare subjective-change expressions with her examples of ''role interpretation'' of the subjects of change predicates. Consider the sentence in (34).

(34) The keynote speaker's paper gets shorter and shorter.

This sentence is interpreted in two ways, due to two different readings of the subject NP. On one reading, *the keynote speaker's paper* refers to a particular paper written by one keynote speaker at a conference, and the sentence says that it gets shorter every time he or she revises it. On the other reading, the subject NP refers to any paper written in any year by any keynote speaker at an annual conference, and the sentence says that the paper written each year for the conference is shorter than the one written in the previous year. In Fauconnier's (1985) terminology, the subject NP in the latter reading represents a *role,* while that in the former reading represents a *filler* of that role. Following this distinction, Sweetser (1990) calls the former interpretation of the subject NP the *individual interpretation* and the latter the *role interpretation.*

Change-of-state predicates with the role interpretation of the subject are similar to subjective-change predicates in that both represent abstract processes: they represent a change that the referent of the subject NP does not undergo in real time. In both cases, a change is noted by comparing two different objects, which are treated as if they were the same entity existing at different periods of time (i.e., before and after the change) in a mentally constructed world. The difference between the two kinds of expression is in the nature of the two compared objects. Role interpretation involves any two instances (fillers) of the same role, while subjective-change expressions involve an unusual instance of an object and a normal one.

The similarity of these two kinds of expression manifests itself in the kinds of predicate that can be used to represent them. Sweetser (1990) observes that predicates that can be used with the role interpretation of their subject are limited in an interesting way. For example, while sentence (34) can be given the role interpretation, (35) cannot.

(35) The keynote speaker's paper shrinks.

Sweetser notes a general tendency for periphrastic change predicates (such as *become shorter*) to permit the role interpretation while lexical change predicates (such as *shrink*) cannot, although lexical predicates representing a nongradient change appear to permit the role interpretation (see below).

She also observes that a similar contrast can be found in sentences like (36a) and (36b) below, in which both subjective change and subjective motion are involved. Sentence (36a) (= (31b)) involves the subjective change that a set of spatially sequential objects are felt to undergo as the focus of attention moves. (The subject NP in this sentence cannot be interpreted as representing a role, and in such a case the subject must be plural, as noted by Talmy (p.c.)).

(36) a.   The telephone poles get taller as you go down the road.

    b. #The telephone poles expand/grow as you go down the road.

The same tendency in the restriction of predicates appears to hold in Japanese sentences with the role interpretation as well as those involving both subjective change and subjective motion. Examples (37a), (38a), and (39a) show that the lexical predicates *hirogaru* 'stretch', *nobiru* 'grow, become longer', and *sebamaru* 'narrow (as a verb)' cannot express a change with the role interpretation of the subject while their periphrastic counterparts can. Examples (37b), (38b), and (39b) show that the same lexical expressions cannot be used to represent subjective change noted of a spatially successive set of objects while their periphrastic counterparts can.

(37) a. Kare no ie no   niwa wa   [hikkosu goto ni]
        he GEN house GEN garden TOP move   every time
        {#hirogaru / hiroku naru}.
        stretch   / broad become
        'The garden of his house gets larger every time he moves.'

b. [Koogai ni   iku ni tsurete] ie no   niwa ga
   suburb GOAL go   as   house GEN garden NOM
   {#hirogaru / hiroku naru}.
   stretch   / broad become
   'The gardens of houses become more spacious as you go to suburban
   districts.'

(38) a. Ue-rararu ki wa   nennen   {#nobiru / takaku naru}.
        plant-PASS tree TOP every-year grow   / tall   become
        'Trees which are planted get taller every year.'

     b. [Yama ni   chikazuku ni tsure] ki ga   dandan
        mountain GOAL approach   as   tree NOM gradually
        {#nobiru / takaku naru}.
        grow   / tall   become
        'Trees get taller as you approach the mountain.'

(39) a. Kooen wa [tsukur-areru goto ni]   {#sebamaru / semaku naru}.
        park TOP   make-PASS every-time narrow   / narrow become
        'Parks become smaller every time they are constructed.'

     b. [Toshi ni chikazuku ni tsurete] kooen wa {#sebamaru / semaku naru}.
        city GOAL approach   as   park TOP narrow   / narrow become
        'Parks become smaller as you approach the city.'

What is most interesting is that the lexical expressions *hirogaru*, *nobiru*,
and *sebamaru* cannot be used in sentences involving subjective change alone
either, as shown in (40).

(40) a. Kare no ie no   niwa dake {#hirogatte iru / hiroku natte   iru}.
        he GEN house GEN garden only be.stretched / broad become RES
        (Lit. 'Only the garden of his house is in the state of having become broad.')
        'Only the garden of his house is spacious.'

     b. Kono denshinbashira dake {#nobite iru / takaku natte   iru}.
        this   telephone pole only become.long / tall   become RES
        (Lit. 'Only this telephone pole is in the state of having become tall.')
        'Only this telephone pole is exceptionally tall.'

    c. Kono kooen dake {#sebamatte iru   / semaku natte   iru}.
       this   park only   narrow   RES / narrow become RES
       'Only this park is exceptionally small.'

Why, then, can many lexical change predicates such as *hirogaru, nobiru,* and *sebamaru* not represent subjective change or change with the role interpretation of the subject?[15] What is crucial is the discontinuous nature of a change involved in subjective change and change in the role interpretation. These changes do not involve a gradual, continuous change process that one entity undergoes; rather, a change is noted as two different entities are compared, and the intermediate stages of the change are absent. Lexical predicates such as *hirogaru, nobiru,* and *sebamaru* represent a gradual, continuous change in relative size. In this respect they are incompatible with subjective change or the role interpretation of change predicates.

This view is consistent with an observation made by Sweetser (1990) about sentences like (41a).

(41) a. The fence {gets higher / rises} as you go toward the back of the yard.

    b. Koko kara kono michi wa shidai ni {semaku naru   / sebamaru}.
      here from this   road TOP gradually narrow become / narrow
      'This road narrows gradually from here.'

In contrast to similar sentences which involve a set of different telephone poles, the subjective change noted in (41a) is a continuous change. Sweetser notes that in such cases lexical change predicates that cannot permit the role interpretation of the subject can be used, and the same seems to hold of Japanese, as shown in (41b), in which the occurrence of *sebamaru* 'narrow' is markedly better than it is in (40c).

Some lexical predicates such as *kuttsuku* 'be attached, stick together', *kireru* 'be cut', and *deru* 'go out' are used in subjective-change expressions, as in examples (3a), (10a), (19), and (23). Note that these predicates can represent a nongradual change from one absolute state to another absolute state with no relevant intermediate states. These verbs thus appear to be compatible with subjective change.[16]

Cognitive and Linguistic Bases of Subjective-Change Expressions

Cognitive Bases

There are both cognitive and linguistic bases for expressions involving subjective change. One cognitive basis of subjective-change expressions is the human tendency to conceptualize a given situation in relation to a typical situation (a reference situation). This is seen most clearly in examples that have ideal categories as reference states. Gestalt psychologists claim that in describing a square with a corner ''cut off,'' the speaker ''sees'' a square with complete corners (cf. Kunihiro 1985). An ideal category like a square is what Rosch (1975) calls a cognitive reference point. This view is further developed by Pentland (1986) and Leyton (1988), who claim that complex shapes can be understood by their changes from simpler (more ideal) shapes. In the expression of subjective change, a similar principle is at work: the expected or normal state functions as a reference state, in relation to which other states are understood.

Second, the use of the resultative form for unexpected states is also based on cognitive mapping between distribution in the world and distribution in time, which shows up in various ways in language. In the case of subjective-change expressions, unexpected or abnormal entities are expressed as if they exist only temporarily: an unusual object such as a round room is treated as if it had previously been ''normal.'' While this idea is not scientifically true, it is consistent with the real-world experience of human beings. When a person perceives various instances of the same kind of object (e.g., a room) he or she does not encounter all the instances simultaneously; they are usually encountered in a temporal sequence. Given this situation, unexpected (abnormal) instances are encountered only on limited occasions. This tendency is one basis for the possibility of expressing an unexpected state as a temporary state.

In fact, there are many expressions in language that are based on a mapping between distribution in the world and distribution in time. Examples include (42a) and (42b).

(42) a. The sum of two natural numbers is sometimes even.

　　　 b. Football players can be sex maniacs.

Sentence (42a) does not mean that the sum of two given natural numbers is even on some occasions and odd on others; it means that the sum of *some* pairs of natural numbers is (always) even (Lewis 1975). Sentence (42b) is ambiguous. It can mean that it is possible that (all) football players are sex maniacs on some temporal occasions, or that it is possible that some football players are sex maniacs (all the time) (Lakoff 1972). In both cases, limited distribution in the world is expressed by a lexical item that expresses limited temporal occurrence. Thus, the use of the resultative form can be regarded as part of a more general phenomenon of expressing distribution in the world in terms of temporal distribution.[17]

Linguistic Bases

As long as the cognitive bases for fictive change noted above are universal, one might expect that all languages have the potential to exploit the notion of subjective change in expressing certain states. However, different languages seem to exploit such a possibility to different degrees. One source of difference appears to be different structural patterns used in expressing meanings. Differences in the lexicalization of aspect appear to be particularly relevant (see Talmy 1985).

Comparison of Japanese subjective-change expressions to English subjective-change expressions is revealing in this respect. English does have expressions based on subjective change (e.g., *a square with its corners cut off*), as noted above. English subjective-change expressions seem to be limited to those involving the "passive of result" (e.g., *cut off*). I know of no example of an English intransitive verb used to represent subjective change (unless subjective motion is also involved). For this reason, most of the Japanese resultative subjective-change expressions discussed in this paper do not have English counterparts. For example, the sentences in (43) are the English equivalents of the Japanese subjective-change sentences given in (23).

(43) a. His eyes protrude.

b. The house sticks out onto the sidewalk.

c. His handwriting leans to the right.

These expressions are not resultative, and there is no evidence that they involve subjective change.

This difference between Japanese and English is due to the different lexicalization patterns of Japanese verbs and English verbs. Languages differ in the situations that the resultative form is used to describe (Nedjalkov and Jaxontov 1988 (p. 7)). Japanese seems to utilize the resultative form to describe more situations than English does. There are many cases in which the same state is described as a result of a change in Japanese, but as a simple state without reference to a possible change in English. Consider the following contrast (Talmy 1985).[18]

(44) a. I stood there for two hours.

    b. Boku wa ni-jikan   tatte ita.
      I TOP   two hours arise RES-PAST
      (Lit. 'I was in the state of having arisen for two hours.')
      'I stood for two hours.'

Japanese expresses the state of a standing person as the result of a change of state (i.e., standing up), while English expresses it without reference to the change that has produced that state. In this case, English lexicalizes stative aspect in a simple form, while Japanese lexicalizes the change of state and uses the resultative form to describe a resulting state. The same is true of descriptions of many other states. The states described by English *know, wear, have, resemble,* and *lie,* for example, are all expressed in Japanese by the resultative form of the inchoative verbs *shiru* 'come to know', *kiru* 'put on', *motsu* 'come to have', *niru* 'become similar', and *yokotawaru* 'lie down'.

This difference in lexicalization patterns can be seen in the differences between the English sentences in (43) and their Japanese equivalents (cf. (23) above). The reason that English does not express these states in terms of the results of a change is the possibility of using verbs like *protrude, stick out,* and *incline* as stative verbs. Such stative verbs are absent in Japanese, and these states must be expressed in some other way. Thus, the lexicalization pattern of aspect in Japanese verbs makes it easier to exploit the cognitive possibility of expressing certain states as a result of subjective change.[19]

This point is consistent with the view that I have proposed with respect to subjective-motion expressions in Japanese and English. In Matsumoto (1996a) I point out that an examination of subjective-motion expressions in the two languages suggests that they are constrained both by the nature of subjective motion as a cognitive phenomenon and by the aspectual system of a particular language in which subjective motion is used to express a certain situation. A similar point can be made about subjective-change expressions: subjective change is a cognitive phenomenon, but the linguistic expressions based on it are constrained by the structure of a language, in particular the lexicalization of aspect.

Concluding Remarks

In this paper I have examined certain resultative expressions in Japanese that are used to describe a state that did not actually come to exist as a result of a change as if it had. I argue that they involve "subjective change of state," or a change in a mentally constructed world. Subjective change is a fictive change that is induced when an object in an unusual state is felt to have undergone a change from its expected or usual state. I have pointed out that subjective change is different from subjective motion in terms of the undergoer of change or motion, the source of the induction of these processes, and the relevant stages of these processes for the description of objects. I have also noted the similarity of subjective-change expressions to expressions with the role interpretation of change predicates, and pointed out that this can be attributed to the abstract, discontinuous nature of their change. I also argue that subjective change is based on a cognitive tendency to look at a situation in relation to a typical case, as well as the human tendency to experience different entities nonsimultaneously (or the mapping between distribution in the world and distribution in time). Furthermore, the lexicalization pattern of aspect in language explains the different degrees to which languages exploit the possibility of expressing states in terms of subjective change.

Notes

1. In writing this paper, I have been aided by the insights of helpful colleagues; I am especially grateful to Chuck Fillmore, Yoko Hasegawa, Yoshihiko Ikegami, Tetsuya Kunihiro, Jeff Lansing, George Lakoff, Jo Rubba, Eve Sweetser, and Leonard Talmy. I am also indebted to anonymous reviewers of this paper for valuable suggestions. An earlier version of this paper was written in 1988 and presented at the Berkeley–San Diego Cognitive Linguistics Workshop in 1990.

2. It has often been claimed that the class of verbs whose -te iru forms indicate the resultative is the class of momentary verbs, or verbs that indicate a process that does not have extended duration (Kindaichi 1950, Soga 1983). However, as Fujii (1976) points out, momentariness is not the real factor here, since the -te iru form of a momentary verb like *ichibetsu suru* 'glance' does not mark a resultative meaning.

Moreover, it is not a property of a verb per se but of the real world situation that the whole sentence refers to that determines whether the process that a verb indicates results in a change of state of the subject NP. Consider the following sentence.

(i) Taroo wa mada seetaa ni   akai hane o   tsukete iru.
    Taroo TOP still sweater LOC red feather ACC attach ASP
    'Taro is still in the state of attaching a red feather on a sweater.'
    or 'Taro is still in the state of having attached a red feather on his sweater.'

This sentence can be interpreted with a resultative reading only when the sweater that Taro puts a red feather on is the one on his own body, which is the only case in which the process represented by the verb is interpreted as affecting the state of the referent of the subject NP.

3. Kunihiro (1987) claims that -te iru expressions like *bakagete iru* can also be

dealt with by reference to possible changes in the same way as (1a), (2a), and (3a). There is, however, no evidence to show the involvement of any change in these examples like the ones I point out below. In fact, these -*te iru* forms do not have the crucial property of subjective-change expressions; unlike true subjective-change expressions such as (1a), (2a), and (3a), they do not describe unusual states.

4. This sentence is acceptable if the speaker has somehow expected the room to be round (e.g., if all the surrounding rooms are round). See the discussion of kinds of reference states below.

5. This sentence sounds more polite than (14a). Perhaps it is a politeness strategy for a speaker to describe a situation as unexpected.

6. The status of some other -*te iru* forms such as *hutotte iru* 'fat', *yasete iru* 'skinny', and *yogorete iru* 'dirty, contaminated (with some foreign object)' is somewhat more complicated. These -*te iru* forms have sometimes been treated as simple stative expressions in the same way as -*te iru* forms like *bakagete iru* above, although these differ from *bakagete iru* in that these verbs can be used in their simple nonpast tense (e.g., *hutoru* 'become fat, gain weight') (see Fujii 1976). These -*te iru* forms are also different from *bakagete iru* in that both -*ta* forms and -*te iru* forms are acceptable as modifiers of a noun, and the -*ta* forms are interpreted with a past-tense reading. For example, *hutotta* is not possible in (i) below, suggesting that the use of this form presupposes an actual process of becoming fat.

(i) sukoshi yaseta   keredo (mada) {??hutot-ta / hutotte iru} hito
    little   lose.weight-PAST but   still   become.fat-PAST become.fat RES person
    'a person who lost a little weight but is still fat.'

However, unlike subjective-change expressions, the meaning of *hutotte iru* in (i) does not necessarily suggest the sense of unusualness that characterizes subjective-change resultative expressions. In this respect, *hutotte iru* is a simple stative expression. Note here that Japanese does not have any adjective that can be used to describe the fatness of a person, and this -*te iru* form fills in this gap. (The adjective *hutoi* 'thick, wide' cannot be used for a human body, for which *hutotte iru* is used.)

The reason *hutotte iru* cannot be interpreted as representing subjective change is the semantic nature of the verb *hutoru*. As I point out below, many lexical change-of-state predicates are restricted to the description of a gradual, continuous change of state, and cannot represent subjective change, which is a discontinuous change process.

7. The view that a description of a change intrinsically involves a comparison explains the phenomenon that the comparison of two entities and the change from one state to another are often expressed by the same formal device in language. For example, the same adposition (e.g., the source marker) is often used to indicate the original state of change (e.g., change *from* A to B) and the state in relation to which the comparison is made (e.g., A is different *from* B) (see also Lichtenberk 1991). Note also that English-speaking children often mark a sandard of comparison with *from,* as has been observed by Clark and Carpenter (1989). In explaining this phenomenon, they state that "comparison . . . can be conceived of as requiring (abstract)

movement away from a standard toward the element being compared to that standard''
(p. 8).

8. As Langacker (p.c.) points out, the fact that Japanese treats the expected or
normal state as if it were a temporally prior state is consistent with the general
tendency for temporally prior events or states to serve as the background for the
description of later events or states (Talmy 1978).

9. The following sentences are also real-change expressions in which a certain
temporally prior reference state is presupposed on the basis of the expected state of
the referent of the subject NP.

> (i) Doa ga   hanbun aite   iru.
>   door NOM half   open RES
>   (Lit. 'The door is in the state of having half-opened.')
>   'The door is half open.'

> (ii) Doa ga   hanbun shimatte iru.
>   door NOM half   close   RES
>   (Lit. 'The door is in the state of having half-closed.')
>   'The door is half closed.'

The expression *hanbun aite iru* 'half open' is used with the expectation that the door
might be completely closed, and *hanbun shimatte iru* 'half closed' is used with the
expectation that it might be completely open (cf. Langacker 1988 (p. 67)).

10. Examples like these cannot be explained simply by saying that the verb *run*
in (25a) indicates extent over a path and that no motion is involved. Temporal expressions that indicate the duration of some process, such as *for a while,* are compatible
with subjective-motion sentences, as shown in (i). This shows that some process (i.e.,
motion) is involved in these sentences (see Matsumoto 1996a).

> (i) The road proceeds along the coast for a while.

11. This sentence involves what I call the participial complex-motion predicate,
in which a participial verb (*haitte*) represents the manner and other action that accom-
panies the motion represented by the main verb (see Matsumoto 1991, in press).

12. Access-path expressions like (25b) are also clear examples which show that a
moving entity is not the referent of a subject NP.

13. Subjective motion represented in prepositions in English is triggered in a different way. It is induced by the location of the subject NP in relation to the location of
some reference object (e.g., the speaker).

14. The *-te iru* form used in subjective-motion expressions does not mark resultative aspect; subjective-motion sentences therefore do not describe the final stage of a
process. As I point out above, the *-te iru* form of a verb is interpreted as resultative
only when the verb represents a change of state of the referent of the subject NP. In
this regard, some of the verbs used to represent subjective motion do not represent a

change of state. For example, the verb *hashiru* 'run' is an activity verb (Ikegami 1981). Its *-te iru* form does not represent the resultative when used to represent real motion, and there is no reason to believe that it does in the case of subjective motion. The meaning that this form indicates when it represents subjective motion is a special case of the progressive, as in the following sentence (Matsumoto 1996a).

(i) Nagai gyooretsu wa ima kawa no soba o   tootte iru.
    long   procession TOP now river GEN side ACC pass ASP
    'A long procession is now passing by a river.'

In this sentence the continuous flow of persons is expressed. Similarly, (26a) above expresses continuous occurrences or a flow of subjective motion: subjective motion can be induced at any moment, and therefore the motion can be regarded as occurring successively. Thus the function of the *-te iru* form is different in subjective-change and subjective-motion expressions.

15. With respect to role interpretation, Sweetser (1990) attributes this to the general nature of lexical expressions: they represent canonical or conventional situations (see Shibatani 1976).

16. Also note the use of *disappear* in the following sentence (which I owe to Len Talmy (p.c.)).

(i) As I went along, paint spots became smaller and smaller and finally they disappeared.

17. Another instance of this phenomenon is Talmy's (1988) example, given in (i).

(i) There is a house every now and then through the valley.

This sentence expresses the distribution of houses in terms of the temporal expression *every now and then*. The speaker (conceptualizer) is moving his or her focus of attention through the valley, and notes the occurrence of houses during his or her survey. The examples given in the text do not depend on such a moving perspective.

18. Other examples include the following.

(i) Yuku ga   niwa ni   takusan tsumotte iru.
    snow NOM garden LOC much   pile.up RES
    (Lit. 'Much snow is in the state of having piled up in the garden.')
    'There is much snow in the garden.'

(ii) Mary wa koko ni kite   iru.
     Mary TOP here LOC come   RES
     (Lit. 'Mary is in the state of having come here.')
     'Mary is here.'

19. How extensively subjective-change expressions can be found in other languages has not been examined. In this connection, it is worthwhile to note the following observation made by Nedjalkov and Jaxontov (1988): "In a number of languages, natural states and qualities are expressed by resultative (stative) form of verbs that denote coming into being of a state or quality. . . . For instance, in Fula the quality "tall" is expressed by the stative form of the verb meaning 'to become tall' (p. 13).

References

Bybee, Joan, Revere Perkins, and William Pagliuca. 1994. *The Evolution of Grammar: Tense, Aspect, and Modality in the Languages of the World.* Chicago: University of Chicago Press.

Clark, Eve V., and Kathie Carpenter. 1989. The Notion of Source in Language Acquisition. *Language* 65:1–30.

Clark, Herbert. 1973. Space, Time, Semantics and the Child. In Timothy Moore, ed., *Cognitive Development and the Acquisition of Language,* 27–63. New York: Academic Press.

Fauconnier, Gilles. 1985. *Mental Spaces: Aspects of Meaning Construction in Natural Language.* Cambridge, Mass.: MIT Press. Reprinted 1994, Cambridge: Cambridge University Press.

Fujii, Tadashi. 1976. 'Dooshi + *te iru* no Imi (The Meaning of a verb + *te iru*). In Haruhiko Kindaichi, ed., *Nihongo Dooshi no Asupekuto* (Japanese Verbal Aspect), 97–116. Tokyo: Mugi Shobo.

Honda, Akira. 1994. From Spatial Cognition to Semantic Structure: The Role of Subjective Motion in Cognition and Language. *English Linguistics* 11:197–219.

Ikegami, Yoshihiko. 1981. Suru *to* Naru *no Gengogaku* (The Linguistics of *Do* and *Become*). Tokyo: Taishukan.

Kindaichi, Haruhiko. 1950. Nihongo dooshi no ichibunrui (A Classification of Japanese Verbs). *Gengo Kenkyuu* 15:48–63.

Kinsui, Satoshi. 1994. Rentai-shuushoku no *-ta* ni tsuite (On the Prenominal *-ta* Modifier). In Yukinori Takubo, ed., *Nihongo no Meishi-shuushoku Hyoogen* (Noun Modifiers in Japanese), 29–65. Tokyo: Kurosio.

Kunihiro, Tetsuya. 1985. Ninchi to Gengo-Hyoogen (Cognition and Linguistic Expressions). *Gengo Kenkyuu* 88:1–19.

———. 1987. Asupekutoji *-te iru* no Kinoo (The Function of the Aspect Carrier *-te iru*). *Tokyo Daigaku Gengogaku Ronshuu* (University of Tokyo Linguistic Papers): 1–7.

Lakoff, Robin T. 1972. The Pragmatics of Modality. *Papers from the Eighth Annual Regional Meeting of the Chicago Linguistic Society,* 229–46. University of Chicago.

Langacker, Ronald W. 1987. *Foundations of Cognitive Grammar.* Vol. 1: *Theoretical Prerequisites.* Stanford, Calif.: Stanford University Press.

———. 1988. A View of Linguistic Semantics. In Brygida Rudzka-Ostyn, ed., *Topics in Cognitive Linguistics.* Amsterdam: John Benjamins.

Leisi, Ernst. 1953. *Der Wortinhalt: Seine Struktur im Deutschen und Englischen.* Heidelberg: Quelle & Meyer.

Lewis, David. 1975. Adverbs of Quantification. In Edward Keenan, ed., *Formal Semantics of Natural Languages,* 3–15. Cambridge: Cambridge University Press.

Leyton, Michael. 1988. A Process-Grammar for Shape. *Artificial Intelligence* 34: 213–43.

Lichtenberk, Frantisek. 1991. Semantic Change and Heterosemy in Grammaticalization. *Language* 67:475–509.

Matsumoto, Yo. 1991. On the Lexical Nature of the Purposive and Participial Complex Motion Predicates. *Proceedings of the Seventeenth Annual Meeting of the Berkeley Linguistics Society,* 180–91. Berkeley, CA: Berkeley Linguistics Society.

———. 1996a. Subjective Motion and English and Japanese Verbs. *Cognitive Linguistics* 7:124–56.

———. 1996b. How Abstract is Subjective Motion? A Comparison of Coverage Path Expressions and Access Path Expressions. In Adele E. Goldberg, ed., *Conceptual Structure, Language, and Discourse.* Stanford, Calif.: CSLI Publications. 359–73.

——— n.d. *Japanese Complex Predicates: A Syntactic and Semantic Study of the Notion 'Word.'* Stanford, CA: CSLI Publications. In press.

Nedjalkov, Vladimir P., and Sergej Je Jaxontov. 1988. The Typology of Resultative Constructions. In Vladimr P. Nedjalkov, ed., *Typology of Resultative Constructions,* 3–62. Amsterdam: John Benjamins.

Okuda, Yasui. 1985. Asupekuto no kenkyuu o megutte (On the Study of Aspect). In *Kotoba no Kenkyuu: Josetsu* (The Study of Words: An Introduction), 105–43. Tokyo: Mugi Shobo.

Pentland, A.P. 1986. Perceptual Organization and the Representation of Natural Form. *Artificial Intelligence* 28:293–331.

Rosch, Eleanor. 1975. Cognitive Reference Points. *Cognitive Psychology* 7:532–47.

Sapir, Edward. 1944. Grading: A Study in Semantics. *Philosophy of Science* 11: 93–116.

Shibatani, Masayoshi. 1976. The Grammar of Causative Constructions: A Conspectus. In Masayoshi Shibatani, ed., *The Grammar of Causative Constructions,* 5–41. Syntax and Semantics, vol. 6. New York: Academic Press.

Soga, Matsuo. 1983. *Tense and Aspect in Modern Colloquial Japanese.* Vancouver: University of British Columbia Press.

Sweetser, Eve. 1990. Role and Individual Interpretations of Change Predicates. Paper presented at the Berkeley—San Diego Cognitive Linguistics Workshop. (Revised version to appear 1996, in *Language and Conceptualization,* eds. Jan Nuyts and Eric Pederson. Oxford: Oxford University Press.)

Takahashi, Taro. 1969. Sugata to mokuromi (Aspect and Purpose). In Haruhiko Kindaichi, ed., *Nihongo Dooshi no Asupekuto* (Aspect of Japanese Verbs), 117–53. Tokyo: Mugi Shobo.

Talmy, Leonard. 1978. Figure and Ground in Complex Sentences. In Joseph H. Greenberg, ed., *Universals of Human Language.* Vol. 4: *Syntax,* 625–49. Stanford, Calif.: Stanford University Press.

————. 1983. How Language Structures Space. In H. Pick and L. Acredolo, eds., *Spatial Orientation: Theory, Research, and Application,* 225–82. New York: Plenum.

———— 1985. Lexicalization Patterns: Semantic Structure in Lexical Forms. In Tim Shopen, ed., *Language Typology and Syntactic Descriptions 3: Grammatical Categories and the Lexicon,* 57–149. Cambridge: Cambridge University Press.

————. 1988. The Relation of Grammar to Cognition. In Brygida Rudzka-Ostyn, ed., *Topics in Cognitive Linguistics,* 165–205. Amsterdam: John Benjamins.

————. 1989. Fictive Motion in Language and Perception. Paper presented at the Conference on Meaning and Perception, French-Canadian Association for the Advancement of Science, University of Quebec.

————. 1990. Fictive Motion and Change in Language and Cognition. Paper presented at the Conference of the International Pragmatics Association, Barcelona.

————. 1996. Fictive Motion in Language and "ception." In Paul Bloom, Mary A. Peterson, Lynn Nadel, and Merrill F. Garrett, eds., *Language and Space.* Cambridge, Mass.: MIT Press.

Teramura, Hideo. 1984. *Nihongo no Shintakkusu to Imi* (The Syntax and Semantics of Japanese). Vol. 2. Tokyo: Taishuukan.

Errapel Mejías-Bikandi

6 *Space Accessibility and Mood in Spanish*

.
.
.
.

This paper examines linguistic contexts in Spanish in which either the indicative or the subjunctive mood can be used. These contexts are illustrated in examples (1) and (2).[1]

(1) a. Probablemente Pedro está enfermo.
      'Probably Peter is-IND sick.'

    b. Probablemente Pedro esté enfermo.
      'Probably Peter is-SUBJ sick.'

(2) a. No es cierto que Pedro está enfermo.
      'It is not the case that Peter is-IND sick.'

    b. No es cierto que Pedro esté enfermo.
      'It is not the case that Peter is-SUBJ sick.'

My goal is to characterize explicitly the role that mood plays in the semantic distinction between minimal pairs such as the ones illustrated in (1) and (2). I examine the interaction of mood with three different phenomena—presupposition inheritance, the establishment of discourse referents by indefinite phrases, and control into adverbial infinitival clauses—and I make some empirical observations regarding the interaction of mood with these three phenomena. I then rephrase these observations using the notions and terminology of the mental spaces framework (Fauconnier 1985). The technical apparatus provided by this framework allows us to state the interaction of mood with these phenomena in a consistent and systematic way, and the systematicity of this interaction in turn enables us to isolate and characterize the contribution of mood to the semantic representation of sentences such as those in (1) and (2). I then present an analysis (restricted to contexts such as the ones illustrated in (1) and (2)) in which mood in Spanish is regarded as a grammatical mechanism that controls the sharing of information among different domains in the representation of a discourse. Specifically, the indicative mood allows information contained within a mental space M to be accessible to M's parent space M'. The use of the indicative mood also allows access to elements in M via counterparts in M'. The subjunctive mood, however, does not allow access to elements in M via counterparts in M', nor does it allow information contained in M to be transferred to M'. From this perspective, mood can be regarded as a grammatical marker that indicates the current viewpoint space. The indicative mood maintains M' as the viewpoint space, even if M is the focus space, whereas the subjunctive mood indicates a shift in viewpoint, making M the viewpoint space.

The paper is organized as follows. In the first section I consider the phenomenon of presupposition inheritance. In the second section I examine indefinite phrases and the conditions under which they can establish discourse referents. I then present cases of control into adjunct clauses and state a generalization over the three phenomena considered. I relate the analysis and phenomena under discussion to some previous analyses of the use of the indicative and the subjunctive in Spanish. Finally, I point out the significance of the work presented here and give some concluding remarks.

Presupposition Inheritance

Fauconnier (1985:85–108) has discussed the phenomenon of "presupposition inheritance."[2] This term refers to cases in which presuppositions introduced by expressions in a space M are also presuppositions in M's parent space, M'. Fauconnier considers the following examples. The speaker A and the hearer B see Max in the street. Max looks glum. A knows Max and B assumes that A knows whether Max has a son. A utters the sentence in (3).

(3) Maybe Max's son is giving him trouble.

In (3), the expression *maybe* creates a possibility space M, and the sentence establishes relations between elements in this space. The parent space of M is the space of the speaker's reality R.[3] The presupposition P_3, "Max has a son" is associated with the use of the definite expression *Max's son*.[4] Thus, P_3 is a presupposition in the possibility space *M*. However, since B assumes that A knows whether Max has a son, it must be the case that P_3 is inherited in the parent space R.[5] Consequently, the presupposition P_3 associated with the expression *Max's son* in (3) is also a presupposition in R; that is, B assumes that A presupposes that Max has a son in the real world (as perceived by A),[6] and not that A is merely speculating about the possibility that Max might have a son.

Consider on the other hand the following context. A and B see a man on the street who looks glum. A utters the sentence in (4).

(4) Maybe that guy's son is giving him trouble.

B does not assume that A knows this man or whether he has a son. The presupposition associated with the expression *that guy's son* is P_4, "That guy has a son". P_4 is a presupposition in M, the possibility space built by *maybe*. In this case, since B does not assume that A knows anything about "that guy," P_4 is not inherited in R.[7] B does not assume that A presupposes P_4 (in R); in other words, B does not assume that the speaker A presupposes that "that guy" has a real son.

I turn now to the interaction of presupposition inheritance with mood in Spanish, and will show that the use of the indicative mood, but not the use of the subjunctive mood, causes presuppositions to be inherited in a parent space.

The Spanish expression *tal vez* 'maybe' establishes a possibility space M. When this expression is used, the verb in its clause can appear in either the indicative or the subjunctive mood, as sentence (5) illustrates.

(5) Tal vez Pedro tiene/tenga un hijo.
    'Maybe Peter has-IND/has-SUBJ a son.'

Consider now the following scenario. A speaker A and a hearer B see a person C in the street. C looks glum, and A utters the sentence in (6).

(6) Tal vez su hijo está en la cárcel.
    'Maybe his son is-IND in jail.'

When a speaker utters a sentence in the indicative mood, such as (6), the hearer assumes that the speaker is talking about something real, in this case a real person who is the son of person C. In other words, the hearer assumes that the speaker takes for granted that the person in question has a son. This intuition can be captured in a mental spaces representation of (6) in the following way. The expression *su hijo* 'his son' in (6) carries the presupposition P_6 "C has a son." P_6 is a presupposition in the possibility space M, which is built by *tal vez* 'maybe'. As we saw above, the use of the indicative

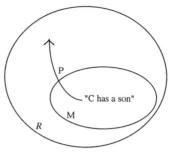

Figure 6.1

mood in (6) causes the hearer B to assume that the speaker A takes for granted that person C has a son (in a situation in which B does not know prior to the utterance of (6) whether A knows C). Consequently, it must be the case that P_6 is inherited in M's parent space R, which is the space of the speaker's (A's) reality; B assumes that A presuppposes that C has a son in the real world. The resulting representation is shown in figure 6.1.[8]

Consider now the same scenario as the one described above, except that in this case the speaker A utters sentence (7).

(7) Tal vez su hijo esté en la cárcel.
    'Maybe his son is-SUBJ in jail.'

Sentence (7) is the same as (6) except that the verb in (7) is in the subjunctive mood. On hearing (7), the hearer B does not assume that the speaker A knows whether person C has a son. In other words, the use of the subjunctive in (7) causes B not to assume that A knows whether C has a son (in a situation, again, in which B does not know whether A knows C). As before, this intuition can be captured in a mental spaces representation. The presupposition P_6 ''C has a son'', which is associated with the expression *su hijo* 'his son', is a presupposition in the possibility space M created by *tal vez* 'maybe'. But, since in hearing (7) the hearer B does not assume that A presupposes that C has a real son, it must be the case that P_6 is not inherited in R, but remains a presupposition in M. The corresponding representation is shown in figure 6.2.

The examples in (6) and (7) show that the use of the indicative mood causes a presupposition to project from the embedded space M into the parent space R. On the other hand, the use of the subjunctive does not cause a presupposition to be inherited from M into R. In other words, the hearer B, upon hearing the indicative sentence (6), assumes that the speaker A knows whether the person C has a son. Consequently, it must be that P_6 is inherited in R. The same is not the case when the subjunctive sentence (7) is uttered;

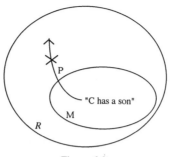

Figure 6.2

that is, it is not the case that upon hearing (7), the hearer B assumes that the speaker A presupposes that C has a son in the real world. In this case, P_6 is not inherited in R.

I now consider some cases in which a different space builder is involved. The scenario is the following: in a press conference, the speaker A denies the rumor that labor unions have stopped supporting the government. A utters the sentence in (8).

(8) No es cierto que los sindicatos han dejado de apoyar al gobierno.
    'It is not the case that the unions have-IND stopped supporting the government.'

The negative *no* establishes a counterfactual space M, where the condition "the unions have stopped supporting the government" is satisfied. Again, the parent space is R, corresponding to the speaker's reality. The presupposition P_8 "The unions supported the government" is associated with the expression *the unions have stopped supporting the government,* and, thus, it is a presupposition in M. In (8) the verb appears in the indicative mood. Upon hearing (8), the hearer B assumes that the speaker A presupposes that the unions supported the government before and continue to do so. Given this intuition, it must be the case that P_8 is inherited and becomes a presupposition in R. On the other hand, consider sentence (9), where the verb of the complement clause appears in the subjunctive mood.

(9) No es cierto que los sindicatos hayan dejado de apoyar al gobierno.
    'It is not the case that the unions have-SUBJ stopped supporting the government.'

In this case, the hearer B does not necessarily assume that the speaker A presupposes that the unions supported the government. Thus, it must be the case that P_8 "The unions supported the government" is a presupposition in the counterfactual space M and is not inherited in R. To illustrate the contrast, consider examples (10) and (11).

(10) ??Los sindicatos nunca han apoyado al gobierno.
Por lo tanto, no es cierto que los sindicatos han dejado de apoyar al gobierno.
'The unions have never supported the government. Consequently, it is not the case that the unions have-IND stopped supporting the government.'

(11) Los sindicatos nunca han apoyado al gobierno. Por lo tanto, no es cierto que los sindicatos hayan dejado de apoyar al gobierno.
'The unions have never supported the government. Consequently, it is not the case that the unions have-SUBJ stopped supporting the government.'

In (10) and (11), the fact that the unions have never supported the government is established in R by the first sentence. The anomaly found in the sequence in (10) can be explained in the following way. The use of the indicative mood in the complement clause of the second sentence causes the presupposition P_8 in M to be inherited in R. This inheritance results in a contradiction, since it has been previously established in R that the unions never supported the government. This contradiction is avoided in (11), where the use of the subjunctive mood allows for P_8 not to be inherited in R.

Consider now a presupposition associated with the word *incluso* 'even'. The speaker A utters the sentence in (12).

(12) Tal vez incluso María está enferma.
'Maybe even Mary is-IND sick.'

The verb in sentence (12) appears in the indicative mood. A presupposition associated with *even Mary is sick* is P_{12}, "Somebody else is also sick".[9] As before, P_{12} is a presupposition in the possibility space M, which is built by *tal vez* 'maybe'. In hearing (12), however, the hearer assumes that there is some other person in the area who is sick; the hearer B assumes that A presupposes that somebody else is sick in the real world. Thus, upon hearing (12), the hearer B might reconstruct the following scenario: there is an epidemic in the area, and many people are sick. The speaker A expects to see Mary at some point, but she does not appear on the scene, so the speaker infers the possibility that even Mary is sick. Consequently, it must be that the presupposition P_{12} in M is inherited in R. Consider, on the other hand, a case in which the speaker A utters the sentence in (13).

(13) Tal vez incluso María esté enferma.
'Maybe even Mary is-SUBJ sick.'

In sentence (13) the subjunctive mood is used. As before, we have a possibility space M built by *tal vez* 'maybe', which is embedded in the space of the speaker's reality, R. There is also the presupposition P_{12} associated with the word *incluso* 'even'. In this case, the hearer B does not assume that A presupposes that someone else is also sick; rather, B understands that the speaker A is just speculating about the possibility that other people might also be sick. In this case, the scenario that B reconstructs from hearing (13) might be the following: the speaker A is speculating about the fact that people in the area look unusually pale, or are absent from their locations of normal activity. A thinks that perhaps everybody is sick, even Mary. Under this scenario, P_{12} is a presupposition in M and is not inherited in R.

Thus, when the indicative mood is used, a presupposition associated with an expression that establishes a condition in a space M is inherited in M's parent space R. That is, the use of the indicative allows the hearer B to infer that the speaker A presupposed some presupposition P (associated with an expression that establishes a condition in M) in the space of the speaker's reality R. The use of the subjunctive mood does not cause a presupposition associated with an expression in a space M to be inherited in M's parent space R. In the next section, I examine the property of some indefinite phrases of establishing discourse referents and consider the extent to which that property is affected by the mood of the verb.

Indefinite Phrases and Discourse Referents

Fauconnier (1985) proposes the following interpretation of indefinite noun phrases:

Indefinite Interpretation
The noun phrase *a N* in a linguistic expression sets up a new element w in some space, such that N (w) holds in that space.

According to this principle, an indefinite expression introduces a new element in some particular mental space. Thus, in a sentence such as (14) the indefinite phrase *a man* introduces a new element w, such that man (w) holds in a space R, the space of the speaker's reality; in this case the new element w is introduced in R, since there is no other space in the representation of (14).

(14) A man is walking down the street.

However, the rule for the interpretation of indefinites leaves undetermined in which space a new element is introduced. This ambiguity provides an account of the specific/nonspecific contrast in sentences with an indefinite. Consider, for example, the sentence in (15) (taken from Fauconnier 1985).

(15) John Paul hopes that a former quarterback will adopt needy children.

In (15) the expression *hopes that* builds a hope space M. Let us assume that M's parent space is R, the space of the speaker's reality. The sentence in (15) is ambiguous between a specific reading for the indefinite and a nonspecific reading. Under the specific reading there is a real quarterback, and John Paul hopes that he will adopt needy children. Under the nonspecific reading there is no real quarterback, but John Paul hopes that there is (somewhere) a quarterback who will adopt needy children. The two readings are accounted for in the following way. The expression *a former quarterback* must identify an element w in the space M built by the space builder *John Paul hopes* satisfying the condition of being a former quarterback. This can be done in two ways. First, the noun phrase *a former quarterback* can introduce w directly in M, the hope space. In this case, there is no counterpart of w in R, M's parent space; that is, there is no real quarterback. This results in the nonspecific reading. Second, the noun phrase *a former quarterback* introduces an element w in R, this element being connected via a pragmatic function F, which maps reality onto hopes, to a counterpart w' in M. In this case there is a real quarterback, and we have the specific reading.

One property of specific indefinites is that they can establish discourse referents (in the sense of Karttunen 1968); that is, it is possible to talk about them later in discourse by using a personal pronoun or a definite expression. Thus, consider the sentences in (16).

(16) a. The mayor hopes that a former quarterback$_i$ will adopt two needy children.

b. This former quarterback$_i$ is very respected in the community.

In (16), the indefinite *a former quarterback* can be coreferential with the definite expression *This former quarterback*, but only if this indefinite is

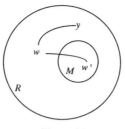

Figure 6.3

interpreted as specific. As we saw above, the expression *hopes* in (16a) builds a hope space M, which is embedded in the space of the speaker's reality R. As before, the expression *a former quarterback will adopt two needy children* establishes a condition in M. Sentence (16b), on the other hand, does not describe the hopes of the mayor and, consequently, it establishes a condition in R. The definite expression *This former quarterback* in (16b) points to an element y in R. I represent the fact that a definite expression and an indefinite are coreferential by linking the element w introduced by the indefinite with the element y pointed to by the definite expression or anaphor.[10] Since the discourse in (16a) and (16b) is possible with the specific reading of the indefinite, it must be the case that the element y can be linked to a new element w introduced in R, but y cannot be linked to a new element w introduced in M (in the nonspecific reading of the indefinite in (16a)). This is illustrated in figures 6.3 and 6.4, respectively.

There are some contexts that do not allow the interpretation of an indefinite as specific. In other words, there are some contexts that do not allow an indefinite to introduce a new element w in the parent space. Consider, for instance, the discourse in (17), taken from Karttunen 1968.

(17) ??Bill does not have a car$_i$. It$_i$/This car$_i$ is black.

The negation in (17) makes it impossible for the indefinite to be interpreted

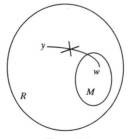

Figure 6.4

as specific, and that renders the anaphoric linking with a subsequent pronoun impossible. The indefinite in (17) must introduce the new element w in the counterfactual space M built by *no*. Since the pronoun *it* points to an element y in M's parent space R, the anaphoric linking is impossible, as in figure 6.4.[11]

Let us now examine the extent to which an indefinite can establish a discourse referent in contexts where either the indicative or the subjunctive mood can be used in Spanish and consider whether the choice of mood has an effect on the ability of an indefinite to be interpreted as specific and, consequently, to establish a discourse referent. Consider sentences (18) and (19). The complement clause of (18) is in the indicative mood, whereas the complement clause of (19) is in the subjunctive mood.

(18) No creo que te he enseñado una foto de mis padres.
     'I don't think I have-IND shown you a picture of my parents.'

(19) No creo que te haya enseñado una foto de mis padres.
     'I don't think I have-SUBJ shown you a picture of my parents.'

The indefinite in (18) is interpreted as specific, whereas the indefinite in (19) is interpreted as nonspecific. That is, the speaker who utters (18) is indicating that he has a particular picture of his parents in mind that he wants to show to the hearer. On the other hand, in the interpretation of (19), the speaker does not have a particular picture of his parents in mind. In (18) and (19) the negative establishes a counterfactual space M, embedded in a space R, the space of the speaker's reality. The complement clause establishes a relation between elements in M. Since the indefinite in (18) is interpreted as specific, it must be the case that this indefinite introduces a new element w in R, which is linked to a counterpart w' in M. On the other hand, the indefinite in (19) introduces a new element w directly in M. Consider now the discourse in the sentences in (20).

(20) a.   No creo que te he enseñado una foto$_i$ de mis padres. . . . Espera, que la$_i$ tengo guardada aquí.
          'I don't think I have-IND shown you a picture$_i$ of my parents. . . . Wait, I have it$_i$ here.'

     b.   ??No creo que te haya enseñado una foto$_i$ de mis padres. . . . Espera, que la$_i$ tengo guardada aquí.
          'I don't think I have-SUBJ shown you a picture$_i$ of my parents. . . . Wait, I have it$_i$ here.'

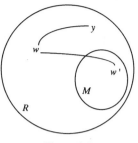

Figure 6.5

In the examples in (20), the second sentence establishes a relation between elements in R; this sentence is outside the scope of the negation in the first sentence. In (20a), the use of the indicative in the complement clause of the first sentence allows the anaphoric pronoun in the second sentence to be linked to the indefinite phrase *una foto* 'a picture'. This is possible in (20a) because, as we have seen, the indefinite introduces a new element w in R. This new element may be pointed to by the anaphoric pronoun *la* 'it' in the second sentence. Example (20b) is unnatural because the indefinite phrase *una foto* 'a picture' cannot introduce a new element w in R. Consequently, the anaphoric pronoun *la* 'it' cannot point to w. The situation can be represented as in figures 6.5 and 6.6.

The examples in (20) illustrate contexts whose representations involve two mental spaces, a space M and M's parent space R, the space of the speaker's reality. The verb V that establishes a relation in M can appear either in the indicative or in the subjunctive mood. In each case there is an indefinite expression that introduces a new element which is an argument of the relation expressed by V. When V is in the indicative mood, the indefinite phrase can introduce a new element w in R, linked to a counterpart w' in M, but this possibility does not exist when V is in the subjunctive mood. In that case, the new element w must be introduced directly in M. As a result, the indefinite phrase can establish a discourse referent when V is in the indicative

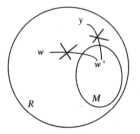

Figure 6.6

mood, but not when V is in the subjunctive mood. In the next section I discuss the phenomenon of control into adjunct clauses in Spanish and its interaction with mood. Control into an adjunct clause is possible from a clause with the verb in the indicative mood, but not from a clause with a verb in the subjunctive mood.

Control

A preverbal subject in Spanish can be interpreted as the subject of a sentence-initial adverbial clause, as sentence (21) illustrates.

(21) Habiendo robado el banco, Pedro se escondió en este almacén.
'Having robbed the bank, Peter hid in this warehouse.'

The verbal form in the adverbial clause in (21), *habiendo robado,* is not marked for person or number. The grammatical subject of the main clause, *Pedro* 'Peter', is interpreted as the subject of the adverbial clause. In a mental spaces representation of sentences such as (21), the subject argument of the relation established by *escondió* 'hid' must somehow be linked to the subject argument of the relation established by *robar* 'rob'. The hearer of the utterance represented in (21) must be able to fill the gap in the argument structure of the relation established by *robar* 'rob' with a counterpart of the element pointed to by *Pedro* 'Peter'. In this section, I consider this phenomenon in its interaction with mood and show that when the verb of the main clause is in the indicative mood, the subject of that clause can be interpreted as the subject of the adverbial clause. On the other hand, when the verb of the main clause is in the subjunctive mood, the subject of the main clause is not naturally interpreted as the subject of the adverbial clause.

Consider a sentence such as (22).

(22) Habiendo robado el banco, probablemente el ladrón se escondió en este almacén.
'Having robbed the bank, probably the robber hid-IND in this warehouse.'

In (22), the verb of the main clause is in the indicative mood and its subject is interpreted as the subject of the adjunct clause, as in (21). In (22), the expression *probablemente* 'probably' builds a possibility space M. The main clause establishes a relation between elements in M. The adverbial clause *habiendo robado el banco* 'having robbed the bank' is outside the scope of *probablemente* 'probably', and thus establishes a relation between elements

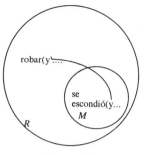

Figure 6.7

in the space of the speaker's reality R, the parent space of M. In this case, the subject argument of the relation established by *se escondió* 'hid' in M can be linked to the subject argument of the relation established by *habiendo robado* 'having robbed' in R. This is represented in figure 6.7. On the other hand, consider the case of (23), where the verb of the main clause is in the subjunctive mood.

(23) ??Habiendo robado el banco, probablemente el ladrón se escondiera
        en este almacén.
        'Having robbed the bank, probably the robber hid-SUBJ in this
        warehouse.'

In (23), it is difficult to obtain an interpretation under which the subject of the main clause is also the subject of the adjunct clause. As a consequence, (23) is an awkward, unnatural sentence. Informally, the problem with (23) is that it is difficult to relate the content of the adjunct clause to the content of the main clause. The representation of (23) also involves two mental spaces, the possibility space M built by *probablemente* 'probably', and its parent space R, the space of the speaker's reality. As in the case of (22), the main clause establishes a relation between elements in M and the adverbial clause establishes a relation between elements in R. However, in (23) a link cannot be established between the subject argument of *robar* 'rob' in R and the subject argument of *se escondiera* 'hid' in M. This is represented in figure 6.8. The example in (22) shows that an argument of a relation established in a space M by a verb in the indicative mood can be linked to the argument of a relation established by a verb in R. On the other hand, the example in (23) shows that the argument of a relation established in M by a verb in the subjunctive mood cannot be linked to the argument of a relation in R.

 I now turn to the question of how mental space representations will allow

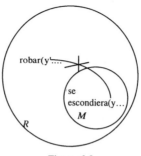

Figure 6.8

us to state a generalization about the way mood in Spanish interacts with presupposition inheritance, the ability of an indefinite phrase to be interpreted as specific and to establish a discourse referent, and the ability of a grammatical subject in the main clause of a sentence to control into an adverbial clause.

Generalization

The data examined in the preceding sections involve a representation that can be informally schematized as in figure 6.9. The representation in figure 6.9 involves two mental spaces: the space of speaker's reality, R, and either a counterfactual or a possibility space M. The space M is built by a linguistic expression that allows the use of either the indicative or the subjunctive mood in the verb that establishes a relation in M. The cases examined above involve some kind of relationship or link between M and R. In the case of presupposition inheritance, a presupposition in M is or is not inherited in R. In the case of indefinite phrases, a new element w is or is not introduced in R and linked

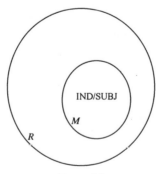

Figure 6.9

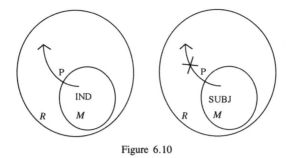

Figure 6.10

to a counterpart w' in M. In the case of control structures, an element in M is or is not linked to an element in R. In all cases, the indicative mood makes these links or relations between R and M possible, whereas the subjunctive mood renders them difficult. Thus, presupposition inheritance occurs when the verb establishing a relation in M is in the indicative mood, but not when this verb is in the subjunctive mood, as represented in figure 6.10. Moreover, an element w in R can be linked to a counterpart w' in M when the verb that establishes the relation in M is in the indicative mood, but not when the verb is in the subjunctive mood, as represented in figure 6.11. Finally, an element that is an argument of a relation in M can be linked to an element in R when the verb that establishes the relation in M is in the indicative mood, but not when this verb is in the subjunctive mood. This can be represented as in figure 6.12. The observations and the representations given above point to the following generalization. Informally, the indicative mood opens a space M, allowing elements within M to be linked to elements in a higher space, or allowing presuppositions within M to be inherited in a higher space. The subjunctive mood, however, closes a space M to any such relations, so that elements within M cannot be linked to elements in a higher space, and presuppositions within M are not typically inherited. From this perspective, mood in Spanish can be viewed as a grammatical marker that indicates whether a particular space M is open or closed; that is, it indicates whether

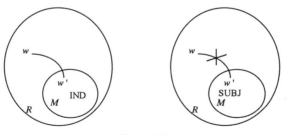

Figure 6.11

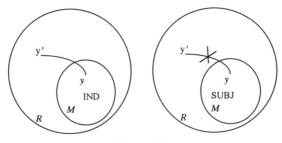

Figure 6.12

a particular space R can have access to information contained within an embedded space M. The analysis of mood presented in this paper can be schematized as in figure 6.13.

This analysis can be situated against the more general background of the shifting of viewpoint in discourse. The data suggest that when the indicative mood is used, the viewpoint space is still R, although the focus space is M. This accounts for the possibility of accessing elements in M via counterparts in R. This also explains why presuppositions are inherited from M into R (although this idea needs to be developed further). On the other hand, the use of the subjunctive mood indicates a shift of viewpoint space from R to M. As a consequence, elements in M cannot be accessed via counterparts in R. In the next section I relate this view of mood to previous accounts of the difference between sentences with a verb in the indicative mood and sentences with a verb in the subjunctive mood in Spanish.

Previous Analyses

The most widely accepted analyses of mood in Spanish account for the semantic difference between indicative/subjunctive pairs by appealing to one of two parameters: the speaker's attitude toward the truth of the complement (see, for instance, Rivero 1971 and Bergen 1978); or assertion versus non-

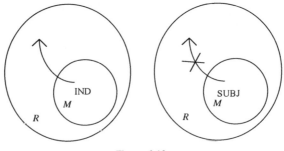

Figure 6.13

assertion (Terrell and Hooper 1974, Terrell 1976, Bell 1980). Consider the sentences in (24) and (25).

(24) Juan no cree que tu hijo está enfermo.
'John doesn't believe that your son is-IND sick.'

(25) Juan no cree que tu hijo esté enfermo.
'John doesn't believe that your son is-SUBJ sick.'

Under Rivero and Bergen's analysis, the speaker who utters the indicative sentence in (24) believes that the proposition expressed by the complement is true, and that she is just reporting the fact that John does not believe in the truth of such a proposition. On the other hand, the speaker who utters the subjunctive sentence in (25) does not commit herself to the truth of the proposition expressed by the complement. An alternative analysis is provided by Terrell, Hooper, and Bell, who claim that the indicative is the mood of assertion, whereas the subjunctive is the mood of non-assertion. Consider, for example, sentences (1a) and (1b), repeated here as (26) and (27).

(26) Probablemente Pedro está enfermo.
'Probably Peter is-IND sick.'

(27) Probablemente Pedro esté enfermo.
'Probably Peter is-SUBJ sick.'

Under Terrell, Hooper, and Bell's analysis the difference between (26) and (27) is that (26) (indicative) is more assertive than (27) (subjunctive), and (26) thus expresses a higher degree of probability. Under this analysis, the speaker who utters (26) regards the fact that Peter is sick as very probably true, whereas the speaker who utters (27) considers it less likely that Peter is sick.

The analysis presented in this paper and the previous analyses discussed above try to capture the same basic intuition regarding mood in Spanish. This intuition can be informally stated as follows: when the indicative mood is used instead of the subjunctive mood in a particular context, the speaker assumes some responsibility over, or feels closer to, the content of the proposition expressed by the complement clause. The two previous analyses discussed here embody this intuition in two different ways: either the speaker commits herself to the truth of the proposition expressed by the complement, or the speaker asserts this proposition.[12] This same intuition is captured by the analysis proposed here. In examples (24) and (25), for instance, we have a counterfactual space M, set up by the expression *no,* and its parent space R, the space of the speaker's reality. The use of the indicative marks the fact that some relation holds between R and M, or that information contained within M is accessible to R. This conforms to the intuition that R and M are, informally, closer and more interdependent. On the other hand, when the subjunctive mood is used, information contained within M is not accessible to R. This conforms to the intuition that R and M are more distant. The aim of all the analyses presented here is to give explicit content to the informal intuition stated above regarding the use of mood in Spanish. In this sense, these analyses are to some extent compatible with each other.

The previous analyses do, however, exhibit some empirical inadequacies. Rivero and Bergen's analysis runs into problems in sentences such as (28).

(28) No creo que tu hijo está enfermo.
      'I do not believe that your son is-IND sick.'

Under Rivero and Bergen's analysis, the speaker of (28) would be negating the truth of what she is presupposing to be true. Consequently, under this analysis sentence (28) is incorrectly predicted to be unnatural.[13] It is not clear how Terrell, Hooper, and Bergen's analysis would account for the difference between sentences such as (2a) and (2b), repeated here as (29) and (30).

(29) No es cierto que Pedro está enfermo.
      'It is not the case that Peter is-IND sick.'

(30) No es cierto que Pedro esté enfermo.
      'It is not the case that Peter is-SUBJ sick.'

In the case of (26) and (27), it was said that (26) is more assertive, and thus indicates a higher degree of probability, than (27). Similarly, we could say that (29) is more assertive than (30), and, thus indicates a higher degree of certainty than (30). Consequently, the speaker who utters (29) is sure that Peter is not sick, whereas the speaker who utters (30) is not so sure. However, this characterization is not intuitively correct. Both (29) and (30) indicate that the speaker is sure about the fact that Peter is not sick. Any attempt to explain the contrast between (29) and (30) by appealing to different degrees of certainty thus becomes circular.[14]

The framework developed in Fauconnier 1985 allows us to give explicit content to the guiding intuition behind previous analyses of mood in Spanish while avoiding the empirical problems that they face. How would the analysis presented in this paper explain the contrast between (26) and (27) on the one hand, and (29) and (30) on the other? The use of the indicative mood instead of the subjunctive mood in (26) and (29) produces a certain effect which, as pointed out above, is very difficult to state explicitly, but which can be informally characterized as the speaker feeling closer to the propositional content of the clause in the indicative mood. Under the analysis presented here, this intuition results from the fact that when the indicative mood is used, the embedded space M can be accessed via R.

Final Remarks

In this paper I have considered linguistic contexts in Spanish in which either the indicative or the subjunctive mood can be used. I have analyzed mood in these contexts as a grammatical marker that indicates whether a particular space M is accessible to its parent space R. The claim is that the indicative mood makes it possible for some relations to hold between M and R, whereas the subjunctive mood makes any such relation difficult. The analysis presents mood in Spanish under a new light. Mood is viewed as a mechanism that regulates the sharing of information among mental spaces. The indicative mood opens a particular space M, so that information contained in it can be passed on to a higher space. The subjunctive mood on the other hand closes a space M, so that information contained in it cannot flow to higher spaces.

The work presented here relates to some extent to work done in dynamic semantics (see, for instance, Barwise 1987) and, in particular, in Dynamic Predicate Logic (DPL) (Groenendijk and Stokhof 1991; see also Chierchia 1992). Using DPL terminology, the indicative creates dynamic contexts, contexts that allow the flow of information, whereas the subjunctive makes a particular context static, preventing the flow of information out of that context. From this perspective, the work presented here can be considered an exploration of the grammatical manifestations of the dynamic/static distinction. However, in Groenendijk and Stokhof 1991 only one phenomenon is shown to be sensitive to the static/dynamic distinction: the possibility of a quantifier binding a variable outside its scope. The present paper shows that there are other phenomena that might be sensitive to the static/dynamic contrast, such as presupposition inheritance and control, that cannot be easily accommodated within the formalism developed in DPL.[15]

I have considered the interaction of mood with three phenomena (presupposition inheritance, specificity, and control) that typically are considered to fall within three different modules of the grammar (pragmatics, semantics, and syntax). Mental spaces representations of the relevant data show that mood interacts with the three phenomena in a systematic way and that a unified account of this interaction can be given. Thus, the analysis shows that phenomena that are typically considered to belong to different modules of the grammar and are consequently given different explanations in certain formal theories can in fact be treated uniformly.

Notes

1. Throughout this paper, IND indicates indicative mood and SUBJ indicates subjunctive mood.

2. I discuss this phenomenon in its interaction with mood in Spanish in Mejías-Bikandi 1995, from which this section is partly extracted. See also Kay 1992.

3. I use R consistently to refer to the space of a speaker's reality that is the parent space of another space M.

4. I use the symbol P to refer to presuppositions. The subscript indicates the number of the example in the text with which the presupposition is associated. Presuppositions are enclosed in double quotation marks, whereas English expressions are italicized.

5. Fauconnier (1985) gives a set of rules, definitions, and strategic principles that account for the results described. Thus, if B assumes that A knows whether Max has a son, then P_3 will be regarded by B as a presupposition in R. This is so by the optimization strategic principle, which requires B to structure M and R as closely as possible with respect to presuppositions and background assumptions as long as contradiction does not arise.

6. The expression *the real world* should be understood to mean "the real world as perceived by the speaker."

7. This is the case in order to avoid a possible contradiction in R.

8. I represent spaces as circles or ovals and indicate that a space M is embedded in a space R by including M in R. In figure 6.1 M is included in R, indicating that R is the parent space of M. M should not be interpreted as a subset of R in the standard set-theoretic sense.

9. There is another kind of presupposition associated with the word *even* that I do not consider. This is the scalar presupposition that Mary is the most unlikely person (within a particular set) to get sick.

10. In fact, when y and w are linked, y = w. That is, the definite expression points to the element introduced by the indefinite.

11. A possible extension of (16a) could be (i):

(i) This quarterback would be very much admired in the community.

The definite expression in (i) can be interpreted as coreferential with the indefinite *a former quarterback* in (16a), even if this indefinite is interpreted as nonspecific. This interpretation is made possible by the use of the conditional in (i). In a sense, then, the nonspecific indefinite can also establish a discourse referent. In (i) the use of the conditional indicates that the clause in (i) is not establishing a relation between elements in R, but rather between elements in M. This makes the coreference between the definite expression and the indefinite possible. Here I am concerned with cases in which an indefinite can be linked to an element in a higher space (in the case of the sentences in (16), to an element in R). Consequently, when I say that an indefinite N can or cannot establish a discourse referent, I mean that the new element introduced by N can or cannot be linked to an element in R.

12. Schane (1995) argues for a notion of "subject responsibility" to account for which matrix clauses in Spanish govern the indicative mood and which govern the subjunctive mood. When the meaning of a matrix clause exemplifies this property of subject responsibility, the indicative mood is used. This analysis captures the same basic intuition expressed above.

13. Contrast (28) with the English sentence (i) from Kiparsky and Kiparsky 1970.

(i) *I do not realize that he has gone.

The unnaturalness of (i) arises from the fact that the speaker is negating what he is supposed to be presupposing (since *realize* is a factive verb).

14. Researchers such as Lavandera (1983) and Lunn (1989) have pointed out a correlation between the indicative mood and information regarded as relevant for the speaker. Although I will not discuss these analyses in detail, an analysis of mood based on the notion of relevance would probably also be compatible with the analysis presented here.

15. Szabolcsi and Zwarts (1990) suggest that *wh*-extractions might also be sensitive to the static/dynamic contrast.

References

Barwise, Jon. 1987. Noun Phrases, Generalized Quantifiers, and Anaphora. In Peter Gärdenfors, ed., *Generalized Quantifiers,* 1–29. Dordrecht: Reidel Publishing Company.

Bell, Anthony. 1980. Mood in Spanish: A Discussion of Some Recent Proposals. *Hispania* 63:377–90.

Bergen, John J. 1978. One Rule for the Spanish Subjunctive. *Hispania* 61:218–33.

Chierchia, Gennaro. 1992. Anaphora and Dynamic Binding. *Linguistics and Philosophy* 15:111–83.

Fauconnier, Gilles. 1985. *Mental Spaces: Aspects of Meaning Construction in Natural Language.* Cambridge, Mass.: MIT Press. Reprinted 1994, Cambridge: Cambridge University Press.

Groenendijk, Jeroen, and Martin Stokhof. 1991. Dynamic Predicate Logic. *Linguistics and Philosophy* 14:39–100.

Karttunen, Lauri. 1968. *What Do Referential Indices Refer To?* Bloomington, Ind.: Indiana University Linguistics Club.

Kay, Paul. 1992. The Inheritance of Presuppositions. *Linguistics and Philosophy* 15: 333–79.

Kiparsky, Paul, and Carol Kiparsky. 1970. Fact. In Danny Steinberg and Leon Jakobovits, eds., *Semantics: An Interdisciplinary Reader,* 345–69. Cambridge: Cambridge University Press. Originally published in M. Bierwisch and K. Heidolph, eds., *Progress in Linguistics* (The Hague: Mouton, 1970).

Lavandera, Beatriz. 1983. Shifting Moods in Spanish Discourse. In Flora Klein, eds., *Discourse Perspectives on Syntax,* 209–36. New York: Academic Press.

Lunn, Patricia. 1989. Spanish Mood and the Prototype of Assertability. *Linguistics* 27:687–702.

Mejías-Bikandi, Errapel. 1995. Presupposition Inheritance and Mood in Spanish. In Richard Barrutia, Thalia Dorwick, Peggy Hashemipour, Ricardo Maldonado Soto, and Margaret van Naerssen, eds., *Studies in Language Learning and Spanish Linguistics in Honor of Tracy D. Terrell,* 375–84. New York: McGraw-Hill.

Rivero, María Luisa. 1971. Mood and Presupposition in Spanish. *Foundations of Language* 7:197–229.

Schane, Sanford A. 1995. Illocutionary Verbs, Subject Responsibility, and Presupposition: The Indicative vs. the Subjunctive in Spanish. In Richard Barrutia, Thalia Dorwick, Peggy Hashemipour, Ricardo Maldonado Soto, and Margaret van Naerssen, eds., *Studies in Language Learning and Spanish Linguistics in Honor of Tracy D. Terrell,* 360–74. New York: McGraw-Hill.

Szabolsci, Anna, and Frans Zwarts. 1990. Semantic Properties of Composed Functions and the Distribution of Wh-Phrases. *Proceedings of the Seventh Amsterdam Colloquium,* ITLI.

Terrell, Tracy. 1976. Assertion and Presupposition in Spanish Complements. In Marta Luján and Fritz Hensey, eds., *Current Studies in Romance Linguistics,* 221–45. Washington, D.C.: Georgetown University Press.

Terrell, Tracy, and Joan Hooper. 1974. A Semantically Based Analysis of Mood in Spanish. *Hispania* 57:484–94.

Laura A. Michaelis

7 Cross-World Continuity and the Polysemy of Adverbial still

·
·
·
·

This paper focuses on the semantic structure of the English adverb *still*—in particular, on the interrelations among its temporal and nontemporal senses.[1] The nontemporal meanings to be investigated will be termed the adversative (or concessive) sense and the marginality sense. They are exemplified in (2) and (3), respectively. An example of the temporal usage is given in (1).

(1) Uncle Harry is still pruning the shrubs.

(2) We told Bill not to come, but he still showed up.

(3) Death Valley is still in California.

The meanings at issue can be described in broad terms as follows. The temporal sense refers to the extension of a state of affairs through to a given reference time (in (1), the present). The concessive sense, paraphraseable by *nevertheless,* indicates that a given event occurred despite the presence of conditions known to militate against it. Hence (2) portrays Bill's arrival as having transpired in the face of efforts to prevent it. The marginality sense, perhaps first noted by König (1977) for German *noch,* is used to locate an entity at the margin of a graded category. Thus in (3), Death Valley is presented as a marginal instance of California territory, where better exemplars of this (geographically defined) category are presumed to lie at points further removed from the eastern border of the state.

This repertoire of meanings, and its etiology, has been of interest to semanticists concerned with the manner in which temporally based lexical schemata sanction nontemporal meaning extensions of various kinds. König and Traugott (1982), for example, have investigated the development of the concessive use from the historically antecedent temporal use. They maintain, as will be noted below, that this development exemplifies the pragmatic strengthening of a quantity-based implicature associated with uses of temporal *still* (Traugott 1988). What is the relation between such historical developments and the links, if any, which connect these senses within the modern speaker's "dictionary entry"?

It has been presumed (e.g., by Traugott (1986)) that where a lexeme instantiates a synchronic polysemy network (in terms of Lakoff 1987), the structure of that network reflects the sequence of diachronic trajectories from which the modern array of senses arose. Thus, for example, the basic or central sense within a polysemy network is that sense from which extended meanings were derived historically. This situation occurs in, e.g., Sweetser's (1990) analysis of polysemous sensory vocabulary, and in her analysis of modal verbs. Sweetser argues convincingly that the motivation for certain diachronic sense extensions is revealed through an examination of meaning connections forged by modern speakers. In particular, she proposes that extant metaphorical mappings, which link conceptual domains, also licensed meaning shifts in which certain lexical items acquired readings referring to the metaphorical "target domain." Thus, e.g., an array of terms denoting vision come to refer to the domain of understanding (as Classical Greek *oida* 'I know' $<eid\bar{o}$ 'I see'). In such cases, the synchronic link between the senses of a polysemous vision term (e.g., *see*) closely resembles the evolutionary path (metaphorical extension) by which the secondary sense arose. Further evidence for the relationship between meaning change and synchronically valid inference is provided by Horn (1984), who notes the role of quantity implicature in lexical change (e.g., in the formation of autohyponyms).

Such studies demonstrate that one can profitably examine synchronic linguistic conceptual structure for clues about the mechanisms of meaning change. The present case study does not deny the validity of this approach. It does, however, question the tacit assumption that the interconnections among meanings of a polysemous lexical item recapitulate the evolutionary paths leading to those distinct senses. That is, one need not presume that an early meaning is a core sense, and that senses developing later in a lexeme's history are "extended senses." I argue that the temporal sense of *still* cannot plausibly be regarded as a central sense, nor can, e.g., the synchronic inference link between temporal and concessive *still* be equated with the path of historical development which yielded the latter. Historically, the sense extensions crystallized quantity-based implicatures associated with temporal *still*. These implicatures are present today, but, as will be seen, do not in themselves create a cohesive category of senses.

This situation, in which the historical links relating a repertoire of senses to a single proto-etymon are not transparent to modern speakers, has been examined by Lichtenberk (1991). According to Lichtenberk, instances of grammaticalization involving certain motion verbs in Oceanic can be regarded as examples of *heterosemy,* defined as follows: "In heterosemy, the semantic (as well as the formal) properties of the elements are too different to form a single conceptual category. Rather, the category has only a historical basis: what unites its members is their common ultimate source" (p. 480).

The theory of lexical meaning presumed by Lichtenberk is that of Lakoff (1987), in which polysemous lexical items constitute categories of (related) senses. The sense relations within such categories—e.g., metonymic links and image-schema transformations—are of a general nature: they represent widely applicable patterns of semantic extension. Thus, for example, prepositions coding paths can also, when coupled with a stative verb, code endpoints: the reading of *around* in *Harry ran around the corner* contrasts with that in *Harry lives around the corner* (Lakoff and Brugman 1986). As noted by Jackendoff (1983), the existence of "formal relations among apparently distinct readings of a polysemous word . . . would make it easier for the language learner to acquire one reading, given another" (p. 13).

Patterns of sense extension are not, however, necessarily reducible to lexical redundancy rules: as argued by Lehrer (1990), the construal rules which create extended readings are only partially productive within semantic classes. Thus, for example, perception verbs like *feel* license both experiencer and stimulus subjects, whereas such verbs as *see* (versus *look*) are not characterized by this polysemy. We might presume that word senses linked via locally productive redundancy rules are most effectively stored and retrieved when they are assimilated to a lexical category, i.e., a conventionalized network of senses (cf. Miller 1978). What can be the psychological status of a heterosemous lexical category, founded upon information of a sort available only to the historical linguist? Such a construct would not qualify as a linguistic generalization. If, however, we can assume that sense networks constitute useful generalizations, there is some reason to suppose that speakers will seek a plausible means of reconciling the disparate descendant readings of a given etymon. The impetus to reconcile such readings may be provided by the presence of suggestively similar use conditions.

The synchronic meaning links forged for this purpose will bear no direct relation to any trajectory of semantic change. In the present case, I argue, the modern speaker has reconciled the senses of *still* by extracting a set of accidental and yet salient semantic commonalities from these senses. The resultant generalization provides a schematic semantic structure under whose rubric all of the senses are grouped. The suggestion that there exist "lexical categories" whose structure parallels that of "referential categories" (Lakoff 1987) is consistent with the dictum that the organization of linguistic knowledge is on a par with that of other sorts of knowledge (Goldberg 1995). The inferencing process involved in the development of the sense network at issue is analogous to that involved in the adduction of conditions upon category membership from ostensive definition. The distinct senses of *still* have common discourse-pragmatic properties; each sense involves a particular form of expectation contravention. The shared use conditions provide the "pointers" to an underlying semantic unity among the usages of *still*.

The category rubric is devised as a means of capturing this semantic unity; it manifests scalar-semantic properties. As noted by König (1977), uses of *still* involve "man's ability to order . . . entities of various kinds [and] to rank them along a scale" (p. 173). Each of the senses, it will be claimed, partakes of and elaborates a general schema involving the maintenance of a given configuration across a sequence of scalar loci. The general schema has a modal component: it evokes an "expected outcome" in which the configuration in question is not so maintained, i.e., is not present at the scalar extreme serving as a reference point. The distinct senses will be said to owe their existence to the compatibility of the general schema with various scalar ontologies (temporal continuance among them). These ontologies accord with conceptual models of temporal extension, concession, and categorization.

It has often been claimed that scalar organization—and scale-based inference—must be invoked in describing the semantics of certain grammatical markers. Most recently, studies by Fillmore, Kay, and O'Connor (1988) and Kay (1990) have suggested that the adverbial elements *let alone* and *even*, respectively, should be analyzed as scalar operators. That is, these operators serve to relate propositions within a scalar model (a set of background assumptions shared by speaker and addressee). The present study provides an additional set of observations about scalar operators. In particular, this study suggests that such an operator may have broad applicability across scalar domains, where such domains are defined by continuance through time, graded category membership, and the relative likelihood of certain situation-outcome pairings. The general semantic structure of the operator constitutes the aforementioned semantic superstructure of *still;* these distinct domains of application yield its distinct senses.

This paper is organized in the following fashion: the next section provides a critical review of previous approaches to the semantics of temporal and concessive *still*—including that of König (1977), which I take as a point of departure. This section also establishes some of the basic properties of the two senses. In the third section I present an analysis of the three distinct senses. The fourth section discusses issues related to the diachronic development of these senses. In the final section I reconcile the senses, presenting the semantic superschema and relating it to Kay's (1989) class of contextual operators. I suggest that "continuance" or "persistence" is best defined for our purposes as an abstract scalar conceptualization, i.e., one that does not necessarily involve temporal extension.

Previous Analyses

Temporal still

According to Hirtle (1977), temporal *still* "expresses continuance of [a] state" (p. 39). While this definition certainly accords with our intuitions, most analysts have sought to provide a somewhat more precise definition of "continuance." Many have followed Horn (1970), in assigning to temporal *still* the function of relating two time phases, both of which are characterized by the presence of the same state of affairs. These phases have commonly been identified with presupposed and assertive components: according to Doherty (1973), Morrissey (1973), König (1977), König and Traugott (1982), and Abraham (1980), *still* (i) asserts that some state of affairs exists or existed at a reference time; and (ii) presupposes that this same state of affairs obtained for some period prior to that reference time. In a tense-logic account of *still*'s German analog, *noch,* Hoepelman and Rohrer (1981) represent this presupposition of prior instantiation by means of overlapping phases: where j is a reference time, *noch* $\emptyset$ *at j* is true if and only if j falls at the rightward boundary of an interval during which $\emptyset$ obtained. As shown in (4), this presupposition is preserved, as required, in polarity contexts. The entailment of (4a), that Bill was here for some period prior to the present moment, remains in a question (4b) and in a conditional protasis (4c).

(4) a. Bill is still here.
   b. Is Bill still here?
   c. If Bill is still here, we'll leave.

(Note that the standard negation test is not used here: the peculiarity of examples in which negation has wide scope over *still* is perhaps due to the presence of a suppletive counterpart, *anymore* (cf. Morrissey 1973).)

As noted by Traugott and Waterhouse (1969), the asserted and presupposed component states belong to a higher-order event whose aspectual class is imperfective. The *still*-bearing predicate then represents an imperfective process, in the sense of Langacker 1987. A process, according to Langacker, is a "relationship scanned sequentially during its evolution through conceived time" (p. 254). Imperfective processes—more commonly referred to as states—are those which do not involve a change over time, whose component relation-states are effectively identical to one another. By contrast, perfective processes (nonstative predicates) portray a dynamic situation, one construed as episodic in character. A grammatical ramification of the perfective/imperfective distinction is that, as noted by Langacker, at least in English, predicates of the former type do not occur in the simple present without a special interpretation (e.g., a habitual reading). As shown in (5), perfective predicates clash with the specifications imposed by temporal *still* (the reader is asked to ignore the acceptable concessive reading of *still*).

(5) a. Bill (*still) caught the cat.
   b. Bill (*still) recognized Harry.
   c. Bill (*still) jogged.

One can note that the class of perfective predicates subsumes both telic predicates (accomplishments and achievements, as shown in (5a) and (5b), respectively) and atelic predicates (activities, as shown in (5c)).

Presumably, the unacceptability of (5a) and (5b) can be explained within any of the aforementioned analyses simply by invoking a salient property of those predicates which Bennett and Partee (1978) have called *nonsubinterval verbs*. Such predicates (more commonly known as *telic verbs*) code "actions that involve a product, upshot, or outcome" (Mourelatos 1981:193); no subpart of that action counts as a valid instance of the whole event. Thus, e.g., the inception of Bill's cat-catching cannot be identified with the entire process. The instantaneous act of recognition simply has no extractable subcomponents. By contrast, a subpart of the action coded by the subinterval verb *jog* is clearly an instance of jogging. The telic/atelic distinction has a number of grammatical ramifications—as pointed out by Dahl (1981), Mourelatos (1981), and Vlach (1981)—and is subject to the following diagnostic: while, e.g., the past progressive version of (5c) entails the preterite (5c), (5a) and (5b) are not entailed by their respective progressive counterparts.

If it is the case that, as claimed by Horn and others, temporal *still* requires that a given state of affairs persist from the presupposed phase to the assertoric phase, then the anomaly of (5a) and (5b) can be said to arise from the nonsubinterval property: telic-verb scenarios do not possess the requisite identity among contiguous component states. In the case of accomplishments, each successive stage of the action is distinct; in the case of achievements, the coded event obtains *within* an interval—"at [an] isolated . . . instant . . . only" (Vlach 1981:277).

The property of continuing throughout an interval then appears to be unique to subinterval verbs. This property is required by temporal *still*—asserted and presupposed phases must represent identical situations. A problem is that, as noted, subinterval verbs such as *jog* also fail to co-occur with temporal *still*. This fact might cause us to sharpen up our definition of continuation. As far as temporal *still* is concerned, continuance of an activity of jogging (at least one coded by the nonprogressive) is not akin to continuance of the state of being here, etc. The distinction between the two types of subinterval verbs—states and activities—has been noted by Herweg (1991b) and Taylor (1977), among others. According to this analysis, the subinterval property of activity verbs can be said to arise from a "higher order" homogeneity, such that while individual moments within the running scenario are distinct, a given span of running is effectively identical to a contiguous span. (The homogeneity of activity predicates often seems to arise from their cyclicity: in the case of running, the stride involves successive leaping motions characterized by an alternating "trail leg"; the replication of this leaping motion gives the action an overall homogeneity.)

By contrast, the homogeneity of state predicates can be identified at a finer level of granularity. All individual subcomponents of a state are identical to one another. There is no level at which such subcomponents are distinct: if one samples the state of "being here" at two distinct instants, those two samples will appear identical. The homogeneity of state predicates is thus appropriately defined with respect to moments rather than intervals, the former being "the fundamental units of time series" according to Bach (1981: 66). This claim leads to the conclusion that temporal *still* serves to relate moments within the tenure of a state. While this conclusion appears correct, certain examples will require us to refine what is meant by "moment" or "instant." One such example is given in (6).

(6) A: How was Harry this month?
    B: He was still depressed.

In the reply of (6), the assertoric phase represents a time span (a month), while the presupposed phase is probably another such interval. I argue below that a "moment" is best defined as the primitive or minimal unit of a temporally based scalar model (a time line), rather than as a pregiven measure of time (cf. the discussion in the second section of a similar point made in Herweg 1991b). If *still* can be presumed to select from a time scale a point rather than a stretch of points within that scale, then one can account for the fact that temporal *still* appears incompatible with durational phrases over which it has scope (7a). This explanation is parallel to that used to explain the incompatibility of punctual adverbs (like *at 3:00 A.M.*) and durational adverbs, as in (7b).

(7) a. Harry was still asleep (*for two hours).
  b. Harry was asleep (*for two hours) at 3:00 A.M.

As noted by Herweg (1991a), durational adverbs like *for three hours* "fix the minimum amount of time the situation occupies" (p. 368); hence they entail downward with respect to the specified temporal boundary, but not upward. For example, if Harry was here for ten minutes, he was also here for nine minutes, etc. Thus, durational adverbs evoke a set of times at which a homogeneous predicate obtains. Given this feature of durational adverbs, we can explain the anomalous nature of (7b) in the following fashion: it is not coherent to simultaneously assert both that a state obtains at a single moment and that it obtains at a set of moments (irrespective of the reference time involved, which, as we will see, is the final moment of the interval in the case of a durationally bounded state).

It might, however, be difficult to base our account of (7a) on our account of (7b). Examples such as (7b) are problematic, for the following reason: punctual and durational adverbs invoke distinct reference times. While the punctual adverb maps to a reference time (3:00 A.M.) which is properly included within the state, the durational adverb invokes a reference time that is equated with the last moment of the coded interval (i.e., the cessation of the bounded state). The incoherence of (7b) might therefore arise from the fact that it is simply difficult to determine the appropriate time of evaluation for the sentence. (Use of the past perfect rather than the past tense in (7b) would remove this indeterminacy—by identifying 3:00 A.M. with the last moment of the two-hour interval—and render the sentence acceptable.) Thus, one can conclude that the anomaly of (7b) does not stem from an inherent incompatibility between punctual and durational adverbs, but merely from an indeterminacy as to the manner in which the "viewpoints" invoked by the two adverb types are to be reconciled.

Fortunately, there is another type of explanation for the incompatibility exhibited in (7a). Herweg (1991a) observes that states, unlike events, are not situational individuals; therefore, states cannot be counted. The interpretation of *Harry hated cats three times* requires that the count adverbial *three times* refer to occasions upon which the state obtained, rather than to hating "events" *per se* (cf. also Mourelatos 1981). Herweg notes, however, that certain grammatical constructs provide an "external criterion of individuation" (p. 371). The assignment of a duration to a state, for example, creates an individuated situation via the imposition of temporal boundaries upon that state. The state so bounded "loses" the subinterval property: no proper subpart of Harry's being asleep for two hours is a situation akin to the whole. The quantification of states is often said to be analogous to portion extraction in the spatial domain: a mass individuated via portion extraction becomes countable: *two cups of margarine* versus **two margarines*. By the same token, according to Herweg, count adverbials in sentences like *Harry was asleep for two hours three times* count "atomic eventualites" rather than associated occasions.

Given that quantized states are situational individuals, we can account for the clash in (7a) simply by likening this case to cases such as (5a) and (5b). In the latter cases, the failure of temporal *still* to co-occur with telic predicates was attributed to the nonsubinterval property of event predications. A proper part of being asleep for two hours is not an instance of being asleep for two hours; the internal heterogeneity of the quantized state does not allow for temporal extension (i.e., stasis over time). Such states therefore exclude temporal *still*.

One problem with an explanation of this sort is the following: the anomaly of (5a) and (5b) was said to stem from the fact that these events (like that coded by (5c)) lack the internal homogeneity necessary to provide *still* with two phases of like kind: two component parts of an eventive episode are not identical. In the case of (7a), however, one can readily evoke a prior phase in which Harry was asleep. The asserted phase is simply a bounded instance of this same state; the durational adverb would in this case be augmentative: *for **another** two hours*. The identical presupposed phase is not a subpart of the quantized state itself, but a distinct earlier phase of that state. Under this interpretation too, however, (7a) is anomalous. This anomaly can again be attributed to the individuated construal supplied by the durational adverb. With Partee (1984), I assume that a state properly subsumes its reference time; i.e., reference time typically provides an internal perspective on the state. Events, however, are subsumed by reference time; they afford only an external perspective. Quantized states, as events, lack a proper subpart at which the time of reference can be located. Such states then do not provide for the "sampling" of a component moment by *still*. A distinct, although compatible, explanation is the following: in the case at hand, the presupposed phase is a state, while the asserted phase is an event (a quantized state); the two phases thus lack the identity required by *still*. They are not situations of the same type.

An additional co-occurrence restriction, noted by both Hirtle (1977) and Hoepelman and Rohrer (1981), is this: temporal *still* does not welcome the perfect aspect. This restriction will be motivated via reference to a presupposition connected to *still*—that of expected or possible cessation. The restriction is exemplified in (8).

(8) a. **Harry has still been unwilling to go.*
   b. **Harry has still fed the cat.*

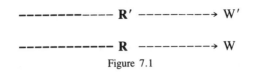

Figure 7.1

If we presume that *still* has wide scope with respect to the perfect operator, examples like (8) appear to undermine the validity of accounts in which the perfect is viewed as an operator that maps an event predication into a state predication denoting a result of that event (Herweg 1991a). The reference time at which this state obtains is established by the tense of the auxiliary head, the stative *have* (Klein 1992). Evidence for the stative nature of perfect predications is provided by facts of the following sort: perfects (i) accept the temporal adverb *now* (i.e., are evaluated for the present moment); and (ii) accept sentential adverbs like *already,* which otherwise scope only state propositions. If perfect-form sentences are state predications, however, why should they fail to accept temporal *still?*

One line of explanation is suggested by Parsons (1990). According to Parsons, the result state entailed by sentences like (8b) is merely that of the event's having culminated at some point prior to now. A more specific result (e.g., the presence of a fed cat) is contextually inferred; the result entailed by the resultative perfect per se is indeterminate (cf. Fenn 1987). Parsons argues that this state of aftermath "cannot cease holding at some later time" (p. 234). A view of this sort is assumed in the Hoepelman and Rohrer account of sentences like (8b). They assume, as do I, that temporal *still* evokes a "world of speaker's expectations" in which the state coded by the *still*-marked predicate has ceased at the evoked reference time (R). This expected cessation contrasts with the state's actual continuance to R. A diagrammatic representation of this situation is given in figure 7.1, adapted from Hoepelman and Rohrer, 1981.

In figure 7.1, the time line of speaker's expectations (W') contains a reference time analogous to that located on the time line of "speaker's reality" (W). A state of affairs (represented by the boldface segmented line) continues up to (and perhaps beyond) R in W. In W', this state of affairs has ceased at some point prior to R' (the counterpart of R in W'). Thus, under the Hoepelman and Rohrer account, *still* has two presuppositions: (i) the presupposition of prior instantiation of the state in W; and (ii) the presupposition of cessation at R' in W'. The latter presupposition is reflected in the intuition that a sentence containing temporal *still* is uttered only when there is some possibility that the state of affairs in question might have ceased at R.[2] Sentences such as (9) are odd.

(9) *Uncle Harry is still dead.

The oddity of (9) is explained by the fact that the speaker cannot (ordinarily) countenance a world W' in which Harry is resurrected at some point following his demise, as would be required by the schema in figure 7.1. Hoepelman and Rohrer argue that this schema also conflicts with the semantics of the resultative perfect. The resultative perfect denotes the occurrence of an event whose resultant state is eternally valid thereafter. With respect to the semantic contributions of *still* and the perfect operator, sentences like (8b) are self-contradictory. Because it is a resultative perfect, sentence (8b) asserts that the aftermath of the past cat-feeding event obtains at present (R). Because it contains *still*, (8b) presupposes that this state of aftermath obtains at some point prior to R. In addition, according to figure 7.1, the sentence presupposes that this state does not continue to R' in W'. However, the speaker who chooses to use the resultative perfect cannot be said to expect that the state of aftermath will have ceased at R. The presupposition of expected cessation at R conflicts with the assertion that the state of aftermath obtains at R.

This situation is complicated somewhat by the interaction of upper-bounding scalar operators with the perfect and wide-scope *still*. As noted by a reviewer, sentences such as (8b') are acceptable.

(8) b'. Harry has still only *fed* the cat.

In (8b'), the italics indicate a point of prosodic prominence denoting a narrow or contrastive focus. This focus is imposed by the scalar operator *only*, which scopes the perfect-form proposition *Harry has fed the cat*. Following McCawley (1987), we can view *only* as indicating that the proposition in which it appears denotes a less ''extreme'' situation with respect to a scale along which situations of a given type are ranked. The situations in this case relate to kindnesses that Harry might bestow upon the cat. This model presupposes that feeding of the cat is a lesser kindness than, say, grooming or entertaining the cat. *Only* imposes an upper bound upon the proposition *Harry has fed the cat*, relative to the scalar model at issue; Harry has performed the kindness specified but no greater kindness. If *only* were absent, the proposition would be upward compatible vis-à-vis the scalar model; it would in fact be entailed by any proposition occupying a more advanced point in the model (Harry has walked the cat, etc.). By removing the upward compatibility of the proposition, *only* creates a proposition which denotes a situation susceptible to change. That is, unlike (8b), (8b') does not denote a state that is eternally valid: the state which consists in the aftermath of a cat-feeding event will never change. By contrast, the state consisting in the aftermath of a cat-feeding event *simpliciter* (i.e., one unaugmented by any further cat-benefaction event) will change at all and any points following the occurrence of a further act of kindness.

The foregoing account of the incompatibility exhibited in (8b) has the advantage of generalizing to that exemplified in (10).

(10) *Uncle Harry is having gone.

As shown in (10), the perfect does not progressivize. This fact does not appear difficult to explain: auxiliary *have* is stative; since the progressive functions to derive a stative predication, stativization of an inherently stative predication is merely redundant (Langacker 1987, McCawley 1971, Vlach 1981). A number of authors have noted, however, that there are conditions under which states do progressivize. One commonly encounters progressive sentences like *Harry is liking your sister more and more.* Such examples are in fact used by Akmajian, Steele, and Wasow (1979) to refute the view that the prohibition against progressivization of the perfect has a semantic basis.

In order to maintain a semantically based account of the anomaly of (10), we must explain why progressives like (10) are unattested. As noted by Langacker (1991), this requires that one identify the conditions under which stative verbs can progressivize. According to Langacker, statives amenable to progressivization are those which denote an unstable state of affairs—one which is subject to imminent or incremental change. (Under the heading of imminent change, we include transition to a state of "failure to obtain," i.e., cessation.) If, as in our example, the degree of affection exhibited by Harry is increasing each day, then the situation is evolving toward a point of culmination. The progressive operator in some sense arrests the development of that situation toward its endpoint, capturing its "in progress" state. The impossibility of sentences like (10) is said to arise from the fact that the state of aftermath can never change—it can neither culminate nor cease. It is thus inherently nondynamic. Since the progressive operator, like temporal *still*, presupposes that the "input" situation is one susceptible to change, it is incompatible with the resultative perfect.

Given this mode of explanation, we preserve the assumption that the perfect, like the progressive, is a stativizing operator. The aspectual class of the perfect is then identical to that of its auxiliary head. Another type of explanation sees the perfect not as a stativizing operator but as a completive marker upon event predications. This type of explanation is offered by Hirtle (1977). According to Hirtle, there exists an effective equivalency between *still* and the temporal adverb *during.* In essence, this claim reflects the intuition, mentioned above, that reference time provides an internal perspective upon a state. Hirtle provides the following account of sentences like (8b): "one cannot reconcile the position of interiority expressed lexically by *still* with the position of posteriority expressed grammatically by the [perfect] aspect'' (p. 38). With respect to its "position of posteriority" vis-à-vis an event, the present perfect does not differ from the preterite; both present an event as having culminated at some time prior to speech time. In this respect, Hirtle's account of (8b) resembles that provided for the starred sentences in (5): temporal *still* does not accept perfective predicates, i.e., those which denote events that are fully instantiated upon reporting of their occurrence. The question now arises as to whether either account of (8b) extends to that perfect involving an imperfective complement—the continuative (8a).

The validity of Hirtle's account hinges upon the assumption that the continuative equates R with the time of cessation of the coded state. As noted by Morrissey (1973), however, continuative perfects are in general ambiguous as to whether or not R provides a "rightward boundary" upon that state. In sentences such as (11), continuation of the state beyond the reference time is a virtual certainty.

(11) Our dalmatian has been deaf since birth.

Hence, the continuative perfect does not evoke a posterior reference point in the sense that the state at issue ceases at or before R. Instead, according to Chafe (1970), sentences like (8a) and (11) evoke a construal in which "everything is understood to obtain at the time of reference, as in a nonperfective [= nonperfect] sentence, except that the beginning of the state . . . is pushed back to an earlier time" (p. 172). In other words, the continuative asserts the existence of a span of time stretching from the inception of the state to (at least) R. The left boundary of this span may be marked by a *since* adverbial (as in (11)), or the span itself may be denoted by a durational adverb (e.g., *for the last three years*). Like a durational, the continuative is downward entailing (with respect to the right boundary): if, in 1992, Harry has been in therapy since 1989, then he has also been in therapy since 1991, 1990, etc. Further, the continuative resembles a durational in that the state denoted by the complement verb is not upper bounded with respect to the right boundary: the state in question might continue beyond R. Finally, the continuative, like a durational adverb, represents a grammatical means of individuating a state. As noted by Herweg (1991a), "the occurrence of a phase of a state is an event" (p. 371). Our explanation for the anomaly of (7a) is then applicable to (8a) as well. Bounded states, as events, lack the subinterval property, and thereby reject temporal *still*. As in the case of (7a), the anomaly of (8a) persists even when an apparently identical prior phase is invoked. Sentences like the following are peculiar: ??*Harry had been unwilling to go until yesterday, in fact, since then he has still been unwilling to go.* Here again, the two phases are only superficially similar; as bounded states, each is a distinct episode.

Historical evidence indicates that the incompatibilty exhibited by (8a) was not always present: temporal *still* at one time served as a durational adverb akin to *constantly* or *continually* (Kemmer 1990). In this capacity, *still* co-occurred with the continuative perfect, the former being in the scope of the latter. Kemmer provides the following citation from 1704: ". . . his past reign, which *still* has been attended with one continu'd Series of Misfortunes.'' The diachronic meaning shift in which, according to Kemmer, temporal *still* changes from a frequency adverb to a temporal reference point yields a concomitant prohibition on its co-occurrence with the continuative perfect. States quantized by the continuative have an episodic construal, and hence cannot properly subsume this reference point. For this reason, (8a) is anomalous.

A difficulty with this line of explanation arises when one recalls that the aspectual character of the perfect, continuative or otherwise, is determined by that of the auxiliary head, not by that of the complement (the latter being a state phase in the case of the continuative). As the auxiliary head here is a straightforward state, why should there not be the possibility of a scoping in which the stative predication represented by the perfect auxiliary falls within the scope of *still?* One answer to this question is suggested by Mittwoch's (1988) analysis of the continuative. In providing truth conditions for the continuative, Mittwoch specifies (p. 218) that the reference time must be the final moment of an interval in which the particular state obtains. In this respect, the continuative perfect does provide a posterior reference point: reference time is equated with the cessation of one phase of the state, in much the same way that reference time is equated with the culmination (or endpoint) of an event. Here again, use of *still* is incompatible with the retrospective or external viewpoint invoked by the continuative perfect (and by event predications in general). Of course, as noted, the continuative perfect, like the resultative perfect, differs from a preterite-form event predication in that only the former is stative. Nevertheless, the state at issue is one which cannot be regarded as persisting from an earlier point. The state is the last moment of a phase; no earlier point within that phase is identical to this moment. The interaction of *still* and continuative is further constrained by the presupposition of possible cessation: the situation denoted by a continuative perfect is one in which a phase of a state has occurred. This phase cannot "cease" to exist once it has culminated. Therefore, a speaker cannot be said to evoke a possible world in which the phase has ended. Of course, this explanation is identical to that given for the anomaly produced by the interaction of *still* with a resultative perfect (8b).

It should be noted that the incompatibility of perfect and temporal *still* does not extend to negated perfects: such sentences as *You still haven't answered my question* are acceptable. Negated perfects are construable as continuative (i.e., universal): for all times within a present-inclusive range there is no event of question answering. These perfects are also construable as existential perfects bearing external negation (cf. Mittwoch 1988): it is not the case that there was an event of question answering with a present-inclusive range of times. The equivalence between existential and continuative understandings disappears when a downward entailing bounding durational is added: *He hasn't answered my question for twenty minutes* can only be continuative. As such, this sentence will reject temporal *still* for the reasons given above.

Negated perfects accept *still* on the externally negated existential reading only. Why should this be the case? Under (external) negation, the existential perfect simply denies the existence of some event within a specified range of times; the continuance asserted by *still* is not directly related to that event but is simply a continuance of this deniability. The interaction of *still* and negated existential perfect is constrained by the presupposition of possible cessation. The state of there not having been an event of a given kind must be a state capable of ceasing. The state of there having been no answer to a given question would cease were that question to be answered. Nonnegated existential-perfect sentences like **Harry has still been there three times* are, however, anomalous. Our explanation for this fact will closely resemble the explanation given for the oddity of (8b'). Numerals are downward entailing and, crucially, upward compatible (barring upper-bounding implicata). Therefore, any further accumulation of visits by Harry will not negate the truth of the proposition *Harry has visited three times*. This proposition will be entailed by, e.g., *Harry has visited fifteen times*. However, as noted with respect to the resultative and continuative perfect examples in (8), existential perfects containing an upper-bounding scalar adverb do accept *still*: *Harry has still **only** visited three times*. Here, the presence of *only* (like *at most*) removes the upward compatibility of the numeral expression. The numeral expression no longer denotes the ascending half line from three to infinity. Therefore, one can imagine the cessation of a state of there having been three visits; cessation of this state will occur when there is any additional visit. Hence, the possible-cessation presupposition of *still* is satisfied in such instances.

Given that the foregoing account has made reference to the notion of expected (or possible) cessation, we must ask the following question: is the oddity of (9) in fact due to presupposition failure? König (1977) has suggested that sentences like (9) simply flout a quantity implicature, owing to their lack of information value. It is useless to assert the continuance of a state where the situation could not be otherwise. In this respect, (9) does not differ from the corresponding sentence without *still,* when the latter sentence is not newsworthy. Quantity implicatures attach to assertions. For this reason, we would expect that nonassertive versions of (9) would be acceptable. This expectation is not confirmed. As shown in (12), (9) is not improved when it is cast as a yes/no question or conditional protasis.

(12) a. *Is Uncle Harry still dead?
      b. *If Uncle Harry is still dead, we'll be upset.

Because it is present in nonassertoric contexts, we will regard the constraint of expected cessation as a presupposition of temporal *still,* rather than a quantity implicature. As will be shown, the paired-scales schema which represents this presupposition (figure 7.1) also underlies the nontemporal senses of *still.*[3]

Concessive still

Most analysts concerned with temporal *still* have also focused upon its non-temporal descendant, the concessive or adversative sense. In this usage, according to Quirk et al. (1972), *still* expresses "the unexpected, surprising nature of what is said in view of what was said before that" (p. 164). For a number of these analysts (notably, Greenbaum (1969), Hirtle (1977), and König and Traugott (1982)) the use of the word *still* to express both temporal and concessive meanings provides evidence for a "strong relationship between 'continuation' and 'concessiveness'" (König and Traugott 1982:178). There is general agreement on the nature of this relationship: continuance of a given state of affairs is akin to persistence despite adversity whenever the context evokes a factor which would seem to militate against the continuance of this state of affairs. Thus, Hirtle (1977) remarks, ". . . [adversative] *still* characterizes the relationship as continuation in spite of an intervening element" (p. 42). König and Traugott (1982) maintain that "the assertion that '*q* continues' given another fact *p* gives rise to the generalized conversational implicature that this persistence is remarkable or unexpected and that therefore *p* and *q* do not normally go together" (p. 178).

Conventionalization of this implicature of expectation controversion is said to underlie the diachronic shift in which markers of temporal extension develop concessive meanings. This shift occurred by 1700 (Kemmer 1990). The adversative implicature, although calculable, might nevertheless be regarded as conventional. It resembles a "short-circuited" conversational implicature, in the sense of Morgan (1978). Since it is inferrable, the relationship between continuance and concession is synchronically transparent; persistence of a state despite adversity entails the continuance of that state. In examples such as (13), the two understandings are present simultaneously.

(13) I studied all night, and I still don't understand it.

Speakers would be hard pressed to resolve the ambiguity of (13) in favor of one or the other sense: the state of ignorance continues despite the intervention of an effort to end it. Temporal continuance is also involved in such adversative examples as (14).

(14) Yes, Harry beats his dog. Still, he's a nice guy.

In (14), a "true concessive" (see the section on transspatial persistence below), the validity of a claim is upheld despite the presence of an apparently reasonable counterargument. We might say here that the validity of the original assertion "persists" despite an effort to impugn it. The lexeme *still* might then be said to subsume both an implicature-free understanding and an understanding linked with König and Traugott's adversative implicature. This appears to be the analysis that König and Traugott (1982) have in mind when they say, "the original meaning . . . of . . . *still* account[s] for . . . the concessive use . . . of [this] particle" (p. 170).

A seemingly insurmountable difficulty for a polysemy analysis of this sort is, however, posed by sentences of the class exemplified in (15) and (16), for which we lack early citations.

(15) Even though he studied all night, Larry still failed the test.

(16) Even if you gave him a raise, Harry would still quit.

In (15) and (16), *still* is coupled with verbs denoting events, *fail* and *quit*. There is no possibility of regarding the event in question as having persisted despite hostile factors. We understand in such sentences that the event in question (Larry's failing the test, Harry's quitting his job) happened or would have happened despite the presence of circumstances which one would expect to preclude that event. In such sentences, *still* does not evoke the continuance of a state over time.

Although it is not clear what diachronic meaning shift yielded that variety of concessive *still* compatible with event predications, this usage is clearly not related to the temporal usage in the manner suggested by König and Traugott. These examples provide evidence against the claim that the temporal and adversative senses are synchronically related in a manner which mirrors their historical development.

Given such evidence, we might either (i) presume that the adversative sense is synchronically unrelated to the temporal sense, or (ii) propose that the senses are linked by another synchronically valid inference pattern, distinct from the adversative implicature. Alternative (ii) will be investigated here. Admittedly, this choice reflects a theoretical bias: a presumption in favor of lexical polysemy over homonymy, i.e., that speakers will forge sense relations where such generalizations are plausible. Aside from this, however, it would seem that the presence of examples like (13), in which the senses coexist, would induce speakers to view adversative and temporal understandings as closely related. As mentioned, this relationship appears to involve scalar semantic properties. The scalar nature of adversative *still,* and of concessive semantics in general, has been noted by König (1977) with respect to examples like (17).

(17) Even if Bill pays me $200, I'm still not going to do it.

According to König, *still* makes the following semantic contribution to (17): "*still* induces an ordering in which various favors (including sums of money) are bestowed upon the speaker by Bill. The situation described in the first clause is the 'advanced case'" (p. 195).

According to König, sentences containing adversative *still* can be translated into a logical formula in which *still* is in construction with a clause and an abstract. The abstract contains a conditional operator, as well as the conditional apodosis. The formula is given in (18).

(18) $<$still, p $<\lambda$x, $<$NOT $<$x $\to$ q $\ggg$

A rough paraphrase of (18) is as follows: "it is still the case that a given situation (here, p) does not entail another situation (q)." In other words, the state of affairs p is one of several situations which fail to bring about situation q. A translation of (17) via (18) is the following: "payment to me of $200 by Bill still will not have the result of causing me to do the task in question." The protasis is a scalar extreme; König (1977) notes that "*still* induces an ordering between the situation described and other comparable situations. None of these situations can bring about the situation described in the conse-quent, even though the situation denoted by p is an advanced case which could be expected to have this effect'' (p. 195).

Although this analysis captures certain important insights about adversative *still*, the formula of (18) appears to diverge too widely from the syntax to which it is mapped. The formula introduces a negative operator which does not necessarily have a surface realization. In (19), the apodosis is positive.

(19) They didn't offer him first aid, but he still survived.

The formula in (18) would require us to translate the assertion that the patient survived under adverse circumstances into a proposition of the following sort: the extreme case (lack of help) still failed to cause the eventuality of dying. A similar type of decomposition is necessary in (20).

(20) They tried to help him, but he still died.

König's logical representation would rework (20) into a proposition of the following sort: the extreme case (rendering of aid) still failed to cause the eventuality of survival. That is, living is failure to die, while dying is failure to survive! The presence of such circularity in our logical translations of concessive assertions is an undesirable result. An additional problem with König's analysis is that it does not give us any insight into the meaning that *still* contributes to concessive constructions. König notes that *still* is omissible in sentences like (17); from this fact, he concludes that *still* might not provide the interpretive framework (18) in concessive sentences. He does not consider the option that *still* reflects, rather than imposes, the concessive understanding. Further, König's analysis fails to account for the speaker's strong intuition that sentences such as (17), (19) and (20) code an event that violates expectation. He notes with respect to (17) that the situation expressed by the protasis would otherwise be expected to have an opposite effect (the speaker's doing the requested task). He does not, however, explicate the manner in which expectation contravention arises from concessive semantics—particularly, the scalar properties of this semantic structure.

While his treatment of the concessive sense is problematic, König's analysis does succeed in delineating unifying semantic features of the senses. He states that ''our analysis . . . shows that there is a close relationship between [the] interpretations of *noch* [''still''] . . . and thus accounts for the fact that they are associated with the same phonetic form. *Noch* [is] implicative under [all] interpretations. [All] interpretations involve the selection of certain entities, points in time, or entities of a different sort, as well as the introduction of an order relation for them'' (p. 187).

Of course, the temporal sense does not merely involve the ordering of "points in time," but also the disposition of some state of affairs across these time points. Further, the nature of the ordered "entities" remains to be explained; what are the scalar ontologies in question? It is the task of the present analysis to provide a clearer picture of the semantic commonalities observed by König.

The Senses

Temporal Extension

Temporal *still* can be regarded as a scopal operator (Kay 1990). Operators of this type express a relationship between two propositions; one of these propositions is represented by the assertion containing the operator. The assertion is termed the "scope" of the operator. Hence, in (21) the scope is *Grandma lives on the Lower East Side*.

(21) Grandma still lives on the Lower East Side.

Temporal *still,* as noted by König (1977), is thus implicative, in the sense of Karttunen 1971. The scope carries a tense specification; the tense has narrow scope with respect to *still* (*pace* König 1977). The tense can be represented as a two-place relation, "obtains at" (cf. Taylor 1977, in which the tense specifier is an additional argument of the main predicator of the proposition). The first argument of this relation is the scope. The second argument is a time point, which is identified with the reference time invoked by the tense operator. This reference time is the present in (21). As mentioned, I follow Partee (1984) in proposing that a state subsumes its reference time. As noted above, reference time provides an internal perspective upon the state. Events are characterized as having an opposite "direction of inclusion": events are contained within the reference time. This reference time is necessarily interpreted as an interval, capable of accommodating the dynamic profile of the perfective episode. The rightward boundary of the reference interval is equated with the event's point of culmination. Parsons (1990) uses a two-place operator, *Cul (e,t),* to indicate that an event culminates at a point, this point being properly included within the reference interval.

By distinguishing between events and states in this fashion, we account for the following intuition: an episode (event) is wholly instantiated within the reference interval; whereas a state obtains for an indefinite period. We can say that a state "overflows" the bounds of the reference time, insofar as an interpreter is free to imagine a larger interval, which encompasses the time for which the state is asserted, and for which that same state also obtains.

In arguing against this view, Herweg (1991a:384) provides examples like the following, in which reference time apparently exhausts the tenure of the state: *Yesterday, Harry was in London.* Here, the reference time, *yesterday,* is readily construed as subsuming the state. (A reading in which *yesterday* is subsumed by the state is perhaps dispreferred via quantity: if the speaker knows that Harry *lives* in London, why should she assert his presence there with respect to one day?) An answer to Herweg's objection is the following. Reichenbach-style theories of tense assume that the reference time is the time of adverbial reference. Klein (1992) has shown that this is not necessarily the case; he notes, for example, that a temporal adverbial accompanying the past perfect can refer to either event or reference time. Whereas we must retain the claim that all tenses have a reference time (whether or not distinct from event time), we need not assume that all temporal adverbs denote the reference time.

With respect to Herweg's counterexample, it is useful to follow Parsons (1990) in distinguishing between reference time and time-limiting adverbials. According to Parsons, "the same period of time that is constrained by the tense of the sentence may also be constrained by temporal modifiers" (p. 209). Parsons notes sentences like *Yesterday, Brutus stabbed Caesar,* in which the temporal adverb *yesterday* properly includes the temporal interval (i.e., the reference time) in which the stabbing event culminated. In Parsons's example, tense and temporal modifier interact in the same way that they do in the more felicitous reading of Herweg's example. The temporal modifier subsumes the reference time. There is nothing to prevent us from maintaining that the reference time itself is subsumed by the state.

However, given the requirement that reference time represent a proper subpart of the interval denoted by the time-limiting adverbial, one cannot account for the alternate reading of Herweg's example. In this reading, *yesterday* refers to the reference time; the reference time is again subsumed by the state of Harry's presence in London. The presence of this reading suggests that the reference time should be *improperly* included within the interval referred to by a temporal adverb. The possibility of coalescence between the two forms of time reference (tense and time adverb) does not detract from the claim that they are otherwise distinct; identity of the two is simply the limiting case of inclusion. The distinction between reference time and time-constraining adverbials allows us to preserve the assumption that the reference time of a state is properly included within that state. Thus, the state referred to by the proposition within the scope of *still* subsumes its reference time in all cases.

Still serves to relate the tensed state proposition within its scope to a presupposed proposition. The presupposed proposition is identical to the scoped proposition, except that the former represents the state of affairs as obtaining at some point prior to the reference time. As noted by König and Traugott (1982), sentences like (21) bear a presupposition of "prior instantiation": (21) presupposes that Grandma lived on the Lower East Side at some point prior to now. Note that the presupposed proposition need not bear a tense specification distinct from that of the asserted proposition. In (22), both asserted and presupposed propositions bear past tense; the presupposed interval is simply prior to the (implicitly specified) past reference time.

(22) Harry was still upset.

Following König and Traugott, among others, we can represent the propositions mediated by *still* in (22) as in (23).

(23) asserted: [[Harry be upset] obtains at' t]
     presupposed: [[Harry be upset] obtains at' t − 1]

The question arises as to whether times associated with the presupposed and asserted phases mediated by *still* are best described as moments or as intervals. With respect to the asserted phase, the question can be framed in the following manner: is the reference time situated within the state a point or a span of time? Earlier, we concluded that temporal *still* has a punctual character: it functions to "highlight" a component moment of an imperfective process (Langacker 1987). An apparent difficulty with this view arises when one considers sentences like (24).

(24) This week, Clinton is still the frontrunner.

The "moment" at which the scoped proposition obtains is a week-long interval. One need not, however, regard (24) as a counterexample to the claim that temporal *still* selects a "moment." As noted in the first section, we need not view a moment as a temporal unit of any particular length. Intuitively, a moment is a minute or so, and it seems odd to refer to a week as a moment. Equally intuitive, however, is the notion that every time line has a minimal unit of measure, and this unit may be small or large with respect to "absolute" measures of time. Herweg (1991b) makes a similar point, noting that it is futile to attempt to distinguish intervals from moments without considering the temporal units relevant to the cognizer: "Since on the conceptual level we deal with mental representations of time, we should rather say that viewing a period of time as pointlike means that its internal structure is cognitively neglected as a matter of the granularity of perspective

$$\ldots > \begin{bmatrix} R/ti \\ C \end{bmatrix} T_i > \begin{bmatrix} \begin{bmatrix} R/t_{i+1} \\ C \end{bmatrix} T_{i+1} \end{bmatrix} > \begin{bmatrix} R/t_{i+2} \\ C \end{bmatrix} T_{i+2} > \ldots$$

Figure 7.2

taken by the subject. Thus, we allow that one and the same temporal entity be represented as a pointlike or complex time depending on the situation" (p. 982).

In the context of this analysis, "situation" is to be construed as the particular time line invoked in the interpretation of the *still*-bearing sentence. A time line is a two-dimensional scalar model (Fillmore, Kay, and O'Connor 1988, Kay 1990) in which some situation (a component state of a process) is coupled with a point at which it obtains. Sentence (24) presupposes a time-line model for a presidential campaign. Its "primitive" is a week. The minimal unit of the time line evoked in (21) may be a year. Given this framework, we use the term "moment" to code any minimal unit of a time scale. A moment is, as usual, opposed to an interval—a grouping of moments. Under this view, *still* "selects" that portion of a state which obtains at a moment, rather than that which obtains at an interval.

While time lines often code a course of development, the time line at issue here codes persistence of a given state of affairs. The sequence of component states arrayed across the time line are identical to one another. An overall perception of stasis is evoked by the conjunction of two component moments of an imperfective process. It should be noted that this analysis explicates the semantics of temporal *still* at two levels. At one level, *still* is viewed as a scopal operator, which mediates between presupposed and asserted propositions. The two propositions code the same state of affairs. At another level, *still* is said to express persistence of a state of affairs across time; it highlights an "advanced" instance of that state, which obtains at reference time. It is at this second level that the scalar nature of temporal *still* emerges most clearly; *still* operates on a scalar model of persistence. The origin of this scale is equated with the inception of the state in question. A diagrammatic representation of the second type of explanation is provided by the scalar model shown in figure 7.2.

At first glance, this representation does not seem to qualify as a scalar model in the terms of Fillmore, Kay, and O'Connor (1988) and Kay (1990). In models presented by these authors, an "argument space" is represented as a set of coordinates, such that the resulting structure is a lattice. An argument space is a set of diads, each member of which is culled from a distinct ordered set or scale. The two distinct scales are the two dimensions of the model: values along one dimension are arrayed along the ordinate;

$$\underline{\quad\quad}Harry\ upset\ <\sim Harry\ upset\underline{\quad\quad}\longrightarrow W'$$
$$R'$$

$$\underline{\quad\quad}Harry\ upset\ <\ Harry\ upset\underline{\quad\quad}\longrightarrow W$$
$$R$$

Figure 7.3

values along another dimension are arrayed along the abscissa. In this analysis, scalar models, temporal and otherwise, will be "collapsed," with one dimension (e.g., states of affairs) superimposed upon the other (e.g., times). One reason for doing this is simply that readers are more accustomed to horizontal representations of time lines, in which some succession of developmental stages is arrayed along a time scale composed of ascending values arrayed from left to right. The use of this linear format for nontemporal scalar models as well will afford a clearer view of what is meant by "scalar continuity."

In figure 7.2., the semantic contribution of temporal *still* is schematized by a boxed component state within the imperfectivity scenario described by Langacker (1987). This component corresponds to the reference time—the point at which, in Langacker's terms, the conceptualizer situates herself. This representation does not show us the presuppositional properties of temporal *still:* the presupposition of prior instantation and of expected cessation at R. These are more clearly portrayed in a representation of (22) given in figure 7.3, analogous to figure 7.1.

In figure 7.3, as in figure 7.1, the paired time lines represent models of the speaker's expectation (W') and of reality as conceived of by the speaker (W). As shown, both "worlds" are defined by the presence of Harry's upset state prior to reference time (R). We can view the tenseless propositions in figure 7.3 as component states of the imperfective process schematized in figure 7.2. As shown, a component state of the process obtains at R in W. There is no component of that state at reference time in W'. Thus, figure 7.3 represents the digitization of figure 7.1: persistence is represented as the presence of two identical component states at contiguous scalar loci; cessation is represented by the lack of such a component state at the more advanced of these loci.

The two levels of representation—propositional and scalar—are compatible insofar as temporal *still* represents a scalar operator. Scalar operators, like *even* and *only* (Kay 1990, McCawley 1987), relate two propositions within a scalar model. In the case of *even,* according to Kay, the *even*-bearing assertion or text proposition (TP) unilaterally entails a contextually given proposition (CP). An example is given in (25).

(25) A: Did Harry come by? (CP)
　　　B: Yes. Even Fred showed up. (TP)

The reply in (25) evokes a scalar model in which invitees are ordered with respect to the likelihood of their arrival. Fred is regarded as less likely to come than Harry. His presence at the event then unilaterally entails Harry's presence. The semantic material shared by CP and TP can be represented as a propositional function: [x showed up]. The TP contains a focus: that constituent that contrasts with some constituent within the CP, and which is represented by a variable in the propositional function. The focus in this case is *Fred,* which accordingly receives prosodic prominence (cf. Lambrecht (1994) on the prosodic realization of narrow focus).

One difficulty with assimilating temporal *still* to the class of scalar operators is the following: while *still* mediates between propositions within a scalar model, it does not appear to select a focus within its "text proposition." No linguistic element within this proposition receives focus accent. Nevertheless, there is a contrastive element in the semantic representation: the time specification of the text proposition, which contrasts with that of the presupposed proposition. The time specification of the assertion has a higher value than the time specification of the presupposed proposition; the former is further removed from the origin of the time line. Thus, the semantic material shared by the asserted and presupposed propositions in (23) can be represented as a propositional function of the sort shown in (26).

(26) [[Harry is upset] obtains at$'$ x]

In (26), the variable ranges over time specifications. To summarize, then, temporal *still* evokes a two-dimensional scalar model, termed a time line. This time line matches some subpart of a state with the time point at which it obtains. In particular, temporal *still* requires a time line characterized by effective homogeneity of these subparts. This type of time line is identical to Langacker's imperfective process, in which a moment of conceived time is linked to a single relation state (trajector-landmark pairing). Temporal *still* "samples" from the imperfective process at reference time, licensing the inference that one or more components of this same process lie at points closer to the origin of the processual sequence in question. On the propositional level, temporal *still* relates two tensed propositions within a time-line model. The text proposition presupposes the context proposition (i.e., entails the CP in both assertive and nonassertive contexts).

Transspatial Persistence

Concessive *still,* as its name implies, is found in various concessive constructions. The term *concessive construction* is used here in a rather imprecise sense; it is not the case that each concessive type represents a unique form-meaning pairing. As observed by König (1986), diverse syntactic templates are drafted into service as concessives: conditionals, coordinate structures, and temporal clauses. The class of concessive constructs (although having such reliable formal concomitants as the factive subordinator *although*) is more readily definable in semantic and pragmatic terms. Such a definition will be provided in what follows. First, it is necessary to draw a functional distinction between "true concessives" and those concessives which might more accurately be referred to as "adversative constructions." As mentioned previously, concessives of the former type refer to the domain of argumentation. An example is given in the reply of (27).

(27) A: There are a lot of strange people around here.
    B: Even so, I'd still rather live in Berkeley than anywhere else.

In (27), speaker A provides a potential counterargument to the claim that Berkeley is a desirable habitat. While conceding the validity of this argument, speaker B asserts that the claim so impugned can nonetheless be upheld. Hence, the reply in (27) includes both a concession to the conversational opponent and a reassertion of the impeached claim. The concession is coded by *even so,* which is anaphoric to A's counterargument. The reassertion is coded by the main clause. The reply need not contain the concessive clause, in which case the concession is implicit in the reassertion.

This type of concessive can be juxtaposed to those exemplified in (28) and (29).

(28) Even though Harry apologized, Marge still left in a huff.

(29) Even if he lost twenty pounds, Harry would still fail the physical.

In (28), a factive concessive, Marge's leaving is asserted to have occurred despite an effort that might have obviated the event. In (29), a concessive conditional, it is asserted that Harry's weight loss would not prevent his failing the physical. These concessives do not refer to the domain of argumentation. Since they do not function to concede the validity of a counterargument, they are not concessives in the strict sense. The antecedent and conse-quent code real-world situations, which are understood to be antithetical to one another. The sentences presuppose that the situation described by the protasis ordinarily entails the lack of that situation coded by the apodosis.[4] In the terminology used here, the protasis establishes a world (whether actual or hypothetical) which is *adverse* to that situation or outcome coded by the apodosis.

As mentioned previously, there are certain concessives in which *still* ap-pears to have both temporal and adversative understandings. These are sen-tences in which the main predicator of the apodosis bears imperfective aspect. An example is given in (30).

(30) Mom has starved herself for a month, and she's still thirty pounds overweight.

In (30), a state of affairs—Mom's obesity—is said to obtain despite an effort to prevent its continuance. As mentioned, earlier approaches to conces-sive *still* have focused exclusively on sentences like (30), in which the conces-sive understanding of *still* is reducible to the temporal understanding plus a contextual implication that the state in question continues despite adversity. Such sentences are thus ambiguous in the manner described by Norvig (1988): temporal and adversative understandings of *still* are mutually compatible. The interpreter need not resolve this ambiguity in favor of one or the other reading.[5] Such ambiguity also characterizes true concessives like (27): the assertability of an earlier claim endures despite an intervening counterar-gument.

There is evidence, however, that the imperfective concessive *still* is not equivalent to the temporal usage couple: it does not accept bounding dura-tional adverbs, nor does it welcome the continuative perfect. These co-occurrence restrictions were attributed (in part) to the fact that the variety of temporal extension evoked by temporal *still* is defined with respect to a homogeneous predicate. As shown in (31) and (32), however, concessive *still* accepts both individuating operators.

(31) She hated the noise, but she still lived there for several months.

(32) The political climate has improved, but times have still been difficult in Dubrovnik.

In addition, as already noted, concessive *still* accepts inherently perfective predicates, while temporal *still* does not. An example of the former situation is given in, e.g., (28): *still* is coupled with *leave,* an achievement verb. These grammatical differences can be attributed to the distinct scalar ontologies evoked by concessive and temporal *still.* While temporal *still* codes the continuation of an imperfective process from one moment to the next, concessive *still* codes the persistence of an outcome (or state of affairs) from one set of circumstances to another. Sentence (29), for example, asserts that the outcome of Harry's failing the physical will obtain whether Harry is twenty pounds overweight (as he is now) or whether he sheds this weight (at some future point). Temporal *still* takes an internal perspective on a state: it "samples" a component of this state at an advanced time point. By contrast, concessive *still* views the event or state in its entirety—as an episode or situation that obtains under specific (unfavorable) conditions. A state so viewed may represent an individuated situation, and hence that state may be described via the continuative perfect, as in (32), or bounded by a durational adverb, as in (31).

Adversative *still,* like temporal *still,* represents a scopal operator: it serves to relate the assertion within its scope to a presupposed proposition. Following Kay (1990), we may refer to the former as the text proposition (TP) and the latter as the context proposition (CP). The scope of *still* (the TP) is the entire concessive sentence, excluding the scopal operators *even* and *still.* In sentence (28), for example, the scope is (33).

(33) If Harry loses twenty pounds (i.e., is slightly overweight), he'll fail the physical.

In (33), Harry's failure is asserted with respect to a hypothetical space (Fauconnier 1985) in which weight loss has occurred. The TP presupposes a CP of conditional form, in which Harry's failure is established with respect to another mental space. Let us assume that the CP of (33) is (34).

(34) If Harry is obese, he'll fail the physical.

In (34), the world of the CP happens to correspond to the speaker's reality space: Harry is in fact overweight. (This situation differs from that of factive concessives, to be discussed below.) The semantic material shared by CP and TP can be represented by the propositional function in (35).

(35) Under x circumstances, Harry will fail the physical.

In (35), the variable ranges over worlds in which the outcome coded by the apodosis obtains. Thus, the focus of the TP is its protasis. The TP estab-

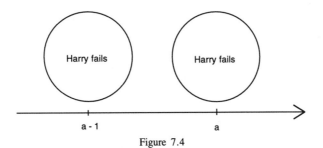

Figure 7.4

lishes a world that is less favorable (or, equivalently, more hostile) to Harry's failing the physical than is the world of the CP. As I note below, the CP expresses a cause-and-effect scenario that is more consonant with general background assumptions.

The CP and TP are related within a two-dimensional scalar model that matches events with the circumstances under which they transpire. Within this model, worlds are arrayed with respect to the degree to which they favor the outcome in question; the least adverse (or most favorable) world is nearest the origin. This is the world of the CP. In the case of (29), this is the world in which Harry is grossly overweight. Failure of the physical is accordingly assured. The world of the TP is located at a more extreme point on this "adversity scale." This is the world in which Harry is only somewhat corpulent. The outcome at issue, Harry's failure of the physical, obtains in both of these worlds. A diagrammatic representation of this model (in which the two dimensions are "collapsed") is shown in figure 7.4.

In figure 7.4, the world of the CP is given the value a − 1; it is less adverse to failure than the world of the TP (a). This model licenses an inference: if Harry's failure transpires under circumstances unfavorable to failure (lack of obesity), then it will also transpire under circumstances that are favorable to failure (obesity). That is, the TP unilaterally entails the CP. In Kay's terms, the TP is more *informative* than the CP. Kay's definition of informativeness allows us to account for the close association of *even* with *still,* and with concessive semantics in general: *even* typically introduces the protases of both factive and conditional concessives (hence the subordinators *even if* and *even though*). According to Kay, *even* "indicates that the sentence . . . in which it occurs expresses, in context, a proposition which is more informative (equivalently "stronger") than some particular distinct proposition taken to be already present in the context" (p. 66).

Thus, for example, the sentence *Even some thin people have high cholesterol* can be taken as unilaterally entailing a less informative CP, *Overweight people have high cholesterol.* The semantic material shared by CP and TP here can be represented as an open proposition: "x type of people have high cholesterol." The focus of the TP, thin people, ranks higher on the relevant dimension of the model (say, persons ranked with respect to their immunity to disease) than does the equivalent argument of the CP, overweight people. Therefore, the proposition resulting from integration of focal argument and propositional function ranks higher (i.e., unidirectionally entails) the CP within the relevant scalar model.

In the concessive sentence (29), the relationship between CP and TP that is mediated by *still* is identical to that which is mediated by *even* in this sentence. The semantic material shared by CP and TP is in both cases represented by the propositional function (35). The focus of both operators is the protasis of the TP. As noted by Kay, the syntactic position of *even* commonly reflects its focus (cf. (25)). Thus, in concessives like (29), *even* is placed before the protasis. Note, however, that *even* and adversative *still* cannot be said to be synonymous. While *even* can be used wherever the requisite scalar entailment is present, adversative *still* must relate propositions relativizable to a scalar model of the sort represented in figure 7.4. Within this model, *still* codes the continuity of an outcome across worlds; *even* simply flags the entailment relation that is licensed by this model.

This model is not uniquely associated with *still,* but is linked to concessive semantics in general. *Still* is simply sympathetic to concessive semantics. For this reason, we find that, as König notes, *still* is redundant in hypotactic concessives of the sort exemplified in (28) and (29). In addition, it need not appear in paratactic concessives containing the connective *but,* as in (36).

(36) The interview went well, but he (still) didn't get hired.

These syntactic templates are clearly devoted to the expression of concessive semantics. As König (1986) observes, however, biclausal templates of a less specialized function can also serve as concessives (coordinate structures, temporal-clause constructions, etc.). In such instances, the concessive understanding can arise from the presence of adversative *still* alone. The concessive interpretation of coordinate structures like (37) can be attributed to the presence of *still.*

(37) Harry came and Marge still left.

A concessive reading of (37) would also be licensed by the presence of *nevertheless* or *yet* in the second conjunct. These particles may be said to function in a manner similar to *still,* with the latter sharing some temporal uses (König and Traugott 1982).[6] Because adversative *still* —among other adverbial elements—mirrors the semantics of concession, concessive constructions operate in tandem with *still*. As noted, however, either can evoke the requisite semantic structure without the other.

Our account of this semantic structure requires some refinement. We have established that concessives require the presence of identical outcomes in two worlds or mental spaces. In the case of concessive conditionals, the "adverse world" is equated with Fauconnier's hypothetical space H. This mental space is established by conditionals whether or not they are characterizable as concessives. The world of the CP is akin to the world of speaker's reality (R). By the same token, the requisite pairing of mental spaces is evoked by sentences containing an instance of *still* that is interpretable as both temporal and concessive. In sentences such as (30), the world favoring obesity (in which Mom is not dieting) is established by the presupposition of prior instantiation. This world is the (past) time space described by Fauconnier (1985).

In the case of factive concessives like (28), the adverse world of the TP is identified with R. We might say that the factive concessive induces the conceptualizer to compare this world with an alternative reality, which is defined by the lack of those hostile conditions which define R. In this case, then, the world of the CP is equated with a hypothetical mental space. In interpreting (28), we bring to bear our conception of a (more prototypical) alternate reality in which the failure to profer an apology leads to the outcome in question.

This analysis leads us to speculate about the ontological status of the concessive CP. In general, the CP, as described by Kay, is construed as being "in the context" at the time at which the TP is uttered. As Kay points out, however, the CP need not represent a conversational contribution per se. In such cases, the CP often represents general background knowledge, which can be presumed to be accessible to the hearer and which is exploited by the concessive assertion. In the present case, the CP is cast in the form of an implicational statement. Sentence (28) might be uttered in a situation in which the addressee has explicitly committed herself to the conditional proposition in (38).

(38) If Harry failed to apologize, Marge left in a huff.

The concessive (28) need not, however, rely upon the presence of a CP having precisely this form. The CP need not involve these particular participants. It need not have been asserted at all. Under such circumstances, the CP is a theoretical construct; it simply codifies the conversants' shared understanding of the conditions which favor the outcome at issue. This maximally general CP can be stated as in (39).

(39) If someone fails to apologize, the offended party will storm away.

This general conception of the CP provides some difficulty for accounts which use a Gricean mechanism to account for the association of concessives (and concessive *still*) with the violation of an expectation. One such account is Fauconnier 1985. Fauconnier (following de Cornulier) notes that conditional sentences are upper-bounded via quantity implicature, such that sentences like (39) yield the implicatum in (40).

(40) Only if someone fails to apologize will the offended party storm away.

This implicatum can be restated in scalar-semantic terms: the world coded by the protasis is the most hostile (or least favorable) in which the eventuality coded by the apodosis will obtain. The conditional (40) will generate the inference in (41).

(41) If someone apologizes, then the offended party will be mollified.

It is precisely this type of inference that, as Fauconnier points out, is contravened by concessives like (28). Thus, the concessive TP must by definition contravene an upper-bounding implicature associated with its CP. Given this fact, we have a ready explanation of the association of concessives with expectation contravention. This account, however, relies upon the assumption that the conditional CP is a conversational contribution. Upper-bounding implicature arises from the assumption that any given assertion is maximally informative. We cannot presume that this implicature attaches to a conditional sentence which has not been uttered in the relevant discourse. For this reason, we must assume that an inference like (41), which relates to an expected outcome, does not necessarily arise from upper-bounding implicature. We might assume instead that this sort of inference represents a presupposition of adversative *still* (and concessives in general).

This presupposition is the concessive analog of the presupposition of expected cessation (discussed with respect to the temporal sense). It can be described as follows: the outcome in question will not typically obtain in the world of the TP. With respect to (29), represented in figure 7.4, this presupposition is the following: if Harry is not grossly overweight (i.e., if

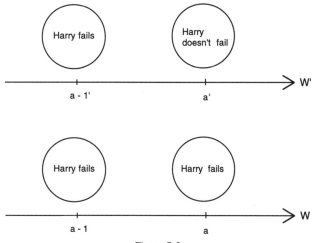

Figure 7.5

he loses the twenty pounds), he will not fail the physical. This presupposition is represented in figure 7.5, a modified version of figure 7.4.

In figure 7.5, the upper adversity scale (W') represents the general expectation that the world of the CP (in which Harry is obese) represents an adversity threshold: no world more adverse to the failure outcome will support that outcome. As shown, a lighter Harry does not fail the physical in the world of the TP (a') within W'. In W, by contrast, failure does occur in a world which disfavors it (a). While there is a persistence of outcomes across worlds a − 1 and a in W, there is no such persistence in W'. The contrast in threshold values on the two adversity scales W' and W is responsible for the flavor of expectation contravention associated with both concessive constructions and adversative *still*.

Marginality within Scalar Regions

As noted by König (1977), sentences like those in (3) and (42) "do not establish a relation between various points in time . . . but between various entities comparable" to one another (p. 184).

(42) a. Compact cars are still fairly safe; subcompacts start to get dangerous.
b. Disturbing the peace is still an infraction; malicious mischief is a misdemeanor.

According to König's analysis, such sentences presuppose that the entity in question represents a "borderline case" of the category defined by the

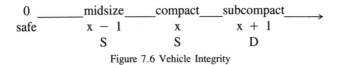

Figure 7.6 Vehicle Integrity

descriptor. Thus, for example, (42a) presupposes that compact cars are located at the periphery of the graded category of safe vehicles. At the same time, (42a) asserts that compacts nonetheless fall within the "safe region" of a general scale upon which cars are ranked with respect to the accident protection afforded their occupants.

Sentences like those in (42) again access a two-dimensional scalar model, analogous to the time line and adversity scale discussed with respect to the temporal and concessive senses of *still*. This scale ranks entities in accordance with the degree to which they manifest a given property; an entity manifesting the property to a high degree will be placed at an advanced point, i.e., at some distance from the origin. The scale also contains a threshold, such that those entities above this threshold and those at or below the threshold are partitioned into distinct "regions." In König's terms, the scale is "divided up by two (or more) predications" (p. 184). In the case of (42a), cars are ranked with respect to their increasing lack of structural integrity. This scale is partitioned into "safe" and "dangerous" regions. Entities arrayed between the origin and transition point lie within the "safe region" of that scale. The entity described in (42) is "located" at or very near the transition point for the scale. A diagrammatic representation of the scale evoked by (42a) is shown in figure 7.6.

In figure 7.6, the scalar loci at which entities are placed are represented by numerical values ($x - 1$, etc.). The subscript beneath these values indicates the region within which the ranked entities fall. Thus, both midsize cars and compacts are in the safe region (S), while subcompacts fall within the dangerous region (D). Marginality *still* selects an entity at the periphery of the safety region, the class of compact cars. It presupposes that there are entities ranked closer to the origin of the scale; these entities are better exemplars of vehicle integrity.

Like the other senses, marginality *still* can be regarded as a scalar operator. The asserted and presupposed propositions related by *still* in (42a) are given in (43).

(43) asserted: Compacts are safe.
    presupposed: Midsize cars are safe, etc.

That is, (42a) presupposes that there is at least one other class of vehicles that can be described as safe. As in the case of adversative *still,* the asserted proposition unilaterally entails the presupposed proposition within the scalar model. Within the model represented in figure 7.6, the proposition that compacts are safe unilaterally entails that midsize cars are safe. The semantic material shared by the asserted and presupposed propositions in (43) can be represented as a propositional function, as in (44).

(44) x is safe.

This propositional function differs from those which have been adduced in the analyses of temporal and adversative *still.* In (44), the variable occupies an argument place, rather than an adjunct position (cf. (26) and (35)). This difference can be attributed to the distinct properties of the scalar models evoked by temporal and adversative *still,* on the one hand, and marginality *still,* on the other. In the former case, homogeneous situations are matched with corresponding scalar loci—points in time or worlds. The succession of moments or of worlds represents an autonomous ordered sequence. (Thus, for example, the passage of time exists independently of the situations which obtain at any given moment.) In the latter case, entities (rather than situations) are ranked with respect to one another. These entities derive their homogeneity from a shared property. The property scale involved (auto safety, etc.) does not exist independently of the entities ranked within it (although we may assign a numerical value to a given position in this ranking).

In all cases, however, the focus of the asserted proposition creates a proposition which ranks higher than a presupposed proposition within the scalar model at issue. In the case of the temporal and adversative senses, "advancement" within the scalar model occurs via replacement of a less advanced scalar locus (time point or world) by a more advanced locus within the appropriate propositional function. That is, in these cases the divergence between presupposed and asserted propositions arises from the fact that these propositions (i) bear distinct time specifications or (ii) establish distinct mental spaces. In the case of the marginality sense, the divergence between asserted and presupposed propositions arises simply via substitution of one entity for a higher-ranked entity within the same scalar region. Such substitution allows the requisite "advancement" along the relevant scale, while preserving the overall homogeneity provided by the entities' shared membership in a given scalar region.

Thus, the nature of the propositional function is determined by the scalar ontology evoked by an assertion involving *still.* The homogeneous contiguous elements can be situations or entities. Analogously, the invariant portion of the open proposition may be either a full clause (an adjunct is supplied by the focus) or a predicate (an argument is supplied by the focus). That is, addition of the focus may either derive a proposition from a proposition or derive a proposition from a predicate. König captures this distinction by assigning the marginality sense the categorial index $<0, 1, <0, 1\gg$: the proposition is derived via addition of a name to a propositional function. Note that König does not regard *still* as a scopal operator; his account does not invoke a relation between asserted and presupposed propositions. Hence, the categorical index amalgamates the focus of the asserted proposition and the propositional function which that focal element completes. Categorical indices for the other two senses derive a proposition from a complex or simple proposition. (Thus, the concessive sense has the category index $<0, <0, 0\gg$, while the temporal sense has the index $<0, 0>$.)

This distinction has a grammatical ramification. As noted by König, marginality *still* does not function as a sentence adverb. It cannot be placed in pre- or postclausal position. In this respect, its syntax differs from that of temporal and concessive *still*. These differences are shown in (45), (46), and (47).

(45)   Good. Harry is here still. (temporal)

(46)   I apologized, and still she left in a huff. (concessive)

(47)   *Still, Death Valley is in California. (marginality)

Although *still* always mediates between full propositions *semantically*, it has syntactic sentential scope only when the requisite identity between scalar elements is an identity between states of affairs, rather than an identity between entities. Only in the former case are the compared scalar elements mapped directly to propositions. In the latter case, the compared elements are mapped to arguments, and the continuation asserted by *still* is not akin to the continued instantiation of a proposition.

It should be noted that the argument variable in open propositions like (44) need not fill the subject position. Strictly speaking, therefore, the invariant portion is not a predicate. König has discussed such examples as (48).

(48) I can still beat PAUL. Peter is too good for me.

Sentence (48) presupposes a proposition with which it which shares some semantic material. This shared material can be represented as the propositional function in (49).

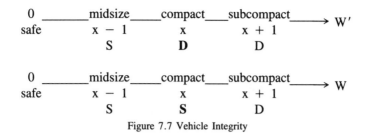

Figure 7.7 Vehicle Integrity

(49) I can beat x.

Sentence (49) evokes a property scale upon which players are ranked according to their skills. This scale is divided into two regions: those players whom the speaker can beat, and those whom she cannot. Sentence (48) asserts that Paul is a borderline case with respect to the former region; it presupposes that there are players whom the speaker can more readily defeat.

As it stands, this analysis has not accounted for a prominent use condition upon assertions involving marginality *still:* assertions like those in (3) and (42) are most felicitously uttered when there is reason to doubt that the descriptor in question is applicable to the entity under discussion. Sentence (42b), for example, is most appropriately directed toward an addressee who has expressed the belief that disturbing the peace is a misdemeanor, i.e., is more serious than an infraction. This sentence would not typically be used to enumerate various offenses and legal sanctions to an apparently uncommitted listener. Marginality *still,* like the other senses, expresses expectation contravention. This property can be represented as a presupposition, again using parallel scales. A representation of this presupposition is given in figure 7.7 for sentence (42a).

In figure 7.7, the model W' within the speaker's expectations places the class of compact cars beyond the threshold for safety, and within the "danger region." The model W contrasts with W': the class of compact cars lies within the safety region. Here, as in the earlier cases, persistence of a property (as against a situation) across two contiguous scalar loci contrasts with an expected transition at the more advanced of these loci.

One can note that particular scalar regions, like the scales themselves, do not exist independently of the entities ordered within them. The point of transition to a contiguous scalar region will be identified with the point at which one situates the lowest-ranking entity (vis-à-vis the scale as a whole) that can be characterized as possessing the property defining that region. Locating this entity within the scalar region entails that all higher-ranking entities will also be located within that scalar region. The ''dangerous'' regions within W and W' have distinct sets of members; this difference arises from the fact that compacts qualify as dangerous vehicles in W', but not in W.

Diachronic Issues

One of the major claims of this study is that the network of senses associated with the lexeme *still* can be examined without reference to the diachronic sense extensions through which those senses arose. It is nonetheless useful to examine the limitations of a diachronic account based solely on pragmatic strengthening (Traugott 1988). We noted earlier that according to König and Traugott (1982), a quantity implicature—or rather its conventionalization—was responsible for the development of the adversative sense. The speaker asserts both continuance of a state of affairs and the existence of factors which might militate against this continuance. Quantity-based considerations dictate that the conjunction of these two assertions have some informational value. In such contexts, continuance comes to implicate continuance despite adversity. It was argued earlier, however, that this ''adversative implicatum'' cannot be said to attach to concessive assertions involving perfective predicates. Thus, the development of a concessive sense compatible with perfective predicates cannot be attributed to this implicature. Instead, semantic broadening may be responsible: the concept of existence despite adversity comes to subsume the existence (under unfavorable circumstances) of two types of eventualities—states and events. In the latter case, *still* evokes occurrence rather than persistence despite hostile circumstances. This broadening cannot, however, account for the emergence of the marginality sense, which does not evoke the domain of eventualities.

The existence of the marginality sense is also inexplicable given a diachronic account involving pragmatic strengthening alone. This sense does conventionalize a quantity implicature as the presupposition of expected transition: the speaker's assertion that an entity bears some scalar property is informative only insofar as the entity's location within the relevant scalar region, as against a contiguous region, is subject to debate. The equivocal nature of the entity's membership within a subregion of a property scale arises from its being situated at or near a transition point within that scale. That is, the presupposition of expected cessation is readily translated into the presupposition of an expected transition from one scalar ''region'' to another.

Nonetheless, the transition at issue is not situated within the temporal domain. The scale is here a graded category within which entities are ranked (and relegated to subclasses) according to the degree to which they manifest a given property. A certain degree of that property, rather than a time point, represents the threshold at which the transition occurs. There is evidence, however, that a semantic extension of the type represented by the marginality sense can arise from a temporal understanding. An example of such a meaning shift is provided by nontemporal scalar uses of inchoatives. Sentence (42a), repeated here for convenience, contains an example of such an extension:

(42) a. Compact cars are still fairly safe; subcompacts start to get dangerous.

In the second clause of (42a), the inchoative *start to get* is not used to assert that subcompacts as a class are becoming increasingly dangerous these days. Instead, the inchoative is used to assert that subcompacts as a class can be located at the point of origin of a scalar region containing dangerous vehicles. This scalar region is properly included within the vehicle-integrity scale shown in figure 7.7. Sentences like (42a) presuppose that more dangerous vehicles (less structurally sound subcompacts) are located at points beyond this transition point, i.e., further removed from the origin of the vehicle-integrity scale. Note that this use of the inchoative is not an instance of abstract motion, as defined by Langacker (1987). Langacker has noted examples like (50), in which a motion verb is predicated of a static entity.

(50) Frontage Road runs along Interstate 80.

Here, according to Langacker, a motion predicate is called for, owing to the fact that the conceptualizer is in essence "tracing" the static configuration. In so doing, she notes the manner in which the configuration present at one spatial point differs from that located at a previous point. In the case of (42a), however, motion does not define the conceptual domain which gave rise to the atemporal meaning extension. In this case, the semantic extension consists in (i) "replacing" time points with rankings (degrees) along a property scale; and (ii) defining a transition over like entities located at contiguous scalar loci rather than over subepisodes of a state at contiguous "moments."

It should be noted, however, that abstract-motion predicates and nontemporal inchoactives share a particular aspectual property: in these usages, a perfective predicate can occur in the simple present without a special interpretation (e.g., habitual). Ordinarily, these predicates cannot be used in the simple present to report events ongoing at speech time, as in (42').

(42') *Harry starts to get forgetful.

(50') *Look! Harry runs past the house.

$$\underline{\quad\quad}\text{It's light} < \text{It's light} < \text{It's dark}\underline{\quad\quad} \longrightarrow \text{W}'$$
$$\mathbf{R}'$$

$$\underline{\quad\quad}\text{It's light} < \text{It's dark} < \text{It's dark}\underline{\quad\quad} \longrightarrow \text{W}$$
$$\mathbf{R}$$

Figure 7.8

Aspectually, both abstract-motion predicates and nontemporal inchoatives qualify as states.

Another nontemporal inchoative is the marginality usage of *already*, noted by König with respect to German *schon*. As argued in Michaelis 1992, temporal *already* represents a pragmatically ambiguous marker of temporal priority. It asserts the existence of a state prior to a reference interval containing a state of a like type. One usage of *already* codes anteriority of a state with respect to an expected point of eventuation, as in (51).

(51) Only five o'clock and it's already dark out.

In this usage, *already* resembles temporal *still:* the time line in W is paralleled in W' by a time line of speaker's expectations. Each adverb requires that the proposition within its scope obtain at the reference time specified by the tense; each presupposes the lack of the state in question at reference time in W'. In the case of *already*, however, lack of the state in question is presupposed for all times prior to reference time in W and W'. Further, in W', the state obtains at some more distant point in the course of development at issue. A representation of (51) is given in figure 7.8 (again following Hoepelman and Rohrer 1981).

In this usage of *already*, what is at issue is not merely a sequence of phases of a given state, but a transition from one state to another. The transition that has occurred at reference time in W is premature with respect to a canonical course of development, represented as the time line within W'. In its nontemporal usage, *already* is the counterpart of marginality *still*. An example of the temporal usage is given in (52).

(52) Compacts are already safe.

Here, as in (42a), a scale of vehicle integrity is invoked. In this case, however, the orientation or direction of the scale is different:[7] the most dangerous cars are nearest the origin. As in (42a), what is asserted is that compact cars are safe. Here, however, the "safe region" does not include the origin of the scale. What is presupposed is that cars safer than compacts

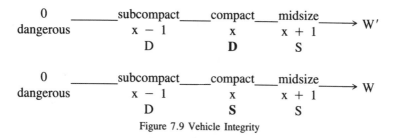

Figure 7.9 Vehicle Integrity

(e.g., midsize cars) are located at points further removed from the origin within the region at issue. *Already* here also presupposes a world of speaker's expectations in which compacts do not qualify as safe, but larger cars do. The model, given in figure 7.9, is analogous to the temporal model shown in figure 7.8.

Marginality *still* (figure 7.7) asserts that the property of being a safe vehicle obtains at a more extreme point in the integrity ranking for vehicles than expected; the origin of the scale is equated with the safest vehicle. By contrast, marginality *already* asserts that the safety property obtains at a less extreme point than expected; the onset of the scale is the point of least structural soundness. In both cases, the temporal and nontemporal scalar models are structurally isomorphic. In the case of *already,* as in the case of inchoatives in general, the nontemporal reading represents a conceptual mapping of a temporal model onto a model of graded categorization.

It was claimed above, however, that the development of marginality *still* was not so direct: this sense was said to represent a refinement of an atemporal schema which subsumed both temporal and concessive uses. Perhaps this claim cannot be maintained in light of examples involving nontemporal uses of inchoatives. If we do allow that marginality *still* developed directly from temporal *still,* this does not impeach the argument that pragmatic strengthening alone does not account for the development of a concessive use compatible with perfective predicates or of the marginality sense. Further, whatever path of diachronic development yielded marginality *still,* it would seem that only a superstructure involving abstract continuation can create a coherent conceptual grouping of senses synchronically.

Conclusion

A representation of the semantic commonalities which unite the three senses of *still* is given in figure 7.10.

The common traits schematized in figure 7.10 can be enumerated as follows. A scale in W contains two homogeneous elements, S. These elements are located at two contiguous scalar loci. The more advanced of these loci

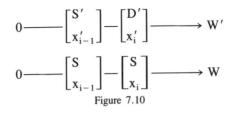

Figure 7.10

is "highlighted" by the predication. This highlighting is indicated by the boldface brackets. The assertion that S obtains at the more advanced scalar locus licenses the inference (whether by lexical presupposition or scalar entailment) that S also obtains at (at least) one scalar point located closer to the origin of the scale. The scale in W is paralleled by an analogous scale in W', the world of speaker's expectations. On this scale, the scalar element (S') obtains at the less advanced point; the more advanced point x_i' is characterized by the lack of S (or by the presence of another element—entity or outcome).

The scalar loci in question may be time points, worlds, or simply rankings within a property scale. The elements ordered may be states of affairs (outcomes or situations) or entities. Thus, the schema given in figure 7.10 is an abstraction over scalar ontologies. The distinct scalar ontologies yield the distinct senses. Thus, *still* is a polysemous lexical item. Evidence for the existence of distinct senses is provided by co-occurrence restrictions and syntactic restrictions: for example, temporal *still* does not accept the continuative perfect, and marginality *still* cannot be placed in pre- or postclausal position. The distinct semantic structures are nonetheless isomorphic. As shown in figure 7.10, the shared semantic properties can be represented in a straightforward fashion. It does not stretch credulity to suggest that figure 7.10 represents a semantic generalization grasped by the speaker. As mentioned, a speaker will arrive at this generalization only once she has access to the full array of senses. A full grasp of the senses includes knowledge of the conditions under which they are appropriately used in discourse. All assertions involving *still* represent assertions of sameness despite expectation of change. This shared pragmatic content might induce one to reconcile senses with respect to their semantic content. The formation of this semantic generalization then resembles the process by which type information is extracted from tokens (Jackendoff 1983). Use conditions shared by the senses are analogous to the set of ostensive definitions from which the speaker extrapolates conditions upon category membership.

The general semantic structure diagrammed in figure 7.10 is then a rubric under which the distinct senses are grouped. This grouping is a "natural category of senses'' (Lakoff 1987). As mentioned, a polysemy network of this sort does not represent a radial category of the kind described by Lakoff. It does not contain a ''core sense.'' Instead, the distinct senses cohere by virtue of their common link to an abstract semantic superstructure. This type of analysis avoids the need to posit a polysemy structure which recapitulates the series of diachronic meaning extensions that gave rise to the distinct senses. Although such polysemy structures exist, it was argued that, in the present case, the diachronic trajectory connecting temporal to concessive *still* cannot represent a synchronic ''sense link.'' The historically primary temporal sense is not the central sense. The senses are related not by their resemblance to a core sense, but by their resemblance to the semantic superstructure. The semantic superstructure is computed only once the full array of senses is available. A polysemy network of this type is then by definition discontinuous with the historical developments which yielded the individual senses.

In addition to augmenting the repertoire of sense networks available within a theory of lexical polysemy, this study has also provided further evidence that use conditions and ''meaning proper'' must be examined in tandem. *Still* is a scalar operator possessed of ''direct pragmatic interpretation'' (Kay 1990: 63). It thus belongs to the family of linguistic constructs which Kay has elsewhere termed *contextual operators:* ''lexical items or grammatical constructions whose semantic value consists, at least in part, of instructions to find in . . . the context a certain kind of information structure'' (1989: 181). The information structure evoked by *still* is a scalar model, ''a set of propositions which are part of the shared background of speaker and hearer at the time of the utterance'' (Kay 1990:63). As argued here, *still* evokes various types of scalar models: a time line, an ''adversity scale,'' and graded categorization. These models are represented by distinct schemata. As noted, the discourse function of *still* is more amenable to a propositional representation. In discourse, *still* functions to relate propositions within a scalar model. A proposition pertaining to a less advanced scalar locus in the model is regarded as part of the discourse context, whether or not this proposition has been asserted as such. The ''text proposition'' containing *still* entails this context proposition. In all of its senses, *still* presupposes a world of speaker's expectations, in which that situation coded by the TP does not obtain at the scalar point in question. In positing this semantic presupposition, we codify the intuition that assertions involving *still* violate expectation. Thus, contextual meaning—and discourse function—are not here extricable from ''literal meaning.''

An additional consequence of this study is the following: the existence of the lexical network, and its organizing rubric, provides evidence for the ability of speakers to derive an abstract conceptualization of "continuance," or "persistence," a notion which is prototypically defined with respect to the temporal domain. Continuance can be viewed at a level of abstraction at which its scalar-semantic properties emerge. This abstraction consists in the "digitization" of a continuum, such that persistence is equivalent to the presence of effectively identical elements at two contiguous scalar loci. An assertion of persistence is equivalent to an assertion that one such element is present at the more advanced of these loci. This abstract scalar conceptualization provides the basis for an analogy within event structure: the notion of continuation is applicable both to the endurance of a situation through time and to the persistence of an outcome across worlds.

Notes

1. For their help in developing the present analysis, I would like to thank John Dinsmore, Gilles Fauconnier, Charles Fillmore, George Lakoff, Knud Lambrecht, and Eve Sweetser. I am especially grateful for the advice of Paul Kay and Jean-Pierre Koenig. An earlier version of this paper appeared in *Journal of Semantics* 10 (1993).

2. Doherty (1973) has attempted to represent the semantics of *still* in terms of three phases. In phase 1, prior to reference time, a state obtains; in phase 2, located at reference time, that same state obtains. In phase three, following reference time, the state does not obtain. As noted by König (1977), however, examples like (i) impugn the validity of this analysis.

(i) Our house is still standing!

The speaker of (i) certainly does not presuppose that the house in question will not be standing at some point following her utterance. We can say, however, that this speaker presupposes that the house *might not* have been standing at R. This is the "modal component" in the meaning of temporal *still* that is captured by the twin time lines in Hoepelman and Rohrer's analysis. By including reference to a parallel possible world in which the state in question ceases at R, this model represents the presupposition of expected cessation.

The term *expected cessation* is used with considerable hesitation. The speaker need not *expect* cessation of the state of affairs in question, but merely view such cessation as a fair possibility. A reviewer notes that sentences such as (ii) are possible.

(ii) As everyone expected, Uncle Harry was still pruning the shrubs.

Thus, the term *expected cessation,* while a convenient shorthand for the modal component of the Hoepelman and Rohrer time-line model, is misleading. The reader is asked to interpret this term as referring to a presumption of *possible* cessation at

R. Given this understanding of the term, one retains the ability to explain the anomaly of such sentences as *Harry is still dead:* under ordinary circumstances, one is loath to invoke a possible world wherein the state of death obtains for some period and then ceases to obtain at a later period.

3. A synthesis of the implicature and presupposition analyses is possible. Traugott (1988) has noted cases of "pragmatic strengthening," in which conversational implicatures associated with certain lexical items become conventionalized. It is possible that, in the present case, the (quantity-based) implicature of expected cessation associated with temporal *still* became a conventional concomitant of both the temporal and nontemporal uses. As noted in the section on diachronic issues, however, our definition of the temporally based notion *cessation* must be broadened to cover cases in which the scale in question does not represent a time line. This broad definition will be entailed by the atemporal scalar definition of continuity suggested here.

4. The term *protasis* is used here in an extended sense: it refers not only to the antecedent of a conditional, but also to the subordinate clause of a factive concessive. This terminological extension is justified by the fact that the two subordinate clauses function in a similar fashion with respect to concessives: both code the "adverse world" within which some eventuality obtains.

5. C. Fillmore (p.c.) has noted that sentences such as (ii) (as against (i)) are peculiar:

(i) Although he's sixty, he is still vigorous.
(ii) ?Although he's only twenty, he is still feeble.

Sentence (i) accesses both temporal and adversative understandings of *still*. In sentence (ii), the temporal understanding is not available. Its peculiarity stems from the fact that the coupling of *still* and an imperfective misleadingly evokes the temporal interpretation. E. Sweetser (p.c.) has pointed out that (ii) is acceptable under an epistemic interpretation (Sweetser 1990): "I conclude that he is feeble, despite the existence of otherwise valid counterevidence (indicating his youth)." An additional example of the epistemic reading of concessive *still* is given in (iii):

(iii) Timber wolves eat a lot of meat, but they're still omnivorous.

Sentence (iii) can be paraphrased in the following fashion: "Despite evidence to the contrary, the conclusion that timber wolves are omnivorous continues to have validity." The enduring validity of a conclusion in epistemic concessives is directly analogous to the enduring assertability of a claim in argumentative (or "true") concessives like (27).

6. Although it has not been discussed, I assume that the concessive use of *yet,* as in (i), is another example of transspatial persistence.

(i) I raced down there, yet I missed the train.

As argued by König and Traugott (1982), *yet* and *still* are distinct in the following respect: *yet* presupposes that the expected cessation of the state of affairs in question will end at a point following reference time. Thus, *He's not here yet* presupposes that this (negative) state will terminate later; the analogous sentence with *still* bears no such presupposition. Both adverbs are, however, markers of temporal persistence, and as such exhibit analogous temporal-concessive polysemy.

7. This scalar directionality can be literal. Sentence (3) is an appropriate response to the eastward-bound motorist who assumes that Death Valley is in Nevada. However, only sentence (i) is appropriate if that same individual is traveling westward.

(i) Death Valley is already in California.

I thank C. Fillmore for making the foregoing observation.

References

Abraham, Werner. 1980. The Synchronic and Diachronic Semantics of German Temporal *noch* and *schon,* with Aspects of English *still, yet,* and *already. Studies in Language* 4:3–24.

Akmajian, Adrian, Susan M. Steele, and Thomas Wasow. 1979. The Category AUX in Universal Grammar. *Linguistic Inquiry* 10:1–64.

Bach, Emmon. 1981. On Time, Tense, and Aspect: An Essay in English Metaphysics. In Peter Cole, ed., *Radical Pragmatics,* 63–81. New York: Academic Press.

Bennett, Michael, and Barbara Partee. 1978. *Toward the Logic of Tense and Aspect in English.* Bloomington, Ind.: Indiana University Linguistics Club.

Chafe, Wallace. 1970. *Meaning and the Structure of Language.* Chicago: University of Chicago Press.

Dahl, Östen. 1981. On the Definition of the Telic-Atelic (Bounded-Nonbounded) Distinction. In P. Tedeschi and A. Zaenen, eds., *Tense and Aspect,* 79–90. Syntax and Semantics, vol. 14. New York: Academic Press.

Doherty, Monika. 1973. 'Noch' and 'Schon' and Their Presuppositions. In F. Kiefer and Nicolas Ruwet, eds., *Generative Grammar in Europe,* 154–77. Dordrecht: Reidel Publishing Company.

Fauconnier, Gilles. 1985. *Mental Spaces: Aspects of Meaning Construction in Natural Language.* Cambridge, Mass.: MIT Press. Reprinted 1994, Cambridge: Cambridge University Press.

Fenn, Peter. 1987. *A Semantic and Pragmatic Examination of the English Perfect.* Tübingen: Gunter Narr Verlag.

Fillmore, Charles J., Paul Kay, and M.C. O'Connor. 1988. Regularity and Idiomaticity in Grammatical Constructions: The Case of *let alone. Language* 64:501–38.

Goldberg, Adele E. 1995. *Constructions: A Construction Grammar Approach to Argument Structure.* Chicago: University of Chicago Press.

Greenbaum, Sidney. 1969. *Studies in English Adverbial Usage.* Miami: University of Miami Press.

Herweg, Michael. 1991a. A Critical Examination of Two Classical Approaches to Aspect. *Journal of Semantics* 8:363–402.

————. 1991b. Perfective and Imperfective Aspect and the Theory of Events and States. *Linguistics* 29:1011–51.

Hirtle, W.H. 1977. *Already, Still,* and *Yet. Archivum Linguisticum* 8:28–45.

Hoepelman, J., and C. Rohrer. 1981. Remarks on *noch* and *schon* in German. In P. Tedeschi and A. Zaenen, eds., *Tense and Aspect,* 103–26. Syntax and Semantics, vol. 14. New York: Academic Press.

Horn, Laurence R. 1970. Ain't it Hard (Anymore). *Papers from the Sixth Annual Regional Meeting of the Chicago Linguistic Society,* 318–27. University of Chicago.

————. 1984. Toward a New Taxonomy for Pragmatic Inference: Q-Based and R-Based Implicature. In D. Schiffrin, ed., *Meaning, Form and Use in Context,* 11–42. Washington, D.C.: Georgetown University Press.

Jackendoff, Ray. 1983. *Semantics and Cognition.* Cambridge, Mass.: MIT Press.

Karttunen, Lauri. 1971. Implicative Verbs. *Language* 47:340–58.

Kay, Paul. 1989. Contextual Operators: *respectively, respective,* and *vice versa. Proceedings of the Fifteenth Annual Meeting of the Berkeley Linguistics Society,* 181–92. Berkeley, CA: Berkeley Linguistics Society.

————. 1990. *Even. Linguistics and Philosophy* 13:59–112.

Kemmer, Suzanne. 1990. *Still.* Paper presented at the fourth annual Berkeley—San Diego Cognitive Linguistics Workshop.

Klein, Wolfgang. 1992. The Present-Perfect Puzzle. *Language* 68:525–52.

König, Ekkehard. 1977. Temporal and Nontemporal Uses of *Noch* and *Schon* in German. *Linguistics and Philosophy* 1:173–98.

————. 1986. Conditionals, Concessive Conditionals, and Concessives: Areas of Contrast, Overlap, and Neutralization. In Elizabeth C. Traugott, Alice ter Meulen, J. Snitzer Reilly, and Charles A. Ferguson, eds., *On Conditionals,* 229–46. Cambridge: Cambridge University Press.

König, Ekkehard, and Elizabeth C. Traugott. 1982. Divergence and Apparent Convergence in the Development of *Yet* and *Still. Proceedings of the Eighth Annual Meeting of the Berkeley Linguistics Society,* 170–79. Berkeley, CA: Berkeley Linguistics Society.

Lakoff, George. 1987. *Women, Fire, and Dangerous Things: What Categories Reveal about the Mind.* Chicago: University of Chicago Press.

Lakoff, George, and Claudia Brugman. 1986. Argument Forms in Lexical Semantics. *Proceedings of the Twelfth Annual Meeting of the Berkeley Linguistics Society,* 442–54. Berkeley, CA: Berkeley Linguistics Society.

Lambrecht, Knud. 1994. *Information Structure and Sentence Form.* Cambridge: Cambridge University Press.

Langacker, Ronald W. 1987. *Foundations of Cognitive Grammar.* Vol. 1: *Theoretical Prerequisites.* Stanford, Calif.: Stanford University Press.

————. 1991. *Foundations of Cognitive Grammar.* Vol. 2: *Descriptive Application.* Stanford, Calif.: Stanford University Press.

Lehrer, Adrienne. 1990. Polysemy, Conventionality and the Structure of the Lexicon. *Cognitive Linguistics* 1:207–46.

Lichtenberk, Frantisek. 1991. Semantic Change and Heterosemy in Grammaticalization. *Language* 67:475–509.

McCawley, James D. 1971. Tense and Time Reference in English. In Charles J. Fillmore and D. Terence Langendoen, eds., *Studies in Linguistic Semantics,* 96–113. New York: Holt, Rinehart and Winston.

———. 1987. The Focus and Scope of *only.* Manuscript, University of Chicago.

Michaelis, Laura A. 1992. Aspect and the Semantics-Pragmatics Interface: The Case of *Already, Lingua* 87:321–39.

Miller, George. 1978. Semantic Relations among Words. In Morris Halle, Joan Bresnan, and George Miller, eds., *Linguistic Theory and Psychological Reality,* 60–118. Cambridge, Mass.: MIT Press.

Mittwoch, Anita. 1988. Aspects of English Aspect: On the Interaction of Perfect, Progressive and Durational Phrases. *Linguistics and Philosophy* 11:203–254.

Morgan, Jerry L. 1978. Two Types of Convention in Indirect Speech Acts. In Peter Cole, ed., *Pragmatics,* 261–80. Syntax and Semantics, vol. 9. New York: Academic Press.

Morrissey, Michael. 1973. The English Perfective and 'still/anymore.' *Journal of Linguistics* 9:65–69.

Mourelatos, Alexander. 1981. Events, Process and States. In P. Tedeschi and A. Zaenen, eds., *Tense and Aspect,* 191–212. Syntax and Semantics, vol. 14. New York: Academic Press.

Norvig, Peter. 1988. Interpretation under Ambiguity. *Proceedings of the Fourteenth Annual Meeting of the Berkeley Linguistics Society,* 188–201. Berkeley, CA: Berkeley Linguistics Society.

Parsons, Terence. 1990. *Events in the Semantics of English.* Cambridge, Mass.: MIT Press.

Partee, Barbara. 1984. Nominal and Temporal Anaphora. *Linguistics and Philosophy* 7:243–86.

Quirk, Randolph, Sidney Greenbaum, Geoffrey Leech, and Jan Svartvik. 1972. *A Grammar of Contemporary English.* London: Longman.

Sweetser, Eve. 1990. *From Etymology to Pragmatics: Metaphorical and Cultural Aspects of Semantic Structure.* Cambridge: Cambridge University Press.

Taylor, Barry. 1977. Tense and Continuity. *Linguistics and Philosophy* 1:199–220.

Traugott, Elizabeth C. 1986. From Polysemy to Internal Semantic Reconstruction. *Proceedings of the Twelfth Annual Meeting of the Berkeley Linguistics Society,* 539–50. Berkeley, CA: Berkeley Linguistics Society.

———. 1988. Pragmatic Strengthening and Grammaticalization. *Proceedings of the Fourteenth Annual Meeting of the Berkeley Linguistics Society,* 406–16. Berkeley, CA: Berkeley Linguistics Society.

Traugott, Elizabeth C., and John Waterhouse. 1969. 'Already' and 'Yet': A Suppletive Set of Aspect Markers? *Journal of Linguistics* 5:287–304.

Vlach, Frank. 1981. The Semantics of the Progressive. In P. Tedeschi and A. Zaenen, eds., *Tense and Aspect,* 271–92. Syntax and Semantics, vol. 14: New York: Academic Press.

8 Alternate Grounds in the Interpretation of Deictic Expressions

·
·
·
·

The introduction to this volume makes clear that cognitive linguistics views language processing as a problem-solving activity in which diverse strategies and knowledge bases are exploited. Discourse processing is seen as an active process of constructing a representation of the speaker's intended meaning, through language the speaker uses as well as the exploitation of pre-existing knowledge structures the listener possesses. One of the most intriguing problems facing the discourse analyst is accounting for how a hearer finds referents for nominals in the discourse, including pronouns and other deictic elements. This paper addresses the problem of finding referents for locational deictic expressions such as *this place, that place, here, there,* and personal pronouns.[1]

Finding referents for such expressions is far from simple. Deictic expressions are usually thought of as referring to entities in the immediate utterance situation—*I* refers to the speaker, *you* to the hearer, *here* to a location construed as proximal to the discourse participants in some sense, and so forth. In actual usage, however, deictic elements are not always used to refer to elements of the immediate utterance situation. This paper addresses usages of this type. Consider the examples in (1), taken from interview data.[2]

(1) JF16: There's a part of southeast San Diego where *you* do go down, *you* see all these Vietnamese theaters and everything in Vietnamese and when I see that I just kind of feel, well, *I* don't belong in *this* place, *this* is where the Vietnamese people are, I don't belong *here.* (italics added)

It is clear to speakers of English that the pronoun *you* in this utterance does not refer to the listener in the discourse situation. Rather, it is a generic, and could felicitously be replaced by generic *one.* In addition, the locative deictic expressions—*this place, here*—refer not to a location perceived as proximal to the participants in the interview, but to a distant neighborhood. This is clear from substitution tests: replacing the locational deictics with a proximal location, such as *your office* (where the interview took place) or *La Jolla* (the neighborhood where the interview was set) renders quite a different, and seemingly wrong, interpretation, while substituting a nominal such as *a Vietnamese neighborhood* preserves what we believe to be the speaker's intended meaning. Thus the immediate discourse situation cannot be taken as the domain for finding referents for these deictic expressions; nonetheless, we have no trouble finding referents and hence understanding the speaker. How do we accomplish this? In this paper, I bring to bear on this question devices from complementary theories within cognitive linguistics: the theories of cognitive grammar (Langacker 1987, 1991), mental spaces (Fauconnier 1985), and cognitive models (Lakoff 1987).

Factors in the Interpretation of Deictics

There are numerous factors that must enter into the interpretation of deictics in discourse processing. The first is the inherent semantic content or value of deictic expressions (cf. Rauh 1981); I refer here to their basic or default values, e.g., *I* as speaker, *you* as hearer, *this* (nominal) as a proximally construed entity, etc. The meanings of deictics are highly *schematic*. That is, they are only partially specified, and therefore may apply across a large number of actual discourse situations: all speakers in a discourse, on their turns, can refer to themselves using the pronoun *I,* and no confusion will result. The pronoun *I* is applicable to any person who is currently taking the role of speaker; no further features of that individual are specified. This schematicity can be problematic, however. In some cases the listener must work to find a referent for a deictic expression. Suppose two graduate students are strolling across campus on a fine day. There has been a lull in the conversation when one of them suddenly utters the sentence in (2).

(2) I'm tired of this place.

Several candidate locations suggest themselves as referents for the expression *this place:* the campus as a physical location; the university as an abstract location; the town in which the university is situated; or perhaps even the state or country in which the campus is situated. Without further context, the hearer will not be able to definitively settle on one of these candidates. It is typical that, in the absence of further clarification on the part of the speaker, the hearer may utter a request for clarification, such as the sentence in (3).

(3) What do you mean, this campus, or this university, or what?

In many, if not most, cases, the discourse topic or domain serves to narrow the field of candidates enough so that the hearer can assume one of the candidates. Thus a second factor in the interpretation of deictics is the limitation of candidate referents by the discourse topic or domain. So, for example, if the utterance in (2) is uttered toward the end of a long diatribe against the students' department, the rigors of the graduate program, the indignities of graduate student labor, etc., the hearer would feel satisfied in concluding that the university as an abstract location is the referent that the speaker had in mind. If, however, the preceding conversation concerned the hot weather, traffic jams, general lack of events of cultural interest, and so on, of the university town, the hearer may feel that the town is the most suitable referent. With sufficient context, the hearer is spared a good deal of work in finding a referent, because one of the candidates has been primed by the foregoing conversation.

A third resource available for the determination of suitable referents is the extended use of deictics that are conventional for the language in question. So, for example, if (4) is the response to a request for clarification on how to make *crêpes à la française,* the listener is hardly likely to object with sentence (5).

(4) Well, you take half a cup of flour; you beat an egg together with some milk, and then you mix this fluid in with the flour in small quantities until . . .

(5) Hey, why do you say *you?* I've never done this before. If I had, I wouldn't be asking for the recipe!

Speakers of English know that a sanctioned use of the second-person pronoun *you* is as a generic; that is, its use to stand for "any person" in such utterances. Numerous extended uses of deictics are allowed in English, and in this paper I shall examine (i) deictics in utterances that may be characterized as quotes or as free indirect speech; and (ii) uses such as generic *you* which do not appear to exploit an utterance context at all.

I will concern myself primarily with the first and third factors in this paper, assuming the second and leaving the investigation of its complexities for future research. Cognitive grammar (Langacker 1987, 1991) will be used to depict the semantic value of deictic expressions as referring to some aspect of the utterance *ground,* i.e., the utterance context. I will then explore how we get extended uses which do not exploit this context (or at least do not obviously or solely exploit it)—uses which involve *alternate grounds* to the actual discourse context, with reference to which we may find referents for deictic expressions. As sources of such alternate grounds I will consider mental spaces (Fauconnier 1985), which provide alternate utterance contexts within which deictics may be used, and cognitive models (Lakoff 1987), which provide frames with roles or relationships which deictics may refer to. I will examine how mental space construction, as discourse proceeds, provides access to contexts permitting interpretation of deictics that are inappropriate if we take the actual discourse context as ground; and how cognitive models provide a viewpoint which is in accord with deictic semantics.

The concept of alternate grounds is not new. It is intuitively given in Fillmore's "taking the other fellow's point of view" (1971:41), in Rauh's shift of the "center of orientation" (1981:46), and Talmy's "decoupling" (1986). As Rauh describes it, "The encoder gives up his real center of orientation and imagines himself located within an imagined space. . . . He establishes a center of orientation to which he relates objects of the imagined space" (1981:45). Langacker (1978) discusses a similar concept, which he refers to as a "surrogate ground": "The ground . . . can be regarded as a platform or perspective from which a situation is viewed. Certain embedded predicates, in varying degrees, introduce a further viewpoint (though not necessarily a new viewer), and can be regarded as platforms for viewing the situation reported by predicates embedded to them; an example is the predicate *say*" (f. 857).

Here Langacker expresses in other terms the notion that the verb *say* is a space builder, and that the space this verb builds may serve as an alternate ground for the interpretation of expressions within the clause following *say*. He revives this concept in discussing "cross-world identification" (1985: 127–30), in which "our capacity for conceptual displacement" allows us to "describe a situation from a vantage point distinct from our actual one" (1985:127). He speaks in this discussion of divergent conceptual "worlds," which are the functional equivalent of Fauconnier's mental spaces.[3]

Hanks (1990; see especially chapter 5) gives a detailed account of this phenomenon, which he terms "decentering," for Maya. He examines several kinds of discourse in which alternate grounds are set up, noting that the various types of discourse "rest on displacement or alteration of the indexical ground of utterances. In the clearest cases, the [indexical] ground of demonstrative reference is transposed from the current corporeal sphere of utterance and projected into some other sphere" (1990:197).

The upshot of these analyses by different scholars is that the viewpoint— the reference point—is displaced or shifted away from the default ground, which is the actual speech situation, and an alternate ground is adopted within

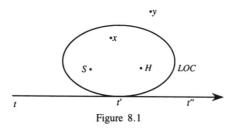

Figure 8.1

which the reference point for a given deictic is located. Mental space theory provides a set of theoretical constructs and principles which can be used to describe this phenomenon.

An analysis by Bolinger (1979) suggests cognitive models as another source of alternate grounds, although he does not explicitly formulate the analysis in these terms. The thrust of the cognitive model analysis is that metaphor is involved: the image-schematic properties of deictic semantics are preserved, such as the designation of an entity and the specification of the proximal or distal relation of that entity to some reference point; but this semantic structure is imported into a new base domain. The base of the expression is no longer the physical situation of an utterance event, but some other domain. Two cases are looked at here: In one (*that part of the city*), the new base is an oriented cognitive model. For the second case, two meanings for impersonal *you* are offered, one involving normative models (cf. Bolinger 1979) and one involving roles in constructed spaces.

The Semantics of Deictics

Among the factors used in interpreting deictic expressions is their inherent semantic content (Rauh 1981). Crucial to the cognitive grammar view, as laid out by Langacker (1985), is the notion of the *ground,* a technical term referring to "the speech event, its setting, and its participants" (Langacker 1985:113). The setting includes the time and place of the speech event. A deictic expression is "one that includes the ground—or some facet of the ground—in its scope of predication [i.e., its meaning]" (Langacker 1985: 113). Specifically, a deictic expression designates some entity—a person, object, time, or location—and specifies a relation between that entity and a reference point within the ground. Figure 8.1 is a composite diagram which may be used to illustrate the meaning of numerous deictics.

The oval in the diagram represents the speech situation. *S* stands for the speaker, *H* for the hearer; *t* labels the arrow representing time, and *t'* is the time of the speech event; *LOC* represents the location of the speech event. One of the elements within the ground serves as a reference point relative to which other elements are judged proximal or distal—let us take the speaker S as reference point, as both Langacker (1978) and Talmy (1988) point out that it is the default reference point for deictic expressions. The dot labeled x signifies an object that is construed as proximal to the reference point; the dot labeled y signifies an object that is construed as distal to the reference point. A particular deictic expression would designate one of the elements represented in figure 8.1; and its relation to the reference point would feature prominently in the semantics of the expression. For English deictics, only two relations are coded, proximal and distal. Talmy characterizes these relations as being, respectively, "on the speaker side or non-speaker side of a conceptual partition drawn through space, time, or some other qualitative dimension" (1988:168). Note that Talmy leaves open a broad spectrum of domains through which the partition is drawn. In extended uses of deictics, the domain is one other than an utterance ground (see the section below, Cognitive Models as Alternate Grounds, on metaphorical extensions of deictic semantics).

Adopting the spatial and temporal boundaries of the speech event as the partition determining proximal vs. distal relations, we may use figure 8.1 to illustrate the semantics of various deictics in their most basic senses. In cognitive grammar, an expression derives its semantic value by virtue of the elements contained within its base, plus the *profiling* of one of these elements. Profiling is equivalent to designation—the profiled elements of the base are the elements which the expression designates or names. For example, profiling S in figure 8.1 creates a linguistic expression which designates the speaker in a speech event—the pronoun I. Profiling H, on the other hand, creates an expression designating the hearer or addressee—the pronoun *you*. Profiling LOC would give the meaning of *here*, profiling t' would give *now*. Profiling x would give the meaning of *this* in its nominal sense. Shifting to entities construed as distal to the reference point, profiling y would give the meaning of nominal *that* if y is a thing, or *there* if y is a location; supposing we were to profile t'', we would have the semantics of *then*.

Thus, according to the cognitive-grammar view of deictic semantics, in order to interpret deictics in discourse we must have in our representation of the import of the discourse a conception of the ground, as well as entities, one or more of which is a reference point for assessing the others; and relations between the entities and the reference point within the ground. But as we saw in (1), the actual discourse setting cannot be taken as the ground in every case. It is at best the default ground, as Fillmore suggests (1971: 41–42), and hence my characterization of the meanings of deictics in the discussion of figure 8.1 as their basic or central (default) senses. In support of this characterization, Hanks writes, "the concept of decentering is tied inevitably to the idea of a normal, automatic, nondecentered usage, in which the indexical ground is right where it should be, so to speak. We recognize cases of decentering by their failure to correspond to the normal cases. It is relevant to the plausability of this view that speakers make basic-level assumptions and routinize their indexical usage so as to privilege the corporeal frame [= actual utterance ground] as the one that is available until further notice. This is significant, since it weighs the actual frame more heavily than the other possible ones" (1990:228). Thus the actual utterance ground is the prototypical base for deictics, since it is "privileged"—it serves as automatic ground and as a standard against which decentered uses are measured; and it is the default in the sense that it is assumed to be "available until further notice."

Mental space theory gives us other important aspects of basic deictic semantics. Pronouns have in their semantics *connectors* (in the sense of the technical term explained in the introduction to this volume) between the discourse ground—i.e., the actual utterance ground, which is a mental space, insofar as it is mentally comprehended by the discourse participants and it is the subject of language within the discourse—and other spaces constructed in ongoing conversation. Because of these connectors, pronouns may function as *triggers,* which are expressions used to identify a *target* element in a mental space. Consider example (6).

(6) In this picture, I'm wearing a gorilla suit.

The expression *in this picture* builds a mental space. The connector and other semantic features inherent in the pronoun *I* allow a listener to use the pronoun as a trigger to identify the person wearing the gorilla suit in the picture (the target) with the speaker of the sentence in the actual discourse context (in spite of the obscuring function of the gorilla suit). This role of pronouns as triggers is basic in both aspects of my analysis—in the role of mental spaces as alternate grounds and in the role of cognitive models as alternate grounds. This will become apparent in following sections.

Analysis

Mental Spaces as Alternate Grounds

In this section I explore the role of mental spaces in providing alternate grounds for the interpretation of deictic expressions. I discuss how a mental space provides a new domain peopled with entities in relation to each other, accessible to deictic reference, and how a viewpoint or reference point different from that of the actual discourse participants may be set up.

The mental space structure of even a short segment of discourse, such as a single entry in my interview data, is an extraordinarily complex affair: mental spaces are constructed and sometimes multiple embeddings of spaces occur; each space is peopled with objects and relations by the language following space-building expressions; the focus or currently active space may switch several times in a multiclausal sequence; and background knowledge is imported into constructed spaces. To make the explication of mental spaces as alternate grounds manageable, I simplify the description to a large extent. Thus my diagrams and descriptions of mental space structure in the data are radically simplified.

The examples analyzed in this section illustrate how mental spaces provide grounds for interpreting deictics in quoted speech and in free indirect speech.[4] The role of mental spaces in providing such alternate grounds is to provide the discourse participants with alternative domains to the actual discourse situation; they may people these domains with entities, predicate attributes of them, and compute relations among them. One state of affairs which can occur within a constructed space is an utterance event—i.e., an individual within a space speaks or has thoughts similar to internal speech; the space then serves as the ground for that utterance. The relations between the speaker in the space and other elements in it may sanction uses of deictics that conflict with what we would expect if the actual discourse situation were taken as the ground. An example from the interview data that illustrates this is given in (7).

(7) JF16: . . . or the same with when I go to, like, a Spanish part of town, you know, see everything in Spanish, and I say, well, you know, *this* is not where I belong. (italics added)

The italicized proximal deictic *this* in example (7) cannot be felicitously read as referring to the location of the actual speech event where this sentence was uttered, the interview site. But if we substitute the phrase *a Spanish neighborhood* for *this*, a felicitous reading within the context of the utterance is maintained. We must find an alternate ground for interpreting *this*—an alternate domain wherein proximal relations hold between the reference point (the speaker) and other elements, such as the location of the speech event. A simplified mental space diagram for this segment is shown in figure 8.2. Note the multiple embedding of spaces. The space marked R is the origin space, the speaker's conception of reality (reality is mentally comprehended by speakers and is thus just another mental space; see Fauconnier 1985 (p. 14–16)). This space would include the interview situation and hence the default ground for the speaker's utterances. S, the speaker, is the only element

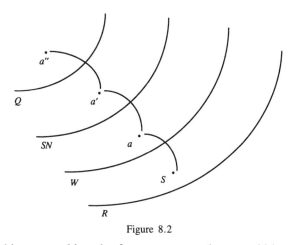

Figure 8.2

shown in this space, although of course many others would be present, for instance, myself as her interlocutor.

The word *when* is a space builder, instructing the listener to construct a time space, marked W. The pronoun I, a nominal, sets up an element, marked a, in W. Relations in R can be used to find a reading for I. Without explicit blockage by certain linguistic expressions, relations in R are available for interpretation of deictics in later spaces; recall also the discussion above of pronouns as triggers. Thus we understand that it is the speaker in R who goes to the Spanish part of town on some occasions. Within W, the location nominal *a Spanish neighborhood* sets up another space, a location space, marked SN. The relation *go to*, which has as its subject the pronoun I, places the speaker in SN, hence the element a', which corresponds to a in W and to S in R. Then within SN we have yet another space, a quote space built by the verb *say*—this is marked Q in the diagram. By virtue of the meaning of the verb, this space portrays an utterance and hence all the appurtenances of an utterance event, namely, a ground, including a speaker, a location of the speech event, etc. This speaker is explicitly set up by the pronoun I of *this is not where I belong,* and is shown as element a'' in the diagram. We can connect this element with a' of SN, by virtue of a's subject relation to *say,* and thence with a of W and S of R.

Note that a different interpretation for I could be available in a different discourse situation. Suppose, for example, that JF had been describing not her own feelings but her brother's. She could easily utter the statement in (8), and the listener could easily read I as the brother, not the speaker JF.

(8) . . . when he goes to a Spanish part of town . . . and he says, this is not where I belong.

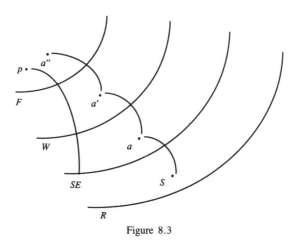

Figure 8.3

Because a quoting verb like *say* sets up an utterance event and therefore a ground, an alternate ground is easily available for the interpretation of deictics in the quoted utterance.

A location for the utterance event portrayed by the words following *say* is available from among the spaces constructed so far, namely, *SN,* the Spanish neighborhood. The quote space is situated within this space, i.e., the speaker of the quoted clause has been placed in *SN* by preceding language. This sets the Spanish neighborhood up as a location which can be construed as proximal to the speaker (the subject of *say* in *SN*). Therefore taking the Spanish neighborhood as a referent for *this* gives a felicitous reading, indeed the only felicitous reading in context.

A more complex example illustrates the crucial role of mental spaces in these extended uses of deictics. Consider the segment of JF16 cited above in (1), and repeated here as (9).

(9) JF16: There's a part of southeast San Diego where you do go down, you see all these Vietnamese theaters and everything in Vietnamese and when I see that I just kind of feel, well, I don't belong in *this place, this* is where the Vietnamese people are, I don't belong *here.* (italics added)

Again we find that a suitable paraphrase for the italicized proximal deictic expressions in this segment is a phrase like *a Vietnamese neighborhood,* and not phrases indicative of locations truly proximal to the interview event such as *La Jolla* or *your office.* What sanctions proximal deictics in this example? Figure 8.3 gives a partial diagram of the spaces constructed in this segment.

To simplify the discussion somewhat, let us say that the first sentence, beginning with *There's,* sets up a locational space, *SE* (southeast San Diego) within *R*. This space is the setting for the segment I wish to focus on, which begins with the word *when*. As we saw above, *when* is a space-building expression and creates a time space in which events may be postulated. The event postulated is *I see that,* where *that* refers to the previously mentioned Vietnamese theaters and shop signs and such in Vietnamese. Another event is postulated within the *when* space, namely, *I feel*. Now *feel,* as a propositional-attitude verb, sets up a space *F* in *W*. In *F* we find the feelings and responses of the speaker. Three expressions of her feelings follow. These expressions set up elements and predicate relations among them: a speaker *a''* (*I*) and a location *p* (*this place, this, here*). The relations *not belong in p* of *a''* and the equation of *p* with yet another space, *where the Vietnamese people are* are set up (these are, for simplicity's sake, not shown in the diagram). We have already seen how we may find a reading of the actual discourse speaker for *I* in such a space construction by virtue of the connector semantics of pronouns; of greater interest is the presence of the proximal locational deictics *this place, this,* and *here,* for which we unproblematically identify the Vietnamese neighborhood as referent. Is this a case of a quote, with an utterance ground automatically set up by a quotative verb, as in the Spanish neighborhood example above?[5]

The answer to this question is no. The verb *feel* introduces language about the internal responses of the speaker to a given situation; these responses may be given in the form of a quote, exploiting proximal relations between the experiencer (the subject of *feel*) and the location; but it is not the verb *feel* alone which supplies all the specifics of an utterance situation and therefore sanctions the proximal deictics, as I argued was the case with the quotative verb *say* in the previous example. Rather it is the collective contribution of several space-building expressions which, taken together, supply all the necessary specifications of an utterance ground (location from *where;* time from *when,* and a reference point from the subject of *feel*). Taken together, these expressions build a scenario in which proximal deictics are sanctioned and allow us to read the language after *well* as a quote (even if as a quote of internal speech or thought to oneself). This is clear when we remove some of the space-building expressions (and their subsequent clauses): use of proximal deictics becomes marginal or disallowed under these circumstances. Removing both the *when* clause and the *feel* clause has the result of making proximal deictics bad, as in (10); note, however, that distal deictics, exploiting the distal relations between the speaker and the Vietnamese neighborhood in *R* (reality), are fine, as in (11).

(10) ???There's a part of southeast San Diego where you do go down, you
see all these Vietnamese theaters and everything in Vietnamese;
and I just don't belong in this place, this is where the Vietnamese
people are, I don't belong here.

(11) There's a part of southeast San Diego where you do go down, you
see all these Vietnamese theaters and everything in Vietnamese;
and I just don't belong in that place, that is where the Vietnamese
people are, I don't belong there.

My intuitions tell me that (10), without the space-building *when I see that*
and *I just kind of feel,* is far less acceptable than (11), which lacks the space
builders but uses distal deictics, in accord with the actual relations between
the reference point (the interviewee) and the topic location (the Vietnamese
neighborhood). It is especially clear that the language after *and* cannot be
read as a quote. Some readers may believe that the switch from generic *you*
to *I* influences these judgments, but the reader is invited to substitute *I* for
you across the board in both versions; it does not change the judgments.

Just what is needed to sanction the proximal locational deictics? Let us try
the segment with one or the other of the two space-building expressions
which are missing from (10) and (11).

(12) a. ???There's a part of southeast San Diego where you do go down,
you see all these Vietnamese theaters and everything in Vietnamese; and when I see that, well, I don't belong in this place,
this is where the Vietnamese people are, I don't belong here.
b. ??There's a part of southeast San Diego where you do go down,
you see all these Vietnamese theaters and everything in Vietnamese; and I just kind of feel, well, I don't belong in this
place, this is where the Vietnamese people are, I don't belong
here.

(12a) is quite bad, in my judgment; it seems that supplying an utterance
location and an utterance time is still not enough to get a quote reading on
the clauses with the proximal deictics. (12b), in which the verb *feel* supplies
a viewpoint, is better, but still marginal. In (12b), the reading for *I* is not
the conceptualizer that the discourse participants are imagining as located in
the Vietnamese neighborhood, but rather the speaker in the interview situation,[6] i.e., the interviewee is describing her feelings in general about such
ethnic neighborhoods, not her feelings on particular occasions when she finds
herself actually located in such a neighborhood. Because we use relations in

R to compute a reading for the *I* of *I feel,* and because no space builder intervenes between it and the following clauses to introduce an alternate utterance ground, we expect deictics in those clauses to exploit relations in *R* also; hence the acceptability of distal deictics in those clauses, as seen in (13).

(13) There's a part of southeast San Diego where you do go down, you see all these Vietnamese theaters and everything in Vietnamese; and I just kind of feel, well, I don't belong in that place, that is where the Vietnamese people are, I don't belong there.

It seems that neither space-building expression alone is sufficient to sanction the proximal deictics. Both are needed: *where* provides an utterance location, *when* provides an utterance time, and *feel* provides a viewpoint; both are crucial aspects of an utterance ground. In order to set up an alternative world within which a speech event is to be situated, we must have all ground elements present: location, time, and reference point (speaker). These are given by three space-building expressions in this segment: *where, when,* and *feel.*

These judgments are complicated by the fact that the mere presence of the proximal deictics, with intonation and stress typical of a quotation (acting out the utterance), as well as elements whose contribution I am neglecting, such as *well,* can force the quotation reading and make the segment without space builders or with only one space builder sound better (albeit still marginal). It is important to test the putative quotation with and without real-speech intonation in order to evaluate the various versions accurately. This fact underscores the importance of the inherent semantic content of deictics and their contribution to the interpretation of utterances such as (9).

To sum up, this section has demonstrated how space-building language provides alternate utterance grounds for interpreting deictics. In cases where an explicit quotative verb such as *say* is used, the semantics of the quotative verb set up a space which is an utterance event. In other cases, such as with the verb *feel,* space-building expressions can contribute the necessary features of an utterance ground—time, place, and reference point—and sanction the use of proximal deictics which would otherwise conflict with the specifications found in the actual discourse situation.

Cognitive Models as Alternate Grounds

A cognitive model is another sort of mental representation proposed by cognitive linguistics (see especially Lakoff 1982 and 1987). Unlike a mental space, which is a temporary knowledge base constructed in the course of a particular discourse, a cognitive model is an enduring representation which stores our knowledge of a domain. The term *cognitive model,* especially the term *Idealized Cognitive Model,* or *ICM,* originates with Lakoff (1982), but the notion arises from numerous sources in linguistics and artifical intelligence, such as the notion of a *script* (Schank and Abelson 1977), a *frame* (Fillmore 1982), or a *schema* (Bobrow and Norman 1975; Rumelhart et al. 1986). Cognitive models are built up on the basis of experience as well as innate properties of the mind (Lakoff 1982). The information in cognitive models may be stored in the form of propositions or of images of various sorts, including visual images or images in other sensory modes.

Cognitive models not only store but also organize our knowledge of a given domain. Thus some elements within a cognitive model may be privileged in some psychological sense; or the whole domain stored in a given cognitive model may have the structure of a radial category (Lakoff 1987). It is important to note that cognitive models do not store our knowledge of how things happen in actuality. Rather, they are *idealized;* that is, they are simplified and adjusted in various ways. One important aspect of cognitive models is that they often provide norms for situations or behavior; that is, they store our expectations and perhaps desires as to how particular scenarios should play out, rather than the noisy reality we actually encounter from day to day. Quinn (1987) examines one example, the American cultural model of marriage: how Americans conceive of marriage and what they expect to happen in a marriage, how they expect the partners in a marriage to behave, and so forth. Cognitive models can thus provide us with default assumptions about the world and specifically about the behavior of ourselves and of others (Fauconnier, p.c.).

In this section, I show how cognitive models, which are assumed by the speaker to be shared with her interlocutor and therefore remain implicit, function in alternate-ground phenomena. I discuss examples in which cognitive models provide conceptual connections which sanction metonymic language use; how they provide alternative viewpoints, without explicit space building or explict appeal to the assumed model; and how they provide normative and antinormative scripts or frames with roles that are referred to with pronouns, assuming viewpoints provided by the model.

Given the cognitive-model construct, we would expect idealized models to be entertained regarding such behavior as immigration. One conclusion I reached in the study from which the data in this paper are drawn (Rubba 1988) was that my informants, and probably many other Americans, maintain several idealized cognitive models pertaining to culture and to immigration. I propose three specific models pertinent to the present topic: (i) an ICM of territoriality, or the relation between a culture (an abstract object) and physical space; (ii) a cultural map of San Diego, a particular application of the ICM of territoriality by residents of San Diego; and (iii) an immigration script or scenario, which prescribes the ideal(ized) way in which immigrants to this country should behave, what aspirations they should have, etc. I shall briefly describe each model in turn. We can find evidence for such models in language use, not only in the overt propositional content of statements, but also in the use of a number of linguistic expressions, such as *but* or *still,* that indicate that a given situation corresponds to or conflicts with such a model. Examples of this type are given below.

The ICM of territoriality contains several maxims or principles. I give these here in propositional form, without making a commitment as to whether they are actually comprehended propositionally or in some other fashion. This ICM must include some sort of definition of a culture as a group of people related by ethnicity, beliefs, language, cultural practices, etc. (definitions of these complex concepts will be neglected here). Most directly relevant is the idea that members of the same culture live in spatial proximity to one another, and that the space they occupy is contiguous. The space they occupy is then their territory, i.e., their physical space is conceived of as belonging to them. No more than one culture can occupy a given space in the model. There are different cultures, which occupy different territories that are discretely bounded off from one another. Additionally, every human being is assumed to belong to one and only one culture. My evidence for this ICM is in large measure introspective, but a number of items in the data support its maxims. For example, another informant, KS, illustrates his belief in the last maxim (one cultural affiliation per individual) in his objections to code mixing or switching languages, as shown in (14).

(14) a. KS71: The fact that they're mixing language is a symbol that they're losing their culture.
   b. KS63: I hate to say it this way but I see [people who mix languages] as confused themselves about who they are. . . . They're emitting mixed signals because part of them is Mexican or Filipino or whatever and another part of them is American.

It is clear from these statements that KS believes that, ideally, an individual should have only one cultural affiliation; cultural affiliations are so exclusive for KS that, in order to have dual membership, each culture must somehow be relegated to a distinct "part" of the individual.

The very notion of *ethnic neighborhoods* demonstrates the territoriality ICM. Ethnic neighborhoods prove the ICM by claiming an area belonging to one culture—mainstream American culture—for a different culture, be it Latino, Asian, Middle Eastern, or whatever. But they violate the ICM in that they attempt to place two cultures in one spatial region—the physical space is undeniably in America, as legal jurisdiction, schooling, etc. show; yet the cultural affiliation of most of the residents is, by some observers, not perceived to be American. The discomfort many mainstream Americans feel with ethnic neighborhoods probably lies in their feeling that this kind of setup violates the normative model they entertain regarding the relation of culture to space.

The association of culture with space in this territoriality ICM is a pragmatic function, or connector, as discussed in the introduction to this volume—a conceptual link between subfacets of a cognitive model, in this case a cultural group and the physical territory it occupies. This connector, like others, sanctions metonymic language use. JF speaks on several occasions of *belonging in a place*. This is such common language that it is hard to see the metonymy. However, one must acknowledge that two domains are being mixed: the notion of *belonging*, which has to do with abstract identification or affiliation with an abstract entity such as a group or culture, and physical space, which, apart from impositions upon it by human conceptualizers, has no boundaries or inherent affiliations. When JF makes statements like the one in (15), she is invoking the deeply held association between culture and territory, and using the spatial expression *here* to identify the culture that occupies the space.

(15) JF16: This is where the Vietnamese people are, I don't belong here. . . .
     When I go to, like, a Spanish part of town, you know, see everything in Spanish, and I say, well, you know, this is not where I belong.

It is clear that JF is not talking literally about her physical location, but rather its cultural affiliation; for, if all of the Vietnamese people were to move to other areas, and folk of JF's own ethnic identity were to move into the neighborhood in question, we would not then expect statements reflecting feelings of not belonging from her about this location.[7]

JF also illustrates a default assumption given by reasoning according to the territoriality ICM: if a person is observed in a particular physical location, and that location is recognized as being the territory of a particular culture, then that individual is assumed to be a member of that culture. Hence the *but* of JF16: "I can *be* there, but I don't belong." The default assumption is that being in a physical location entails belonging to the culture occupying that territory; JF's statement here asserts a violation of the default (one of the uses of the word *but* in English), a case in which physical presence does not entail cultural membership.

The second proposed cognitive model is a cultural map of San Diego, i.e., a stored mental representation of the locations of various neighborhoods in San Diego, including information about the ethnicity of the residents there. Obviously, the details and accuracy of such a map will vary from individual to individual depending on factors such as length of time residing in the area, how much the individual knows about San Diego, etc. Importantly, this map is likely to be *oriented*, that is, a given individual will perceive some area of San Diego as her "home" territory, or will perceive certain neighborhoods as being potential homes or not in accordance with her ethnic and cultural affiliation. Areas considered not to be potential home territories will be accorded a different status by the conceptualizer, and this status may be reflected in language use (see the discussion of inheritance of the cultural map below).

The third cultural model is a script or scenario for immigration to one country from another. Since presence in a physical space entails membership in the associated culture, individuals who commit themselves to leaving one physical space and taking up permanent residence in another are expected to change their cultural affiliation also, bringing it in line with the culture associated with the new physical location. Leaving one territory permanently entails abandoning the culture associated with that space; entering another territory with the intention to stay entails adopting the culture of that territory (assimilating to the new culture). JF displays this model, as seen in (16).

(16) a. JF16: They don't wanna give up what they've . . . what they have come from, you know, where they have come from. They don't wanna give all that up. And I just don't think you can really do that in this country, I mean either you have to be here and be a productive member of the society or you know, or you know, or you're just gonna sit there and you're gonna be like in "little Vietnam" or something. . . . Either go back there and, you know, have what you like back there, or be a member here.

b. JF17: You can't just come over here and say, "Okay, I wanna be an American and forget about my past." I mean you've got some cultural ties to your past, but I think you have to throw off a lot of those if you really want to become an American.

"Recalcitrant" immigrants who do not rapidly assimilate violate this scenario, and JF indicates this with the expression *still*, which, in one of its senses, indicates conflict with a normative model, as in (17).

(17) JF16: These people, they've come to America and still, they wanna be
     back [in the home country], you know, they don't want—they wanna
     be here for the advantages, but they don't wanna give up what
     they've . . . where they have come from. . . . And I just don't think
     you can do that in this country.

To summarize, several cognitive models which are interrelated and pertain
to the domain of cultural affiliation—including physical location, immigration, and the ethnic makeup of a particular place (San Diego)—supply the
necessary entities and relationships for comprehending linguistic expressions
in the data. I now turn to the analysis of how these apply in the interpretation
of deictic expressions.

In the discussion of mental spaces, I implied that the use of a deictic entails
the presence in the awareness of the speakers of an utterance ground, and
that the use of a deictic invariably invokes this ground. The discussion of
deictic semantics also assumed that an utterance event invariably forms the
base of the semantics of a deictic. I propose here an extension of the semantics of deictics which does not involve an utterance event as a ground; rather,
some other oriented domain serves as the base set of entities and relations
for interpreting a deictic. It is crucial that the domain is *oriented,* that is,
that it contains a reference point of some sort from the vantage point of which
other entities are evaluated. This will become clear presently. The domains
I have in mind are the cognitive models about culture, territory, and immigration discussed above. I will examine two examples from the interview data.
The first involves the use of a distal deictic to pick out a proximal location.
The second involves the use of the personal pronouns *you* and *they* to identify
not participants in the actual discourse situation, but roles in cognitive models
and individuals in mental spaces.

INHERITANCE OF THE CULTURAL MAP

Consider a statement by JF at the beginning of the segment JF16, given in
(18b).

(18) a. JR: I have kind of, kind of mixed feelings about different things,
        like I, I react in certain ways when I'm, like when I'm on the bus
        and I see an ad all in Spanish or you know, you walk down certain
        streets in a city, 'n you see most of the shop signs in Asian characters
        or something. I wonder, how do you feel when you encounter things
        like that? You know, what are your own, your own personal gut
        reactions? When you see a shop sign in Spanish or . . .

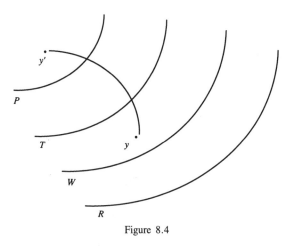

Figure 8.4

b. JF16: [starting over my finish] Well, well the fir, I guess the firs, the first thing you think is, um, you know, that you're in *that* part of the city, and I, I think usually you see that kind of stuff usually in the older part of the city, and um, I know, um, you can go out to like sorta there's a part of southeast San Diego where you do go down, you see all these Vietnamese theaters and everything in Vietnamese . . . (emphasis is JF's)

The point of interest in this example is the use of the distal deictic *that* in the phrase *that part of the city*. Note that the word was pronounced with heavy emphasis. Figure 8.4 gives a mental space diagram of this portion of the segment. With my question *how do you feel when you encounter things like that?* I set up a *when* space W within the origin space R (reality). JF's response remains in the *when* space, where she sets up the element y with the word *you;* this invokes a role paraphrasable as *one* or *someone*.[8] She cues us to remain in this space by using the present tense on the verb *think*. This verb then sets up another space, a thought space (T) which contains the thoughts of the generic individual set up by *you*. These thoughts comprise the clause *that you're in **that** part of the city*. The nominal *that part of the city* sets up another space, a location space, marked P. The word *you* and the relation *be in* of *you're in* set up the element y' in P. The identity of the elements y and y' is established by retention of the second person and by the trigger function of pronouns as discussed above.

Thus the space-building process in this discourse segment places a generic individual *you* in an ethnic neighborhood; *you,* the generic individual, has

thoughts there, including something like "self is in *that* part of the city."
We can identify the part of the city as the ethnic neighborhood by virtue of
the space building—the neighborhood has been set up by me in the question,
and the element *y* place there by virtue of JF's remaining in the space I set
up. We saw in the discussion of the quotative verb example above that just
such space building can provide the relations needed to sanction a proximal
deictic; and we can imagine the use of one, if *y*'s thoughts were to be
portrayed as a quote of internal speech. So what grounds the use of the distal
deictic *that* in this segment?

As I have mentioned previously, relations in *R* are always available for
the grounding of deictics, unless explicitly blocked by, for instance, a quotative verb, and one possible analysis of *that* is that it exploits the actual
distal relation of the neighborhood in question to the interview site. However,
several factors militate against this interpretation. One is the change in interpretation we get if we imagine an alternative scenario. Many neighborhoods
are located distantly enough from the one where the interview took place to
sanction distal deictics. We could have been discussing a distant mainstream,
"non-ethnic" neighborhood, and an expression like *There's no shopping
mall (tram stop/library branch) in that part of the city* would be unremarkable, with the distal deictic simply referring to a spatially distant location.
Another factor is the heavy intonational emphasis on the demonstrative. I
would class this usage not as taking the actual discourse context as ground,
but as being an example of a special use of highly stressed definite determiners to attribute to the modified nominal some special significance, often
already known to both speaker and hearer (at least, the speaker assumes that
the hearer shares the knowledge necessary to appreciate the special status of
the nominal's referent). Consider the examples in (19).

(19) a. My Dad always used to go on and on about how he had met *the*
       Bob Jones, the famous golfer, on his honeymoon.
    b. Upon entering the house I realized that this wasn't just any house.
       It was *the* house—the house where it had all happened, so many
       years ago.
    c. I tossed and turned and couldn't sleep because I couldn't shake the
       knowledge that I was lying in *that* bed—the bed where the old man
       had died.
    d. The first thing you think is . . . you're in *that* part of the city.

Emphatically stressed definite determiners in these sentences indicate a special significance of each nominal's referent; in these examples, I have provided appositive phrases which give a clue as to the nature of this signifi-

cance. The *that* in (18b) is a special definite determiner like the ones in (19). The special significance of the nominal *part of the city* is computed by virtue of importation of knowledge structures held by individuals in *R* and imputed to the generic conceptualizer in *P*. Recall what is going on by virtue of the space construction in this discourse segment: we are imagining the generic person's thoughts and it is this generic person who uses *that* in her thoughts. What is invoked with the deictic is a subpart of the generic individual's encyclopedic knowledge—I suggest the cultural map of San Diego. The emphatic determiner points to an item of encyclopedic knowledge that is shared by the discourse participants (here, generic *you,* plus the interviewer and interviewee). Use of the deictic activates the model or scenario within which the item is relevant, as well as the item itself.[9] In this case, the generic individual is in the ethnic neighborhood, and is at the same time invoking her model of how that part of town fits into her cultural map of San Diego; the deictic *that* indicates that it has marked status.[10]

Note that the speaker—the interviewee—assumes that the hearer will understand what is special about that part of the city with little specification of the factors that underlie its significance. She assumes that the foregoing description in my question is sufficient to establish the markedness of the neighborhood; in other words, she assumes that her interlocutor (as well as the generic individual in space *P!*) shares her classification of that part of the city as an ethnic neighborhood, and that its status as such is sufficiently marked to be deserving of a special definite determiner. This is implicit, background knowledge which is nevertheless necessary to comprehend the use of *that:* a case of semantic freeloading, in which cultural knowledge is available for the interpretation of a linguistic expression by being imported into constructed spaces. We can appreciate this by imagining, as her interlocutor, someone who does not share her model of the city, and does not know what it is about the neighborhood that is special. Such an individual is likely to respond to an utterance like (20a) with something like (20b). Imagine two people, A and B, driving through San Diego; A is familiar with the city and B is a newcomer.

(20) a. A: Uh-oh, we're heading into *that* part of the city.
      b. B: What do you mean, *that* part of the city? What's special about it?

B would probably be able to guess, from the *uh-oh* and from general knowledge about cities in America, that the part of the city in question is objectionable in some sense, but without specific knowledge of the cultural map of San Diego, would not know the specific factors that make it objectionable.

Imagine, further, an interlocutor who does not possess the general knowledge about American cities that tells her that they are likely to have undesirable locations, and that interlocutor's puzzlement increases even more.[11]

The relevant question for this study is: What is the ground for the use of the deictic *that* in this segment? I suggest that the ground is the shared (or presumed shared) model of San Diego's neighborhoods and their cultural affiliation. The usage is similar to, possibly an extension of, the discourse deictic use of *that* to "point" to previously mentioned entities. An example is given in (21).

(21) A: Do you think the doctor made a mistake in your treatment?
B: You bet. And I'm hiring an attorney for *that* reason.

Discourse deictics take the text of the discourse as ground; definite deictics such as *that* point to material that has been mentioned already and is therefore known and accessible to all participants in the discourse. In similar fashion, a usage such as that in (18) relies on knowledge presumed by the speaker to be shared by the discourse partipants. However, the knowledge in question is not a text constructed in discourse (in fact, as we have seen, the discourse is rather impoverished in providing a referent for *that*), but the knowledge stored in a cognitive model. Thus the ground for this kind of usage is the cognitive model in which a classification of San Diego's neighborhoods is given.

GENERIC PRONOUNS AND ROLES IN COGNITIVE MODELS

The reader will have noted the use of impersonal *you* on the part of my interviewee in several discourse segments quoted in this paper. In this section, I offer an analysis of some particular examples. (22) gives a sampling.

(22) a. JF1: If *you* want to get ahead in the United States *you* really have to know English. . . . Just depending on whatever country *you* go to, it's important to learn the language of that country.
b. JF8: In high school I took French and I found that *you* go to French class once a day and, you know, *you* do your French homework and stuff but *you* really don't learn the language that well. It's not until *you* go [to the country] and *you're* actually doing everything . . . in *your* life in that language that *you* really start to learn it.
c. JF16: These people, they've come to America and still, they wanna be back, you know? They wanna be here for the advantages, but they don't wanna give up what . . . they have come from. . . . And

I just don't think *you* can do that in this country, I mean either *you* have to *be* here and be a productive member of the society, or . . .

d. JF17: *You* can't just come over here and say, "Okay, I wanna be an American and forget about my past." I mean *you've* got some cultural ties to *your* past, but I think *you* have to throw off a lot of those, if *you* really want to become an American.

Bolinger (1979) and Lansing (1989) offer analyses of impersonal *you;* here I build on some aspects of these analyses. Bolinger proposes that impersonal *you* is a metaphor: "the participants in a conversation—*I, you, we*—are always present in a communicative act and available for metaphoric transfer" (1979:208). However, he does not explicitly give particulars of the metaphoric mapping involved in impersonal *you*. Precisely which aspects of the meaning of *you* in its basic, nonmetaphorical sense are transferred or mapped? What is the target domain into which they are mapped? The answers—or at least partial answers—to these questions are implicitly given in Bolinger's article. The target domain he proposes is normative behavior: "the use of *you* is somehow **normative**" (1979:201, his emphasis). Several pages of his article are devoted to a demonstration of this fact by noting that other apsects of the constructions in which impersonal *you* appears are compatible with a normative reading, for example imperfective aspect in the verbs of which impersonal *you* is subject (1979:201n). It is clear from some of JF's statements that the activities or obligations of the person designated by impersonal *you* conform to norms for particular situations, for instance her model of the typical or normal language-learning experience in American schools, as given in (22b), or her normative schema for "how much" of one's cultural background should be preserved when immigrating to a new country, as given in (22d).

In cognitive-model terms, we can say that impersonal *you* identifies a role in a script or frame—an idealized cognitive model or ICM. Many of these models are normative, as discussed above—the immigration scenario, for example. (22a), (22c), and (22d) illustrate such normative uses of impersonal *you*.

So the target domain for the metaphoric mapping, Bolinger suggests, is some normative model entertained by the speaker (and, in many cases, assumed by the speaker to be shared with her interlocutors, insofar as she views these as members of her culture). Thus the ground for interpreting this pronoun is not (or not exclusively; see the discussion below) the actual utterance context or default ground, but some normative model.

Which aspects of the source-domain meaning of *you* carry over into this target domain? Bolinger discusses several. One is *speaker viewpoint*. Recall that the reference point for identifying the person *you* designates is the speaker of an utterance; *you* designates the speaker's coparticipant in the discourse. In the normative use, the individual designated by *you* participates in behaviors that are considered normal, expected, or required from the viewpoint of the holder of the model (Bolinger 1979 (p. 205)). Parallel to the fact that the reference point for *you* in the default domain (the actual discourse situation) is the speaker, the reference point for normative behavior in the target domain is the holder of the model, the individual for whom the norms hold true.

Another property which is mapped is inclusiveness. While default *you* identifies a coparticipant in the source domain, the actual discourse, normative *you* identifies a coparticipant in the target domain: culturally normal behavior, behavior the speaker believes she herself would indulge in and that she would therefore identify with (according to Bolinger, "if the reference is to a stage on which the speaker has trouble imagining himself, *you* is proportionately difficult—which is to say that *you* adopts the viewpoint of the speaker" (1979:205)).

My informant may be exploiting this inclusiveness value by setting it up in direct opposition to the exclusive value of another pronoun, *they*. Examine closely the switches between *you* and *they* in the segments in (23).

(23) a. JF3: I don't understand their [= opponents of Proposition 63] logic behind that argument because in order to vote here you have to be a citizen, and in order to become a citizen you have to learn English. . . . So if they expect that they're gonna be voting they have to know English.

 b. JF8: It's not until you go and you're actually doing everything . . . in your life in that language that you really start to learn it. . . . They say that some of these kids even go through the bilingual education, they come out of high school and they can't even, they, they know English but not real well, and that they're still doing everything in their, their native language.

 c. JF16: These people, they've come to America and still, they wanna be back, you know? . . . They wanna be here for the advantages, but they don't wanna give up what . . . they have come from. . . . And I just don't think you can do that in this country, I mean either you have to *be* here and be a productive member of the society or you know, or you know, or you're just gonna sit there and you're gonna be like in "little Vietnam" or something. They're trying to make it just like it is, the way it was at home, but I mean if you're coming here you should try and, you know, try and fit into the society. . . . Either you're gonna have to give up, either go back there and you know, have what you, you know, like back there, or . . . be a member here. You know, I, I just don't think it's right when they come over and, from wherever and try to continue their culture here. You know, like they, they seem unwilling to wanna, um, become a member of the American culture, you know?

d. JF17: You can't just come over here and say, "Okay, I wanna be an American and forget about my past." I mean you've got some cultural ties to your past, but I think you have to throw off a lot of those, if you really want to become an American. And, um, I just don't think you can come over, and just . . . I don't see how they expect to become . . . you know, how much do they really wanna become Americans? You know, the next question. If they want to continue living in their own culture, you know, then you get the question, you know, how much do they really want to become an American?

There are two possible explanations for JF's use of *they* in these passages. One is that she has a specific third-person plural referent in mind—a particular group of real individuals of whom these predications (as far as she is concerned) are true. (23a) and (23b) exemplify this type; most of the exemplars in (23c) are also subject to this intepretation. Such a usage is nonmetaphorical, exploiting the actual discourse context as ground. But another interpretation is possible for these uses of *they*. On this interpretation, *they* serves as plural generic, and the propositions in which *they* appears describe typical behavior of a certain class of individuals, in a fashion similar to generic *you*. The clearest example of this is found at the end of segment (23c), repeated here as (24).

(24) You know, I, I just don't think it's right when they come over and, from wherever and try to continue their culture here. You know, like they, they seem unwilling to wanna, um, become a member of the American culture, you know?

The phrase *from wherever* indicates that JF does not have a particular group in mind; I suggest that what she does have in mind is "typical recalcitrant immigrants," in other words, a role in a model, but in this case the model, rather than being normative, is antinormative or "incorrigible"—it is a model of how uncooperative immigrants behave. The exclusive value of the deictic would appropriately indicate that the speaker conceives of them as being outside of groups to which she conceives herself as belonging.[12]

Some of the aspects of impersonal *you* that Bolinger considers are not metaphorical; that is, they do not involve transfer of semantic properties of utterance-grounded *you* into the target domain of normative models. Some of them seem to exploit directly the default meaning, i.e., the use of normative *you* is simultaneously metaphorical and literal.[13] Bolinger suggests that "impersonal *you* is a courtesy device. When I ask *How do you make a kite?* I defer to your judgment, even take instruction. When I say *You do it like this,* I give instructions without insisting on my role as would be the case if I said *I do it like this*" (1979:205). In his first example, *How do you make a kite?*, it is easy to see how a simultaneous personal and impersonal reading implies the superior knowledge resources of the actual addressee, and defers to this superiority—my reading of a question like this can include the inference that the addressee has made a kite at some point in the past, and it does include deference to the actual addressee's greater wisdom and experience in this domain; at the same time, the impersonal reading is available, implying that there is a standard procedure for kite making and it is this procedure that the speaker intends to elicit.[14]

There may be more to the dual value—literal and metaphorical—of normative *you* than Bolinger discusses. The use of *you* in descriptions of normative behavior may appeal directly to the actual addressee, in the sense that the speaker is implying that the addressee does or would engage in the described behavior under the appropriate circumstances. Thus it is both metaphorically inclusive, in the sense that the speaker includes the individual set up by *you* in a cultural in-group; and literally inclusive, in the sense that the speaker uses the default (second-person inclusive) value of *you* to equate the addressee with this set-up individual. This is accomplished, I suggest, by the value of pronouns as triggers, as discussed above. Accessing the normative model sets up a mental space within which the normal activities of an in-group member (labeled with normative *you*) are portrayed. Normative *you* acts, not only as a nominal designating an individual who conforms to the norm, but also as a trigger to identify the actual addressee. So normative *you* can be analyzed as having three-way reference: by virtue of speaker viewpoint, it refers to the speaker; by virtue of its nominal role in the mental space, it refers to a normal individual; and by virtue of its trigger function it refers to the addressee. All three individuals are seen as belonging to the in-group and as likely to act according to the norm, given the appropriate circumstances.

In the foregoing discussion I pointed out both metaphorical and nonmetaphorical aspects of normative *you*. Are all uses of impersonal *you* normative, and also metaphorical? Bolinger wishes to answer this question positively, motivated by his observations of inaccuracies in a previous analysis (Whitley 1978) which claimed that impersonal *you* is a simple generic, not always normative: "The crucial question is, how generic is *you?* Whitley would have it as generic as 'anyone and everyone' (p. 27), but there are peculiarities of its behavior that suggest a different interpretation'' (1979:199); similarly, ''impersonal *you* and *one* are close, but they cannot 'be used interchangeably, with little if any difference in meaning,' as Whitley claims (p. 20)'' (1979: 202).

Bolinger has a point, and the corrections he makes to Whitley's analysis are valid, but he goes too far in claiming that impersonal *you* is always metaphorical and always normative. There is a non-normative use of impersonal *you,* one which relies on mental space construction. I characterize this function as the mere setting up of a role in a mental space, without assigning a particular value to that role. This is essentially the analysis offered by Lansing (1989). On his analysis, impersonal *you* sets up a character Lansing calls the *focalizer*—a conceptualizer-actor functioning in a constructed space. Propositions and predications about that conceptualizer hold in that space.

Consider the following subsegments of JF16 and JF17, in which the anti-normative behavior of recalcitrant immigrants (those who refuse to assimilate, don't learn the language, etc.) is described (the segments of interest are those with pronouns in bold).

(25) JF16: These people, they've come to America and still, they wanna be back, you know? They wanna be here for the advantages, but they don't wanna give up what . . . they have come from. . . . And I just don't think you can do that in this country, I mean either you have to *be* here and be a productive member of the society or you know, or you know, or **you're** just gonna sit there and **you're** gonna be like in ''little Vietnam'' or something.

Note that in this example, one use of impersonal *you* cannot be considered normative:[15] *you're just gonna sit there and you're gonna be like in ''little Vietnam or something.* The kind of behavior described here—being trapped in an ethnic neighborhood, probably unemployed and hence unproductive, and creating an enclave which is not American (''little Vietnam''), is hardly in accord with the normative models of immigration discussed above and in Rubba 1988. Nor can it plausibly be considered to be referring to the addressee (myself—while graduate students may not be universally considered to be productively employed, I hardly fit the category of the recalcitrant immigrant). To whom is this *you* referring?

Note that impersonal *you* in this segment appears with a space builder, *gonna,* which sets up a future and/or hypothetical space. In this space, *you* sets up a role of which undesirable traits are predicated—*just sit there, be in ''little Vietnam.''* The reading is not normative, but it *is* typical (generic).

If it were normative, we would be able to say that the speaker identifies with this role as a cultural norm, but it is clear from attitudes she has expressed elsewhere that this kind of behavior does not follow the normative script she maintains for the process of immigration. However, it does read as "anyone and everyone in such a situation"—a reading similar to Whitley's "anyone and everyone," but with the stipulation that a situation is set up within which this "anyone and everyone" plays a role. It is a script, but not an in-group script, not an approved script from the cultural viewpoint of the speaker. And the hypothetical situation is set up by space-building expressions in the discourse, *either . . . or* and *gonna* for this particular example.

To see how space building affects the acceptability of impersonal *you,* let us turn now to the segments in which the actual usage is *they.* These statements also describe typical, although unapproved, behavior on the part of immigrants. For some of these segments, substituting impersonal *you* for *they* works better than for others.

(26) JF16: And I just don't think you can do that in this country, I mean either you have to *be* here and be a productive member of the society or you know, or you know, or *you're* just gonna sit there and *you're* gonna be like in "little Vietnam" or something. *They're* trying to make it just like it is, the way it was at home, but I mean if you're coming here you should try and, you know, try and fit into the society.

Substituting *you're* for *they're* in (26) does not work—the impersonal reading is lost, and the reading is personal. This is because the present-progressive tense of the sentence switches the focus out of the space set up by *gonna* in the previous clauses to *R,* the actual discourse space. In that space, no normative reading is available for *you* because the content of the clause does not follow the norms for the situation in question. The default reading is available, of course, since there is an addressee; hence the personal reading. Now notice that adding a space-building expression before this clause restores the impersonal reading.

(27) When you continue your culture here, you're trying to make it just like it is, the way it was at home, but I mean if you're coming here you should . . .

The *when* clause sets up a space within which a generic role can be set up, and the generic reading is available within that space.

In (28b), the substitution works for the two clauses within the *when* space, but fails in the next sentence, where there is no space builder.

(28) a. JF16: You know, I, I just don't think it's right when *they* come over and from wherever and try to continue *their* culture here. You know, like *they, they* seem unwilling to wanna, um, become a member of the American culture, you know?

b. You know, I, I just don't think it's right when *you* come over and, from wherever and try to continue *your* culture here. ??You know, like *you, you* seem unwilling to wanna, um, become a member of the American culture, you know?

c. You know, I, I just don't think it's right when *you* come over and, from wherever and try to continue *your* culture here. You know, *if you do that,* it's like *you, you* seem unwilling to wanna, um, become a member of the American culture, you know?

Adding a space builder—an *if*-clause—in (28c) improves the generic reading considerably.

In (29a), although space builders are present (*think,* which allows an impersonal reading for the first *you*), the situation is not specified in enough detail to attain the generic reading; hence the unacceptability of (29b). Adding the elliptical material which we presume the speaker had in mind with some space-building material makes the generic reading available in (29c). Note also that the space-building *If you want to continue* makes the impersonal reading available for the repetition of the *how much* question at the end of the segment.

(29) a. And, um, I just don't think you can come over, and just . . . I don't see how *they* expect to become . . . you know, how much do *they* really wanna become an American? You know, the next question. If *they* want to continue living in *their* own culture, you know, then you get the question, you know, how much do *they* really want to become an American?

b. And, um, I just don't think you can come over, and just . . . ??I don't see how *you* expect to become . . . ??you know, how much do *you* really wanna become an American? You know, the next question. If *you* want to continue living in *your* own culture, you know, then you get the question, you know, how much do *you* really want to become an American?

c. And, um, I just don't think you can come over, and just continue your culture here. *Under those circumstances,* I don't see how *you* expect to become . . . you know, how much do *you* really wanna become an American? You know, the next question. If *you* want to continue living in *your* own culture, you know, then you get the question, you know, how much do *you* really want to become an American?

These tests show that an impersonal reading for *you* is most readily available inside a constructed space distinct from *R*. We can analyze this use of *you* as an unspecified role in a mental space. It appears that, in some cases, enough other propositional content has to be present to specify the fictive situation being set up as a mental space. This may be the most schematic meaning for nonpersonal *you*.

These facts contradict Bolinger's claim that impersonal *you* is always normative and metaphorical. Apparently, cases persist where impersonal *you* is equivalent to Whitley's "anyone and everyone." This raises the question of whether Bolinger's metaphorical and normative uses can be reduced to the type just explored, a use setting up an unspecified role in a mental space. Alternatively, the latter value may be analyzable as an extension from the normative or from the literal use of *you*. I will not attempt to decide this question here, but leave it for future work. We can make note of some commonalities the unspecified-role use of *you* has with both other uses of *you:* it makes a connection between the fictive conceptualizer (the role in the mental space) and some real people; the discourse participants (the actual speaker and listener) and other people (people who actually engage—have engaged, will engage—in the behaviors imputed to impersonal *you*). Also, the speaker viewpoint is preserved, albeit weakly, since the speaker belongs to the class of values ("anyone and everyone") available to fill the generic role. Lastly, it exploits the invocation of the addressee, implying that the behavior of *you* is behavior that the addressee might herself engage in.

I have given two explanations for impersonal *you*—one normative, one simply generic. For the normative use, I have attempted to make explicit some features of the metaphorical mapping proposed by Bolinger (1979), and have also commented on nonmetaphorical aspects of normative *you*. For the generic sense, I have given a more explicit account of Lansing's *focalizer* in mental space terms, and have demonstrated the necessity of space-building expressions to attaining the generic interpretation.

Conclusion

In this paper, I have analyzed some of the extended uses of deictic expressions in English. I first gave a general outline of the problem—the task of finding referents for deictics in ongoing discourse; factors that enter into solving this problem; and the central notion of the account, alternate grounds. I then reviewed a concept of deictic semantics which offers enough detail to examine specifically which aspects of deictic semantics are exploited in alternate-ground phenomena. These semantic features were shown to be imported into other domains or onto other bases or grounds—alternate utterances, as in quotes and free indirect speech; or, in further extensions, into non-utterance bases, including shared models, such as the cultural map of San Diego; shared norms for behavior; and scripts or scenarios that are typical without necessarily being normative or prescriptive.

The analysis presented here demonstrates how deictic semantics as well as pragmatic and cultural knowledge are intimately intertwined in a particular access problem: accessing the intended referents of deictics in discourse. It also deals with some important viewpoint phenomena, showing how space-building language provides speakers the opportunity to displace the viewpoint relevant for deictic expressions in the discourse, and how the orientedness of some cultural models provides a viewpoint which can be adopted in interpreting deictics such as special *that* and normative *you.* Also illustrated is metaphor, the importation of semantic structure into new domains: deictic semantics are transferred into domains which are not interpretable as utterance or indexical grounds, such as the domains for normative and generic *you,* and special definite determiners such as *that* in the example considered here. Another aspect of the importation of structure is semantic freeloading: the automatic inheritance, into constructed spaces, of models from the origin space (such as the cultural map of San Diego), without explicit language invoking the model; The speaker assumes, when she says "*that* part of the city," that her interlocutor shares the cultural map *and* has access to it within the constructed space. The importance of scripts or frames for situations that form part of our everyday experience is shown in the analysis of *you* as normative; and the general architecture of mental space theory allows us to construct an account of generic uses of *you* that are non-normative.

Overall, I hope to have relayed the complexity of the task language users face when they encounter a deictic expression in discourse and must find a referent for it. I have explored only a small number of cases of what is no doubt a very widespread phenomenon, and have shown that constructs from various branches of cognitive linguistics are useful in explicating this phenomenon. This work is but a beginning to what promises to be a large and fertile area for applications of cognitive linguistics to discourse research.

Notes

1. This paper is an expansion of Rubba 1989, which in turn is based on work done in an earlier project (Rubba 1988). Some of the material included here was presented

in the cognitive science seminar at the University of California, San Diego, in November, 1988, and portions of Rubba 1988 were presented at the annual meeting of the law and Society Association at Berkeley in June, 1990. The data analysis of these previous versions is substantially revised in this paper.

A number of individuals provided guidance and helpful comments in the preparation of these projects. These include Gilles Fauconnier and Ron Langacker, who provided assistance with the theoretical frameworks of mental spaces and cognitive grammar, as well as helpful insights with respect to the particular phenomena treated here. Thanks also to George Lakoff, Jeff Lansing, Teenie Matlock, Naomi Quinn, Eve Sweetser, Karen van Hoek, David Zubin, and the other participants in the Berkeley-San Diego Cognitive Linguistics Workshop held at the University of California, San Diego, in spring, 1991. I am indebted to Roy D'Andrade for guidance on the original project, and to my informants for their candid responses. Two anonymous reviewers made helpful comments and corrections.

2. The data are from queries and responses in an interview between myself and a subject in a sociolinguistic study (Rubba 1988). The purpose of the study was to examine the rhetoric in the political debate that accompanied the passage of California Proposition 63, which, in 1986, made English the official language of California. It is important to note that, in the course of eliciting these data, I was not attempting to elicit interesting uses of deictic expressions. Their interesting nature became apparent to me in the analysis phase of the study.

3. Langacker cites an early version of Fauconnier's work on mental spaces in this discussion.

4. Hanks (1990) offers an analysis of alternate grounds similar to the one offered here, albeit in other than mental space terminology. His *frames* (drawn from work by Goffman (1981) are the equivalent of mental spaces, and he describes the phenomena in question in terms highly compatible with mental space theory. For instance, he exemplifies multiple embeddings of frames or mental spaces and the use of cuing devices (his *shifters*) for tracking reference across embeddings (1990:208); he notes the trigger function of pronouns, and the function of some linguistic expressions as *keys* (some keys that Hanks describes are, in Fauconnier's framework, space builders). Hanks's analysis provides support for the present account from an unrelated language.

5. David Zubin, in personal communication, holds that verbs like *feel* admit quotes. Although the discussion to follow refutes this idea, I am grateful for his incitement to explore the question.

6. We cannot allow the fact that these two individuals—the actual discourse speaker (the interviewee) and the conceptualizer in the Vietnamese neighborhood— are the same person to confuse this discussion. In mental-space terms, these are two distinct entities in distinct spaces; their identity is established by means of connectors, as discussed above, as well as by other aspects of the utterance, such as elements or spaces which would lead us to connect the last *I* to a person other than the speaker.

7. I owe these observations to Gilles Fauconnier (p.c.). David Zubin (p.c.) questions whether this is a "live" or "dead" linguistic metonymy—i.e., whether the

speaker divorces space and culture sufficiently for us to say that she is actively using a metonymic connector in such speech. Zubin's claim is that the tie is direct, and the usage therefore nonmetonymic. This might well be the case; but we must acknowledge that at some point or on some level, metonymy is involved—it could be historically, such that the linguistic metonymy was once alive, but became conventionalized to the point that abstract domains are now the semantic base for extensions of physical-space terms such as *here*. Or it could be a case of metonymic reasoning (see Lakoff 1987 and Rubba 1988), in which one concept (space) stands in for an associated concept (culture) in thinking, and this is reflected in language use.

8. Interestingly, JF performs a switch here from the clearly personal *you* at the end of my question to impersonal *you*. Although this switch is relevant to the present discussion, I will not discuss it here.

9. We can also assume that the discourse topic of ethnic neighborhoods is set up in my question and primes the model so that it is available for interpretation of later language. This priming must be quite general, however; my words *certain streets in a city* are the first mention in this interview of anything related to the notion of ethnic neighborhoods. The complex structure of the model remains implicit.

10. Discussion with Karen van Hoek was very helpful in sorting out this point.

11. In cases like these, emphatic *that* seems to carry a negative connotation. I have not explored other data with emphatic *that* to find out if it always carries this connotation, nor have I considered how this connotation is acquired by the deictic.

12. *They* is often used in this way in making generalizations about people viewed as belonging to some group or class that does not include the other discourse participants. For example, it seems perfectly acceptable to utter (i) in the presence of just a single representative of the class in question (babies).

(i) (On holding a baby and having it squeeze the speaker's finger): It's so cute how they hold your finger so tight!

13. Langacker has also made this point to me in personal communication.

14. For a reply like *You do it like this,* however, my reading is strictly impersonal. I agree with Bolinger that it "flaunts" less than the use of *I* would in such a statement. Thus the speaker uses impersonal *you* to generalize her knowledge and imply that it is nothing special; she is not an unusually superior individual for knowing how to make a kite. This use "spreads the credit" for having some particular skill beyond the speaker and to people in general. I would argue that impersonal *you* is also used to spread not credit, but blame. An example like (i) makes this clear.

(i) I completely forgot the committee meeting. When you're so busy, you lose track of things.

In this statement the speaker switches to impersonal *you* in order to imply that her foibles are shared by everyone in such a circumstance—again, it generalizes her experience. Substituting *I* in this statement localizes the blame and sounds much more like a confession of an individual fault, and not an excuse intended to make the faulty behavior seem more acceptable.

15. I am grateful to Jeff Lansing for pointing out these non-normative uses of *you* (including substitutions of *you* for *they* to be discussed below).

References

Bobrow, Daniel G., and Donald A. Norman. 1975. Some Principles of Memory Schemata. In Daniel G. Bobrow and Allan Collins, eds., *Representation and Understanding*, 131–49. New York: Academic Press.

Bolinger, Dwight. 1979. To Catch a Metaphor: *You* As Norm. *American Speech* 54: 194–209.

Fauconnier, Gilles. 1985. *Mental Spaces: Aspects of Meaning Construction in Natural Language*. Cambridge, Mass.: MIT Press. Reprinted 1994, Cambridge: Cambridge University Press.

Fillmore, Charles J. 1971. *Santa Cruz Lectures on Deixis*. Bloomington, Ind.: Indiana University Linguistics Club.

———. 1982. Frame Semantics. In Linguistic Society of Korea, ed., *Linguistics in the Morning Calm*, 111–38. Seoul: Hanshin.

Goffman, Erving. 1981. *Forms of Talk*. Philadelphia: University of Pennsylvania Press.

Hanks, William. 1990. *Referential Practice: Language and Lived Space Among the Maya*. Chicago: University of Chicago Press.

Lakoff, George. 1982. Categories and Cognitive Models. Cognitive Science Technical Report no. 19, Institute for Cognitive Studies, University of California, Berkeley.

———. 1987. *Women, Fire, and Dangerous Things: What Categories Reveal about the Mind*. Chicago: University of Chicago Press.

Langacker, Ronald W. 1978. The Form and Meaning of the English Auxiliary. *Language* 54.

———. 1985. Observations and Speculations on Subjectivity. In John Haiman, ed., *Iconicity in Syntax*, 109–50. Amsterdam: John Benjamins.

———. 1987. *Foundations of Cognitive Grammar*. Vol. 1: *Theoretical Prerequisites*. Stanford, Calif.: Stanford University Press.

———. 1991. *Foundations of Cognitive Grammar*. Vol. 2: *Descriptive Application*. Stanford, Calif.: Stanford University Press.

Lansing, Jeff. 1989. Impersonal *you*. Manuscript, University of California, San Diego.

Quinn, Naomi. 1987. Convergent Evidence for a Cultural Model of American Marriage. In Dorothy Holland and Naomi Quinn, eds., *Cultural Models in Language and Thought*, 173–92. Cambridge: Cambridge University Press.

Rauh, Gisa. 1981. Aspects of Deixis. In Gisa Rauh, ed., *Essays on Deixis*, 9–60. Tübingen: Gunter Narr Verlag.

Rubba, Jo. 1988. Cognitive Models and California Proposition 63: English as Official Language. Manuscript, University of California, San Diego.

————. 1989. ". . . *That* Part of the City": Mental Spaces and Ethnic Neighbor-hoods. *Proceedings of the Fifteenth Annual Meeting of the Berkeley Linguistics Society,* 268–77. Berkeley, CA: Berkeley Linguistics Society.

Rumelhart, D.E., P. Smolensky, J.L. McClelland, and G.E. Hinton. 1986. Schemata and Sequential Thought Processes in PDP Models. In D.E. Rumelhart, J.L. McClelland, and the PDP Research Group, eds., *Parallel Distributed Processing, Vol. 2,* 7–57. Cambridge, Mass.: MIT Press.

Schank, Roger C., and R.P. Abelson. 1977. *Scripts, Plans, Goals and Understand-ing: An Inquiry into Human Knowledge Structures.* Hillsdale, N.J.: Lawrence Erl-baum Associates.

Talmy, Leonard. 1986. Decoupling in the Semantics of Attention and Perspective. *Proceedings of the Twelfth Annual Meeting of the Berkeley Linguistics Society.* Berkeley, CA: Berkeley Linguistics Society.

————. 1988. The Relation of Grammar to Cognition. In Brygida Rudzka-Ostyn, ed., *Topics in Cognitive Linguistics,* 165–205. Amsterdam: John Benjamins.

Whitley, M. Stanley. 1978. Person and Number in the Use of *we, you,* and *they. American Speech* 53:18–39. [8]

9 Roles and Identificational Copular Sentences

·
·
·
·

Copular sentences with two NPs, NP_1 be NP_2, have at least three uses: predication, identification, and identity statements.[1] Predicational copular sentences such as (1) and (2) ascribe a property denoted by the predicate NP to the referent of the subject NP. Logically, they express class membership or class inclusion of the referent of the subject NP in the class characterized by the predicate NP. Subject NPs of predicational sentences are usually referential but predicate NPs are never referential linguistically.

(1) Jack is a student.

(2) A whale is a mammal.

Identificational sentences such as (3) combine two NPs, one expressing a variable and the other identifying its value. The value-denoting NP is strongly referential, while the variable-denoting one is only weakly so; that is, it purports to refer but it cannot succeed in doing so because its referent is not known to the hearer. The function of identificational sentences is to make it possible for the hearer to identify the unknown value of a variable.

(3) Clinton is the president of the United States.

Copular sentences may be pragmatically ambiguous between predication and identification. For example, sentence (4) is predicational if the predicate *a minor official* is taken to be nonreferential, meaning something like "the head of state is only a nominal position without any substantial power." Sentence (4) may be the answer to a question such as *How powerful is the head of state?* But suppose that the identity of the head of state is known to few people, in order to reduce the danger of assassination. Someone asks a question such as *Who is the head of state?* and (4) is the answer. Then the predicate of (4) is more strongly referential than the subject and (4) is identificational.

(4) The head of state is a minor official.

Identity statements such as (5) express identity of the referents of the two NPs. In this case, the two NPs are both strongly referential.

(5) Tully is Cicero.

What distinguishes these three uses of copular sentences is a difference in referentiality between the two NPs. In predicational sentences, the difference is the greatest, for the subject is referential while the predicate NP can never be. This difference prevents permutation of the two NPs in predicational sentences. Thus, (6) and (7) do not have the same meanings as (1) and (2). The exclamation point preceding these examples indicates that a sentence may be acceptable with a different meaning.

(6) !A student is Jack.

(7) !A mammal is a whale.

In identity statements, there is no such difference between the two NPs and either of them may be the subject, so that permutation does not produce any semantic change; for example, (8) has the same meaning as (5).

(8) Cicero is Tully.

Identificational sentences are in between; a difference remains but it is not as important as for predicational sentences. The strongly referential value denoting NP of identificational sentences is usually taken to be the underlying subject and the incompletely referential variable denoting NP the underlying predicate, but permutation is still possible in this case, so that (3) can be transformed into (9) without semantic effect.

(9) The president of the United States is Clinton.

Sometimes the order of the two NPs helps determine which type of copular sentence is in question. In fact, (3) may be identificational or predicational;

but the only plausible reading of (9) is identificational, for it is extremely difficult for proper names such as *Clinton* to denote a property.

There is also an elliptical type of copular sentence of the form shown in (10), which is drawn from Nunberg 1979.

(10) I am the ham sandwich.

The intended reading of (10) is something like "I'm the one who ordered the ham sandwich." It clearly does not express identity ("I = the ham sandwich") or membership ("I ∈ {ham sandwich}"). This type of copular sentence is called an eel sentence in Japanese linguistics, for the example discussed most intensively happened to be the following, which may also mean that the speaker literally is an eel.

(11) Watasi-wa unagi-da.
     I-TOP   eel-COP
     'I am {an eel/the eel}.'

In this paper, I undertake a description of identificational copular sentences in Japanese, using the notion of role proposed in the Mental Spaces framework (Fauconnier 1985). I first explain the notion of role, define the identificational use of copular sentences with regard to it, and point out some of the differences between identification and predication in Japanese. I then describe in some detail characteristics of identificational copular sentences and show that so-called eel sentences can be explained as elliptical identificational copular sentences with their role missing at the surface level. Finally, I extend the notion of an identificational sentence to the so-called *double subject construction* in Japanese, and show that the notion of role is useful for explaining its multiple readings.

Roles and Their Functional Character

NPs, especially common NPs, do not always refer to the same entity. The referent may change according to contextual parameters such as the speaker's beliefs, the situation, the time, and so on. In order to account for this type of context dependence of NPs in identifying their referents, Fauconnier (1985) proposes the idea of role. A role, which is given by the meaning or descriptive content of an NP, is a kind of function which ranges over parameters such as time, situation, context, etc., and chooses a suitable value from the set of objects satisfying the descriptive content. For example, *president* is a role function whose domain and range are respectively a set of countries and a set of presidents, as in (12).

(12) president (USA) = Clinton
      president (Korea) = Kim Young Sam
      president (France) = Chirac

Certain NPs such as *the author of the Iliad* are roles fully specified for parameters, so that their values are definitely fixed. But when parameters are easily recoverable from the context, they may be omitted. For instance, if we are talking about successive American presidents, we do not have to say *the current president of the United States of America; the current president* will do. Sometimes even *the president* will suffice to refer to Clinton. We thus have roles underspecified for certain parameters (cf. Nishiyama 1990).

There are roles such as *my son* that are underspecified for the parameter of time but immune to changes in it, since once their values are fixed at a certain time point, they point always to the same values in spite of any other changes happening to them. However, roles such as *the prime minister of Japan* are underspecified for the time parameter and sensitive to time changes for identification of their values, so that they may yield multiple values when the sentence in which they appear provides varying parameters, as in (14).

(13) My son has changed recently.

(14) The prime minister of Japan has changed recently.

Sentence (13) means that there has been some change in the speaker's son, while his identity remains intact. Suppose that (14) was uttered on October 17, 1993. It may mean something similar to (13), i.e., that Hosokawa, the actual value of *prime minister of Japan* on that day, had changed recently; e.g., his mood, his political opinions, or his appearance had altered. But it may mean that the value of *prime minister of Japan* had changed. The NP *the prime minister of Japan* denotes an underspecified role in that the parameter relative to time is not specified. The first interpretation is called a value interpretation, in which an NP is used as a convenient means to refer to a particular object which happens to be the value of the role given by the NP. The second interpretation is called a role interpretation, in which the role *prime minister of Japan* associates different values to parameters defined by the adverbial *recently*. Thus, the role interpretation in (14) expresses the very functional character of the role. I call this kind of interpretation in particular a value-changing role interpretation.

The sentence below means that the value of the role *prime minister of Japan* is Hosokawa under the parameter *now*.

(15) Now, the prime minister of Japan is Hosokawa.

This sentence is identificational. The subject NP in (15) is given a value-changing role interpretation and is not fully referential; that is, its referent is not identified by the hearer. I define an identificational sentence, NP_1 *be* NP_2, as follows: one NP denotes a role which is value-changing and nonreferential, and the other identifies the value for the role.[2]

Absurd inferences sometimes appear to be valid, due to the fact that parameters may be omitted when recoverable from the utterance context. A well-known example of this is given in (16).

(16) The temperature is 90°.
　　　The temperature is rising.
　　　*Therefore, 90° is rising.

The first sentence is an elliptical identificational sentence that means that the role *temperature* yields a value *90°* under the implicit parameter *now*. The NP *the temperature* is an underspecified role, but a particular parameter is assigned to it implicitly. The transcription *temperature = 90°* does not correspond accurately to this interpretation; it should be transcribed by *temperature(now) = 90°*. The second sentence means that the underspecified role *temperature* assigns different values to different time points such that for every pair of time points t_0 and t_1, if t_1 is later than t_0, *temperature(t_1)* is higher than *temperature(t_0)*. We cannot substitute *90°* for the second occurrence of *the temperature*, since *90°* can not denote such a value-changing role. *90°* is just the value of the role *temperature* under the parameter *now;* it cannot take any more parameters to yield different values.

The inference in (17), which has (14) as the second premise, is quite similar to (16) in its structure; as noted above, (14) has two interpretations. What is interesting about (17) is that the value interpretation of the second premise renders this inference valid, while the value-changing interpretation still makes it invalid just for the same reason as for (16).

(17) The prime minister is Hosokawa.
　　　The prime minister has changed recently.
　　　Therefore, Hosokawa has changed recently.

A concrete object, such as a person, is more than a bundle of properties and its identity may remain the same even if it changes in a certain property to some extent. In this case, a value interpretation is compatible with changes in some properties. But an abstract object such as the temperature in a certain place is simply a property which consists in a set of values. A change in an abstract object is therefore always a change in values, so that the only acceptable interpretation of the second premise of (16) is a value-changing interpretation, with the effect that there is no reading that can make the inference (16) valid (cf. Sakahara 1990c).

Predication and Identification in Japanese

Japanese copular sentences may be used for predication and identification, just like their English counterparts. The subject of predicational sentences is marked by the topic marker *wa;* a predicational sentence is of the form NP_1 *wa* NP_2 *da,* as in (18).[3]

(18) Homer-wa   Iliad-no   sakusha-da.
      Homer-TOP   Iliad-GEN   author-COP
      'Homer is the author of the Iliad.'

The subject of identificational sentences is marked by the nominative marker *ga,* as in (19).

(19) Homer-ga   Iliad-no   sakusha-da.
      Homer-NOM   Iliad-GEN   author-COP
      'Homer is the author of the Iliad.'

The copular morpheme *da* appears in identificational sentences, as in predicational ones, the only difference in form between (18) and (19) is in the marking of the subject, with *wa* in (18) and *ga* in (19).[4] However, their readings are clearly distinguished. The nominative marker *ga* requires a reading that Kuno (1972) called *exhaustive listing,* which tends to give rise to an implicature that all the suitable values are enumerated, so that (19) could be expressed more accurately by a cleft sentence such as (20) in English.

(20) It is Homer who is the author of the Iliad.

In the predicational sentence (18), the focal item is the predicate, but in the identificational sentence (19), it is the subject; this difference in information structure shows up as soon as these sentences are negated. Sentence (18) is compatible with negation, as in (21), but (19) cannot be negated, as (22) below shows.

(21) Homer-wa   Iliad-no   sakusha-de-nai.
     Homer-TOP Iliad-GEN author-COP-NEG
     'Homer is not the author of the Iliad.'

(22) *Homer-ga   Iliad-no   sakusha-de-nai.
     Homer-NOM Iliad-GEN author-COP-NEG
     'Homer is not the author of the Iliad.'

As Takubo (1983) suggests, Japanese has a constraint on negation such that the focus of negation must be inside VPs. Sentence (22) may only be interpreted, though not very naturally, as an identificational sentence whose VP is negative from the start; that is, this sentence will identify someone who is not an author of the Iliad.

For identificational sentences, permutation is possible without any clear semantic effect, and in this case the surface subject is marked by the topic marker *wa,* as in (23). In this case, the focal item is inside the VP and, as we predict, (23) may be negated as in (24).

(23) Iliad-no   sakusha-wa Homer-da.
     Iliad-GEN author-TOP Homer-COP
     'The author of the Iliad is Homer.'

(24) Iliad-no   sakusha-wa Homer-de-nai.
     Iliad-GEN author-TOP Homer-COP-NEG
     'The author of the Iliad is not Homer.'

It is easy to see that (23) is identificational, since proper names such as *Homer* are not taken to denote a property. Sentences (19) and (23) are equivalent and they are equally appropriate answers to the WH-question in (25), which requires the value for the role of the author of the Iliad to be specified.

(25) Iliad-no   sakusha-wa dare-ka?
     Iliad-GEN author-TOP who-Q
     'Who is the author of the Iliad?'

However, permutation is not possible for predicational sentences; (26) is grammatical by itself, but is not equivalent to (18).

(26) !Iliad-no   sakusha-ga   Homer-da.
     Iliad-GEN   author-NOM   Homer-COP
     'It is the author of the Iliad who is Homer.'

There are several other differences between Japanese predicational and identificational sentences, but we need not be concerned with details here (cf. Sakahara 1990a).

Characteristics of Japanese Identificational Sentences

Four Sentence Patterns

The function of identificational sentences is to make it possible for the hearer to identify the value of the role under certain contextual parameters. Up to this point, I have treated the variable part of identificational sentences as an inseparable block. However, when it is composed of a role-denoting NP and a parameter-denoting one, it may often be divided into two parts. Thus writing the former as R, the latter as P, and a value as V, we can represent the structure of (27) as (28). Furthermore, there are four surface patterns that are roughly equivalent to (28), as in (29). I will refer to them as ①, ②, ③, and ④; they are illustrated in (30).

(27) Iliad-no   sakusha-wa, Homer-da.
     Iliad-GEN   author-TOP   Homer-COP
     'The author of the Iliad is Homer.'

(28) P-no   R-wa, V-da.
     P-GEN   R-TOP V-COP

(29) ① [P-no R-wa], [V-da]. (= (28))   ①————permutation————→③

     ② [P-wa], [R-wa], [V-da].
        P-TOP   R-TOP   V-COP   topicalization of   topicalization of
                                    the parameter   the parameter

     ③ [V-ga], [P-no   R-da].
        V-NOM P-GEN   R-COP

                                          ②————permutation————→④
     ④ [P-wa], [V-ga], [R-da].
        P-TOP   V-NOM R-COP

(30) ① Iliad-no sakusha-wa, Homer-da. (= (27))

② Iliad-wa,   sakusha-wa, Homer-da.
Iliad-TOP   author-TOP   Homer-COP
'As for the Iliad, the author is Homer.'

③ Homer-ga,   Iliad-no   sakusha-da.
Homer-NOM Iliad-GEN   author-COP
'Homer is the author of the Iliad.'

④ Iliad-wa,   Homer-ga,   sakusha-da.
Iliad-GEN   Homer-NOM author-COP
'As for the Iliad, Homer is the author.'

The syntactic clusterings are indicated by brackets in (29). In subject position, role-denoting NPs are marked by *wa,* and value-denoting NPs by *ga.* Parameter-denoting NPs attach to role-denoting NPs in the form of genitive modifiers, as in ① and ③, or they are independent elements directly dominated by a sentence node and marked by *wa,* as in ② and ④.

From the well known difference in information structure between the subjects marked by *wa* and those marked by *ga* in Japanese (cf. Kuno 1972), we see that in identificational sentences, parameters and roles represent given information and values represent new information. The first phrase introduced by the topic marker *wa* sets up a frame in which the sentence that follows holds. For example, (31) has a similar information structure to (32).

(31) Kinou-wa,   watasi-wa Tokyo-ni   itta.
yesterday-TOP I-TOP   Tokyo-GOAL went
'Yesterday, I went to Tokyo.'

(32) On the subject of what I did yesterday, I went to Tokyo.

In ② and ④, the parameter functions as the frame of the following sentence; that is, the parameter is the starting point of the act of identification expressed by the sentence. It is to be noted that in ② and ④, the function of the role, which is to map a parameter onto a value, is especially clear from the surface form itself.

Four Question Patterns

From the four patterns above, WH-questions that require a value for the role to be specified can be easily formed by replacing the value by the WH-word *dare* 'who' or *nani* 'what', depending on whether the question is about a human being or a thing, as in (33).[5] In this case, the question marker *ka* is attached to the end of the sentence and the copula *da* is deleted. This paradigm is exemplified in (34).

(33) ① P-no   R-wa, {dare/nani}-ka?
P-GEN R-TOP {who/what}-Q
'{Who/what} is R of P?'

② P-wa, R-wa, {dare/nani}-ka?
P-TOP R-TOP {who/what}-Q
'As for P, {who/what} is R?'

③ {dare/nani}-ga,   P-no   R-ka?
{who/what}-NOM P-GEN R-Q
'{Who/What} is R of P?'

④ P-wa, {dare/nani}-ga,   R-ka?
P-TOP {who/what}-NOM R-Q
'As for P, {who/what} is R?'

(34) ① Iliad-no   sakusha-wa, dare-ka?
Iliad-GEN author-TOP   who-Q
'Who is the author of the Iliad?'

② Iliad-wa, sakusha-wa, dare-ka?
Iliad-TOP author-TOP   who-Q
'As for the Iliad, who is the author?'

③ Dare-ga,   Iliad-no   sakusha-ka?
who-NOM Iliad-GEN author-Q
'Who is the author of the Iliad?'

④ Iliad-wa, dare-ga,   sakusha-ka?
Iliad-TOP who-NOM author-Q
'As for the Iliad, who is the author?'

But neither questions about the role, such as (35), nor questions about the parameter, such as (36), are acceptable.

(35) ① *Iliad-no   nani-wa, Homer-ka?
     Iliad-GEN what-TOP Homer-Q
     'What of the Iliad is Homer?'

   ② *Iliad-wa, nani-wa, Homer-ka?
     Iliad-TOP what-TOP Homer-Q
     'As for the Iliad, what is Homer?'

   ③ *Homer-ga, Iliad-no   nani-ka?
     Homer-NOM Iliad-GEN what-Q
     'What of the Iliad is Homer?'

   ④ *Iliad-wa, Homer-ga, nani-ka?
     Iliad-TOP Homer-NOM what-Q
     'As for the Iliad, what is Homer?'

(36) ① *Nani-no   sakusha-wa, Homer-ka?
     what-GEN author-TOP   Homer-Q
     'The author of what is Homer?'

   ② *Nani-wa, sakusha-wa, Homer-ka?
     what-TOP author-TOP   Homer-Q
     'As for what, the author is Homer?'

   ③ *Homer-ga, nani-no   sakusha-ka?
     Homer-NOM what-GEN author-Q
     'Homer is the author of what?'

   ④ *Nani-wa, Homer-ga,   sakusha-ka?
     what-TOP Homer-NOM author-Q
     'As for what, Homer is the author?'

However, the situation is exactly the other way around in the case of predicational sentences; the subject (or a part of it) cannot be asked about while the predicate or its part can be.

(37) a. *Dare-wa Iliad-no   sakusha-ka?
     who-TOP Iliad-GEN author-Q
     'Who is the author of the Iliad?'

b. Homer-wa nani-no sakusha-ka?
Homer-TOP what-GEN author-Q
'The author of what is Homer?'

c. Homer-wa Iliad-no nani-ka?
Homer-TOP Iliad-GEN what-Q
'What of the Iliad is Homer?'

I conclude from this that the value is the focal item of identificational sentences composed of a role, a parameter, and a value, and that it is taken to replace a WH-morpheme in corresponding questions, whether such questions are explicitly uttered or not. However, the role and the parameter represent given information, and questions about them are not acceptable. The order of role, value, and parameter in surface patterns is irrelevant to the information structure of identificational sentences. For example, the value is always the focus whether it is at the beginning, the middle, or the end of a sentence. In predicational sentences, the subject always represents given information and the predicate represents new information.

Topicalization of an Element from Inside Values

We saw that parameters may appear as genitive modifiers of roles or as independent topics. The question arises whether genitive modifiers of values, as in (38a), can also be made into topics. But topicalization applied to genitive modifiers inside values proves to be impossible, as (38b) shows.

(38) a. Kono-jiko-no gen'in-wa, Taro-no inemuri-da.
this-accident-GEN cause-TOP Taro-GEN dozing-COP
'The cause of this accident is Taro's dozing.'

b. *Taro-wa, kono-jiko-no gen'in-wa inemuri-da.
Taro-TOP this-accident-GEN cause-TOP dozing-COP
'As for Taro, the cause of this accident is the dozing.'

Sentence (38a) is of pattern ①. The topicalization test will yield the same result for the other three patterns. Thus there is a clear difference between the genitive modifiers which are parameters and those which are not.

Backward Pronominalization

As is well known in English linguistics, the coreference relation in identificational sentences is very similar to that of question-answer pairs (cf. Declerck 1988); indeed, in the question-answer pair in (39b), the nominal *Taro* contained in the answer cannot be taken to be the antecedent of the pronoun *kare* 'he' in the question; likewise, in (40b), the nominal inside the value cannot be the antecedent of the pronoun inside the role, which is its parameter.

(39) a. Nani-ga, Taro$_1$-no rikon-no gen'in-ka? Kare$_1$-no uwaki-da.
  what-NOM Taro-GEN divorce-GEN cause-Q he-GEN infidelity-COP
  'What is the cause of Taro's divorce? His infidelity.'

 b. *Nani-ga, kare$_1$-no rikon-no gen'in-ka? Taro$_1$-no uwaki-da.
  what-NOM he-GEN divorce-GEN cause-Q Taro-GEN infidelity-COP
  'What is the cause of his divorce? Taro's infidelity.'

(40) a. Taro$_1$-no rikon-no gen'in-wa, kare$_1$-no uwaki-da.
  Taro-GEN divorce-GEN cause-TOP he-GEN infidelity-COP
  'The cause of Taro's divorce is his infidelity.'

 b. *Kare$_1$-no rikon-no gen'in-wa, Taro$_1$-no uwaki-da.
  he-GEN divorce-GEN cause-TOP Taro-GEN infidelity-COP
  'His infidelity is the cause of Taro's divorce.'

Furthermore, we see that in (41b) below, when the subject is the value, backward pronominalization becomes possible too, since the parameter, which is given, is apt to be an antecedent for a value-denoting nominal, which expresses new information.

(41) a. Taro$_1$-no uwaki-ga, kare$_1$-no rikon-no gen'in-da.
  Taro-GEN infidelity-NOM he-GEN divorce-GEN cause-COP
  'Taro's infidelity is the cause of his divorce.'

 b. Kare$_1$-no uwaki-ga, Taro$_1$-no riko-no gen'in-da.
  he-GEN infidelity-NOM Taro-GEN divorce-GEN cause-COP
  'His infidelity is the cause of Taro's divorce.'

The topicality of the parameters of identificational sentences is higher than that of any other element and they may trigger a backward pronominalization (cf. Ruwet 1982). But, needless to say, pronominalization is optimal when syntactic reasons and informational structures coincide. In fact, (40a) is far better than (41a) or (41b), in which the two factors justifying pronominalization contradict each other.

Postposing

Although Japanese is a strict verb-final language, parameter-denoting NPs and role-denoting NPs can be postposed after verbs across the sentence boundary, but value-denoting NPs cannot be postposed in this way.

(42) ①   [V-da,] P-no R-wa.
             V-COP P-GEN R-TOP

    ② a. [P-wa, V-da,] R-wa.
             P-TOP V-COP R-TOP

        b. [R-wa V-da,] P-wa.
             R-TOP V-COP P-TOP

    ③   *[P-no R-da,] V-ga.
             P-GEN R-COP V-NOM

    ④ a. *[P-wa, R-da,] V-ga.
             P-TOP R-COP V-NOM

        b. [V-ga R-da,] P-wa.
             V-NOM R-COP P-TOP

(43) ①   Homer-da, Iliad-no   sakusha-wa.
             Homer-COP Iliad-GEN author-TOP
             '[It] is homer, the author of the Iliad.'

    ② a. Iliad-wa, Homer-da, sakusha-wa.
             Iliad-TOP Homer-COP author-TOP
             'As for the Iliad, [it] is Homer, the author.'

        b. Sakusha-wa Homer-da, Iliad-wa.
             author-TOP Homer-COP Iliad-TOP
             'The author is Homer, as for the Iliad.'

③   *Iliad-no   sakusha-da, Homer-ga.
       Iliad-GEN author-COP Homer-NOM
       '[It] is the author of the Iliad, Homer.'

④ a. *Iliad-wa, sakusha-da, Homer-ga.
       Iliad-TOP author-COP Homer-NOM
       'As for the Iliad, [it] is the author, Homer.'

    b. Homer-ga   sakusha-da, Iliad-wa.
       Homer-NOM author-COP Iliad-TOP
       'Homer is the author, as for the Iliad.'

Deletion

Parameter-denoting NPs and role-denoting NPs can be deleted, while value-denoting ones cannot. Thus postposing and deletion coincide. In patterns ① and ③, the deletion of an element will destroy the copular construction; therefore, the cases to be considered are patterns ② and ④, which have three subparts. For greater clarity, I bracket the elements to be deleted in (44).

(44) ② a. [P-wa] R-wa V-da.
      b. P-wa   [R-wa] V-da.

    ④ a. [P-wa] V-ga R-da.
      b. *P-wa [V-ga] R-da.

(45) ② a. Sakusha-wa Homer-da.
         author-TOP Homer-COP
         'The author is Homer.'

      b. Iliad-wa Homer-da.
         Iliad-TOP Homer-COP
         'The Iliad is Homer.'

    ④ a. Homer-ga   sakusha-da.
         Homer-NOM author-COP
         'Homer is the author.'

      b. *Iliad-wa sakusha-da.
         Iliad-TOP author-COP
         'The Iliad is the author.'

Note that (45②b) is a so-called eel sentence; that is, the type of sentence in (10) (*I am the ham sandwich*). It does not express predication ("Iliad ∈ {Homer}") nor identity ("Iliad = Homer"). It is an elliptical identificational sentence in which, after deletion of the role R, the parameter P and the value V are connected directly by the copula as in *P wa V da*. Therefore, we do not have to suppose that eel sentences are a new kind of copular sentence; they are simply elliptical identificational sentences.

Eel Sentences and Pseudo-Clefts

We saw in the section above that eel sentences arise from deletion of a role-denoting nominal. I now examine the generation of eel sentences through pseudo-clefts. Starting with an ordinary sentence, (46), we obtain a pseudo-cleft, (47a), in which *watasi* 'I' may be taken as the parameter, *unagi* 'eel' as the value, and the verbal part of the relative *chuumonsita-no* 'ordered' as the role. In Japanese pseudo-clefts, the genitive marker *no* is usually used as an expletive relative noun, as in (47a). In (47b), the parameter *watasi* 'I' is extracted from the relative to be made a topic, and then the sentential role is deleted in (47c), which is indeed an eel sentence, meaning that the speaker ordered a dish of eel (of course, other interpretations are possible, depending on the content of deleted roles).

(46) Watasi-wa unagi-o chuumonsita.
     I-TOP   eel-ACC ordered
     'I ordered an eel.'

(47) a. Watasi-ga chuumonsita-no-wa, unagi-da.
         I-NOM   ordered-GEN-TOP   eel-COP
         'What I ordered is an eel.'

     b. Watasi-wa, chuumonsita-no-wa, unagi-da.
         I-TOP   ordered-GEN-TOP   eel-COP
         'As for me, what I ordered is an eel.'

     c. Watasi-wa, unagi-da.
         I-TOP   eel-COP
         'I am the eel.'

In fact, (47c) is ambiguous; it may also be a predicational sentence, meaning that the speaker is an eel. Subject-to-object raising filters the reading of eel sentences. Thus, (47c) embedded under *Taro wa . . . to omotta* 'Taro thought that . . .' as in (48a) is still ambiguous in the same way; however, (48b) no longer has the eel-sentence reading, and it is only predication. As for (45②b) (*Iliad-wa Homer-da*), which only has the eel sentence interpretation, subject-to-object raising will dispose of this one reading and, in fact, (49b) is not acceptable.

(48) a. Taro-wa, watasi-wa unagi-da-to   omotta.
    Taro-TOP I-TOP   eel-COP-COMP thought
    'Taro thought that I was {an eel/the eel}.'

    b. Taro-wa, watasi-o unagi-da-to   omotta.
       Taro-TOP I-ACC   eel-COP-COMP thought
       'Taro thought me to be an eel.'

(49) a. Taro-wa, Iliad-wa Homer-da-to   omotta.
    Taro-TOP Iliad-TOP Homer-COP-COMP thought
    'Taro thought that the Iliad was Homer.'

    b. *Taro-wa, Iliad-o   Homer-da-to   omotta.
       Taro-TOP Iliad-ACC Homer-COP-COMP thought
       'Taro thought the Iliad to be Homer.'

What is interesting about a role-denoting relative sentence is that its domain and range are not fixed; it is a proposition from which one can extract practically any of the arguments. Thus in the pseudo-cleft (50a), it is the subject that is the value; topicalization of the object which is the parameter yields (50b); and the deletion of the sentential role yields another eel sentence, (50c).

(50) a. Unagi-o chuumonsita-no-wa, watasi-da.
    eel-ACC ordered-GEN-TOP   I-COP
    'The one who ordered an eel is me.'

    b. Unagi-wa, chuumonsita-no-wa, watasi-da.
      eel-TOP   ordered-GEN-TOP   I-COP
      'As for the eel, the one who ordered it is me.'

    c. Unagi-wa, watasi-da.
      eel-TOP I-COP
      'The eel is me.'

When a verbal element in a relative functions as the role, any of its arguments may freely be either a parameter or a value with regard to the role. As we will see in the next section, this flexibility of a role-denoting relative sentence contrasts sharply with the rigidity of a nominal role.

Rigidity of Nominal Roles

A verb can form a genuine multiple-place function, from which any of the arguments can be abstracted. For example, *kaita* 'wrote' in (51a) below is a two-place function, such as (51b). We can abstract either argument of (51b), as in (52a) or in (52b). Linguistically, they become (53a) and (53b); then, by topicalizing the parameters, as in (54a) and (54b), and by deleting the roles, we obtain eel sentences such as (55a) and (55b).

(51) a. Homer-wa, Iliad-o   kaita.
       Homer-TOP Iliad-ACC wrote
       'Homer wrote the Iliad.'

    b. **kaita**(Homer, Iliad)

(52) a. λ x**kaita**(x, Iliad) (Homer)

    b. λ x**kaita**(Homer, x) (Iliad)

(53) a. Iliad-o   kaita-no-wa,   Homer-da.
       Iliad-ACC wrote-GEN-TOP Homer-COP
       'The one who wrote the Iliad is Homer.'

    b. Homer-ga   kaita-no-wa,   Iliad-da.
       Homer-NOM wrote-GEN-TOP Iliad-COP
       'What Homer wrote is the Iliad.'

(54) a. Iliad-wa, kaita-no-wa,   Homer-da.
       Iliad-TOP wrote-GEN-TOP Homer-COP
       'As for the Iliad, the one who wrote it is Homer.'

    b. Homer-wa, kaita-no-wa,   Iliad-da.
       Homer-TOP wrote-GEN-TOP Iliad-COP
       'As for Homer, what he wrote is the Iliad.'

(55) a. Iliad-wa, Homer-da.
Iliad-TOP Homer-COP
'The Iliad is Homer.'

b. Homer-wa, Iliad-da.
Homer-TOP Iliad-COP
'Homer is the Iliad.'

The nominal role *sakusha* 'author' is a relation that a certain person has
to a certain work; likewise, *sakuhin* 'work' is a relation that a certain work
has to a certain author. Therefore in this case too we may think of two-place
relations as in (56) and (57).

(56) **sakusha**(Homer, Iliad)
(**author**(Homer, Iliad))

(57) **sakuhin**(Iliad, Homer)
(**work**(Iliad, Homer))

But the domain and range of a nominal role are rigid and cannot be inter-
changed, so lambda abstraction is restricted to the first argument. The function name and the abstracted argument must agree; (58a) and (59a) are adequate, but (58b) and (59b) are not.

(58) a. λ x**sakusha**(x, Iliad) (Homer)
(λ x**author**(x, Iliad) (Homer))

b. *λ x**sakusha**(Homer, x) (Iliad)
(λ x**author**(Homer, x) (Iliad))

(59) a. λ x**sakuhin**(x, Homer) (Iliad)
(λ x**work**(x, Homer) (Iliad))

b. *λ x**sakuhin**(x, Iliad) (Homer)
(λ x**work**(x, Iliad) (Homer))

Indeed, (58a) and (59a) become (60a) and (61a), which are grammatical;
but (58b) and (59b), which correspond respectively to (60b) and (61b), arc
nonsensical.

(60) a. Iliad-no   sakusha-wa, Homer-da.
         Iliad-GEN author-TOP   Homer-COP
         'The author of the Iliad is Homer.'

     b. *Homer-no   sakusha-wa, Iliad-da.
         Homer-GEN author-TOP   Iliad-COP
         'The author of Homer is the Iliad.'

(61) a. Homer-no   sakuhin-wa, Iliad-da.
         Homer-GEN work-TOP   Iliad-COP
         'The work of Homer is the Iliad.'

     b. *Iliad-no   sakuhin-wa, Homer-da.
         Iliad-GEN work-TOP   Homer-COP
         'The work of the Iliad is Homer.'

However, rather than putting a restriction on abstraction, it is better to suppose that a noun is basically a one-place function, as in (62) and (63).

(62) **sakuhin**(Homer) = Iliad
     (**work**(Homer) = Iliad)

(63) **sakusha**(Iliad) = Homer
     (**author**(Iliad) = Homer)

Examples (62) and (63) are inverse relations of each other, if we ignore their function names. In other words, it is not possible to make an inverse function out of nominal-role functions without changing function names. We have obtained the eel sentence (55a) from a pseudo-cleft, (54a), but it can also be obtained from (60a), an identificational sentence with a role-denoting noun. Likewise, (55b), obtained from a pseudo-cleft, (54b), can also be obtained from (60a). But it should be noted that the names of the roles to be deleted in (60a) and (61a) are different from the start, for roles denoted by nouns are unilateral functions, whereas in (54a) and (54b), the verb that denotes the roles is the same, for a sentential role is a genuine multiple-place function.

In Japanese linguistics, it is commonly held that eel sentences are always generated through pseudo-clefts, but this position is mistaken. The reason for this erroneous position lies in the fact that most verbs do not have ready-made names for their arguments. For instance, we cannot refer to the subject of the verb *chuumonsuru* 'to order' without using this verb in the definition such as *chuumonsuru-hito* 'the person who orders'; the situation is almost the same for the object. Thus if the intended reading of (64) is *What I ordered is the eel,* we have to resort to a pseudo-cleft to capture this interpretation, since the relation of *watasi* 'I' to *unagi* 'eel' cannot be expressed by using a simple nominal.

(64) Watasi-wa unagi-da.
     I-TOP   eel-COP
     'I am the eel.'

In this respect, *kaku* 'to write', which has *sakusha* 'author' ready for the subject position and *sakuhin* 'work' ready for the object position, is rather an exception. The relation of Homer to the Iliad is that of an author to his work. In this case, it is no longer necessary to resort to a pseudo-cleft sentence to capture the intended reading of (65) (= (55a)) or (66) (= (55b)); the nominals *sakusha* 'author' and *sakuhin* 'work' will suffice.

(65) Iliad-wa, Homer-da.
     Iliad-TOP Homer-COP
     'The Iliad is Homer.'

(66) Homer-wa, Iliad-da.
     Homer-TOP Iliad-COP
     'Homer is the Iliad.'

Pseudo-clefts and identificational sentences with a nominal role have the same information structure, and that is all that is needed to give rise to eel sentences.

The Double-Subject Construction and Identification

The notions of identification and predication may be applied to sentences of other types. For example, the sentence in (67), often discussed as an example of the double-subject construction, is ambiguous.

(67) Zoo-wa,   hana-ga   nagai.
     elephant-TOP trunk-NOM long
     'As for elephants, their trunk is long/The long body part of elephants
     is their trunk.'

First, sentence (67) may be predicational, meaning that elephants have a long trunk; in this interpretation, *ga* is free from its usual exhaustive implicature and the sentence does not exclude the possibility of elephants having another body part that is long. In a way, *hana-ga nagai* is taken to be a composite predicate meaning something like 'to be long-trunked.' Secondly, (67) may be identificational, specifying the body part of elephants that is long; in this interpretation, (67) implies that *hana* 'trunk' is the only body part of elephants that is long. In this case, *zoo* 'elephant', *hana* 'trunk', and *nagai* 'long' correspond in this order to the parameter, value, and role of the identificational sentence (cf. Nishiyama 1989).

What is interesting is that if we topicalize *hana* 'trunk', as in sentence (68), the only interpretation is identificational.

(68) Hana-wa, zoo-ga   nagai.
      trunk-TOP elephant-NOM long
      'The animal that has a long trunk is an elephant.'

The parameter in this example is *hana* 'trunk' and the value is *zoo* 'elephant'; i.e., (68) is an answer to a wh-question such as *What is the animal that has a long trunk?* The reason that (68) is only identificational is perhaps the difficulty in taking *zoo-ga nagai* as a composite predicate meaning something like 'to be long-elephanted'.

Outside the domain of body parts, too, similar pairs of sentences can easily be found, one of them being ambiguous and the other only identificational.

(69) Taro-wa, suiei-ga   umai.
      Taro-TOP swimming-NOM good
      'Taro is good at swimming/As for Taro, swimming is his speciality.'

(70) Suiei-wa,   Taro-ga umai.
      swimming-TOP Taro-NOM good
      'As for swimming, Taro is the expert.'

In examples of this general type, the relation of the range and the domain of a role is not rigid. Take, for example, the adjective role *nagai* 'long'. Suppose that its range is composed of animals and its domain of their body parts. The role *nagai* 'long' is a function that assigns to each animal its long body part. If *zoo* 'elephant' is chosen as the parameter, the role *nagai* 'long' will yield *hana* 'trunk' as the value; that is one of the readings of (67). Now let us interchange the range and domain; now, *nagai* 'long' is a function that assigns to each body part an animal that has a long body part of the kind in question; then, if *hana* 'trunk' is the parameter, *zoo* 'elephant' will be identified as the value; that is the reading of (68).

But sometimes the relation of two things is fixed with regard to a role. Suppose for example that *ii* 'good' is a function that assigns to each species of animal some of its members that are delicious to eat and that, in the case of fish, it identifies sea bream as delicious fish. Thus, the sentence below is interpreted as identificational.

(71) Sakana-wa, tai-ga   ii.
     fish-TOP   sea bream-NOM good
     'As for fish, sea bream is good.'

But for the role *ii* 'good', we cannot interchange the range and domain; the entire category cannot be sorted out of one of its members. Thus if we topicalize *tai* 'sea bream', as in (72), the result is pragmatically unacceptable.

(72) *Tai-wa,   sakana-ga ii.
     sea bream-TOP fish-NOM   good
     'As for sea bream, fish is good.'

Thus, the notion of role can explain the multiple readings of Japanese double-subject constructions as well as the unacceptability of some of their instances.

Conclusion

I began with the hypothesis that the various uses of copular sentences constitute a continuum according to differences in referentiality between the two NPs involved. They are predicational when only the subject is referential and the difference in referentiality is clear; they are identity statements when the two NPs are equal in referentiality; and they are identificational when one NP is strongly referential and the other NP is only weakly so.

The notion of a role that assigns values to parameters provides a particularly useful insight into the analysis of identificational sentences, whose function is precisely to permit this process of assigning values. We found indeed the following interesting tripartite identificational sentence pattern, which reflects directly the structure of the role, mapping parameters into values.

(73) Iliad-wa, sakusha-wa, Homer-da.
     Iliad-TOP author-TOP   Homer-COP
     'As for the Iliad, the author is Homer.'

Identificational sentences are also interesting in that their information structure contradicts their underlying syntactic structure. In fact, many researchers have argued that the "underlying subject" of identificational sentences is the value-denoting NP, which is higher in referentiality but is new information. For this reason, inverted sentences with role-denoting NPs as subjects are far more natural and compatible with negation, while the basic form cannot be negated naturally.

The distinction between identification and predication may not be read off from a surface form such as (74), in which both the subject and the predicate may be referential, though not to the same degree at the same time. This is also the case with the Japanese counterpart (75).

(74) The head of state is a minor official.

(75) Kokka-genshu-wa koyakunin-da.
     state-head-TOP   minor official-COP

But the difference may be detected in diverse ways in different languages. For example, if we modify the predicate of (74) by *only,* as in (76), the only acceptable reading is predicational, for predication is compatible with degrees but identification is not (cf. Fauconnier 1991).

(76) The head of state is only a minor official.

In Japanese, the topic marker *wa* is used to mark the subject of predicational sentences and the role-denoting subject of identificational sentences, while the nominative marker *ga* is used for the value-denoting subject of identificational sentences. So the ambiguity in the English example (77) does not remain in (78) or (79). In this case, unlike (74) or (75), it is clear that the proper noun *Homer* is higher in referentiality and (78) is only predicational.

(77) Homer is the author of the Iliad.

(78) Homer-wa Iliad-no   sakusha-da.
     Homer-TOP Iliad-GEN author-COP

(79) Homer-ga   Iliad-no   sakusha-da.
     Homer-NOM Iliad-GEN author-COP

In Polish, inverted identificational sentences show a special case-marking pattern (cf. note 2). In French, the presence or absence of an indefinite article in predicate nominals sometimes indicates this distinction. Both (80) and (81) may be interpreted as meaning that the husband of the speaker is a student, but (80), which gives information about what the speaker's husband does, is predication, while (81), which gives information about who the speaker's husband is, is identification.[6]

(80) Mon mari est étudiant.

(81) Mon mari est un étudiant.

The four patterns of identificational sentence in Japanese may have counterparts in other languages, although the verbs may be other than the copula. Likewise, eel sentences, discussed especially in Japanese linguistics, may be found in other languages, for the process involved in their generation, i.e., deletion of a filler of a role that stands for given information, is quite natural in any language, and examples (82) and (83) below are indeed eel sentences.

(82) I am the ham sandwich; the quiche is my friend. (Fauconnier 1985)

(83) Moi, c'est la tarte à l'oignon; la quiche, c'est lui. (Fauconnier 1984)

I have also shown that an incomplete relative may function as a sentential role pointing to the missing argument; and that the relation of domain and range is not fixed for a sentential role, which is to say that it can be used as a multiple-place function. On the contrary, a nominal role has a fixed domain and range, and does not accept multiple abstractions.

Notes

1. I am grateful to Brendan Wilson for invaluable comments on an earlier version of this paper. I am particularly indebted to Yuuji Nishiyama for comments on my papers on the copular construction and other subjects, which enlightened me repeatedly on a number of questions. In fact, we have arrived independently at very similar conclusions on many points.

One and the same sentence may accept two different readings, depending on contextual factors, and in particular on assumptions on the part of the hearer. The nature of the differences in the uses of copular sentences is thus pragmatic. When I say a given sentence is predicational, identificational, or equational, I refer to its ordinary reading. This does not exclude the possibility that it may be interpreted differently given an appropriate context.

2. Even roles that purport to refer to human beings must be referred to by a neuter demonstrative pronoun that is reserved for things. For example, suppose that a disagreement arises between two persons as to who is the current prime minister of Japan; A says that Hosokawa is the current prime minister but B claims that it is Miyazawa who is the current prime minister of Japan (in reality, Miyazawa is the former prime minister). In this case, B must use a neuter demonstrative pronoun *sore* 'that' to refer to the role, as in (i) below.

(i) A: genzai-wa shushou-wa   Hosokawa-da.
      now-TOP   prime minister-TOP Hosokawa-COP
      'Now, the prime minister is Hosokawa.'

   B: Iya, {sore/*kare}-wa Miyazawa-da.
      no   {it /he}-TOP   Miyazawa-COP
      'No, {it/he} is Miyazawa.'

The Japanese personal pronouns *kare* 'he' and *kanojo* 'she' are anaphoric only to referential human NPs. The reason a personal pronoun is not acceptable here is simply because role-denoting NPs are not referential in identificational sentences.

Geach (1962) points out that Polish is quite interesting in this respect. Predicates in Polish are ordinarily marked by the instrumental case, as shown in (ii).

(ii) Wałęsa   jest   presydentem.
     Walesa (NOM) be(present 3sg) president (INSTR)
     'Walesa is (the) president.'

Permutation has no effect on the case marking, and role-denoting NPs that are surface subjects are still case marked by the instrumental, as in (iii).

(iii) Presydentem   jest   Wałęsa.
      president (INSTR) be(presnt 3sg) Walesa (NOM)
      'The president is Walesa.'

Case marking in Polish thus directly reflects the semantic functions of those NPs.
   3. I use the following abbreviations in glosses of Japanese examples:

COP: copula (*da, desu, dearu*)
TOP: topic marker (*wa*)
GEN: genitive marker (*no*)
NOM: nominative marker (*ga*)
ACC: accusative marker (*o*)
Q: question marker (*ka*)
COMP: complementizer (*to, no*, etc.)
NEG: negation marker (*nai*)

The usual form of the copula is *da; desu* is its polite form and *dearu* its written form. The copula *da* is deleted before *ka,* though *desu* or *dearu* remain at the surface. There are several complementizers and it is mainly the meaning of verbs that determines which one is used.

4. Topic is a discourse phenomenon. The particle *wa* may appear in subordinate clauses, but it is interpreted as a contrast marker in this case. In the same way, the nominative marker *ga* is often free from exhaustive-listing implicature in subordinate clauses. Thus the distinction between predication and identification will disappear in the surface form of subordinate copular clauses, so that the subordinate clause in (i) may be taken to be predication as well as identification, just like its English counterpart.

(i) Taro-wa Homer-ga   Iliad-no   sakusha-da-to   omotteiru.
Taro-TOP Homer-NOM Iliad-GEN author-COP-COMP thinks
'Taro thinks that Homer is the author of the Iliad.'

5. Sometimes *doko* 'which place' is used when questions are about places, as in (ii).

(i) Nihon-no shuto-wa, Tokyo-da.
Japan-GEN capital-TOP Tokyo-COP
'The capital of Japan is Tokyo.'

(ii) Nihon-no shuto-wa,   doko-ka?
Japan-GEN capital-TOP which place-COP
'Which place is the capital of Japan?'

6. For more details about French copular sentences, see Ruwet 1982, Verheugd-Daatzelaar 1990, Sakahara 1990b, and Fauconnier 1991.

References

Declerck, R. 1988. *Studies on Copular Sentences, Clefts and Pseudo-Clefts.* Dordrecht: Foris Publications; Leuven: Leuven University Press.

Fauconnier, Gilles. 1984. *Espaces Mentaux.* Paris: Editions de Minuit.

———. 1985. *Mental Spaces: Aspects of Meaning Construction in Natural Language.* Cambridge, Mass.: MIT Press. Reprinted 1994, Cambridge: Cambridge University Press.

———. 1991. Roles and Values: The Case of French Copula Constructions. In Carol Georgopoulos and Roberta Ishihara, eds., *Interdisciplinary Approaches to Language: Essays in Honor of S.-Y. Kuroda,* 181–206. Dordrecht: Kluwer Academic Publishers.

Geach, P. 1962. *Reference and Generality.* Ithaca, N.Y.: Cornell University Press.

Kuno, S. 1972. *The Structure of the Japanese Language*. Cambridge, Mass.: MIT Press.

Nishiyama, Y. 1989. 'zoo-wa hana-ga nagai' koubun-nituite (On the "As for Elephants, Their Trunk is Long' Construction). *Reports of the Keio Institute of Cultural and Linguistic Studies* 21:107–133.

———. 1990. 'kaki-ryouri-wa Hiroshima-ga honba-da' koubun-nituite—houwa-meisiku-to hihouwa-meisiku (On the 'As for Oyster Dishes, Hiroshima is the Best Place' Construction—Saturated NP and Unsaturated NP). *Reports of the Keio Institute of Cultural and Linguistic Studies* 22:169–88.

Nunberg, Geoffrey. 1979. The Non-Uniqueness of Semantic Solutions: Polysemy. *Linguistics and Philosophy* 3:143–84.

Ruwet, Nicolas. 1982. Les Phrases Copulatives. In *Grammaire des Insultes et Autres Études*, 207–38. Paris: Editions de Seuil.

Sakahara, Shigeru. 1990a. Yakuwari, ga/wa, unagi-bun (Roles, ga/wa, Eel-Sentences). In Shigeru Sakahara and Makoto Nagao, eds., *Advances in Japanese Cognitive Science*, vol. 3, 29–66. Tokyo: Kodansha Scientific.

———. 1990b. Kijutu-bun/doutei-bun-to furansu-go-no kopyura-bun (Descriptional/Identificational Sentences and French Copular Sentences). *Furansu-Gogaku-Kenkyu* (Studies in French Linguistics) 24:1–13.

———. 1990c. Yakuwari-to kaishaku-no tayousei (Roles and Multiplicity of Interpretations). In *Research Report in 1989: Furansu-Bunka-no tyusin-to shuen* (The Center and the Periphery of French Culture), 107–23. Osaka: Osaka University of Foreign Studies.

Takubo, Y. 1983. On the Scope of the Question and the Negation. In *Papers from the Kyoto Workshop on Japanese Syntax and Semantics*.

Verheugd-Daatzelaar, E. 1990. *Subject Arguments and Predicate Nominals: A Study of French Copular Sentences with Two NPs*. Amsterdam: Ropodi.

José Sanders and Gisela Redeker

10 *Perspective and the Representation of Speech and Thought in Narrative Discourse*

.

.

.

.

Perspective is a ubiquitous phenomenon in many types of discourse and an important factor in discourse production and comprehension (see, for example, Graumann and Sommer 1988).[1] If discourse perspective is broadly defined as a particular vantage point, or point of view in discourse, then, strictly speaking, no sentence in any discourse is free from a certain degree of perspectivization. With respect to clause-level lexical and syntactic choice, perspective can be signaled by grammatical realization or by a particular choice of lexical encoding (see, for example, DeLancey 1982, Kuno 1987, and Zribi-Hertz 1989), as can be observed in example (1).

(1) Accompanied by his son, the informant went out to investigate.

The writer of (1) expresses more "empathy" (Kuno 1987) with the informant than with the son (i) by referring to the father with an independent description and to the son with the dependent description *his son;* and (ii) by making the father the implicit subject of the adjunct *accompanied by.* More generally, any description of an event, activity, process, or state implies a deictic center involving space, time, and person. Explicit indicators of the deictic anchoring of an utterance are first- and second-person pronouns and temporal and spatial deictic expressions. For many scenarios, languages allow alternative framings like *to come* versus *to go, to give* versus *to receive, to buy* versus *to sell,* and so forth (see Fillmore 1982). Whenever such alternatives are available, the choice is dictated by and has consequences for the sentence's implied deictic center. If the narrator in example (1) had chosen to write *came out* instead of *went out,* our vantage point would have been outside the house.

At the discourse level, an even wider range of phenomena can be described in terms of perspective. Most of the research in this area has been concerned with fictional narratives, where perspective mainly serves a dramatizing function by encouraging the reader to imagine the events and to identify with the characters in the story. However, perspective phenomena can be found in other text types as well, and their functions are not restricted to dramatization.

Taking as our point of departure the concept of *focalization*, developed in modern narratology, we will propose a definition of the concept of perspective as *the embedding of a subject's point of view in the narrator's discourse reality*. Focalization stands for a distinct vision of the story that is narrated in a text and should be distinguished from the narration of the story (Genette 1980). Bal (1990) uses focalization in the sense of *subjective vision*, where "subjective" means both *colored* and *bound to a subject*. We investigate here how variations of subjectivity within the narrator's discourse, and the boundaries between the narrator's and the character's subjectivity, can be described in terms of mental space theory. Our goal is to determine, on the basis of linguistic characteristics, whose vision is represented where.

Focalization

The concept of focalization was introduced by Genette (1980) to distinguish the experiencing subject whose *vision* is presented from the narrating agent, the *voice* that verbalizes a story. Three types of narrative can thus be defined: *nonfocalized* narratives, where the (omniscient) narrator knows more than the character; *internal focalization*, or narrative with a "restricted field of vision", where the narrator says only what a given character experiences and believes; and finally, with more severe restriction, *external focalization*, or "vision from without", where the narrator says only what happens to a given character without presenting that character's thoughts.

Genette acknowledges that "the commitment as to focalization is not necessarily steady over the whole length of a narrative" (1980:191). Nevertheless, he analyzes a shift of focalization as "a momentary infraction of the code which governs that context without thereby calling into question the existence of the code" (1980:195). Texts with such infractions of the perspective code are described as containing "variable focalization" or "omniscience with partial restrictions of field" (1980:194). Variable focalization is illustrated in Genette's analysis of Flaubert's *Madame Bovary*. The "focal characters" in this novel are first Charles, then Emma, and finally, again, Charles (1980:189).

Bal (1990) has refined Genette's typology in several important respects, one of which is of particular interest to the present investigation. Bal argues that nonfocalized stories simply do not exist: since strictly objective narration is impossible, the narrator is always a focalizer—in Bal's terminology, an *external focalizer* (not to be confused with Genette's quite different use of this term). This narrator-focalizer may permit *embedded focalization* by assigning a character in the story as focalizer (this is what Genette calls "internal focalization"). Following Genette, Bal emphasizes the importance of the distinction between the narrating "voice" and the experiencing "vision", and argues that the term *focalization* should be reserved for the case of "vision."

Vision versus Narration

The distinction by both Genette and Bal between the agent who sees and the agent who verbalizes has the advantage that "narration" and "vision" can be described as two different acts that sometimes must be attributed to different persons. However, this distinction implies a paradox: the nature of (narrative) texts is such that in order to represent vision, one needs narration. In order to represent perception and thought *one needs a voice*—how else can perception and thought be verbalized? The act of narrating and the act of vision (focalizing) coincide in the person of the narrator (see also van Rees 1985 (p. 449)). The voice of the narrator is always present, and narrative is therefore always subjective, whether it presents a character's vision or that of the narrator. In fact, most literary scholars agree that no narrative can be told without a narrating agent—the so-called "implied author" (Booth 1983; Chatman 1978), whose subjectivity implicitly or explicitly colors the narrative.

How, then, can we determine the extent of focalization in the narrator's voice, when all we have available is the narrator's inescapably subjective representation? Focalization by the narrator is in fact invisible, like a permanent filter that is placed between the stream of information and the reader. With internal focalization—the subjective point of view of a character—this problem does not arise. In this case, there is no paradox, since the narrator can present a character's vision without letting the character narrate. We propose, therefore, to define perspective only with respect to embedded voice or vision, thus shunning the question of the narrator's subjectivity.

The separation of narration and vision in internal (embedded) focalization is particularly clear in what is called *free indirect discourse,* especially the free indirect representation of a character's *consciousness* (Fludernik 1993). However, it is not desirable to restrict discourse perspective to the linguistic form of free indirect representation of consciousness. First, free indirect representation of consciousness (thought) is closely related to and often even indistinguishable from free indirect *speech.* Second, *direct* representation of thought, which combines a character's vision and narration, is functionally very close to free indirect thought. What these have in common, and what distinguishes them from narrative descriptions of speech events or mental states, is that some of the narrator's responsibility for the story is delegated to the character whose speech or thought is represented.

We propose, then, to broaden the concept of embedded perspective to include all direct, indirect, and free indirect representations of a character's speech and thought. In fact, we introduce a more subtle type of perspectivization, where a character's vision is not explicitly presented but is implied by the narrator's choice of referential descriptions.

Perspective as a Mental Space Phenomenon

Mental space theory is a model designed to account for embeddings and restrictions of validity in language. It is based on the assumption that understanding a text involves the creation of domains or *spaces,* with embedded spaces entailing a restriction of the validity or factuality of the embedded material (Fauconnier 1985; Dinsmore 1991). We will show that this conceptual framework allows us to account for the discourse-functional properties of a wide range of perspectivization phenomena.

Definition of Perspective

Given the considerations discussed above, we define perspective as follows: *Perspective* is the introduction of a subjective point of view that restricts the validity of the presented information to a particular subject (person) in the discourse. A discourse segment is perspectivized if its relevant context of interpretation is a person-bound, embedded space within the narrator's reality.

In this definition, the *narrator's reality* is whatever is presented as the discourse world, regardless of its truth or validity outside of the discourse. As a consequence, subjectivity is only considered with respect to the discourse world, and the subjective point of view the definition refers to is always bound to a subject other than the current narrator. This experiencing subject (the *character*) can be any story character other than the narrator in the here and now, including the distanced first-person narrator in the past, in dreams, and so forth.

The realization of an embedded perspective usually (though, as we argue below, not necessarily) involves the representation of a character's spoken and mental discourse in *direct, indirect,* or *free indirect* form. The examples in (2) illustrate various kinds of perspective, that is, ways of introducing subjective points of view into the discourse.[2]

(2) a. According to a spokesman the man was "clearly on the run from the police."

   b. They had heard shots as well, but knew nothing else, they said.

   c. He heard something and turned around. There were the three Englishmen again. Now, could they really be tourists? No, no way! They looked just too shabby.

   d. The police lost track of the car with the kidnapped girl. A little later in the woods, a policeman saw a man who had a girl with him. The kidnapper had released her on a nearby street.

All four of these examples contain material presenting the subjective point of view of one of the characters in the discourse, but the type and degree of perspectivization vary. The examples differ in the distribution of narrator's and character's responsibility for the wording and content of the character's point of view. In the direct quote in (2a), the narrator (writer) distances himself from the exact wording by attributing it to the quoted spokesman. The narrator assigns the responsibility for the validity of both the wording and the content of the information to the quoted speaker. The narrator using the indirect quote in (2b) is less distant, but does not with this utterance commit himself to the belief that the quoted speakers actually didn't know anything else. The content of the utterance can be fully attributed to the quoted speakers, even though the wording may be the narrator's.

Likewise, the third and fourth sentences in (2c) need not reflect the narrator's convictions; the doubts expressed are attributed only to the perceiving character. In the free indirect mode, speaker and character share the responsibility of both wording and content. In (2d), finally, it is the narrator who determines both the wording and the content of the sentence. Yet, an embedded perspective is implicitly introduced by the indefinite reference *a girl*, which is clearly the policeman's and not the narrator's description.

In all these cases, then, the validity of the perspectivized information is somehow restricted to a certain subject in the discourse, but the examples differ in the distribution of responsibility between narrator and character for the perspectivized segment's wording and content. Table 10.1 shows how this can be expressed in terms of the mental space concepts of viewpoint and focus (see Fauconnier and Sweetser, chapter 1 in this volume, and the section on mental space structures below). Table 10.1 also shows how different forms vary in the strength of perspectivization, that is, the embedded repre-

Table 10.1 Different types of perspective, their mental space characteristics, and the resulting strength of perspectivization

| Type of Perspective | Responsibility | | Mental-Space Processing | | Strength of Perspective |
	for Wording	for Content	Viewpoint Location	Focus Location	
direct	subject	subject	embedded space	embedded space	+ +
free indirect	default: subject	subject	default: embedded space	embedded space	+
indirect	narrator and subject	subject	base space and embedded space	embedded space	−
implicit perspective	narrator and subject	narrator and subject	base space and embedded space	base space and embedded space	− −

sentation's immediacy and implicd claim to authenticity. The four categories correspond to the four examples in (2) above.

Mental-Space Structures

In a narrative text, the reality of the narrator (the implied author) is the basic mental space. This *base space* is the starting point of the discourse representation. In the unmarked case, information is valid in the base space. Linguistic markers, such as indicators of quotation and focalization, create new spaces within the narrator's reality; that is, they represent information from a character's subjective point of view.

Each time the narrator lets characters speak or presents their thoughts, an embedded mental space (M) is created within the base space (B). The linguistic markers—space builders—that create these various types of perspective space connect the information to certain persons in the discourse. The linguistic means that establish the embedding of "mental discourse" (thoughts) are very similar to the ones used to represent actual spoken or written discourse.

The representation modes introduced above vary in the degree of explicitness of their embedding of information in the base space. The amount of influence a narrator has with respect to the form and content of the information in the embedded space is represented by the accessibility of the embedded space. If the narrator has minimal influence, as in direct quotation, the viewpoint shifts to M; that is, M is accessed directly. The greater the narrator's influence, the more likely it is that the base space (B) remains the viewpoint and that the information in the embedded subspaces is accessed via B.

This will be exemplified below by mental space structures of the various types of representation of speech and thought in the examples (3) through (5). In examples (6) and (7), other linguistic means are used to represent a subjective point of view, which can be described in terms of mental space structures as well.

DIRECT MODE

In written discourse, direct quotes are by convention assumed to be faithful reproductions of witnessed utterances (cf. Clark and Gerrig 1990). Still, direct perception of an utterance is not always strictly required. Since direct quotes are explicitly introduced as embedded discourse, quotation is a much more flexible device than free indirect style (see the discussion of the free indirect mode below). The quoting speaker can even label the quotation as an approximation (*He said something like* " ... ") or as hypothetical or even counterfactual (*Now if you were to say* " ... "). Such modalized uses are possible because direct quotation, unlike free indirect speech, involves a complete shift of the deictic center of the discourse to the time, space, and person co-ordinates of the quoted utterance or thought. In spontaneous speech, quotations should not be considered as reproductions, but as reconstructions or as demonstrations (see Clark and Gerrig 1990, Mayes 1990, Redeker 1991, and Tannen 1989). Yet the implied claim in all direct quotation is that both the content and the wording of the represented discourse are the quoted speaker's. Consider the sentence in (3), diagrammed in figure 10.1.[3]

(3) "The man was clearly on the run from the police," the spokesman said.

Linguistic markers such as the quotation marks and the parenthetical *the spokesman said* open a subspace (M) within the narrator's base space (B_1); this is represented by the arrow from the character *the spokesman* (s), to whom the utterance is attributed, to the new space. This embedded space is in fact a new base space (B_2), since all aspects of the referential center are moved to the new narrator, i.e., the embedded speaker s. What is the case according to the spokesman is valid only within B_2, and not necessarily for the narrator in B_1. Identity connectors between entities and between predicates to these entities in both spaces are represented by lines between the respective elements.

Mental Space Representation for Direct Mode

(3)   "The man was clearly on the run from the police," the spokesman said.

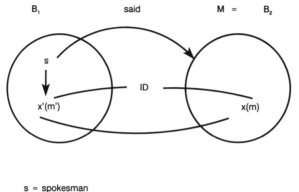

s = spokesman
m = the man
x = clearly on the run from the police
B_1 = Narrator's reality, base space
M = Character's reality, embedded space
B_2 = Character's reality, new base space

Figure 10.1 Mental space representation for direct mode

In the direct mode, both viewpoint and focus are in B_2. This means that in a sentence such as *Piet said, "I hate that bastard,"* *that bastard* can only be interpreted as Piet's words. That is, access to the referent of *that bastard* is only provided from Piet's space. The distance between the base space and the subspace is reflected in the degree to which references to persons can be exchanged between spaces. In the case of direct quotes, access to referents in the quotation is provided only directly in the new base space (B_2), that is, by the quoted speaker. Thus, the subspace is relatively inaccessible to the narrator, and the representation of the quoted material is strictly bound to the character, whose subjectivity can be fully expressed.

Direct quotation can be used whenever it is appropriate to demonstrate a (real or imaginary) speech event to the current listener or reader. In narratives, direct quotation is aimed at heightening liveliness and the reader's involvement by *showing* what happened instead of *reporting* it. This is the dramatic (mimetic) function of direct quotation (Redeker 1991 (p. 342)). By contrast, in reports such as news texts quotation is used to increase the perceived objectivity and accuracy of the account to the reader. Here the (diegetic) documenting function of quotation is prominent. The writer claims authenticity by implying that he has had direct access to the original speech situation.

Mental Space Representation for Partial Direct Quotation

(3') According to the spokesman, the man was "clearly on the run from the police."

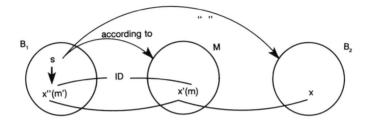

s = spokesman
m = the man
x = clearly on the run from the police
B₁ = Narrator's reality, base space
M = Character's reality, embedded space
B₂ = Character's reality, new base space

Figure 10.2 Mental space representation for partial direct quotation

This documenting function is put to its extreme in *partial quotations,* in which less than a full clause of an utterance is quoted directly. Compare (3) to (3').

(3') According to the spokesman, the man was "clearly on the run from the police."

In figure 10.2, the marker *according to* opens a new space (M) relative to the base space (B_1), indicated by the arrow from the speaker (s) to M. *According to* connects M to the character (S) to whom the utterance is attributed.

The embedded material, which is bound to the person *the spokesman,* is reinforced and altered by the use of quotation marks that signal a direct quote: *"clearly on the run from the police."* The quotation marks open a new base space (B_2), embedded in M, since in the partial quotation the referential center is moved to the new narrator, i.e., the embedded speaker s. As in normal direct mode, focus and viewpoint are located in B_2.

The stretch of discourse within such quotation marks is heavily shielded as subjective, coming from a source other than the narrator. Thus, within the boundaries of the embedded subspace (M), a new base space (B_2) is embedded, which creates a double embedding. By using such heavily marked stretches as *clearly on the run from the police,* the narrator may want to indicate that he will not take responsibility for the validity of this particular part of the claim. Especially in news texts, the function of partial quotation may be to express the narrator's (negative) attitude towards the quoted fragment, i.e., that he does not believe it or does not agree with it (Weizman 1984).

If the whole sentence is presented as a direct quote, the quotation is less distancing than in the case of direct quotation of a part of the claim, as in (3'), because in (3) there is no double embedding: the new base space, created by the direct mode, is not embedded within an embedded subspace. Therefore the distance between narrator's reality (B_1) and the embedded character's space (B_2) is shorter in (3) than in (3'). The reader may *transport* the claim from B_2 to B_1 more easily, i.e., the statement that the man was clearly on the run from the police, which is valid within B_2, may turn out to be valid in, or transportable to, B_1. By default, in the absence of contradictory information, the reader will make this transportation and will infer that the information is true in the narrator's reality.

INDIRECT MODE

In the indirect-representation mode, shown in example (4) and figure 10.3, the embedded speaker's discourse is paraphrased by the narrator and syntactically embedded in the narrator's discourse (*he said that x,* or *x, he said*).

(4) They had heard shots as well, but knew nothing else, they said.

In this case of indirect-representation mode, an embedded subspace (M) is opened by the space builder *they said*. Although M is in focus, viewpoint is at least potentially still from the base (B). Because the referential forms in indirect mode are related to the narrator's reference point, access to the referents is always possible from B. Thus, indirect-mode spaces are more accessible from the base than direct-mode spaces.

Typical of the indirect mode is that it is difficult, if not impossible, to distinguish between the narrator's and the character's words. In (4), the only stretch of discourse not embedded in M is *they said,* which is part of narrator's reality in the base space (B).[4] The rest of the sentence seems to report *what* they said, which is bound to the persons *they* in M. Closer analysis reveals that this embedded part also contains elements that could be words from the narrator. In this example, the actual utterances (x) may have been, in response to questions, *Yes, we did hear some shooting* and *No, we didn't see anybody*. There is no

Mental Space Representation for Indirect Mode

(4) They had heard shots as well, but knew nothing else, they said.

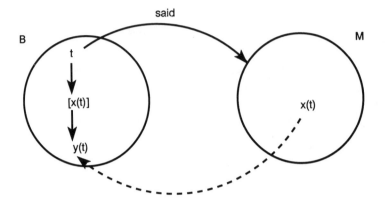

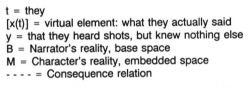

t = they
[x(t)] = virtual element: what they actually said
y = that they heard shots, but knew nothing else
B = Narrator's reality, base space
M = Character's reality, embedded space
- - - - = Consequence relation

Figure 10.3 Mental space representation for indirect mode

way to reconstruct the actual utterance(s) exactly. All we know is that the narrator, on the basis of whatever was said literally, x, reports y.

This means that the relation between what was actually said, x, and what is reported, y, is a relation of *consequence* rather than of *equivalence*. The narrator does not provide an identical representation of the utterance (equivalence, as in the direct mode), but concludes from the utterance what he thinks is right, x, adds elements such as *as well* and *but*, and reports the information in B. The reader will by default represent the propositional content of y as valid in B. As for the wording of the represented discourse, it is not clear whether viewpoint is in B or M. For instance, in a sentence such as *Piet said that he hated that bastard*, it is possible to interpret *that bastard* as the narrator's words.[5] But in the preferred interpretation of such marked lexical choices, access is provided directly from Piet's space, M, with viewpoint in M and M in focus, and the expression *that bastard* attributed to Piet.

In comparison to the direct mode, the narrator is more on stage by his influence on the representation of the embedded discourse. Thus, the indirect mode is less subjective in the sense that the utterance is less exclusively the embedded character's responsibility. The narrator's influence in indirect mode is more limited, however, than it is in narrative descriptions of speech events. Compare (4) with (4').

(4') They admitted hearing shots, but denied knowing anything about it.

When speech events are described or narrated, as in (4'), there is no embedded subspace within the base. The narrator is fully responsible for the validity of the information. This example illustrates how utterances can be reported or narrated without responsibility of the speaking character for either form or content (for a discussion of narrative reports of speech acts, see Leech and Short 1981).

FREE INDIRECT MODE

While the direct and indirect representation of speech and thought are explicitly signaled by linguistic markers such as syntactic embedding, parentheticals, and quotation marks, the free indirect mode is less readily identifiable. In modern literary texts it can occur as a continuous *stream of consciousness,* as noted and studied by many literary theorists (e.g., Pascal 1977, Rimmon-Kenan 1983, and Toolan 1988; see also Cohn 1978 on *narrated monologue* and *free indirect thought;* and Banfield 1982, Wiebe 1990, and Fludernik 1993 on *represented consciousness*). Free indirect mode bears characteristics of both direct and indirect mode: the referential center stays with the narrator, as in the indirect mode, while the embedded speaker's discourse is represented literally, as in the direct mode, as shown in example (5) and figure 10.4.

(5) He heard something and turned around. There were the three Englishmen again. Now, could they really be tourists? No, no way! They looked just too shabby.

Although there is no parenthetical in (5), the presence of the verb of cognition *heard* and the fact that the subject of this hearing event, h, *turned around* (presumably to look), evokes a "subjective" interpretation of the sentences that follow. They can be interpreted as perceptions and thoughts of the charac-

Mental Space Representation for Free Indirect Mode

(5) He heard something and turned around. There were the three Englishmen again. Now, could they really be tourists? No, no way! They looked just too shabby.

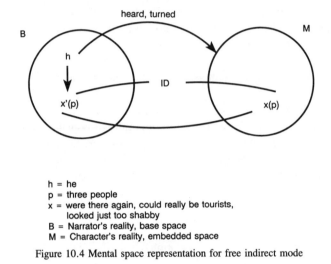

h = he
p = three people
x = were there again, could really be tourists,
    looked just too shabby
B = Narrator's reality, base space
M = Character's reality, embedded space

Figure 10.4 Mental space representation for free indirect mode

ter *he* (h); the stative aspect of sentences enhances their perspectivized inter-pretation (see Caenepeel 1989). Thus, an embedded subspace (M) is opened by *heard* and connected to h.

Viewpoint in free indirect mode can be located in the embedded subspace (M) or in the base (B), just as in indirect mode. While M is in focus, access to the referents of *the three Englishmen* in M is provided both directly by M, connected to *he,* as well as by B. However, the default interpretation that viewpoint is in M is stronger for free indirect mode than for indirect mode. Free indirect mode thus strongly favors direct access in M for referents in the embedded subspace, which is bound to the character who speaks or thinks. It is possible to coerce the viewpoint into B, and thus provide access from B, by interpreting the references as the narrator's words. However, this results in a marked interpretation, in which the implied narrator uses the characters' referential terms as his own "labels". Such marked narration may occur in children's books, but is very unlikely to occur in more mundane texts such as news reports. Therefore, the most natural interpretation is that the character *he* in the example already knows "the three Englishmen" and is thus able to refer to them by this definite reference form.

The free indirect mode, as in example (5), suggests authenticity by expressive, speaker-characteristic elements. The question form in the third sentence, the exclamation, the person-bound vocabulary (*no, no way*), and the expressive elements *now* and *no* are markers of the character's own wording. Thus, not only the content, but also the wording of what is in M, bound to the person *he,* is presented in a more direct way than in the indirect mode. Free indirect mode is thus more closely related to the direct mode than to the indirect mode. Note particularly that the reference point of deictic expressions (*here, now, yesterday,* and so forth) lies with the character, not with the narrator (on mental space constructs and deixis, see Rubba, chapter 8 in this volume). The reader has stronger evidence that the represented discourse was actually thought by the character: the relation between x in M and B is one of equivalence.

The main contrast with the direct mode is that the reference point for tense and person is not moved to the quoted utterance of the character, but stays with the narrator. Furthermore, the utterance or thought is not introduced by a parenthetical (e.g., *Joep said,* '' . . . ''*;* see, for instance, Leech and Short 1981; Banfield 1982). Finally, the free indirect mode allows the narrator to interpret and verbalize a character's mental processes to some extent, for instance, in the representation of a child's discourse by an adult narrator, as in Henry James's novel *What Masie Knew* (see Moore 1989). The conclusion is that the narrator's and character's voices are intertwined.

Free indirect mode, then, occupies a special intermediate position between direct quotation and indirect mode. The literary concept of internal focalization is identified with the free indirect representation of a character's mental discourse, and is considered here as one option for the representation of thought, on a par with free indirect representation of speech. The two do, of course, differ in the preconditions for their acceptability, as the representation of thoughts in nonfictional discourse is generally limited (we will come back to this point in the conclusion). The perspectivization and space-building characteristics, however, are the same.

IMPLICIT PERSPECTIVES

Even in discourse without direct, indirect, or free indirect representation of speech and thought, there may be elements that represent the expressions or perceptions of a character in a more remote way. Consider, for instance, example (6) and figure 10.5.[6]

(6) a. The police lost track of the car with the kidnapped girl.

    b. In the woods near Apeldoorn, a policeman saw a man who had a girl with him.

    c. The kidnapper had released her on a nearby street.

Mental Space Representation for Implicit Perspective

(6) a. The police lost track of the car with the kidnapped girl.
   b. In the woods near Apeldoorn, a policeman saw a man who had a girl with him.
   c. The kidnapper had released her in a nearby street.

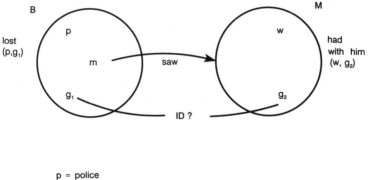

p = police
g_1 = kidnapped girl
m = policeman
w = man in woods
g_2 = girl in woods
B = Narrator's reality, base space
M = Character's reality, embedded space

Figure 10.5 Mental space representation for implicit perspective

In sentence (6b), an embedded subspace (M) is created by the verb of perception *saw*. M is connected to the character *a policeman* (m). In the preceding sentence, the narrator has already introduced *the kidnapped girl* (g_1). To the policeman in the woods, however, this girl was unknown at the time. The referent of *the kidnapped girl* is referred to by an indefinite referential form, *a girl* (g_2) from M, the policeman's belief space; that is, viewpoint is in M.

The kidnapper is implicitly present in (6a) via the predicate *kidnapped* in *the kidnapped girl;* the mention of such a predicate will activate the kidnap scenario with its roles (see, for instance, Fillmore 1982). In the initial representation of (6b), the reader will suspect an identity relation between *the kidnapped girl* (g_1) and *a girl* (g_2), but cannot be certain. Thus, in M, *a girl* is a new referent.

Sentence (6c) gives certainty about the identity relation. Grammatical and pragmatic pressure now causes a space conversion: *her* in (6c) refers strongly to the most recent female referent, which is *a girl* in sentence (6b), whereas at discourse level, *the kidnapper* refers to the implicitly introduced kidnapper in (6a), and the predicate *released* fits into our scripted knowledge about kidnap-

Mental Space Representation for a Modal Construction of Implicit Perspective

(7)   About his motives, the police could say nothing.

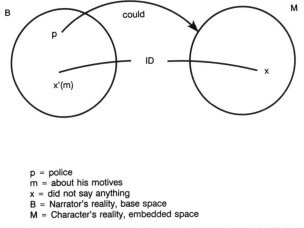

p = police
m = about his motives
x = did not say anything
B = Narrator's reality, base space
M = Character's reality, embedded space

Figure 10.6 Mental space representation for a modal construction of implicit perspective

pings. Once the identity relation between the kidnapper in (6a) and (6c) is established, the identity relation between the girls g_1 and g_2 must be established too.

In this fragment, viewpoint shifts from the base (B) to M in sentence (6b). The referent *a girl* is the counterpart for the referent *the kidnapped girl*, initially set up in the base. In sentence (6b), viewpoint is in M, which means that access to the referent *a girl* is not provided by the counterpart character in B, but directly by M.

This example, then, contains a clearly restricted viewpoint, bound to a person, that can be described in terms of an embedded mental space. Thus, it meets our definition of perspectivization. We call this type of perspectivization *implicit perspectives*. Other markers of implicit perspectives are modal verbs, such as in example (7) and in figure 10.6.

(7) About his motives, the police could say nothing.

Modal expressions such as *could* indicate that a character in the text is represented as an active consciousness, and that the information which is marked by *could* is only valid to this character. The statement *the police could say nothing about his motives* expresses an opinion or evaluation by the character involved, i.e., the police. The variant *the police did not say anything about his motives,* by contrast, does not ascribe any opinion to the police, and is valid in the narrator's base space. Thus, the modal verb opens an embedded mental space in which the validity of the marked information is restricted to the character whose opinion is indicated (for further discussion see Sanders and Spooren 1995 and 1996 and Sanders 1996).

In implicit perspectives, the narrator reports in his own words the interpretation of a perceived event or utterance, but by using a modal verb or marked reference he builds a space in which the validity of the information is restricted to the character involved. Thus, the wording is a shared responsibility between character and narrator. Since the representation of the character's utterance or perception is highly influenced by the narrator, implicit perspectives, as indirect quotes, are less subjective than the direct and free indirect mode.

Perspective in Discourse

In this section we consider the perspective phenomena in the full discourse contexts in which they occur. We first present an analysis of (the relevant parts of) a news text; we then discuss the scope of perspective spaces.

Analysis of a News Text

The text in (8), which is a shortened translation of a Dutch news text, contains some referential choices within a double embedding of perspective spaces that are puzzling at first glance.[7]

(8) a. Two suspected IRA members were arrested after being caught in a shooting exercise by armed Belgian civilians near the Belgian-Dutch border.

   b. A third man, who managed to escape, is still wanted.

   c. On Saturday afternoon, the police were called by a man who owns a house in the neighborhood of Hoogstraten.

   d. He had heard shooting in the woods near his house.

   e. Accompanied by his son, the man went out to investigate, armed with a shotgun.

   f. On their way they met three English-speaking tourists.

g. They had heard shots as well, but knew nothing else, they said.

h. A little further on, the two found a box of explosives and weapons.

i. After some time, the suspects appeared at the spot.

j. They kept them at gunpoint until the police arrived, according to the informant.

k. After their arrest, one of the now-handcuffed men managed to escape anyway.

l. The police are still looking for him.

Notice that the most important (result of an) event is mentioned first in this text. This so-called "lead" (see, e.g., van Dijk 1988) is a typical feature of news texts. This means that the main point of the news story can in principle be treated as "given" before the story is told. However, the mention of the call to the police introduces a subjective viewpoint in this text, which causes liveliness and suspense. Despite the fact that narrator and readers know how the story will end, a slight tension is built because at this stage in the story, police and informant do not know the outcome (see Gerrig 1989).

Although this text does not contain any direct or indirect speech or represented consciousness, a part of it does, in a more remote way, represent at least the content of a character's speech. The information presented in sentences (8c) through (8j) is understood as originally experienced and reported by the caller and passed on to the writer by a police spokesman. Representing the text in a mental space structure shows how these domains are created (see figure 10.7; we restrict our representation and discussion to sentences that mark boundaries between spaces).[8]

The embedded sequence in the IRA text contains several remarkable referential forms in sentences (8c) and (8f) of the original text. Consider first (8f), *On their way they met three English-speaking tourists.* The use of the indefinite description *three English-speaking tourists* suggests that these should be "new" characters that have not yet been introduced (see, e.g., DuBois 1980), but still the interpretation that these are the three suspected IRA members that this text is about is immediate and straightforward.

How does the reader know how to resolve this reference? First of all, readers assume that the information in a text is relevant to that text's topic and aims. Therefore they try to establish coherence and coreference links (some candidate concepts in this text: the arrest of the three IRA members,

Mental Space Representation of Implicit Perspectives in IRA-text

Mental Space Structure	Explanation
Base **caught** (b,i)	[a] Two suspected IRA-members (i) arrested (...) after being caught (...) by armed Belgian civilians (b). [b] ...
no space builders *Focus and Viewpoint in Base*	
M₁ **were called** (m,p)	[c] On Sat. afternoon, the police (p) (...) were called by **a man** (m), who...
*space builders of M₁ : temporal indication: Saturday afternoon; spatial indication 'police **in Turnhout'** ; verb of saying: 'police* **were called'** *; Focus and Viewpoint in M₁, M₁ connected to **police** (p)*	
M₂ **had heard** (m,x)	[d] He (m) had heard (...) (x). [e] ...
*temporal indication for opening M₂ : past perfect **'had heard'; he** is subject Focus and Viewpoint in M₂, M₂ connected to **a man** (m)*	
met (m,e)	[f] (continued) On their way they (m + s) met **three English speaking tourists** (e). [g,h] ....
Focus and Viewpoint in M₂	
appeared (s)	[i] (continued) After some time, one of **the suspects** (s) appeared at the spot.
Focus in M₂, Viewpoint in B / M₁	
kept (m,s)	[j] They kept the suspects (s) at gunpoint **until the police (p) arrived**, according to the informant (m).
*closing marker of M₂ : '**according to the informant'***	
M₁ **managed to escape** (m)	[k] After their arrest, the now handcuffed man (m) managed to escape anyway.
Focus and Viewpoint in M₁	
Base **are looking for** (p, s1)	[l] The police (p) are still looking for him (s1)
temporal indication for closing M₁ : present progressive **'are** *still looking' , Focus and Viewpoint in Base*	

Figure 10.7 Mental space representation of implicit perspectives in IRA text

the sound of machine guns), using knowledge of the world to derive the necessary inferences (the attribution *English-speaking* matches the fact that the IRA is an Irish organization; the shots in the woods—IRA members use guns). But indefinites do not normally trigger such reference resolution. A necessary precondition seems to be that the reader recognizes the possibility that the writer might adopt a character's perspective at this particular point in the text. Reporting an eyewitness account, as in this text, is obviously a perfect environment for such perspective taking to occur. Writer and reader know that the *three English-speaking tourists* will turn out to be the three IRA members. But to the man and his son, walking in the woods, M₂, and to the police, M_1, the three were new persons, who introduced themselves as tourists. The man and his son had no reason (yet) to distrust this information. Thus, the characters are "old" to the narrator and reader, whereas they are "new" to the man and his son and to the police.

At this point, the writer thus has a choice between a definite and an indefinite description. His choice signals which space he is taking to be the current viewpoint. The indefinite form indicates that the writer chooses the perspective of the man and his son (M_2). A definite reference at this point would have placed the description in the narrator's own reality (B), where the identity of the three men is certain:

(8) f'. Accompanied by his son, the informant went out to investigate, armed with a pistol and a shotgun. On their way they met *the three (suspected) IRA members.*

An analogous line of reasoning applies for the marked reference in (8c). *On Saturday afternoon the police in Turnhout were called by a man who . . . .* The informants, one of whom is referred to here with the noun phrase *a man [+ modifier]*, were already introduced in (8a), so they are not new to the writer or the reader. Still, the reference form in (8c) is indefinite. Here, too, the explanation is that the man was introduced in the narrator's reality, whereas he is new to the police at the time of the call. The reader has to interpret (8c) from that embedded perspective (that is, belief space M_1 in figure 10.7).

Marked references, then, can serve to signal embedded points of view or an embedded focalizer (Sanders 1990). Instead of the objective version of the external narrator, the subjective perspective of (one of) the characters is presented. The mental space model thus describes how new, embedded person-bound belief spaces can cause "renewed" introduction of characters that are "old" in higher spaces.

Yet the narrator's influence on the wording in implicit perspective spaces is potentially greater than in any mode of speech and thought representation. For instance, in sentence (8i), the reference *the suspects* is used, which is a police term, while the events are described within M_2, which is bound to the man (m). This can be explained by a shift in viewpoint back to the base space or subspace (M_1), coming from the narrator (B) or the police (M_1), whereas M_2 is still in focus: the events still take place within M_2, the man's embedded subjective story. *The suspects* is linked to *they* in sentence (8g) because there are no other available referents for the definite NP *the suspects;* the suspects must be referents who are already introduced, and they can be neither the police nor the man and his son. This means that in implicit perspectives, not only the wording of the perspectivized information is a shared and shifting responsibility of narrator and character, but also its content: *the suspects* bears content value other than "the Englishmen", which can only be explained from the narrator's knowledge of the eventual outcome.

The Scope of Perspective Subspaces

In fictional narratives, sentences with stative aspect, which do not temporally update the narrative, introduce a perspective focus (Caenepeel 1989:112). Following this theory, all nonstative types are what Caenepeel calls "perspectivally nonsituated" (1989: 110). However, in the IRA news report, sentences (8c) through (8j), which are part of the embedded perspective space (M_2), all have an "event" aspect that moves narrative time forward. They do not describe states, but a sequence of events. The sentences show no marked references, focalizing verbs or other explicit linguistic signals for represented consciousness. On the contrary, temporal updates and spatial phrases can be discerned, such as (8h) (*A little further on, . . .*) or (8i) (*After their arrest, . . .*). Yet, as a result of the perspective markers in the preceding sentences, these sentences can be interpreted as the subjective version of the events given by the informant. The ending of (8j) also supports this interpretation. It is a closing signal for the embedded perspective—*. . . according to the informant*—to signal explicitly that the preceding material had been presented from the perspective of the informant, not the narrator's reality (B). This shows how a perspective marker can have an effect beyond the sentence it occurs in.

Perspective-neutral sentences, then, can fall within the scope of a perspective marker, even if they have the aspect of an event. In other words, the mental space model of perspective offers a description of perspective not only at local-sentence or main-clause level, but also at a more global level. Embedded perspective spaces may span several sequentially narrative events; in fact, they may span major text parts.

We should make it clear, at this point, however, that we do not claim to have solved all problems of perspectivization in narrative texts. Especially in literary narrative it is sometimes simply impossible to decide which sentences do and which don't represent an embedded perspective. The example in (9) is a fragment from the detective novel *Devices and Desires,* by P.D. James.[9] A young girl has hitched a lift with two elderly ladies.

(9) "Does your mother know that you're out, what you're doing?. . ." Silly old cow, she thought, what business is it of hers what I do? She wouldn't have stood the cheek from any of her teachers at school. But she bit back the impulse to rudeness, which was her adolescent response to adult criticism. She had to ride with the two old wrinklies. (p. 5)

By their wording, and by the explicitly embedding clause *she thought,* it is clear that the second and the last sentence of the fragment represent the character's thoughts. In spite of the absence of quotation marks, the second sentence can be recognized as a direct quote by the shift of the reference point (*I* refers to the girl). The last sentence also presents the girl's thoughts, in the wording *two old wrinklies.* The sentence about her adolescent response is presumably an evaluation by the (adult?) narrator. But what about her not having stood the cheek—is this a thought of the girl or of the narrator? There are no clear markers for either interpretation within the sentence itself (for discussion of this type of problem, see also Moore 1989).

The fragments in examples (10) and (11) from the same novel illustrate that the ambiguity remains even when linguistic signals to subjectivity such as evaluative and expressive devices are present.

(10) He turned off the B1149 at Felthorpe to take the country roads across the flat country. It was unnecessary to consult the map. The magnificent fifteenth-century tower with its four pinnacles was an unmistakable landmark and he drove towards it along the almost deserted roads. (p. 142)

(11) But it was time to get back. She gave a vigorous kick, twisted herself over and began her powerful crawl towards the shore, towards that silent watcher waiting for her in the shadow of the trees. (p. 141)

Whose opinion, for instance, is it in (10) that it was *unnecessary to consult the map?* Presumably it should be ascribed to the character who is driving. But is it also his opinion that the tower was *magnificent* and an *unmistakable landmark?* And in (11), whose opinion is it that *it was time to get back?* The answer depends on the preceding context, but most probably is the *she* of the next sentence. The expressive attributions *vigorous* and *powerful* would be interpreted as signals of perspectivization by the external narrator. But the focalizer here could equally well be the character herself. All that is certain is that she does not see the silent watcher, who—as the reader suspects and the narrator knows—is going to kill her.

Conclusion

All perspective phenomena are subjective in the sense that they represent that the validity of information (wording or wording and content) is restricted to a certain person in the text. We have shown in this paper that mental space theory offers a useful representation of embedded perspectives and explains differences in the degree of the embedding force of various perspective types. The restriction of validity in perspectivization is thus placed in a general framework of comparable linguistic phenomena such as restrictions of validity by temporal and spatial modifiers.

Our definition of perspective is based in part on the literary concept of focalization, which figures as a special type of perspectivization in the broader class of perspective phenomena. Focalization can be distinguished from other types of perspective by defining it in terms of the representation of a person's thoughts and perceptions; its typical linguistic realization is the free indirect mode.

The extent to which reference to persons can be transported between spaces signals the accessibility of the embedded space. Different types of speech and thought representation differ in the extent of separation of the embedded mental space, that is, the shielding of the embedded space from the base space. In comparison to the direct mode, the indirect mode and implicit perspectives are less explicitly marked as embeddings; in other words, they are more accessible to the narrator's influence. The more accessible the embedded discourse in a certain perspective type is for alterations by the narrator, the less subjective the embedded information is, and therefore the less restrictions are put on the use of the perspective type in various text genres.

Another functionally relevant feature is, of course, the difference between representations of *spoken* and *mental* discourse. To represent a person's thoughts in the direct or free indirect mode requires the possibility of claiming access to that person's consciousness. This explains why focalization especially is such a prominent device in some text genres and almost absent in others. It is a highly subjective mode of representation with a dramatizing effect. This effect may serve well in text genres with an entertaining or dramatizing function, as has been confirmed by readers' judgments (Sanders and Redeker 1993). While the free indirect mode is very common in fictional narrative (Bronzwaer 1977) as the representation of mostly *mental* discourse, its use to represent *speech* can be found in other text types too, such as newspaper articles on sports, art and other special-topic news. The function of such "soft" news genres is broader than simply to be informative and includes, for instance, entertainment. "Hard news" texts do not normally contain free indirect discourse.

In closing, we want to raise an issue we could not fully explore in this paper. We want to suggest (inspired by Langacker's (1990) discussion of subjectivity) that two types of subjectivity should be distinguished, the narrator's and the character's. For instance, the representation of an utterance in direct mode is subjective with respect to the quoted speaker: it is strictly bound to a certain character in the text. Yet, it is at the same time very objective: the narrator's interference with the representation is minimal. This situation may be clarified by Langacker's model of subjectivity. In this model, there is an inherent asymmetry between a perceiving individual and the entity perceived. In the "optimal viewing arrangement", the perceived object (here, the embedded discourse) is fully foregrounded—i.e., maximally objective—while the perceiving individual (the narrator) is off stage, not influencing the representation—i.e., the narrator is maximally subjective. Conversely, if the perceiving individual is foregrounded, he is objectivized, but at the same time the perceived entity is subjectivized (Langacker 1990).

The situation is complicated in the case of perspective by represented discourse, since there are two perceiving individuals, the narrator and the character. This explains why the direct mode at the same time is and is not subjectively construed. As an entity that is perceived and presented by the narrator, the directly quoted discourse is maximally objective. The perceiving individual within the represented discourse, the character, is maximally subjective, since he is foregrounded and given a free rein. In other words, the stronger the perspectivization, the more the character's subjectivity enters the discourse. But this is compensated for by a reduction in the narrator's influence, i.e., the extent to which his subjectivity can be expressed. We thus get two opposite clines for the four types of perspective, with full character subjectivity and no narrator subjectivity in direct quotation (the strongest type) and full narrator subjectivity and minimal character subjectivity for implicit perspectives (the weakest perspective type).

In indirect reports of speech and thought, what is being reported is accessible to the influence of the narrator (moderate narrator subjectivity), while the characters are given little room for their own verbalization (low character subjectivity). Free indirect mode is ambiguous in this respect. It is relatively weakly marked as embedded (and thus allows some narrator subjectivity), but is nonetheless close to the direct mode in its fairly direct presentation of the embedded character's words (moderate character subjectivity). This is why the free indirect mode was considered higher than the indirect mode in the hierarchy of strength of perspective shown in Table 10.1.

Notes

1. We are indebted to many colleagues for helpful comments on earlier versions of this paper, especially Gilles Fauconnier, Leo Noordman, Gerard Steen, Eve Sweetser, and Ellen van Wolde. The research reported here was supported in part by the Netherlands Organization for Scientific Research (NWO), grant number SIR 01-254, to José Sanders.

2. The samples in this section are translations or adaptations from original Dutch news reports. Short "hard news" texts generally have all the essential characteristics

that are needed in narratives or stories, and they answer to Fleischman's (1990:103) criteria of narrativity. They have a story point, namely, something that makes them relevant or newsworthy; they have past reference time; and they refer to unique events and persons.

3. In the space diagrams, lines with arrows represent connections between the base space and subspaces that are established by space builders. Lines without arrows connect elements that are related through a pragmatic function (cf. Fauconnier 1985, chapter 1). A prime in these diagrams indicates that an element, (x'), is the counterpart in the narrator's reality of the element, (x), in the embedded subspace.

4. The example selected here also provides an illustration of the claim that the difference between direct and indirect mode is not necessarily syntactic. The discourse in (4) is represented indirectly because the deictic center is not that of the reported utterance, but of the narrator (past tense, third person).

5. The ambiguity between narrator's and character' reference to persons is stronger with subordinating *that*-clauses than with so-called discourse parentheticals, as in example (3'). The difference between discourse parentheticals and a subordinating indirect-speech parenthetical is that the latter permits readings of both a narrator perspective and an embedded-character perspective, while the discourse parenthetical permits just one perspective, by default the embedded character's (Reinhart 1983). Compare examples (i) and (ii).

(i) Max said that a famous actress was going to visit him.

(ii) A famous actress was going to visit him, Max said.

The second sentence, with the discourse parenthetical, can only be used when Max really said something very similar to what (ii) claims he said. Given a speech event like the one in (iii), if the narrator knows Max's mother is an actress, he may account for Max's speech event by saying (i), and thus represent his own perspective, while (ii) cannot be considered as an account for the given speech act (examples from Reinhart 1983 (p. 174)).

(iii) Max: My mother is going to visit me.

In this respect, indirect speech with a discourse parenthetical is relatively close to the free indirect-representation mode.

6. These sentences were translated from a Dutch news story. Here is the complete translation:

> de Volkskrant, April 24, 1989
> KIDNAPPED GIRL TURNS OUT WELL AFTER POLICE ACTION
> APELDOORN (ANP)—The kidnapping of a six-year-old girl in Apel-
> doorn on Sunday turned out well after a large-scale action of the police.
> This was announced by the police on Sunday.
> Witnesses saw how the girl was dragged into a car and taken away by a
> man. The police immediately started a pursuit with twenty policemen and

an aircraft from the transport department, but lost the car. About a quarter of an hour later, a policeman who was working on another investigation in the woods outside Apeldoorn discovered a man who had a girl with him. The man appeared to have taken pity on the girl, but there was no trace of the kidnapper.

A little later a witness of the kidnapping who had heard—through listening to the police radio station—where the girl had been found, discovered the car with the presumed kidnapper. According to the police, this led to a wild pursuit through Apeldoorn. The suspect, a 24-year-old man from Apeldoorn, had car trouble and was arrested by the police a little more than an hour and a half after the kidnapping. About his motives the police could not say anything.

7. Here is the complete translation of the text. The original Dutch text has been slightly shortened (a passage with details on the weapons was omitted), but the crucial part (sentences 5–16 in the translation below) remains. Note that some of the examples in the previous sections were taken from this text.

de Volkskrant, June 18, 1990

(1) SUSPECTED IRA MEMBERS CAUGHT WHILE AT SHOOTING EXERCISE

(2) This weekend two suspected IRA members were arrested near the Belgian-Dutch border area after being caught in the process of a shooting exercise by armed Belgian civilians in the neighborhood of Turnhout. (3) A third man, who managed to escape handcuffed and on foot, is still wanted. (4) With these arrests, the supposed offenders in a series of IRA terrorist actions in Belgium, the Netherlands and Germany have been apprehended.

(5) The arrest is the result of a combination of chance and good luck. (6) Saturday afternoon the Rijkswacht in Turnhout was called by a man who owns a bungalow in the neighborhood of Hoogstraten. (7) He had heard the sound of machine guns in the woods near his house. (8) Accompanied by his son, the informant went out to investigate, armed with a pistol and a shotgun. (9) On their way they met three English-speaking tourists. (10) They had heard shots as well, but knew nothing else, they said. (11) A little further on, the two found a piece of ground which had been broken up, where, after some digging, a box of explosives and some weapons appeared.

(12) The son kept watch at this spot, and the father went for help. (13) After some time one of the suspects appeared up at the spot. (14) The son fired a warning shot, after which the man took flight. (15) The father, who had heard the shot, returned to the son with a forester and on the way came across the two other suspects. (16) They kept the two—a man and a woman—at gunpoint until the Rijkswacht arrived, according to the informant.

(17) After their arrest, the now-handcuffed man managed to escape after all. (18) The police are still looking for him.

(19) Late Saturday evening the Dutch police arrested the third suspect in Baarle-Nassau, a few hundred meters across the border. (20) According to a spokesman the man was "clearly on the run from the police." (21) He

did not have any papers and did not want to give his name. (22) It is expected that Belgium will request his extradition.

8. Note that the deictic point of view is also important in this respect: the mere fact that a certain character is mentioned in subject position (as *he* in sentence (8d)), or that someone's description is oriented toward a certain character (Kuno 1987, Zribi-Hertz 1989) can reinforce the impression that the perspective of that character is taken.

9. P.D. James. 1989. *Devices and Desires*. London: Faber & Faber.

References

Bal, M. 1990. *De Theorie van Verhalen en Vertellen: Inleiding in de Narratologie*. 5th ed. Muiderberg: Coutinho. An earlier edition is published in translation as *Narratology: Introduction to the Theory of Narrative* (Toronto: University of Toronto Press, 1985).

Banfield, Ann. 1982. *Unspeakable Sentences: Narration and Representation in the Language of Fiction*. Boston: Routledge and Kegan Paul.

Booth, Wayne. 1983. *The Rhetoric of Fiction*. 2d ed. Chicago: University of Chicago Press.

Bronzwaer, W. 1977. Over het Lezen van Narratieve Teksten (About the Reading of Narrative Texts). In W. Bronzwaer, D. Fokkema, and E. Ibsch, eds., *Tekstboek Algemene Literatuurwetenschap*, 229–54. Baarn: Ambo.

Caenepeel, M. 1989. Aspect, Temporal Ordering and Perspective in Narrative Fiction. Ph.D. diss., University of Edinburgh.

Chatman, S. 1978. *Story and Discourse*. Ithaca, N.Y.: Cornell University Press.

Clark, Herbert, and R. Gerrig. 1990. Quotations as Demonstrations. *Language* 66: 764–805.

Cohn, D. 1978. *Transparent Minds: Narrative Modes for Presenting Consciousness in Fiction*. Princeton, N.J.: Princeton University Press.

DeLancey, Scott. 1982. Aspect, Transitivity and Viewpoint. In P. Hopper, ed., *Between Semantics and Pragmatics: Typological Studies in Language*, 167–83. Amsterdam: John Benjamins.

Dinsmore, John. 1991. *Partitioned Representations*. Dordrecht: Kluwer Academic Publishers.

DuBois, J. 1980. Beyond Definiteness: The Trace of Identity in Discourse. In Wallace Chafe, ed., *The Pear Stories: Cognitive, Cultural and Linguistic Aspects of Narrative Production*, 203–74. Norwood, N.J.: Ablex.

Fauconnier, Gilles. 1985. *Mental Spaces: Aspects of Meaning Construction in Natural Language*. Cambridge, Mass.: MIT Press. Reprinted 1994, Cambridge: Cambridge University Press.

Fillmore, Charles J. 1982. Frame Semantics. In Linguistic Society of Korea, ed., *Linguistics in the Morning Calm*, 111–38. Seoul: Hanshin.

Fleischman, Suzanne. 1990. *Tense and Narrativity: From Medieval Performance to Modern Fiction*. Austin, Tex.: University of Texas Press.

Fludernik, M. 1993. *The Fictions of Language and the Languages of Fiction: The Linguistic Representation of Speech and Consciousness*. London: Routledge.

Genette, G. 1980. *Narrative Discourse*. Oxford: Basil Blackwell.

Gerrig, R. 1989. Suspense in the Absence of Uncertainty. *Journal of Memory and Language* 28:633–48.

Graumann, C., and C. Sommer. 1988. Perspective Structure in Language Production and Comprehension. *Journal of Language and Social Psychology* 7:192–212.

Kuno, S. 1987. *Functional Syntax*. Chicago: University of Chicago Press.

Langacker, Ronald W. 1990. Subjectification. *Cognitive Linguistics* 1:5–38.

Leech, G., and M. Short. 1981. *Style in Fiction: A Linguistic Introduction to English Fictional Prose*. London: Longman.

Mayes, P. 1990. Quotation in Spoken English. *Studies in Language* 14:325–63.

Moore, G. 1989. Focalization and Narrative Voice in *What Maisie Knew*. *Language and Style* 22:3–24.

Pascal, R. 1977. *The Dual Voice: Free Indirect Speech and Its Functioning in the Nineteenth-Century European Novel*. Manchester: Manchester University Press.

Redeker, Gisela. 1991. Quotation in Discourse. In R. van Hout and E. Huls, eds., *Artikelen van de Eerste Sociolinguïstische Conferentie*, 341–55. Delft: Eburon.

Reinhart, T. 1983. Point of View in Language: The Use of Parentheticals. In Gisa Rauh, ed., *Essays on Deixis*, 169–94. Tübingen: Gunter Narr Verlag.

Rimmon-Kenan, S. 1983. *Narrative Fiction: Contemporary Poetics*. London: Methuen.

Sanders, José. 1990. Expliciet of Niet? Referentie-Bepalende Factoren bij Personen in Nieuwsberichten (Explicit or Not? Determining Factors of Reference to Persons in News Reports). *Interdisciplinair Tijdschrift voor Taal- en Tekstwetenschap* 9:159–80.

———. 1996. Degrees of Subjectivity in Epistemic Modals and Perspective Representation. In L. de Stadler, ed., *Proceedings of the Third Conference of the International Cognitive Linguistics Association*. Forthcoming.

Sanders, José, and Gisela Redeker. 1993. Linguistic Perspective in Short News Stories. *Poetics* 22:69–87.

Sanders, José, and W. Spooren. 1995. Perspective, Subjectivity, and Modality from a Cognitive Linguistic Point of View. Manuscript, Tilburg University.

———. 1996. Subjectivity and Certainty in Epistemic Modality: A Study of Dutch Epistemic Modifiers. *Cognitive Linguistics*.

Tannen, Deborah. 1989. *Talking Voices: Repetition, Dialogue, and Imagery in Conversational Discourse*. Cambridge: Cambridge University Press.

Toolan, M. 1988. *Narrative: A Critical Linguistic Introduction*. London: Routledge.

van Dijk, T. 1988. *News as Discourse*. Hillsdale, N.J.: Lawrence Erlbaum Associates.

van Rees, C. 1985. Implicit Premises on Text and Reader in Genette's Study of Narrative Mood. *Poetics* 14:445–64.

Weizman, E. 1984. Some Register Characteristics of Journalistic Language: Are they Universals? *Applied Linguistics* 5:39–50.

Wiebe, J. 1990. Identifying Subjective Characters in Narrative. In *Proceedings of COLING 90*, 401–406.

Zribi-Hertz, A. 1989. Anaphor Binding and Narrative Point of View: English Reflexive Pronouns in Sentence and Discourse. *Language* 65:695–727.

11 Mental Spaces and the Grammar of Conditional Constructions

-
-
-
-

This paper is in essence a footnote to the work of Fauconnier and of Fillmore. I argue that the grammar of English conditionals (as described by Fillmore (1986, 1990a, 1990b)) corresponds saliently to the structure of embeddings in mental spaces which Fauconnier suggested as a basic common denominator of conditional semantics. Fillmore (1990a, 1990b) lays out a comprehensive set of formal aspects of English conditional constructions, and gives concomitant semantics for each constructional grouping of forms. I suggest that certain of these formal constructional aspects should be taken precisely as marking mental space embeddings, and that this will explain some further interactions between constructions which are not touched on by Fillmore. I argue that such an approach adds to the generality and compositionality of Fillmore's analysis.

Fillmore proposes that a basic element of conditional meaning is *epistemic stance,* the speaker's mental association with or dissociation from the world of the protasis (P). One of the differences between (1), (2), and (3), for example, is that in (1) the speaker identifies with P as a description of the real state of affairs; in (2) the speaker does not identify with P or with ¬P; and in (3) the speaker identifies with ¬P instead of with P. Of course we have no way of knowing the speaker's true inner views: these forms portray the speaker as having certain attitudes, which may also not be irreversible. For example, the speaker in (3) may simply be displaying mild skepticism, or may be totally convinced that P is false, but in either case is displaying an association with ¬P.

(1) If/Since he's (so) hungry (as you say he is), he'll want a second helping.

(2) (I don't know, but) if he's hungry, he'll want a second helping.

(3) If he were/was hungry, he'd want a second helping.[1]

In contrasting (1) and (2), we see that *since* can be used to mark identification with an assumption, while *if* in itself does not mark such identification with the protasis. Further lexical material within the protasis (*so, as you say he is*) may at least encourage an interpretation involving a committed epistemic stance, even with the uncommitted *if*. In (3), we note that the verb form *were* in the protasis marks a dissociated epistemic stance. The present-tense verb form used in the protases of (1) and (2) was apparently neither committed nor dissociated, but neutral, since by itself it did not convey commitment to P or to ¬P. The apodoses show similar variation in form. Note that in (1) and (2), *will* verb forms follow present-tense protases to indicate a conditional relationship between present and future. In (3), the *would* conditional marks a greater dissociation from the truth of the proposition.

The claim made by Fillmore, then, is that both our choice of conjunctions and our choice of verb forms mark the kind of epistemic stance we take toward an utterance. This is remarkably close to Fauconnier's (1985) pair of observations: (i) that conjunctions like *if* set up a particular kind of mental space, distinct from our base space and from spaces set up by, e.g., *since;* and (ii) that contrasts such as indicative/subjunctive in French mark not only the setting up of mental spaces, but the relationships between them. Thus, for example, Fauconnier compares (4) and (5).

(4) Je veux qu'elle *mette* une robe qui *soit* belle.

(5) Je veux qu'elle *mette* une robe qui *est* belle.

Loosely, both these examples mean "I want her to put on a beautiful dress." The English translation is ambiguous between a reading where there is supposed to be some particular beautiful dress that the speaker thinks exists and also wants her to put on, and a reading where the speaker doesn't care what dress, as long as it's beautiful. This second reading could be said to embed the description of the dress inside the *want*-space: the speaker's desire is "that she put on a dress and that the dress be beautiful." The first reading, on the other hand, interprets the definite description as applying in the speaker's base belief space: the speaker believes there is a beautiful dress, and wants her to put that dress on.[2] The French sentences are not so ambiguous. The verb "put on" in French is in the subjunctive, since the verb "want" in French requires subjunctive forms in tensed complements. But in (4), "I want that she put on-SUBJ a dress that is-SUBJ beautiful," the dress is not supposed to be a specific extant one: any dress that's beautiful will do; and in (5), "I want that she put on-SUBJ a dress that is-IND beautiful," there is some particular dress assumed to exist and to be the one the speaker wants

Example 4

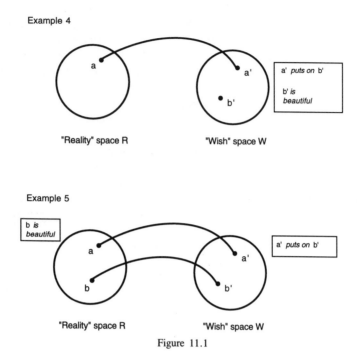

Figure 11.1

her to wear. Fauconnier explains this in terms of the relationship between the mental spaces. In (4) the use of the subjunctive in the relative clause indicates that the description applies *inside* the mental space defined by "want" (and marked by the subjunctive form that "want" requires of its complements. In (5), the indicative form in the relative clause marks the opposite relationship: the description applies outside the *want*-space, very possibly in the base mental space of the speaker, as shown in figure 11.1.

English conditional forms are not identical in behavior to French subjunctives or to definite descriptions. Conditional constructions in general are neither simple markers of a new mental space, nor descriptions which could apply either inside an evoked mental space or outside in the "base" space. The conditional construction exists precisely to set up a relationship between a conditional mental space and a proposition which applies specifically within that space, so subordination of the apodosis content to the protasis space is part of the deal. My argument is that the choice of verb forms in English conditional examples can be shown to follow from this simple fact. Predictably, extra embedding of conditionals (a conditional as the apodosis of a conditional) results in precisely the sort of formal marking of mental space embedding that Fauconnier demonstrated with French indicatives and sub-junctives. Definite descriptions, as we shall see, can apply either within the conditional space or outside it, and their verb forms under some circumstances will reflect that difference, making use again of the same verb-form choices that mark mental space embedding generally in conditionals. Further, there are some ways in which the apodosis can be more independent in content from the *content* of the protasis, and this results in greater freedom of form as well.

I therefore suggest that an analysis in terms of embedded mental spaces helps motivate the regularities to be observed in Fillmore's data, and also explains other general aspects of the choice of verb forms in English, as in embeddings of one conditional in another, or interpretation of embedded definite descriptions.

Fillmore's Basic Analysis

Fillmore (1990a, 1990b) argues that the verb forms of English conditional constructions can be analyzed as depending on two central factors, epistemic stance and tense structure (including temporal relations between the content of the protasis and the apodosis). So a form like *had('ve) gone* is used for a past protasis with negative epistemic stance, while a form like *went* is used for present or future protases with negative epistemic stance, and for past protases with positive or neutral stance; for positive or neutral stance, *go* would replace *went,* and *went* would replace *had('ve) gone.*

(6) If she had gone to his party yesterday, he would've ignored her.

(7) If she went to Joe's party tomorrow, he'd just ignore her.

(8) If she went to Joe's party yesterday, he ignored her.

(9) If she goes to Joe's party tomorrow, he'll just ignore her.

Other constructions besides conditionals show markings of epistemic stance. For example, some verbs of mental state or attitude describe essentially positive stances toward a content (e.g., *believe*), while some describe neutral or negative stances (e.g., *hope* and *wish,* respectively). Thus we find neutral verb forms (present forms with present reference) in (9a) and (9b), but negatively aligned (subjunctive or past for present time) forms in the complements of examples like (9c).

(9) a. I believe she is reading my letter.

   b. I hope she is reading my letter.

   c. I wish she was/were reading my letter.

For conditional constructions, Fillmore characterizes epistemic stance as the speaker's presumed association with or commitment to the world of the *protasis* in each case. This means that each potential verb form for an apodosis has built-in properties of combination with protasis forms. Forms can be incompatible in their demands on interpretation of the construction. For example, (10) is ungrammatical.

(10) *If she were here, they'll be happy.

In (10), the form *were* requires an interpretation of the protasis as present and negative in epistemic stance, while the form *will be* requires interpretation of the apodosis as neutral or hypothetical in stance, and future in time. Fillmore says there is no way to combine these two forms into a unified epistemic stance, and hence into a well-formed conditional sentence.

An Excursus on Tense and Distance

This paper has thus far assumed that past verb forms (ignoring true subjunctive singular *were*) are characteristic of conditional constructions representing negative epistemic stance. The motivation for this has been treated in some detail by other authors, such as Langacker (1978), who treats the past forms of auxiliaries as *distal* in a general sense, which includes both relative past-time location and also epistemic distance. Fleischman (1989) lays out cross-linguistic evidence that past-tense forms generally tend to be used for social and epistemic distance (e.g., politeness and counter-to-expectation, or "counterfactual," meaning) as well as for temporal distance. I shall not here be examining all the details of English past-form usage, some of which clearly derive historically from the use of distinct subjunctive forms. However, for a modern English speaker, the extensive identity of past and negative-stance forms is surely a central fact of grammar. It is generally true that one more layer of "past" morphology adds one more layer of "distance," temporal or epistemic. There is, so to speak, one layer of this "distancing" in the basic backshifting we see in hypothetical conditionals, where present-tense forms represent future in protases (with no backshift in apodoses), and another layer in "counterfactuals," where a genuinely negative epistemic stance

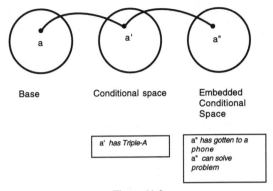

Figure 11.2

is represented by the use of a past form with future reference in protases (with the conditional *would*—historically a backshifted future—in apodoses).

A Mental-Space Analysis

Another way of looking at the problem of (10) is to say that one cannot use a conditional construction to embed material from a reality space or a possible space within a counterfactual space. Conditionals prototypically express a dependency relation between protasis and apodosis. Unlike relative clauses and definite descriptions, which may "pop" levels of embedding and apply in the reality space as well, conditionals are genuinely embedded, and one cannot therefore use a neutral or positively aligned apodosis form inside a space that is established (by the protasis forms) as negatively aligned.

This suggestion has the merit not only of showing how Fillmore's analysis can be made to fit Fauconnier's, but also of predicting the forms which result when conditionals are embedded within each other (a situation not touched on in Fillmore's discussion).

(11) If you have Triple-A, then if you go to a telephone, you can solve your problem.

(12) If you had Triple-A, then if you went to a telephone, you could solve your problem.

In (11) and (12), we see an entire conditional construction embedded as the apodosis of another as shown in figure 11.2. We further see that the entire embedded conditional takes on the verb forms appropriate to the epistemic alignment of the higher protasis. That is to say, both clauses of the embedded conditional are in the present-tense forms characteristic of hypothetical stance in (11), and in (12) both clauses of the embedded conditional are in the "past" (also called "subjunctive") forms which characterize negative or counterfactual stance. As far as we can tell, (12) does not present it as less likely that one will be able to get to a phone, only as less likely that the whole lower conditional will hold (i.e., that getting to a phone will solve one's problems). And this appears to be inherited from the counterfactuality of the higher protasis: getting Triple-A means you can solve your problems by phone just as certainly in both worlds, but (11) presents the mental space where "you have Triple-A" as a more likely one than (12) does. The result is that any space embedded in (12) inherits its distance from the speaker's base mental space, and takes on the verbal forms appropriate to such distance. Compare these examples with (13).

(13) If you had had Triple-A, then if you'd gone to a phone, you could have solved your problems.

Note the difference between (13) and (14), where the same form does result from the counterfactuality of going to a phone.

(14) If you'd gone to a phone, you could have solved your problems.

As an example of a different construction with behavior quite parallel to that of conditionals, let us examine embedding of the *the Xer, the Yer* construction as a conditional apodosis. This construction shares some semantic structure with conditionals, but also has some quite independent semantic aspects (see Fillmore 1986; see also Michaelis 1994 on Latin parallels); importantly, it involves the idea of *paired scales,* wherein a change in the value of one scale influences the value of the other scale.

(15) The colder it gets, the happier we'll be.

(16) The colder it gets, the happier we are (in general).

Although these examples show further structure in that they are specifically pairings of *scales,* they are more generally also examples of unidirectionally dependent mental space structures (if I know what the mental space in question has for a temperature value, I know the happiness value too, but not the other way around), and thus share significant mental-space structuring with conditional structures. And the relationship between the two clauses of a *the*

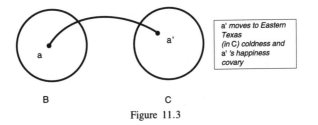

a' moves to Eastern Texas
(in C) coldness and a' 's happiness covary

B   C

Figure 11.3

Xer, the Yer construction is often conditional in nature, as in *If it gets colder, we'll be happier.*

Embedding *the Xer, the Yer* constructions in *if*-conditionals shows the same results we have seen with embedding of conditionals in conditionals: the embedded complex apodosis construction as a whole takes on the verbal forms characteristic of epistemic stance of the higher protasis.

(17) If we move to eastern Texas, (then) the colder it gets, the happier we'll be.

(18) If we moved to eastern Texas, (then) the colder it got, the happier we'd be.

(19) If we had moved to eastern Texas, (then) the colder it got, the happier we'd have been.

The simple past *got* in (19) appears to be acceptable in lieu of a complex past (cf. below, (22) alongside (23)); but otherwise these forms are strikingly like the ones observed above in two-leveled conditional constructions, and the same potential explanation can be offered for their behavior: they show the formal markings of being embedded in the higher conditional mental space set up by the *if*-clause.

(20) If we ate subtraction stew, then the more we ate, the hungrier we would get.

(21) If we eat subtraction stew, then the more we eat, the hungrier we'll get.

(22) If we'd eaten subtraction stew, then the more we'd've eaten, the hungrier we'd've gotten.

(23) If we'd eaten subtraction stew, then the more we ate, the hungrier we'd've gotten.

Definite descriptions, unlike apodoses, can refer either within the embedded conditional space or outside it. Relative clauses (examples (24), (25), and (26)) will thus show the verb form appropriate to the space in which they are taken as referential, just as Fauconnier's relative clauses showed subjunctives when semantically embedded in the subjunctive space. In (24), with a neutral epistemic stance toward its embedded conditional space, the relative clause could be interpreted either as applying inside or outside the conditional commitment to go to a play: either it means the speaker is committing to attending wheatever play gets suggested in the hypothetical world, or it means that a play has already been identified, and that is the play about which the speaker is making a conditional commitment. In (25), where the protasis and apodosis show negative epistemic stance, the corresponding "past" verb form *wanted* in the relative clause marks agreement with that negative stance—hence the description is taken as applying within the conditional space. Sentence (26), on the other hand, shows a similar negative epistemic stance as marked by the protasis and apodosis verb forms, but the relative clause shows a "present" form, marking positive stance, and hence the description applies in the base "reality" space.

(24) If she gives me the tickets, I'll go to the play that she wants me to go to.

(25) If she gave me the tickets, I'd go to the play she wanted me to go to. (i.e., to whatever play she might like)

(26) If she gave me the tickets, I'd go to the play she wants me to go to. (i.e., there is such a specific play)

Epistemic and Speech-Act Conditionals

Sweetser (1990) has argued that conditionals, like many kinds of conjunctions, are interpretable as joining clauses in several different ways. The interpretations most familiar to linguists and philosophers are those where the *content* of the two clauses is semantically related. For example, in (27), a likely interpretation is that Mary's absence (in the described hypothetical world) will causally influence John's. In (28), a similar relationship holds between the contents of the clauses, except that the world described is seen through a negative epistemic stance.

(25)

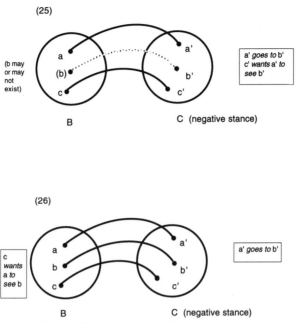

Figure 11.4

(27) If Mary doesn't go, John won't either.

(28) If Mary hadn't gone, John wouldn't have either.

Dancygier (1992, 1993) calls these conditionals *predictive* conditionals, meaning that they share a function of connecting the contents of the two clauses in such a way that the apodosis content at least *would* be predictable from the protasis content.

Considerable attention has also been given in the pragmatic and philosophical literature to examples like (29) and (30), sometimes called conditional speech acts. In these cases, the speaker presents the performance of a speech act as taking place in the conditional mental space established by the protasis.[3]

(29) a. If you're not too busy, what's Sue's phone number?
b. If you will be going to Paris, why not buy your ticket now?

(30) If you need any help, my name is Chris.

Thus, in (29a), the speaker at least *presents* the question about Sue's phone number as conditional on the addressee's not being too busy to answer it. In (30), the

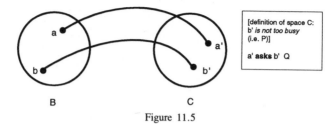

Figure 11.5

speaker offers his or her name as a means of summoning assistance, and purports to do so on condition of assistance being needed. Crucially, there is no way that the listener can take the fact of the name itself as contingent on somebody's needing help: it is very difficult to get a content-level reading for this example.

Finally, there are cases where the conditional relationship has to do not with content or with speech-act structure, but with the speaker's purported reasoning processes. Sweetser (1990, chapter 5) labeled such cases *epistemic* conditionals. In (31a), the speaker may mean to say that the contents of the two clauses are conditionally related, that loving her may cause him to type her thesis. But in (31b), the likeliest interpretation is not that typing was a (causal?) precondition for loving, but that the speaker's knowledge about the typing is a precondition for a conclusion about loving. A parallel contrast can be observed between the causal-conjunction examples in (32a) and (32b), where (32a) shows a content causal relation between the two clauses, and (32b) is most readily interpreted as expressing an epistemic causal relation.

(31) a. If he loves her, he'll type her thesis.
    (The love will bring about the typing, in the real world.)

   b. If he typed her thesis, he loves her.
    (My knowledge that the typing happened is a precondition for my conclusion that he loves her.)

(32) a. He typed her thesis because he loves her.
    (The love causes the action of typing.)

   b. He loves her, because he typed her thesis.
    (Knowledge about typing causes conclusion about loving.)

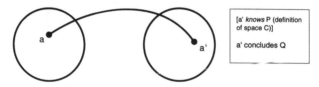

Figure 11.6

The contrast between these three classes of conditional interpretations turns out to be an important one for determining verb-form use in conditional sentences. Dancygier has pointed out a number of formal differences between predictive and nonpredictive conditionals, some of which involve the distribution of the verb forms discussed above.[4] In discussion with Fillmore at the time he was writing Fillmore 1990a, and 1990b, I pointed out that the restrictions on tenses in conditional protases and apodoses are largely relaxed when the conditional link is not intended to be at the level of the contents of the two clauses, but at the level of their epistemic or speech-act relationships. This can be seen as a particular kind of mental-space link, and the forms reflect the difference.

First, as Fillmore remarks, the possible use of future forms in conditionals is restricted. Conditional protases often allow *will* only in the volitional, not in the future sense. Note, for example, examples (33), (34), and (35).

(33)   If he's better tomorrow, he'll go to the show.

(34)   *If he'll be better tomorrow, he'll go to the show.

(35)   If he'll write that book, he'll make a lot of money.

Sentence (35) allows a volitional interpretation: "if he's just willing to write that book, if he agrees to write it" and it is therefore acceptable in the protasis; (34), lacking such an interpretation, gives us trouble. Sentence (33), with a present tense used with future reference, is the standard form for future reference in hypothetical conditional protases. Dancygier (1992) has argued persuasively that the use of present rather than future forms in conditional protases is part of the general phenomenon of tense-*backshifting,* which characterizes specifically predictive conditionals, as opposed to epistemic and speech-act conditionals.

However, when the conditional relationship is epistemic, for example, these restrictions vanish. So imagine (34) in a context where speaker A has just said "Don't worry, he'll certainly be better tomorrow." Speaker B replies, "Oh, great, if he'll be better tomorrow, then (that means) he'll go to the show, and I shouldn't give his ticket away." Here the future is present in the content, but the conditional relationship is not between a future event and a further future one, but between a present belief and a present conclusion. Compare examples (36) and (37).

(36)   If it rains tomorrow, then we'll bring our umbrellas.

(37)   If it'll rain tomorrow, then we'll bring our umbrellas.

Sentence (36) is about a conditional relationship between two future events, while (37) is about a present belief resulting in a present decision about the future. Examples (38) and (39) are further data (from Fillmore 1990a) showing that the protasis in (37) is indeed a true future: it can't take the *only* that volitional *will* allows.

(38) *If it'll only rain tomorrow . . .

(39) If he'll only write that book . . .

We also find in epistemic conditionals many other tense-restriction violations, as in (40) and (41).

(40) If he's going to the play, then he got tickets yesterday.

(41) If she had opened the window (before she got captured), then they'll escape. (from Fillmore)

Speech-act conditionals show almost no connection whatsoever between the verb forms of protasis and apodosis.

(42) If you will be going to Paris, why did you buy a ticket to Tokyo?

(43) If you're interested, I gave/will give/had just given a paper on speech-act conditionals.

Some of these "violations" of tense restrictions follow naturally from the functional differences between predictive and nonpredictive conditionals. If there is a causal connection between the content of protasis and apodosis, it is natural that there will be restricted temporal relations between clauses: a real-world cause cannot follow its effect. However, in reasoning we may move from knowledge about an effect to a conclusion about a cause or enabling condition, or vice versa ("If he got the tickets, then he's going to the play" or "If he's going to the play, then he got the tickets"). So there is no need to find it odd for a "wrong" sequence of tenses to occur in nonpredictive conditionals, at least insofar as tense-form use is based on temporal reference.

Insofar as tense forms indicate epistemic stance rather than temporal reference, we may say that "counterfactual" negative-stance uses of tense backshifting would naturally show concord between protasis and apodosis in predictive cases, where the content of the apodosis applies only within the mental space set up by supposing the truth of the content of the protasis. But in cases where no such relationship exists between the two contents, where the only conditional relationship is between the epistemic states or speech acts instantiated by the two clauses, there is less reason to expect a close relationship between the forms expressing the contents of protasis and apodosis. In Sweetser 1990 and Nikiforidou 1990, evidence is presented to suggest that speech-act conditionals in particular, but also epistemic ones, tend to have given protases much more often than predictive conditionals do. (Reasons for this difference are also put forward.) This being so, we would not expect to find much need for negatively aligned protases in such examples in any case, and hence there should be little need for apodoses that agree with them. Dancygier has brought to my attention the following interesting contrast, where the nongiven protasis in (44) forces a predictive "content" conditional reading, while the given protasis in (45) tends to get a speech-act reading.

(44) If you were interested, she'd be his wife. (sounds as if your interest could influence their marriage status)

(45) If you're interested, she's his wife.

However, supposing we take (44) to mean something like "All the interesting guys are married; look at that guy over there, for instance—if you were interested, (I bet it would turn out that) the woman with him would be his wife." This is an example of an epistemic conditional where the speaker is presenting the likely conclusion or discovery as depending on a negative-stance protasis—and here, in this unusual example, we do find the dependence of forms which would be predicted by the conditional connection.

My claim, then, is that when conditionals involve different structures of mental space embeddings than content conditionals, this is reflected in their freer form. But where there is real predictive conditionality involved in the mental space structure, the restrictions on form which apply to predictive conditionals will be followed. And where there are constraints on the temporal relationships of causally related events, those restrictions will be reflected in corresponding restrictions on sequence of tenses in conditionals describing those events. In general, tense use in conditional structures in English does reflect semantics, including mental space structure.

Conclusions

First of all, I hope to have shown that Fillmore's analysis extends beyond his original data set to account for verb forms not only in predictive conditionals and in embeddings under mental space predicates, but also in embedded relative clauses, in conditionals and paired-scale constructions embedded within conditionals, and in epistemic and speech-act conditionals. Motivating his analysis by looking at the mental space structures needed to represent such conditionals allows us to motivate the behavior of the other constructions as well.

It should be possible to vastly increase our ability to regularly predict conditional form choices (probably in other languages as well as in English), based on a fuller understanding of mental space embeddings. This paper is by no means a full treatment of the problems addressed by Fillmore, who in turn admits that he tackles only part of the larger problem of verb-form usage. However, I have attempted to show that there are motivations for the forms Fillmore discusses, that mental spaces are a crucial part of the semantics of conditionals, and that mental space embeddings are a crucial part of the semantics of English tense forms.

Notes

1. The variation between *was,* a past form, and *were,* a true subjunctive form, is characteristic only of *be* in English. The subjunctive forms will not be discussed in this paper.

2. Fauconnier convincingly shows that the traditional contrasts between opaque and transparent, referential and attributive, fall out of our ability to interpret descriptions relative to different mental spaces, such as the speaker's belief space and the intentional space of the speaker's wishes, and our further ability to take descriptions as either identifying roles or values.

3. Probably the first celebrated examples of conditional speech acts are found in Austin 1979. Van der Auwera 1986 provides an excellent discussion of many of the semantic and pragmatic difficulties involved in such constructions. For further discussion and references, see Sweetser 1990, chapter 5.

4. I have here omitted discussion of another group of nonpredictive conditionals, Dancygier's (1992, 1993) *metalinguistic* conditionals (see also Sweetser 1990, chapter 5). They display similar formal differences from the predictive class of conditionals.

References

Austin, J.L. 1979. Ifs and Cans. In *Philosophical Papers.* 3d ed, 153–80. Edited by J.O. Urmson and G.J. Warnock. Oxford: Oxford University Press. Originally published 1961.

Dancygier, Barbara. 1992. Two Metatextual Operators: Negation and Conditionality in Polish. *Proceedings of the Eighteenth Annual Meeting of the Berkeley Linguistics Society,* 61–75. Berkeley, CA: Berkeley Linguistics Society.

————. 1993. Interpreting Conditionals: Time, Knowledge and Causation. *Journal of Pragmatics,* 403–34.

Fauconnier, Gilles. 1985. *Mental Spaces: Aspects of Meaning Construction in Natural Language.* Cambridge, Mass.: MIT Press. Reprinted 1994, Cambridge: Cambridge University Press.

Fillmore, Charles J. 1986. Varieties of Conditional Sentences. *ESCOL* 3:163–82.

————. 1990a. Epistemic Stance and Grammatical Form in English Conditional Sentences. *Papers from the Twenty-Sixth Regional Meeting of the Chicago Linguistic Society,* 137–62. University of Chicago.

————. 1990b. The Contribution of Linguistics to Language Understanding. In Aura Bocaz, ed., *Proceedings of the First Symposium on Cognition, Language and Culture,* 109–28. Santiago: Universidad de Chile.

Fleischman, Suzanne. 1989. Temporal Distance: A Basic Linguistic Metaphor. *Studies in Language* 13:1–51.

Langacker, Ronald W. 1978. The Form and Meaning of the English Auxiliary. *Language* 54.

Michaelis, Laura A. 1994. A Case of Constructional Polysemy in Latin. *Studies in Language* 18:23–48.

Nikiforidou, Vassiliki. 1990. Conditional and Concessive Clauses in Modern Greek: A Syntactic and Semantic Description. Ph.D. diss., University of California, Berkeley.

Sweetser, Eve. 1990. *From Etymology to Pragmatics: Metaphorical and Cultural Aspects of Semantic Structure.* Cambridge: Cambridge University Press.

Van der Auwera, Johan. 1986. Conditionals and Speech Acts. In Elizabeth C. Traugott, Alice ter Meulen, J. Snitzer Reilly, and Charles A. Ferguson, eds., *On Conditionals,* 197–214. Cambridge: Cambridge University Press.

Karen van Hoek

12 Conceptual Locations for Reference in American Sign Language

•

•

•

•

American Sign Language (ASL) is the visual-gestural language used by approximately half a million Deaf people in North America.[1] It is not based on English, but is rather a separate language, with its own lexicon and grammatical mechanisms which have evolved within the visual-gestural modality (Klima and Bellugi 1979). It is in its devices for marking coreference that ASL most clearly shows the stamp of the visual modality. Referents introduced into a signed discourse are associated with points in the signing space, termed *referential loci*. Pronouns may then be directed to these loci, and verb signs move between loci, marking "agreement" with their arguments.[2]

The precise nature of the referential loci is still controversial. Liddell (1990, 1995) describes them as "surrogates," which are visual images of referents occupying various locations, as if they were present in the signing space. Many other researchers have assumed (implicitly or explicitly) that the loci are merely points in space, and can be thought of as spatial representations of syntactic or semantic indices (cf. Lillo-Martin and Klima 1990). I assume that the loci may vary in their imagistic content; in one discourse (or at one moment in a particular discourse) a locus may be conceived as a detailed, highly specific mental image of the referent, and in another discourse (or another point in time) may be a highly schematized, nonspecific image—which includes the possibility that the image may consist of an association between the referent and the point in space, with no other visual-imagistic content.

I demonstrate below that these quasi-imagistic associations between referents and loci may involve much more than simply the establishment of the referent, as an isolated notion, with a particular point in space. Referential loci are frequently associated with the larger "scenes" or spatial settings which the referent occupies. This point is roughly equivalent to an observation made in other terms by Liddell (1990, 1995), who notes that the locus is not merely associated with the referent, but rather represents the referent's conceived location. The import of this for the application of mental spaces theory (Fauconnier 1985) is illustrated by a number of examples in the next section.

Multiple Loci for Reference

Although the typical pattern is for each referent to be associated with one locus (and vice versa), it is not uncommon in ASL discourse for one referent to be associated with more than one locus. This is illustrated in (1) below. The notation used for ASL examples is as follows: ASL signs are represented by English glosses; where more than one word is needed to gloss a single sign, the glosses are joined by hyphens. Some of the glosses have small semicircles under them, representing the space in front of the signer. Arrows represent the direction of movement for a sign which is articulated with a path movement; Xs represent the space in which a stationary sign is articulated. The third-person pronoun and the sign meaning 'there' are articulated almost identically, as both consist of a pointing gesture. They are frequently distinguished by differences in palm orientation, but in some contexts they are phonologically identical. The data reported here have largely been transcribed by native deaf signers, who have reported clear intuitions as to the correct gloss in each case.

(1) NIGHT, WE-TWO TALK INDEX-THERE HIS ROOM. INDEX-PRO

BAWL-OUT. I TELL I SORRY, INDEX-PRO FORGIVE ME.

MORNING, I GO OUT Y-A-R-D, SEE INDEX-PRO AGAIN.

BAWL-OUT AGAIN. STRANGE. BEFORE, INDEX-PRO TELL

INDEX-PRO FORGIVE ME, MORNING, INDEX-PRO ANGRY

AGAIN.

'In the evening, we talked in his room. He bawled me out. I told him I was sorry, and he forgave me. In the morning, I went out to the yard, and saw him again. He bawled me out again. It was strange. Before, he told me he forgave me, but in the morning, he was angry again.'

The two conceived situations—the conversations in the room and in the yard—constitute mental spaces, each of which is associated with a locus in signing space. The pronominal forms used for reference directly reflect the mental space within which the referent is accessed in each case.

Although any number of mental spaces may be established in a sign discourse, the vast majority of them will not be associated with distinct loci in the signing space. In van Hoek 1992 I note that multiple loci are associated with a single referent only when that referent is described as occupying multiple spatial locations. Other kinds of mental spaces do not give rise to the use of multiple loci; for example, if the referent is described as occupying the same spatial location at two different points in time, a single referential locus would be used (see van Hoek 1992 for examples).

Principles of Accessibility

Although multiple loci may be set up in a given discourse, corresponding to different mental spaces, these loci are not all equally likely to be used at a given point in the discourse. Signers instead select certain loci for pronominal reference, and may judge other loci to be unacceptable for use in a particular context. In (2), the signer first establishes one locus associated with the referent's location in Chicago, then mentions that the person moved to New York. Subsequent pronouns are directed to the locus associated with New York, even where the signer is talking about the person's experiences in Chicago.

(2) THAT FRIEND INDEX-HE FROM CHICAGO. MOVE NEW-YORK

INDEX-HE. [approximately five sentences omitted] THAT TIME IN

CHICAGO INDEX-HE MISERABLE LITTLE-BIT. INDEX-HE

BECOME-INVOLVED-WITH D-R-U-G-S. SOME PEOPLE

GO-ALONG-WITH-HIM. PERSONALITY SAME BUT GUESS

D-R-U-G-S INDEX-THERE IN HIS WAY.

'That friend of mine, he's from Chicago. He moved to New York. [. . .] When he was in Chicago, he was kind of unhappy. He got involved with drugs. It was some people he was with. His personality hasn't changed—I guess there (in Chicago), drugs were in his way.'

The final sentence describes the referent's experience in Chicago, but accesses the referent via the locus associated with New York. The conception of the referent in New York functions as a trigger accessing the target, the conception of the referent in Chicago. This is analogous to the use, in English, of a nominal description which directly pertains to a referent in one mental space (e.g., *the girl with green eyes,* in reference to a painting depicting a girl who has green eyes), but which indirectly accesses a referent in a different mental space (such as the conception of the real-life model for the painting, who may in fact have blue eyes).

The principles of locus selection in ASL discourse, as they have been worked out so far (cf. van Hoek 1989, 1992), seem congruent with general principles of the theory of accessibility developed by Givón (1989) and Ariel (1988, 1990), among others. Accessibility Theory holds that a particular nominal form is selected for reference in a given context to reflect the degree of accessibility (roughly "retrievability") of the referent in that context. Cross-linguistically, full nominals (names and descriptive phrases) are markers of relatively low accessibility, used when the referent is not highly active in the addressee's awareness. Pronouns are markers of relatively high accessibility, and null anaphora (i.e., no phonological marking of coreference) marks still higher accessibility.

The ordering of elements on the Accessibility Scale appears to be fairly constant cross-linguistically, in the sense that full noun phrases always mark lower accessibility than overt pronouns, which in turn mark lower accessibility than null anaphora (cf. Givón 1989, Ariel 1990). The precise degree of accessibility indicated by a particular nominal form is, however, quite variable cross-linguistically. In English, unstressed pronouns are used for reference to the current discourse topic; null anaphora is reserved for referents of greater accessibility (e.g., in a sentence such as *John wants to go,* the subject of *to go* is not phonologically marked, as it corefers with the subject of the higher clause). ASL makes extensive use of null anaphora (Lillo-Martin 1986). I assume that the range of accessibility covered by unstressed pronouns in English corresponds to the range covered by null anaphora and by unstressed pronouns in ASL. In other words, the semantic range for overt pronouns in ASL partially overlaps with the range for pronouns in English, though overt pronouns in ASL tend to mark somewhat lower accessibility than those in English.

In ASL, principles of Accessibility explain the selection of loci for pronominal reference in contexts in which more than one locus has been previously established in the discourse. The same can be said for the choice of descriptive full nominals in English. When a speaker, looking at a painting which depicts a girl with green eyes, says something like, "The girl with green eyes has blue eyes," she is selecting the nominal *the girl with green eyes* to access the conception of the real-world model. Presumably she chooses this particular description because the painting is physically present and perceptible, therefore salient in the discourse space. The speaker's choice of a nominal description for a particular referent is not dictated by these considerations, however. Full nominals (such as *the girl with green eyes* or *the girl who posed for this picture*) can be selected to highlight different facets of the referent and/or the referent's relationship to one discourse context or another.

Pronominal reference in ASL seems to differ slightly from full-nominal reference in either English or ASL, in that the choice of a pronominal locus is in many contexts (perhaps not all) dictated by considerations of accessibility. Signers frequently judge certain referential loci to be unacceptable for use in a given context, while full nominal descriptions can be chosen more freely. The data presented here are taken from elicited discourse, and grammaticality judgments have not been consistently elicited for alternative choices of loci in the same contexts.[3] Here I focus on exploring the motivations for the pronominal forms which were actually used in these discourse segments, but I report grammaticality judgments where they are available.

Ariel (1988, 1990) and Givón (1989), among others, have identified a small number of cross-linguistic factors which determine the accessibility of a referent in a given discourse. Similar factors affect the selection of a specific spatial locus for reference in ASL. Accessibility is essentially a matter of how "active" a referent is in a conceptualizer's awareness. It is influenced by salience, both perceptual and conceptual.

In van Hoek 1992 I claim that the choice of a locus for reference in an ASL discourse is determined by the interaction of two considerations, *specificity* and *salience*. Here I propose a slight revision of this analysis. The import of specificity is that, other things being equal, the signer chooses the locus for pronominal reference which most directly represents the mental space which is elaborated by the clause containing the pronoun. In (1), for example, the signer uses different pronouns to describe the referent in two different contexts; each pronoun corresponds to a specific mental space. Specificity need not be stated as an independent principle, however; it is simply another manifestation of accessibility principles. The mental space which is being elaborated, the focus space, is highly activated; an element within it is therefore highly accessible. Unless other factors make some other, corresponding element more accessible, the signer will access the referent in question by means of the spatial locus corresponding to the element in the focus space. The question to be addressed is why any space other than the focus space would be more accessible, or, in other words, why the signer would select a locus other than the one corresponding to the focus space.

Perceptual salience is a significant factor. An image of the referent which is visible to both the signer and the addressee will typically be selected as the locus for pronominal reference, as in (3). Note that the picture is used as the locus for pronominal reference even where the signer is discussing the referent's personality in real life, *not* in the world of the picture, and even though the signer had established a different locus for this referent before introducing the picture.

(3) I HAVE FRIEND, INDEX-SHE NAME K-C. HERE, HAVE PICTURE.

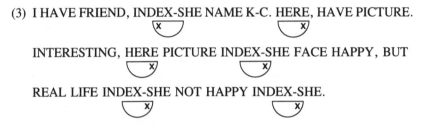

INTERESTING, HERE PICTURE INDEX-SHE FACE HAPPY, BUT

REAL LIFE INDEX-SHE NOT HAPPY INDEX-SHE.

'I have a friend named K.C. Here, I have a picture of her. It's interesting, in the picture here she looks happy, but in real life she's not happy.'

When the image is near at hand and clearly visible to both signer and addressee, signers report that it is anomalous to fail to use the image as the locus for subsequent reference (particularly if the picture has actually been mentioned in the discourse). A less salient image (such as a painting hanging on the wall several feet away from the signer and addressee) would be less likely to be used as a referential locus.

When the referent is physically present, his or her actual location is obligatorily used as the referential locus. This is true even if the signer had previously set up an "abstract" locus before the referent entered the room; in actual elicitation sessions in which a person under discussion entered the room, the signer immediately abandoned the locus which had previously been used for reference to that person, and directed all subsequent pronouns to her or his actual location.

Conceptual Salience

Relative accessibility among more abstract loci (those which do not correlate with an image or with the referent's physical presence) is influenced by subtle factors involving discourse focus and point of view. As the conceptualizer mentally tracks a discourse, certain mental spaces are brought into the center of attention, while others become relatively peripheral. The influence of these shifts on locus selection is illustrated by a number of examples below. It should be borne in mind however that the discussion here is in many respects preliminary, as a great deal more data will be required to conclusively prove the validity of the analyses offered for these examples. The analyses given are of the nature of hypotheses and suggestions for future investigation rather than fully established fact.

A locus which is understood to represent the referent's current location will be selected in preference to a locus representing a past or future location (except in certain contexts to be discussed below). The signers I have consulted all report the clear intuition that contexts such as that in (4) require the use of the locus representing the referent's current location, even where the signer is describing the person's behavior in a past or future situation. (4) is taken from a larger discourse in which a locus on the signer's right has been associated with the referent's current location in New York (indicated by an X in the leftmost corner of the semicircle representing sign space). The signer compares the referent's situations in New York and Chicago, using the New York locus for pronominal reference in both sentences.

(4) MAYBE THAT WHY INDEX-HE NOT CORRESPOND BECAUSE

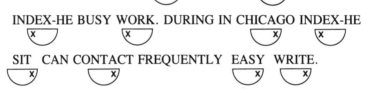

INDEX-HE BUSY WORK. DURING IN CHICAGO INDEX-HE SIT CAN CONTACT FREQUENTLY EASY WRITE.

'Maybe that's why he hasn't been corresponding with me, because he's busy working. When he was in Chicago he was just sitting around, so we could make contact frequently and it was easy for him to write.'

It can easily be seen in examples such as these that the locus representing the past or future location has not been entirely forgotten or "erased," as evidenced by the fact that verbs describing events in the past or future are articulated in the corresponding regions in signing space.[4] In (4), for example, the signs SIT, CONTACT and WRITE are all articulated in the space associated with Chicago, despite the fact that the subject pronoun is direct to the space associated with New York.

In van Hoek 1992, I suggested that the locus associated with the referent's current location tends to be selected as the trigger (the locus used for pronominal reference) because it bears a special relationship to the current discourse situation as the space where the referent is "now." This explanation can be refined somewhat. We can assume that some spaces are construed as more "active" or more "topical" than others, as the focus of attention shifts from space to space throughout the discourse.

Within a narrative, there will typically be a foreground and a background, determined by the speaker's sense of "what the story is about." A narrative describing the changes a person has undergone from past to present tends to be construed as being "about" the person's present situation, against which the past situations are presented as points of comparison. Since these past situations are construed in relation to the present situation, rather than being independent foci of attention, the space most closely associated with the referent's present situation tends to be construed as the more active, accessible space for pronominal reference.

Narratives set entirely in the past provide evidence in support of this interpretation. When the narrative involves multiple past locations, there is a tendency for one locus to be selected as the trigger through which other mental spaces may be accessed. Only a few examples have been collected so far, but the preliminary findings suggest that the locus selected is typically the one which corresponds to the referent's most recent location, in the chronological sequence of the narrative. Example (5), from a signed description of the life of Abraham Lincoln, illustrates this. Passages which focus on details of his life within just one location have been omitted; the crucial data involve the indexing of pronouns in sentences comparing Lincoln's life in two locations.

(5) LINCOLN LONG-TIME-AGO INDEX-HE GROW-UP KID

INDEX-HE. [five sentences omitted] OLD-20 INDEX-HE MOVE

OTHER CITY S-P-R-I-N-G-F-I-E-L-D I-L-L INDEX-HE MOVE.

INDEX-HE MARRY PROGRESS. PEOPLE NOTICE INDEX-HE

DEPRESSED. INDEX-HE SULLEN-WALK SOMETIMES WANDER

NOTHING ETC. PEOPLE LOOK-AT-HIM. SEEM INDEX-HE KID

THERE GROW-UP NONE. [approximately twenty sentences omitted,

describing Lincoln's life in Springfield] BUT STRANGE INDEX-HE

HIMSELF THAT TIME KID GROW-UP INDEX-HE FINE NO

DEPRESSION ETC.

'Lincoln grew up a long time ago. . . . When he was twenty, he moved to another city, Springfield, Illinois. He got married and his life went along for a while. People noticed he was depressed. He would walk around looking sullen, sometimes he'd wander around doing nothing. People would look at him. It seems that when he was a kid growing up, there was none of this (i.e., depression). [lengthy anecdote about Springfield omitted] But it was strange, when he was a kid growing up he was fine, with no depression or anything.'

Again we can see that, although the signer focused exclusively on Lincoln's adult life in Springfield throughout an extensive passage (approximately twenty sentences, which have been omitted here), the locus associated with Lincoln's childhood home remained "active" in the discourse—as evidenced by its use with the verb GROW-UP in the last sentence. Despite the potential availability of that locus, pronouns referring to Lincoln are indexed to the locus associated with his adult location, in a manner analogous to the use of a referent's current location for pronominal reference in sentences describing past events. This usage can be explained if we assume that Lincoln's adult situation is being taken as the focus of the discourse, relative to which the description of his childhood situation is presented merely as a side comment. It seems intuitively clear that Lincoln's childhood is not the focus of the discourse in these passages, and so the space associated with his childhood location is not the most accessible and is not selected for pronominal reference.

Focus Shift

The analysis outlined above suggests that "current location," which in van Hoek 1992 was considered to play a major role in locus selection, is in fact a privileged notion only insofar as the referent's current situation is understood to be "what the discourse is about" and discussion of past situations is construed as commentary on current reality. Further support for this analysis is provided by the observation that the "current location" locus is not used in preference to other loci, such as loci associated with past locations, if the discourse is clearly focused on the past. When the signer mentions the referent's current location only in passing, the signer may continue using a past-location locus for reference (cf. van Hoek 1992).

Moreover, when the focus of the discourse shifts so that the emphasis is clearly on narrating a past event, there is a tendency for the signer to shift back to the use of a past-location locus for pronominal reference, rather than continuing to access the conception of the referent through the current-location locus. This is illustrated by the contrast between examples (6) and (7).

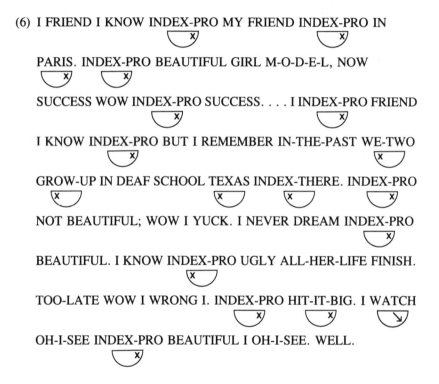

(6) I FRIEND I KNOW INDEX-PRO MY FRIEND INDEX-PRO IN

PARIS. INDEX-PRO BEAUTIFUL GIRL M-O-D-E-L, NOW

SUCCESS WOW INDEX-PRO SUCCESS. . . . I INDEX-PRO FRIEND

I KNOW INDEX-PRO BUT I REMEMBER IN-THE-PAST WE-TWO

GROW-UP IN DEAF SCHOOL TEXAS INDEX-THERE. INDEX-PRO

NOT BEAUTIFUL; WOW I YUCK. I NEVER DREAM INDEX-PRO

BEAUTIFUL. I KNOW INDEX-PRO UGLY ALL-HER-LIFE FINISH.

TOO-LATE WOW I WRONG I. INDEX-PRO HIT-IT-BIG. I WATCH

OH-I-SEE INDEX-PRO BEAUTIFUL I OH-I-SEE. WELL.

'My friend, I know her—my friend, she's in Paris. She's a beautiful girl, a model now, and wow is she successful. . . . I—she's a friend, I know her, but I remember in the past, we grew up together in the deaf school in Texas. She wasn't beautiful; I would think, "Yuck." I never dreamed she would become beautiful. I knew she would be ugly all her life. Too late I realized I was wrong. She hit it big. I look at her and I think, ''Oh, I see, she's beautiful, I see. . . . Well . . .''

Immediately after the consultant signed (6), he was asked, ''Tell me a little bit more about what you remember'' (signed as TELL-ME MORE WHAT YOU REMEMBER WHAT; note that, although the signer was describing an imaginary situation, he was not *translating* from English to ASL, but rather was role playing, inventing ''memories'' in his own words). He continued with the following passage, which seems to involve more clear focus on the past time, rather than comparison with the present. Note that the pronouns are at first directed to the locus associated with the referent's current location (Paris), but then shift to the locus associated with the past location, Texas. The second sentence includes the verb PICK-ON, which is indexed to the locus associated with Texas; subsequent pronominal reference is directed to that same locus, until the final sentence when the signer again compares the present and the past.

(7) I REMEMBER IN-THE-PAST WE-TWO IN SCHOOL INDEX-THERE

TEXAS. I AWFUL I PICK-ON INDEX-PRO THROW M-U-D WOW

TEND CALL INDEX-PRO P-I-Z-Z-A FACE AWFUL WOW TRUE.

INDEX-PRO CRY. I LOOK, FRIEND, BUT I QUOTE WE-TWO

FRIEND YES BUT I NEVER THINK INDEX-PRO BEAUTIFUL. I

LOOK QUOTE TOO-LATE INDEX-PRO NEVER MARRY, ETC.

NOW TRANSFORM. I LOOK WOW INDEX-PRO BEAUTIFUL

WOW.

'I remember in the past, we were in school in Texas. I was awful, I picked on her, I threw mud at her, wow, I used to call her pizza-face, really awful. She would cry. I would look at her—we were kind of friends, but I never thought she would be beautiful. I would always look at her like ''It's too late for her, she'll never marry,'' and so on. Now she's transformed. I look at her and wow, she's beautiful.'

It appears that the shift in focus, from present to the past, promotes the use of the locus associated with the past for pronominal reference. Example (8) may also be an example of this phenomenon, though here the length of the discourse focused on the past is much shorter than in (7). Here once again the referent has been associated with a locus to the signer's right, which is understood to represent the referent's current location in New York.

(8) INDEX-HE THAT TIME INDEX-HE IN CHICAGO INDEX-HE

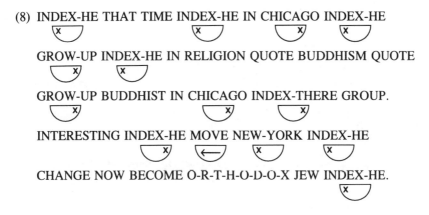

GROW-UP INDEX-HE IN RELIGION QUOTE BUDDHISM QUOTE

GROW-UP BUDDHIST IN CHICAGO INDEX-THERE GROUP.

INTERESTING INDEX-HE MOVE NEW-YORK INDEX-HE

CHANGE NOW BECOME O-R-T-H-O-D-O-X JEW INDEX-HE.

'That time when he was in Chicago he grew up in the religion of Buddhism; he grew up Buddhist in a group there, in Chicago. It's interesting, when he moved to New York he changed and became an Orthodox Jew.'

In (9), the signer describes a hypothetical future situation in which a friend (whose current location has been associated with a locus to the signer's right) might take a trip to an island (associated with a locus to the left). After lengthy enumeration of all the things that might go wrong on the trip, involving a large number of verbs articulated in the space associated with the island, the signer eventually directs a pronoun to that locus as well, in the sentence which translates as 'I think he'd better stay home.'

(9) SUPPOSE FRIEND INDEX-THERE PLAN GONE ISLAND FOR

VACATION. TELL GONE FINE BUT I TEND WORRY. SUPPOSE

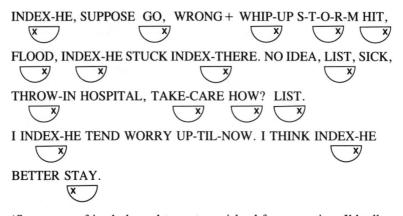

INDEX-HE, SUPPOSE GO, WRONG+ WHIP-UP S-T-O-R-M HIT,

FLOOD, INDEX-HE STUCK INDEX-THERE. NO IDEA, LIST, SICK,

THROW-IN HOSPITAL, TAKE-CARE HOW? LIST.

I INDEX-HE TEND WORRY UP-TIL-NOW. I THINK INDEX-HE

BETTER STAY.

'Suppose my friend planned to go to an island for a vacation. I'd tell him fine, go, but I'd tend to worry. Suppose he goes, there might be a sudden storm or a flood and he could be stuck there. I have no idea— there are a lot of possibilities; he might get sick, get thrown in the hospital, how would he be taken care of? There are a lot of possibilities. I tend to worry about him. I think he'd better stay home.'

An additional factor influencing the accessibility of mental spaces in the discourse is the presence of a "point of view" distinct from that of the signer. A point of view is associated with a mental space representing the thoughts or perceptions of the conceived viewer or cognizer. Elements which are construed as belonging to that mental space (i.e., as part of that person's thoughts or perceptions) are tightly connected conceptually with the point of view, which is therefore highly accessible relative to those elements. This suggests that, for a pronoun which is conceived as "viewed" from a particular point of view, the locus associated with that point of view will also be highly accessible.

In (10), the signer uses a present-location locus for pronominal reference even when describing things which happened to the referent in the past, with the exception of one sentence in which a past-location pronoun is used within a clause which is associated with a conceived cognizer situated in the past location.

(10) FRIEND INDEX-HE LIVE F-L-A NOW. REALLY LONG-TIME-AGO

TEXAS GROW-UP INDEX-HE INDEX-THERE HE

LONG-TIME-AGO. KID INDEX-HE TEND MINGLE EASY INDEX-HE

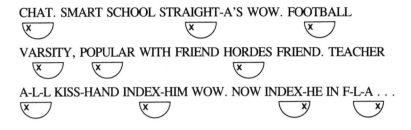

CHAT. SMART SCHOOL STRAIGHT-A'S WOW. FOOTBALL

VARSITY, POPULAR WITH FRIEND HORDES FRIEND. TEACHER

A-L-L KISS-HAND INDEX-HIM WOW. NOW INDEX-HE IN F-L-A . . .

'My friend lives in Florida now. He grew up in Texas a long time ago. As a kid he tended to mix with people easily and chat people up. He was smart in school, got straight As. He was a varsity football player; he was really popular—he had hordes of friends. The teachers all had a really high opinion of him. Now he's in Florida . . .'

The pronoun of interest is in the sentence TEACHER A-L-L KISS-HAND IN-DEX-HIM WOW meaning 'The teachers all had a really high opinion of him' (the sign normally written as KISS-HAND does not describe the action of kissing someone's hand, but rather means 'have a very high opinion (of someone or something)'; the glass has become conventional because it describes the articulation of the sign). Other pronouns in this discourse are directed to the space associated with the referent's current location, in accordance with the general preference for current-location spaces for pronominal reference. The indexing of this one object pronoun may be explained by the fact that it appears within a sentence describing the teacher's opinion; the space which is conceived as including the teachers becomes more accessible.

Example (11) contrasts with (7) above. In (7), the signer switched to the use of a past-location locus when the focus of the discourse was clearly on the past events. In (11), which also involves fairly lengthy narration concerning the past, there is no switch to the past-location locus. In this case, the statements about the past are explicitly associated with the point of view of a referent which is conceived as having a particular location at the present time. The focus of the discourse therefore does not entirely shift to the past; instead the focus is on this referent's memories, and so the locus associated with the referent's present location remains highly accessible and is used for pronominal reference throughout.

(11) MAN FROM CHICAGO MOVE NEW-YORK, INDEX-HE

PROGRESS WORK PROGRESS THAT INDEX-HE. REMEMBER

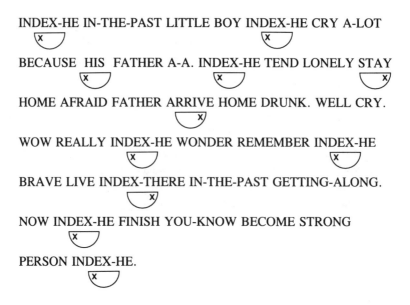

INDEX-HE IN-THE-PAST LITTLE BOY INDEX-HE CRY A-LOT

BECAUSE HIS FATHER A-A. INDEX-HE TEND LONELY STAY

HOME AFRAID FATHER ARRIVE HOME DRUNK. WELL CRY.

WOW REALLY INDEX-HE WONDER REMEMBER INDEX-HE

BRAVE LIVE INDEX-THERE IN-THE-PAST GETTING-ALONG.

NOW INDEX-HE FINISH YOU-KNOW BECOME STRONG

PERSON INDEX-HE.

'This man from Chicago moved to New York, where he's worked and gotten ahead. He remembers when he was a little boy, he cried a lot because his father was an alcoholic. He tended to be lonely and to stay at home afraid of his father coming home drunk. He would cry. Now he really thinks about it a lot, remembering how he was brave, living there and getting by. Now, you know, he's become a strong person.'

The signer reestablishes the fact that he is describing the man's reminiscences about the past, as opposed to the signer's own recollection. The association with the man's current point of view may promote the accessibility of the locus representing the man's current location, facilitating its selection as the locus for pronominal reference.

Conclusion

The pronominal system in ASL involves much more than merely remembering one-to-one associations between referents and spatial loci. Determining which locus to use for reference frequently involves assessing the relative salience, both perceptual and conceptual, of various loci and their corresponding mental spaces. Although the data and analysis presented here are highly preliminary, they suggest that the patterns of spatialized pronominal indexing in ASL can provide a unique perspective on issues of focus shift and salience in discourse. Clearly a great deal remains to be investigated; areas for future investigation would include further examination of the effects of discourse-focus shift and the presence of one or more points of view.

Notes

1. This research was supported in part by National Institutes of Health grants R01 DC00301, R01 DC00146, R37 HD13249, and P0 NS19632, as well as National Science Foundation grant BNS 8911486 to Dr. Ursula Bellugi of the Salk Institute for Biological Studies, La Jolla, California. It was also supported in part by a faculty grant from the Horace H. Rackham School of Graduate Studies and the Office of the Vice President for Research of the University of Michigan. I would like to thank my consultants Freda Norman, Lucinda O'Grady-Batch, and George Zein. Thanks also to Ursula Bellugi, Gilles Fauconnier, Edward Klima, and two anonymous reviewers for helpful discussion.

2. Ordinary pronouns (equivalent to 'I', 'you', 'she/he', etc.) consist of a pointing gesture articulated with the index finger. There is no distinction between nominative and oblique cases (e.g., 'I' vs. 'me') and no distinction for gender. Dual and trial forms (e.g., 'the two of you', 'the three of them') are used as well. Reflexive pronouns ('myself', 'himself/herself', etc.) are articulated with an *A* handshape—a fist with the thumb extended. Possessive pronouns ('my/mine', 'your/yours', etc.) are articulated with a flat handshape.

3. The data presented here were elicited from native deaf signers, i.e., deaf signers with deaf parents. The signers were given an imagined scenario or historical information (e.g., the life of Abraham Lincoln) and asked to make up a narrative about it in ASL. Signers would often produce flowing ASL discourse on a topic for one or two minutes; the examples given here are excerpted from the longer discourses. These data are therefore not perfectly naturalistic, as they are not taken from spontaneous signed discourse, but they are more naturalistic than translations of English sentences or grammaticality judgments elicited in response to invented ASL sentences.

4. It appears to be a property of certain verbs, which may form a natural class, that they are obligatorily articulated in the space which most accurately reflects the spatial location of the event they described. The principles governing these verbs have not yet been investigated in detail.

References

Ariel, Mira. 1988. Referring and Accessibility. *Journal of Linguistics* 24:65–87.

———. 1990. *Accessing Noun Phrase Antecedents*. New York: Routledge.

Fauconnier, Gilles. 1985. *Mental Spaces: Aspects of Meaning Construction in Natural Language*. Cambridge, Mass.: MIT Press. Reprinted 1994, Cambridge: Cambridge University Press.

Givón, Talmy. 1989. The Grammar of Referential Coherence as Mental Processing Instructions. Technical Report No. 89-7, University of Oregon.

Klima, Edward S., and Ursula Bellugi. 1979. *The Signs of Language*. Cambridge, Mass.: Harvard University Press.

Liddell, Scott. 1990. Four Functions of a Locus: Reexamining the Structure of Space in ASL. In Ceil Lucas, ed., *Sign Language Research: Theoretical Issues*, 176–98. Washington, D.C.: Gallaudet University Press.

———. 1995. Real, Surrogate, and Token Space: Grammatical Consequences in ASL. In K. Emmorey and J. Reilly, eds., *Language, Gesture, and Space*, 19–41. Hillsdale, N.J.: Lawrence Erlbaum Associates.

Lillo-Martin, Diane. 1986. Two Kinds of Null Arguments in American Sign Language. *Natural Language and Linguistic Theory* 4:415–44.

Lillo-Martin, Diane, and Edward S. Klima. 1990. Pointing Out Differences: ASL Pronouns in Syntactic Theory. In Susan Fischer and Patricia Siple, eds., *Theoretical Issues in Sign Language Research*. Volume 1: *Linguistics*, 191–210. Chicago: University of Chicago Press.

van Hoek, Karen. 1989. Locus Splitting in American Sign Language. In Robert Carlson, Scott DeLancey, Spike Gildea, Doris Payne, and Anju Saxena, eds., *Proceedings of the Fourth Meeting of the Pacific Linguistics Conference*, 239–55. Eugene, Oreg.: University of Oregon Press.

———. 1992. Conceptual Spaces and Pronominal Reference in American Sign Language. *Nordic Journal of Linguistics* 15:183–99.

INDEX